The Little 500

50

The Story of the World's Greatest College Weekend

The Little

By John Schwarb

INDIANA UNIVERSITY PRESS   BLOOMINGTON AND INDIANAPOLIS

This book is a publication of
Indiana University Press
601 North Morton Street
Bloomington, IN 47404-3797 USA
http://www.indiana.edu/~iupress
Telephone orders 800-842-6796
Fax orders 812-855-7931
Orders by e-mail iuporder@indiana.edu
© 1999 by The Indiana University Foundation

Printed in China

Schwarb, John.
The Little 500: the story of the world's greatest college weekend/by John Schwarb.
p. cm.
ISBN 0-253-33573-6 (cl)
1. Little 500 (Bicycle race) I. Title. II. Title: Little Five Hundred.
GV1049.2.L57S35   1999
796.6'2'09772255—dc21   99-22906

1 2 3 4 5 04 03 02 01 00 99

In loving memory of
Bruce Schwarb

CONTENTS

The Little
500

Foreword by Howdy Wilcox

Almost 50 years ago, the Little 500 was conceived as a desperate effort to utilize the unbounded energies and efforts of the new Student Foundation Committee—some 36 outstanding juniors and seniors at Indiana University.

As Executive Director of the Indiana University Foundation, just completing my first year on the job, I sent a letter to President Herman B Wells suggesting the organization of the student leaders, pointing out that the Foundation would never be the organization it was intended to be unless the student body was involved during its four-year stay on the campus. Dr. Wells agreed.

The first get-together of the student group was a lovely banquet in the Union Building, where both Herman and I told the group of the goals and aspirations of the Foundation—of the hopes and dreams of the first Foundation's Board of Directors. We asked the student leaders to recognize the needs for alumni support and to understand that the Foundation was indeed "the margin of excellence" that could take the university to greater heights. Unanimously, the students agreed to carry the message to the whole student body, and in less than 60 days they reported that the job had been done—and asked what else they could do to further the cause.

I knew I had to challenge their imagination and their energies.

In a matter of days, I witnessed an event that set the stage for what would become the "Little 500." I saw four or five men, racing bicycles around one of the temporary dormitories on the southeast corner of campus. Girls, leaning out of windows, cheered them on. One boy, with the bill of his cap turned up, acted like a reporter, monitoring every lap.

Two nights later, I convened the Student Foundation Committee at my house on Fess Avenue, told them of the impromptu event I had witnessed and asked them how they would like to sponsor a "Little 500" bicycle race, with all the proceeds going into scholarships for boys and girls who were working their way through IU. A little of my personal life went into that suggestion.

The idea took hold, the Committee unanimously liked it, and the Little 500 was born.

The following months were hectic, as we organized the rules for the race and collected sponsors. But in the end that first Little 500 netted $7,000 with every cent going into scholarships for working students and, nearly fifty years later, the formula is essentially the same.

The Little
500

Foreword by Bill Armstrong

When I arrived in 1952, President Wells made it very clear that he wanted the Student Foundation program that was started by my friend Howdy Wilcox to continue. He felt it had great value. I questioned whether this was the type of event that I wanted to be involved with, but I was convinced in the short period of two months that Dr. Wells and Howdy had a powerful idea.

We're not playing games. We have a great purpose, and that purpose is to bring the students closer to the university, to bring about a realization as to why a tax-assisted state university needs their support when they have graduated. Along with that, we want to make it fun, and the best way to instill the great things about the university is to have events and a place where they can participate for an entire year, where they will become close to other students and administrators of the university. Then by working on these events, we hope they will get a big thrill and see the results of their efforts as they unfold.

All of these goals have been realized during these 48 years, and it's all been worth the effort. We've developed and inspired the leaders of the future, and without a question, those diligent workers have learned so much to carry along with them for the rest of their lives. I've always said that being a steering committee member is equivalent to 10 hours of credit, and in most every case, with a grade of "A."

As for our Little 500—what other intramural event has had a movie produced about it and seen all over the world, been written up in glowing terms and recognized as the best of its kind by *Sports Illustrated* and many other publications, welcomed national television coverage, and enjoyed practically every other way as an event like this can be recognized and publicized? The proof of its contribution and success has been brought to light year after year, and the leaders of the past from this program have become the leaders of today in so many of the university's activities and endeavors.

Now, after being around the activity for 46 years, I have overwhelming love and respect for the many students, now alumni, who have worked diligently for the good of the university. I'm so grateful for the close relationships that I have with so many of these dedicated workers. I would certainly like to salute the past steering committees, the various committee chairmen, the riders, and the participants in all events for their great work. We have had impressive and inspiring staff members who have contributed beyond their line of duty to bring everything around to reality.

All of us involved in this program have only wanted to add to the life of the university, but in so doing there's only one way to describe the activity, and that is to say it's the World's Greatest College Weekend.

Author's Note: Mr. Armstrong wrote this foreword in December 1997. He died July 17, 1998.

The Little
500

Acknowledgments

My single greatest regret from my days as a student at Indiana University is that I never rode in a Little 500. From the moment I attended my first race as a freshman in 1993, supporting my fraternity team that was long on heart but somewhat short on speed, I was hooked. I volunteered to serve as the Little 500 beat writer for the *Indiana Daily Student* prior to my junior year (ignoring the newsroom doctrine that writers never *volunteered* to cover Little 500, with all the work that the beat entailed), and from then on lived vicariously through each of the 33 teams.

I've often thought of Little 500 riders as akin to the college golfers, cross-country runners, and other athletes from the so-called "non-revenue" sports. All of them train and practice in relative obscurity—the bicyclists often being alone on the Bloomington roads or in the dark corners of greek houses or dormitory basements—and those who don't finish at the very top are sometimes forgotten. Every year in a Little 500 race only four riders can fit on the winners' stand, while the other 128 participants are left to ponder the "what ifs" and take some degree of happiness in the sheer act of competing. It was the competition and the tradition of the race that lured me in as a student, and motivated me to learn more about the event's history and mark on the IU campus.

Looking back to when I began research for this book, I realize that I had no idea what I was getting into. Writing for the newspaper as strictly a race reporter was one thing, but learning about the culture of the Little 500 led me down paths I never knew existed. I knew about Wilcox and Armstrong and many of the winners, but nothing about what built the great teams and the star-studded weekends. I knew about the Mini, but not about its once-raging popularity; I knew Bob Hope had visited, but not how he wholeheartedly embraced IU; I knew about the Cutters, but little about their eviction-to-elation story. I tried to include as many stories as possible in these pages, hopefully showing that as an event, the Little 500 was indeed much more than just a bicycle race. From the sideshow events to an Academy Award–winning film, the scope of the Little 500 stretched far from the cinders of two stadiums; indeed it has extended across 50 years of Indiana University history.

Among the many stories here are mostly tales of winning teams, but it is important to note that their achievements couldn't have come without supporting casts, namely, hundreds of other teams—some who rode to win, but many who rode just to be a part of the story. In the appendixes an attempt was made to include all teams and as many individuals as possible, all vital players in the story of the Little 500. While collecting the stories of the winning teams and significant others in the event's history, I also compiled countless personal stories—unfortunately, too many to include in these pages. The stories of students who used the event as a stepping stone to future careers and relationships (I know of riders, Student Foundation workers, and fans from nearly every year between 1951–1996 who found spouses through the event) are not all here, but they, too, inherently add to the aura of the Little 500.

My goal in writing this book is that alumni may pick it up and reminisce about their era while learning about others, that friends of IU may learn more about an event they might have only known from *Breaking Away* and that yet others with no ties to IU may read and marvel at an event whose boundaries were only limited by the imaginations of its participants and fans.

I hope you all enjoy the trip.

I owe a tremendous amount of gratitude to Dick Bishop, Randy Rogers, and Curt Simic, three passionate Little 500 fans who entrusted a young college graduate with 50 years of history. Their enthusiasm and dedication to this project helped it along every step of the way, and I am extremely grateful. I am also very much appreciative of John Gallman and the gracious staff of Indiana University Press, whose outside-the-box thinking helps so many books like these see the light of day.

It would be easy to use the clichéd phrase "without (blank) person this book would not have been possible" on any number of people, but those words suit Howdy Wilcox and Bill Armstrong best. The time I spent with each of them was delightful; their memories were invaluable.

Two fellow authors and mentors from my days as a student, Murray Sperber and James Madison, helped me get started on this project and boosted my confidence. May all their future writing efforts be fruitful.

The staff of the Indiana University Foundation and Student Foundation, especially Jewel Baker, Mike Foote, and B. J. Walls, were always available to answer a near-endless stream of questions, and I thank them for their answers. Many other university offices were helpful, including the Main Library, Registrar's Office, and the IU Athletic Department.

Finding photographs for this book was no small task, and many parties are to be thanked for their generosity, usually after deep searches into their respective archives. The Indiana University Archives, Indianapolis *Star* and *News*, Bloomington *Herald-Times*, *Indiana Alumni* Magazine, IU Photographic Services, and Dave Repp were tremendous sources for snapshots of Little 500 history, as were several other private donors who delved into their scrapbooks to help. A former colleague, Ruth Witmer, also made my life much easier by lending a second eye to the photo selection process.

Brandon Grimes assisted in collating appendix material, and he and several other friends eagerly helped with the proofreading process. Greg Bardonner, Tom Biersdorfer, JR Ross, and Ronny Whitworth were all supportive friends, patiently listening to more than their fair share of Little 500 stories on the golf course.

While researching this book I met hundreds of past and present Student Foundation members, Little 500 riders, and other race fans, all of whom provided stories and insights into the event. The following people provided formal interviews and/or particularly useful information: Jay Allardt, Bill Armstrong, Martha Lea Armstrong, Dave Atha, Tom Battle, Adam Beck, Julie Beck, Chappie Blackwell, Dave Blase, Brock Blosser, Bob Bolyard, Lisa Braun, George Carlin, Dennis Christopher, Terry Clapacs, Ritter Collett, Lew Cook, Jim Cusick, Ron David, Mark Dayton, Clarence Doninger, Mark Edwards, Rita Erickson, Jon Foote, Mike Foote, Ken Frost, Sara Gardner, Adam Giles, Chris Gutowsky, Kendall Harnett, Kerry Hellmuth, Jeff Hilligoss, Steve Hoeferle, Mike Howard, Alex Ihnen, Jill Janov, John Jones, Tim Kappes, Lara Keeley, Bob Kirkwood, Walter Koch, Eddie Krause, Jim Law, Charlie Lyons, Jim Mahaffey, Ralph Martin, Jamie McEwen, Tom McGlasson, Richard McKaig, Joel McKay, Al Moellering, Bob Moore, Melissa Munkwitz, Gina Murray, Bill Naas, Karl Napper, Greg O'Brien, John Odusch, Alan Ogden, Mike Orr, Leigh Parker, Jim Pollak, Jay Polsgrove, Steve Powell, Spero Pulos, Jonathan Purvis, Steve Reisinger, Scott Ricke, Randy Rogers, Jerry Ruff, Debbie Satterfield, Liz Schoettle, Richard Schultz, Tom Schwoegler, Mark Senese, David Shaw, Curt Simic, John Skomp, Ken Sloo, Glenn Spiczak, Wayne Stetina, Kirsten Swanson, Jerry Tardy, Lee Ann Terhune, Rebecca Tesich, Eddy Van Guyse, Hilary "Moose" Walterhouse, Jack Wehner, Herman B Wells, Howdy Wilcox, Glen Wilson, Nancy Wilson, Peter Yates, and Jerry Yeagley.

Finally, my deepest thanks are for my family, for Mom, Dad, Jeremy, and Jenny, who were always there. And for Amy, who came aboard a bit later but feels like she's been there forever, too.

The Little 500

1. Setting the Pace

The men of Trees Center's Hickory Hall had outdone themselves this time. Months of battling between the west and east wings in everything from tug-of-war to snowball fights to mudslinging never seemed to prove one side's supremacy over the other, but maybe this event would. Two teams of three men on bicycles in a grueling six-day, 500-mile race around the dorm, for ultimate bragging rights.

On a warm spring day in early May 1950, Hickory residents assembled around the east campus hall to cheer on their teams. The gathering was not only competitive but lighthearted, as a few students donned caps with "press" tabs, parading about as imaginary sportswriters. The men's units were surrounded by ladies' dorms, and over the next two days the women would join the cheering and general mayhem that was the Hickory Hall "500."

About 200 yards away, entertaining guests in his back yard, Howdy Wilcox heard the roars and walked over to take a look. Just a few months earlier, as the new executive director of the Indiana University Foundation, he had created the first IU Student Foundation Committee to help promote the school through student-oriented activities. At the time Wilcox wasn't exactly sure what the activities would be, but after that walk to Hickory Hall one idea came to mind.

In 1950, Indiana University was celebrating. It had met the challenges the G.I. Bill placed on all American universities in the post-war years with remarkable grace, even emerging as a model for other institutions. The campus population tripled between 1944 and 1946, as married veterans with young children converged on the university, changing the face of the Bloomington campus. Temporary trailer communities were set up around campus, construction was started on residence halls exclusively for married students, and even IU President Herman B Wells briefly opened his home to veterans' families on the housing waiting list.

The blossoming campus population required substantial extra housing, and additional faculty were hired. Libraries were expanded, laboratories were updated and by 1950 IU was suddenly capable of hosting major research programs. "For the first time in almost a century and a half," Thomas D. Clark wrote in his four-volume *Indiana University: Mid-western Pioneer,* "Indiana began to feel the satisfying impulse of having achieved true university status."

Yet while the university was expanding its research capabilities, the student psyche was branching out in a different direction. The students' generation in 1950 was torn between the postwar glow of their adolescence and the anxiousness of the Korean War that followed them into adulthood. Undergraduate men of the early 1950s took part in what have become clichéd scenes of the era: they ate goldfish, tested how many of themselves they could cram into telephone booths, and staged panty raids. So many students arrived on campus in automobiles that the dean of students prohibited freshmen from having cars, in an attempt to keep the grounds from turning into an overgrown parking lot. Into this fray walked Wilcox, charged with harnessing student energies into activities that would promote goodwill and, eventually, money for an expanding university.

Sandwiched between the greatest triumph and tragedy of his father's life, Howard S. "Howdy" Wilcox was born on February 3, 1920. Howard Wilcox Sr. lived the nomadic life of an automobile racer in the sport's formative years, when man and machine were just beginning to test the limits. Less than a year before his son's birth Howard Sr. reached racing's pinnacle with a win in the 1919 Indianapolis 500, but became a casualty of the sport four years later in a fatal crash at an Altoona, Pennsylvania, race. Howdy's mother had died earlier while delivering his younger sister, and his father's death left him an orphan at age three. His paternal grandmother took him into her Indianapolis home, supporting the family on just the $100 per month she received from the government after losing a son in World War I. Money was always tight, so Wilcox began earning his own keep when he was seven by selling newspapers. He would go on to hold many jobs—at a drug store, a bowling alley, almost anywhere—and worked constantly when not in school.

Despite the busy schedule, Wilcox maintained high grades and was offered a full scholarship to The University of Louisville, but he opted to follow his high school friends and attend Indiana University. He arrived in Bloomington in the fall of 1938 with just $150, the proceeds from the sale of his Model "A" Ford. The money didn't last long (in a stroke of bad

Howard Wilcox, Sr., 1919.

luck, it was stolen during registration), and Wilcox again found himself on a job hunt. And find employment he did—at the IU News Bureau, in the Reserve Officer Training Corps, as a waiter in his own fraternity house. "The dollar sign was always ticking in my head," Wilcox would say. Nevertheless, he found time to be involved on campus, serving as president of the Alpha Tau Omega fraternity and the honorary Skull & Crest Society. He also edited IU's student newspaper, the *Indiana Daily Student,* for one week in March 1942. By the end of the week, Wilcox was called to Fort Benning, Georgia, for Army training. In just a few weeks he would be off to France to help fight World War II.

Three years later Wilcox, a company and battalion commander, returned to civilian life a decorated soldier. Back home again in Indiana, Wilcox remained active with the National Guard while holding down positions in advertising agencies. By 1949 he was married with a family, and settling back into life in Indianapolis. Then came the call from IU President Herman B Wells. There was yet another job in Wilcox's future—back on his old college turf.

The roots of the Indiana University Foundation date to the school's 1920 centennial, with a fund-raiser that provided for three new campus buildings. The projects, intended to honor Hoosiers who died in World War I, included Memorial Stadium, Memorial Hall, and the first wing of the Indiana Memorial Union. The campaign was successful, though the majority of the funds came from current students and faculty rather than alumni. Such an unbalanced scale helped illustrate how the university's fund-raising techniques needed revamping, and the nationwide Depression of the late 1920s and early 1930s added to the urgency of the project. A group of interested alumni, working in conjunction with Alumni Secretary George "Dixie" Heighway, discussed the principles of fund-raising and concluded alumni contributions were the key to sustaining the school's financial and institutional well-being. The best way to solicit and maintain these donations, the group decided, would be through a non-profit foundation, independent of the university in its administration but working solely for the good of the university. Through this aptly named "Indiana University Foundation," private citizens could pledge gifts, financial or otherwise, without state-imposed restrictions and with the understanding that their donation would only be used for the school's benefit. And to ensure that the alumni involved in the Foundation would not attempt to run the actual university (as some administrators feared when the Foundation formally came into existence in 1936), provisions were made in the Foundation bylaws that required its Board of Directors to include the president of the school, the president of the school's Board of Trustees, and two other Trustees.

Herman B Wells joined the Foundation Board of Directors in 1937, when he became president of IU. During his 25-year term as university president, from 1937 to 1962, he served as both president of the Foundation and chairman of its board (he passed the chair on to Elvis Stahr when Stahr took over as IU president in July 1962, but he remained Foundation president until 1969). As for employees, the Foundation relied only on volunteers and Heighway, who was hired part-time. In 1944 Lawrence Wheeler became the first Foundation director, hired by Wells to devote full-time energy to IU's new annual fund-raising campaigns. When Wheeler retired in 1949, Wells faced the task of hiring another director. The name that immediately surfaced was Howdy Wilcox, who was then working in advertising in Indianapolis. In his autobiography, *Being Lucky*, Wells described Wilcox as an "innovative and energetic" leader with "a natural flair for public relations."

Upon beginning his term as Foundation executive director in July 1949, one of Wilcox's first duties was to oversee the 1949–50 school year's fund-raising campaign. Considering IU's 10,000-plus alumni base, the results were only fair: 1,403 donors contributed $46,487. Wilcox wondered whether alumni understood the Foundation and its goals. "If our alumni today had been exposed to the Foundation and its activities before they became alumni, the response to mailings would be considerably greater," he explained in a January 30, 1950, letter to Wells. In other words, Wilcox wanted to make a pitch to the current students about the Foundation, in order to ensure their future alumni gifts and word-of-mouth influence with other alums. To head such an effort he created the first Student Foundation Committee, recruiting 36 of the most active and influential juniors and seniors on campus—both male and female, greek and non-greek—to spread the word. Wilcox and Wells educated them on the motives of the Foundation during a dinner in their honor on February 19, 1950, and then sent them off to work. For two months the committee members visited every dormitory, fraternity, and sorority to spread awareness and gain support for the Foundation. The campaign was successful, but once everyone on campus had heard the clarion call of the Foundation, the committee was left with little else to do.

Not long after the committee became idle, Wilcox took the walk to Hickory Hall. He was awestruck at the amount of excitement generated by the impromptu bicycle race, and his mind, too, started racing. In the wee hours of that night he called one of his Student Committee members, Al Moellering, waking him with this new idea. A bicycle race, Wilcox explained, could be the first signature student event sponsored by the Foundation in the continuing quest to build future alumni support. He pictured students enjoying the race, remembering the good times as alums, and responding in kind with open checkbooks (a somewhat oversimplified process, to be sure, but essentially the end result). And that would just be the long-term goal, as in the short term Wilcox aimed to win over the community and take care of students whose plight mirrored his of a decade earlier. He wanted to use race profits to fund scholarships for working students.

Having already sold his student committee on the event during fall 1950, Wilcox called some 400 other student leaders, faculty, and staff to Alumni Hall in the student union on January 20, 1951, to formally

The first Indiana University Foundation Student Committee, February 1950.

announce his creation and its upcoming May 12 premiere at Memorial Stadium. On stage with Wilcox and President Wells were numerous Student Committee officers, Dean of Students Col. R. L. Shoemaker, and Bloomington Mayor Tom Lemon, and above all of them in foot-high letters read the theme of the event: "To Help Those Who Help Themselves." Wells addressed the throng and proclaimed Wilcox's idea "a great promotion," and one that would "gain friends for the Foundation and gain funds for the scholarship drive." Lemon promised the coop-

eration of the city, proclaiming "what's good for IU is good for Bloomington." As always, Wilcox the P.R. man put on a well-choreographed affair, even making headlines. The *Daily Student* published a special Sunday edition to publicize the announcement, with the lead story written by newspaper editor Charlie Lyons, whom Wilcox shrewdly picked to serve as Student Committee Public Relations Director.

Wilcox barely remembered his father, the 1919 Indianapolis 500 champion, but maintaining a great love for the automobile race was one

HE SERVES BEST
WHO SERVES
THE TRUTH

THE WEATHER
Turning much colder,
snow.

THE INDIANA DAILY STUDENT

VOL. LXXX—No. 71—Z 173.   INDIANA UNIVERSITY   SUNDAY, JANUARY 21, 1951.   BLOOMINGTON, INDIANA   Established 1867

Mickey McCarty Says:

(Editor's Note — Walter McCarty is a member of the University's Board of Trustees. As editor of The Indianapolis News, his column, Mickey McCarty, Says, appears daily in The News.)

FELLOW IU ALUMNI AND TAXPAYERS: When the sad and solemn Wilcox told a small group of his Indianapolis Fourth Estaters

I.U. TO STAGE 'LITTLE 500' BICYCLE RACE IN STADIUM

Howdy Wilcox's plan for his Little 500 was to pattern it after the Indianapolis 500, the race that made his father a champion. His connections with the Indianapolis Motor Speedway led to some valuable early publicity, such as this early 1951 photo opportunity at the snowy speedway. Pictured with women from the Foundation Student Committee are Speedway President Wilbur Shaw (on bike) and official Indianapolis 500 starter Seth Klein. Indianapolis Star cartoonist Charlie Werner also got into the spirit with a drawing of Speedway owner Tony Hulman waving the checkered flag to Shaw (front) and IU President Herman B Wells (note the obstacle about to fell their front tire).

Setting the Pace   5

way Howdy kept his father's memory alive. In a way, Howard Wilcox Sr. would live on through his son, as the format of the IU bicycle race was designed to be a carbon copy of the Indianapolis 500. Everyone in Bloomington could relate to that event, and the Foundation's would be a spin-off, literally a "Little" 500. Just like the automobile race his father had won three decades earlier, this one would also be run in May, only earlier in the month so as not to conflict with students' final exams. Just like Indy, a field of 33 teams would gather at 11 A.M., aligned in 11 rows of three. A pace car would give the field a flying start to 200 laps around an oval track, albeit only for 50 miles instead of the 500 raced by Indy cars and the 1950 Hickory Hall teams (who, incidentally, tired and gave up well before their planned six-day race was complete). Each team would have a financial sponsor, with the business's name featured prominently on riders' jerseys and pit areas. The Little 500 would be regulated much like its big brother, with auto racing rules modified to fit the bike format. Those rules would be enforced on race day by the Bloomington Bicycle Bureau, a local cycling group. Teams would earn a spot in the field in qualifications held roughly one month prior to the race. Each team would include four men, with one rider on the quarter-mile track at a time. When one rider became fatigued, he could ride to his designated pit and pass his bike to a teammate.

At the Indianapolis 500 some of the fiercest competition took place in the weeks prior to the event, as teams constantly tinkered with cars to generate the best combination of speed and handling. Although the same could be done with bicycles, Wilcox took it upon himself to provide the bicycles for the Little 500, ensuring that his race would be won by riders and not by disparities in the quality of equipment. Working on a shoestring budget, he called the Schwinn bicycle company in Chicago and asked if they would donate bicycles in exchange for promotional consideration. Schwinn officials balked at offering freebies for a first-time race but offered to sell Wilcox some 40 bicycles at wholesale cost. "Spending money I didn't have," Wilcox later said, he accepted the offer and paid $1,700 for the bikes. "With conventional frames, gears and tires," the 1951 Little 500 guidelines read, "these bicycles are equipped with English racing saddles, racing handle bars and with racing pedals. No major adjustments in the bicycles will be permitted." Each team was allotted one bike with which to practice, qualify, and compete.

With the support of much of the campus guaranteed following Wilcox's January announcement, the race to organize The Race began. Howdy took care of securing the sponsors, calling on a few Indianapolis friends and local businesses (12 of which signed up immediately in January, upon first hearing the announcement). By race day, Wilcox had 33 sponsors at $100 each. Each sponsor was randomly assigned a bike team, and the Student Committee recruited those teams—a task that may have been the easiest of the year. Every men's housing unit would be allowed to enter one team, and few wanted to be left out of the newest event on campus. By the March 15 entry deadline the committee was flooded with entries, as 57 of Indiana's 64 men's housing units (24 fraternities and 33 dormitories) submitted the required entry forms and $10 fee. It was a participation rate of 89 percent—an overwhelming figure for an unproven commodity.

One of many bumps in the road to race day involved scheduling qualifications for the field, as IU track and field coach Gordon Fisher vehemently opposed allowing bicycles on his soft-cindered Memorial Stadium running surface any time before race day. A compromise was struck, and qualifications were moved to the University Auditorium on April 7, 14, and 21. The planning was sound, but the fickle Indiana weather forced some shuffling. Rain canceled the first date, and when riders returned for the second date they were greeted by stiff headwinds through the north stretch of the Auditorium course. And with or without wind, the route was quite odd and difficult.

For a qualifying attempt, each team's first rider started on the road in front of the Auditorium doors, headed for the southwest corner of the building, then turned and pedaled out of sight on a path more naturally square than oval in shape. The next rider, waiting at the start for the bike, wouldn't see his teammate again until he made a sharp turn off the northwest corner and back onto the main strip. Riders had to complete their exchange within a 15-foot space surrounding the start/finish line—an area that proved too narrow to make an exchange with any speed. (A few years later, it would be widened to 32 feet.) The exchange itself was a unique and treacherous maneuver few teams ever completely perfected, as one rider would jump off the bike, and the next would take control of the bike in the allotted space. The second rider was permitted to run out of the zone with the bike before mounting, but without the

The Little
500

Qualifications for the first race were at the IU Auditorium, with the first day of attempts held on April 14, 1951. Officials worried about riders falling onto the unforgiving concrete permitted the use of "catchers" in assisting riders dismounting the bike on exchanges (catcher is to the left of the riders in photo, and the Wildermuth Fieldhouse is in the background).

first rider's help. During an exchange, an early dismount by the first man or a late controlling of the bike by the second man constituted a foul, and the team would have to take a second attempt later in the day. Each team was permitted three tries, and fouls on all three would mean no race. Three legal exchanges were required to complete the successful attempt, with all four riders circling one lap. Exchange fouls were very common, as were wipeouts, even though teams employed "catchers" to help the man jumping off the bike. The concrete surface at the Auditorium caused more than a few scrapes and bruises.

The Phi Delta Theta fraternity team posted the fastest time of the April 14 qualifiers, finishing in 3 minutes, 5.9 seconds and securing the pole position. A total of 26 teams attempted qualifying on the windy day, with 15 succeeding. The first six qualifiers of the day were permitted an opportunity to try again the next week, as there were no previous records to help gauge whether their first times would be good enough for the field. Three teams (the North Hall Barons dorm team and the Sigma Alpha Mu and Sigma Phi Epsilon fraternities) took the chance and failed. At the April 21 qualifications the Phi Kappa Psi fraternity broke the week-old track record with a 3:04.6 time. But in accordance with Indianapolis Motor Speedway rules, the Phi Delts kept the pole position

Student Committee workers kept track of qualifications results on typewriters and a chalkboard near the start/finish line (the Auditorium is in the background). Among the results shown on the board are the times of the North Hall Barons, Sigma Alpha Mu and Sigma Phi Epsilon teams—all three opted to waive the posted times and make another attempt the following week, but failed on the second try and lost their chances to ride in the race.

by posting the fastest time on the first day of qualifying. Rain once again interrupted the proceedings, forcing three more teams to qualify on April 22 in windier conditions than the two previous days (six teams that simply failed to appear at all for qualifying were disqualified). Once the dust settled and the field was set, a glimpse at the lineup showed fraternities faring better overall in qualifying, as 20 of the 24 entered cracked the top 33, compared with 13 of the 33 residence hall entrants.

One of the residence hall teams came from venerable South Hall,

the oldest dormitory on campus. Nicknamed the Buccaneers, the same name used by the dorm's intramural teams, this group brought an especially impressive athletic resumé to the track. Bob Moore, a graduate student and the team's oldest rider, was a three-year letterman on the IU cross-country team. Russ Keller, a junior, competed for IU as a wrestler. Both men were well conditioned and had even served as guinea pigs for university researchers, running for hours on treadmills for a study on the effects of extended physical activity. The Bucs' team also included a

former football player, Glen Wilson, who had competed for two years at Hanover College before transferring to IU. While in high school he rode seven miles to and from school and boasted he could make the trip in 20 minutes.

Since February, the Buccaneers had been doing something few other Little 500 teams had even thought of—heavy bike training on the roads in and around Bloomington. Moore, Keller, Wilson, and freshman John Skomp completed 10- to 15-mile rides every day, not only around Bloomington but to other towns in Monroe County such as Ellettsville and Stanford. To them these daily trips weren't chores, but rituals to look forward to. To them the Little 500 would not be a parade on bicycles, but a race to be won. South Hall even engineered its own exchange maneuver, handing off the bike by hopping off the back of the seat, not the side, as other teams were doing. An amateur Indianapolis cyclist (whose identity was kept secret by team captain Keller) taught them the maneuver three days before the race, and the team worked incessantly on it. Armed with this odd, new technique and a few other secrets, the seventh-qualifying dorm team looked increasingly like the favorites to win the first Little 500.

On the eve of race day, Wilcox and the Student Committee were sure every possible detail had been taken care of for their showcase event. Part of the master plan involved pairing each bicycle team with a women's housing unit, preferably a sorority for a fraternity and a women's dorm for a men's dorm. The women would be the bikers' "coed sponsors," and—in 1950s fashion—they designed racers' jerseys, decorated pits, and most of all, supported their men loudly on race day. Despite the race weekend conflicting with Mother's Day, traditionally a well-celebrated holiday among students and especially among the women's housing units, the Foundation successfully petitioned the women to fit Little 500 into their weekends. Wilcox promised everyone a great spectacle and gathered a host of familiar faces from the Indianapolis Motor

Speedway to help out. Speedway Board Chairman Tony Hulman attended, along with Speedway President Wilbur Shaw, a three-time Indianapolis 500 winner. Shaw's responsibility was to drive the official Indy pace car, a 1952 Chrysler New Yorker convertible, around the track to give the Little 500 a flying start. Waving the checkered flag would be Seth Klein, duplicating the task he had performed at every Indy 500 since 1920. Tommy Milton, chief steward at Indy, would serve in the same capacity for the bicyclists, as would track announcer Sid Collins. The event Wilcox created to mirror the Indianapolis 500 was about to do just that, not only in form, but in sheer star power.

Only Mother Nature could thwart the beautifully laid designs, and in a repeat of April's qualifications, try she did. Throughout the evening and into the night before the race, rain pelted the city. Nevertheless, a Friday night parade continued as scheduled, as did the "Little 500 Bicycle Bounce," a free campus dance sponsored by Alpha Chi Omega and Theta Chi (held indoors at Theta Chi instead of on the lawn as planned). Wilcox, however, wasn't in a festive mood Friday night. He faced the possibility of a washed-out race, and he rushed to track down friend and IU alumnus F. McKinley Blough at a Sigma Alpha Epsilon fraternity party for a much-needed weather report. Blough had a connection at a St. Louis weather center, and, fortunately, the report he received was promising: a sunny, warm front would move in the next day. Wilcox still stayed up until 5 A.M., fearing the worst, but by morning his fears had dissipated and the race would continue as scheduled.

By late Saturday morning, May 12, 1951, the results of the Foundation's massive publicity efforts for the Little 500 were evident at Memorial Stadium. Some 7,000 spectators gathered in the stands, accompanied by media from all over the region in the press box and infield. Newspapers from Bloomington, Indianapolis, Louisville, and many towns in between sent reporters, as did the Associated Press. Local radio stations WFIU and WTTS prepared to broadcast the race, and Paramount News sent a film crew. And, true to Wilcox's history of chasing

Above left: Howdy Wilcox's Indianapolis friends joined in the festivities on race day, May 12, 1951 (From left to right are Wilcox, Seth Klein, Wilbur Shaw and Tony Hulman). Above: before the race Shaw addressed the riders, reminding them to be aware of each other during the race, and Klein explained the various flags to the crowd (on the left is an official from the Bloomington Bicycle Bureau, and holding the microphone is Indianapolis Motor Speedway track announcer Sid Collins, who would also announce the Little 500).

Just like the Indianapolis 500, a pace car gave the 11 rows of three riders a "flying" start to 200 laps of competition. Driving the Chrysler is Wilbur Shaw, with President Herman B Wells alongside in the front seat. Both pictures were taken roughly at the same time, one from the infield looking toward the frontstretch stands, the other from just ahead of the start/finish line looking into the east end of the stadium.

money, *everyone* paid to get in—media, vendors, riders and coaches, President Wells, even Wilcox himself. Tickets cost $5 for box seats, $2 for adults, $1 for students and faculty, and 60 cents for children. Programs cost a quarter.

As 11 A.M. approached, a few pre-race ceremonies filled time on the infield podium. All-American basketball player Bill Garrett was named the outstanding senior athlete and received the Jerry Stuteville Award, named for a basketball player killed one year earlier in an automobile accident. On the track, Wilbur Shaw addressed the riders, wishing them luck and asking them to take care of themselves and be conscious of their competitors. Following Shaw's greeting the 33 Schwinn bicycles were assembled on the track in eleven rows of three, Indy-style, as the teams

The well-trained South Hall Buccaneers claimed the lead of the race in the 11th lap and cruised through the first half with ease. Bob Moore (shown behind front wheel, handing off to John Skomp) was the team's most talented rider, and rode the majority of the team's laps. Looking on are fellow Buccaneer Glen Wilson (left) and team trainer Walter Koch (in hat behind Moore).

were introduced to the crowd and the pace car loaded up its distinguished passengers. Shaw drove, President Wells rode shotgun, and Tony Hulman rode in the backseat, along with Foundation Student Committee co-chairs Kenneth Kress and Robert Skiles. The car took a few parade laps with the field in tow, then sped off the track while the riders continued on at full speed with the drop of the green flag. At the start, Phi Delta Theta's rider opened with a furious but foolish dead-sprint effort, building nearly a one-half lap lead before falling exhaustibly back to the field just as quickly as he had left it. Meanwhile, Bob Moore of the South Hall Buccaneers held steady from his position on the inside of the third starting row, moving up to third by the 10th lap. On the following lap he took South Hall into the lead—for good.

Months of preparation combined with a few savvy race-day tactics helped the Buccaneers turn the 1951 Little 500 into a runaway. The preparation even extended to the team's pit, where a stationary bike and a trainer helped keep them loose throughout the race. Few teams had the foresight to hire an athletic trainer, thinking either that the 50-mile race wouldn't be overly strenuous or that the infield first-aid tent would be more than enough. But the Bucs had their own man, Walter Koch, a graduate student in health and safety, who turned the 15-foot pit into a miniature health center. Koch supplied the pit with necessary supplies for the inevitable scrapes and bruises, and he rubbed and iced down each rider after his shift.

"They were the only ones out there who knew what they were doing," North Hall Friar rider Jerry Ruff said of the Bucs, who outlasted the field with a unique strategy for rotating riders. While most teams divided up the race's 200 laps into sets of five or 10 laps per rider before an exchange (at least, that was the *plan*—by the end of the race many teams ran single-lap shifts), South Hall let a stopwatch dictate when a rider needed a rest. Prior to race day the team estimated that a 47-second lap pace could win the race (judging from Phi Delta Theta's pole time of 3:05.9, which averaged 47-second laps on a more difficult course), so on race day the goal was to ride every lap at or under that time. If a rider exceeded that magic number, another would take over. As the race settled into its middle stages South Hall started to lap the competition with ease, proving the estimate accurate. Moore clearly was the best of the Bucs and took the bulk of the work, riding 114 laps overall. Wilson and Skomp contrib-

uted some hard, short shifts, while Keller added a bit more endurance and longer shifts. Other teams weakened as the race wore on, some to the point of the one-lap shifts, and the combination of such fatigue and the knowledge that first place was out of reach made South Hall's day all the easier.

Late in the race it became clear that the only way the Bucs could avoid victory would be to somehow knock themselves out, and they almost did. On lap 146 Wilson came in for an exchange, made a sloppy dismount and bent the pedals into the frame. South Hall's personal pit mechanic (brought along by Moore in another well-thought idea) hammered the pedals back into place, and Skomp rode off. He didn't get far, however, as the Schwinn's chain broke, sending Skomp back for a more complex repair. Though South Hall wasn't the only team to suffer crippling bike problems—the Ferguson House team spent some 19 minutes of race time stuck in the pits, thanks to a broken spoke on the first lap and later two flat tires—it was the only team that could lead the race even when *not* riding. When the chain broke, the Bucs held a five-minute lead over the field, so the ensuing three-minute, 11-second wait for repairs failed to knock them out of first place. The incident did, however, liven up the last hour of the race and give other teams' riders and fans some glimmer of hope, if only for a moment.

Back on track safely for the final quarter of the race, team No. 7 again rebuilt its lead and crossed the finish line first with a time of 2 hours, 39 minutes, averaging 18.99 miles per hour. Second-place Sigma Alpha Epsilon finished its 200th lap 4 minutes, 35 seconds later. Thirteen more teams were allowed to complete 200 laps before the red flag was shown and the race halted. South Hall, the team that believed 47-second laps could win the race, rode at just that clip and rejoiced as Little 500 champions. The elapsed time for turning the 200 laps, minus the three minutes for bike repair, averaged 46.5 seconds per lap. On the victors' stand Skomp tried to account for his team's success by noting that none of his teammates smoked or drank alcohol, and though such a proclamation probably made the South Hall Buccaneers unique on a college campus, it didn't even begin to explain their thorough dominance of the first Little 500.

For their impressive victory, the Bucs collected an equally impressive bounty of prizes to take back to the dormitory. Indiana Lt. Gov. John

How good were the 1951 South Hall Buccaneers? Late in the race they suffered major bicycle problems and had to spend over three minutes idle in the pits while undergoing repairs, but upon re-entry into the race still held first place.

Watkins presented the riders with a three-foot-high winner's trophy immediately following the race, and each individual received his own small trophy with a built-in clock. In keeping with an Indianapolis 500 tradition, L. Strauss & Co. of Indianapolis commissioned an artist's portrait of the winning team, to be displayed in South Hall. Prior to the race local merchants donated money for lap prizes, with $20 awarded to the team in the lead at every 20-lap interval. South Hall led from lap 11 to the end, sweeping all the prizes and netting $200. Even South Hall's

coed sponsor, Maple Hall, received a $100 mirror from a local mirror company for backing the winning team, while Alpha Chi Omega sorority picked up a separate trophy for best pit decorations. Topping the list of prizes was a giant RCA television-radio-phonograph console, compliments of the local RCA plant. The second- and third-place finishers also received RCA televisions, but South Hall's model was a top-of-the-line beauty that few families, much less college students, had in their homes. In fact, after May 1951 many students from all over campus flocked to

The Little
500

Spoils and smiles were all around on the winners' stand, as South Hall emerged on top in the first Little 500. The winning riders, from left to right, were Glen Wilson, Bob Moore, Russ Keller and John Skomp (Moore is enthusiastically thanking Maple Hall coed sponsor Joyce Hilgemeier, and Keller is posing with the three-foot-high winner's trophy). Along with the team trophy and individual trophies, the riders brought home to South Hall a team portrait and a state-of-the-art RCA television-radio-phonograph console.

South Hall on Friday nights to watch top boxing matches on NBC's popular *Gillette Cavalcade of Sports*.

When the final gate receipts were tallied and all expenses paid from the 1951 Little 500, including $2,000 for bicycles and equipment and $1,400 in Federal Amusement Tax, Howdy Wilcox's creation showed a profit of nearly $6,000. As promised, the money went toward working students, in the form of sixty $100 scholarships. Two weeks after the race, the South Hall Buccaneers were invited to the Indianapolis 500 as guests of Wilbur Shaw, and before the automobile race he let the team take a spin around the track in Glen Wilson's 1928 Rolls Royce. Just as Wilcox's vision had become a reality on May 12, 1951, his race came full circle that day at the Indianapolis Motor Speedway: his champions rode on the track that had made his father a champion.

2. "We Have a Good Thing Going Here"

Not surprisingly, Howdy Wilcox's quick turnaround of the IU Foundation drew the attention of outside businesses. In under two years' time, the man had accepted a new job with a stagnant organization and turned it into a dynamic force, thanks to a signature event he created from scratch. And by forming a student group to run the Little 500, Wilcox provided the product with a structure to help it last long after his time at IU.

The *Indianapolis Star* and *News* newspapers were particularly impressed with Wilcox's accomplishments, and in 1952 offered him the position of personnel and promotions director. Having collected a $9,000 yearly salary from the Foundation, he couldn't pass up the newspapers' offer of $12,000. Trading campus life for the "real world," Wilcox remained in the newspaper industry until 1966, both in Indianapolis and at subsidiary papers in Phoenix. His final business coup began in midlife, at age 46, when he started his own public relations firm in Indianapolis. Twenty years later he sold his firm for one million dollars.

Wilcox remained with the Foundation part-time to help oversee the second running of the Little 500, which ran just as smoothly as the first, at least off the track. The 1952 race enjoyed a higher turnout, with about 8,500 spectators, and an increased amount of scholarships—$8,200 worth—for working students. On the track, however, riders experienced a different race than 1951's relatively slow and tame affair. The overall pace of the event picked up, helped in part by riders with a year's experience under their belts, but consequently so did the number of accidents. Some 50 riders tumbled to the cinders during the course of the 200 laps, and the *Daily Student*'s account of the spills revealed everything from the comical to the downright scary. Freshman Stan Solomon of Kappa Delta Rho crashed on his very first lap and was rushed to the hospital with a fractured cheekbone. Stan Dusseau of Rogers West W wrecked on an exchange and cracked a rib when he fell into a cot in an adjoining pit. Dodds House captain Robert Primavera crashed near the starting line and hit his head on a box of camera flash bulbs ("a photo finish," one writer quipped). Many teams sent one or more members to the infield hospital tent, victims of not only a faster race but of a still somewhat unfamiliar one. Riders in 1952 had again qualified at the

After just two and a half years with the IU Foundation, Howdy Wilcox traded Bloomington for Indianapolis and a position with the Indianapolis Star *and* News *in 1952. He continued to closely follow his creation, however, and served as the Little 500 starter for several years (1958 race shown).*

Auditorium, and prior to race day few had experience on a cinder surface.

Considering those factors, one would have expected the '52 winning team to be loaded with seasoned Little 500 veterans. Enter the North Hall Friars, another team from the campus's Men's Residence Center, today known as Collins Living-Learning Center. Sandy Franklin and Jerry Ruff returned from the sixth-place Friar team of 1951, and South Hall Buccaneer Russ Keller moved over to the North team. Of the four victorious 1951 Buccaneers, only Keller had returned to the Little 500. John Skomp and Glen Wilson had left school for the armed forces, and superstar Bob Moore finished his graduate work and prepared for the 1952 Olympic trials (though a collision with a truck prior to the trials ended his Olympic bid). "Conditioning paid off again," proclaimed Keller after North Hall held off Rogers East V and Phi Kappa Psi to win. Keller himself was the catalyst of the conditioning efforts, instilling in the Friars the same work ethic of the Bucs, with daily training regimens focused on long rides and dedication to winning.

The race's successful second running answered any lingering questions about its staying power (the 1952 race program cover went a step further, boldly advertising the Little 500 as "The Greatest Collegiate Bicycle Race in the World"), but Wilcox's official departure from the Foundation in August 1952 left a leadership hole. President Wells again stepped in to hand-pick the next Foundation head man, just as he had done in 1949. During a summer visit to a state park, Wells found his man in the form of William S. Armstrong—a man who, like Wilcox, had honed his people skills as an IU student.

While growing up in Owensboro, Kentucky, Bill Armstrong dreamed not of the IU cream and crimson but of Purdue Boilermaker black and gold. An uncle had played football and baseball for the Boilers, and young Bill thought he would follow the same path. By playing football, baseball, and basketball he did continue the family athletic tradition, but instead in Bloomington and not West Lafayette. He also stayed active around campus, with the Sigma Nu fraternity, Sphinx Club, and the Intramural Athletic Association. For varsity athletes he organized and served as first president of the I-Men's Club, and in 1941 he inaugurated the Cream and Crimson intrasquad football game, a spring tradition ever

Former South Hall champion Russ Keller returned to the Little 500 in 1952, racing for neighboring North Hall. He took charge of the Friars' training regimens, and guided the team to its first of two consecutive wins (Keller, left, is taking the bike from teammate Jerry Ruff).

For decades the pace car for the Little 500 was borrowed from the Indianapolis 500, including this 1952 Studebaker, shown off creatively by members of the Student Committee.

Herman B Wells (left) would not take "no" for an answer as he actively pursued Bill Armstrong (right) for the vacant IU Foundation executive director's position. Gregarious and popular as an IU student, Armstrong would pick up right where he left off after accepting the job.

The Little
500

since. Staying involved in student life and standing over six feet, if there was ever a prototype "Big Man on Campus," Armstrong was it.

After serving in World War II, Armstrong returned to Owensboro and started a family with wife Martha. There he juggled activities much as he did in his college days, lending help to community groups and youth sports leagues while working as a broadcaster and as director of sales and advertising for the Ideal Milk Company. When first approached by Wells in 1952, he confessed to knowing nothing about the Foundation and declined the offer. But Wells knew about Armstrong's former stature on campus a decade earlier, and that his outgoing personality was perfect to further the Foundation's growth. "We have a good thing going here," Wells explained. "Much more than just a bicycle race."

Armstrong finally relented, and he arrived in Bloomington on December 1, 1952, to take over as Foundation executive director. Intending to take the task of building the Foundation seriously, he didn't think running a bike race would be part of fulfilling his duties. One of the first students he met in the Foundation offices was a 23-year-old senior named Jim Pauloski, who had served on the 1951–52 Student Committee. A few months before Armstrong had arrived, Pauloski was appointed by George Heighway and the exiting Wilcox (who would return to future races as official starter) to serve as Little 500 coordinator. Since Armstrong didn't care for the race, he didn't immediately care for Pauloski either. But Armstrong soon promoted Pauloski to the presidency of the Steering Committee (originally the Student Committee, but renamed as the top governing body of the new "Student Foundation"), and stepped back as preparations for the 1953 race began. When Indianapolis Motor Speedway dignitaries like Wilbur Shaw and Sid Collins again volunteered their help on race day, and 48 housing units signed up for qualifying, Armstrong's negative attitude toward the Little 500 began to change.

Armstrong had little involvement in the running of the 1953 race, but he did call on some of his connections in the entertainment industry to lure Lu Ann Simms, a performer from the CBS variety show *Arthur Godfrey and His Friends,* to the Little 500. She was to serve as the "Little 500 Sweetheart," appearing at events throughout the weekend and, most importantly, kissing each member of the winning bike team. In Armstrong's opinion, having an attractive female celebrity on hand would

Helping to bridge the transition between Armstrong (far right) and Wilcox (second from right) was Jim Pauloski (left), a member of the 1951–52 Student Committee and Little 500 coordinator in Wilcox's absence. Armstrong didn't immediately take to Pauloski or the bicycle race, but made the senior his first Steering Committee President and watched with growing enthusiasm as the 1953 Little 500 played out to a crowd of 10,000.

"add class" to the overall weekend, not to mention generate some extra Little 500 publicity.

Talking to reporters after the 1953 race, the North Hall Friar riders complained that the 20-year-old Simms "didn't put enough passion" into her post-race responsibilities. Perhaps they were speaking the truth or perhaps they were slightly bored, having just completed a clean sweep of the Little 500 season. During qualifications at the University School

After two years at the Auditorium, Little 500 qualifications moved to a much more bicycle-friendly facility, the University School track. Located northeast of campus, the track would hum throughout the spring with cyclists practicing for qualifications and the race. (Helmets, incidentally, were not required equipment in Little 500 riding until 1957.)

cinder track (which replaced the Auditorium for 1953 qualifications), the Friars secured the pole position with an attempt three seconds faster than the second-qualifying Phi Gamma Deltas. On race day, North Hall defended its '52 title with ease. Jerry Ruff and Gene Strause returned from the previous year, and added Leonard Border and Robert Sedam to complete a foursome which finished more than three minutes ahead of its closest followers. Ten-dollar lap prizes were awarded to the race's leader at every 10-lap interval, and of the 20 available, North Hall took all but four. Team manager Keller said the men were in better shape than in 1952, thanks in part to veterans Ruff and Strause, who

pioneered a Little 500 training tradition by riding in Florida over spring vacation.

The 1953 Little 500, while not especially competitive on the track, again recorded strong attendance figures. Ten thousand people came to the race, marking the first time attendance was higher than the IU student population. (Such numbers do not imply that every student attended, but that many did, along with other friends and fans of IU.) Also, proceeds from the Foundation's 1952–53 alumni fund-raising drive topped the $100,000 mark—more than doubling the take from just two

years earlier, when the Little 500 premiered. With these figures, Bill Armstrong was finally convinced. His job really *was* in part about running a bike race, and that was fine. The challenge would be to make it bigger and better every year.

And so the expansion began. Armstrong started becoming a details man, taking it upon himself to know the entire operation. It all started with the Student Foundation members, and Armstrong made a point of getting to know each one. He would personally appoint the top few men and women for the one-year steering committee terms, an agonizing job that got increasingly tough as the Little 500 grew. The Student Foundation was becoming one of the most prestigious organizations on campus, joining mainstays such as Union Board and student government, and with its popularity came many students gunning for a few precious openings. A top spot in the Student Foundation even evolved into an instant post-graduate success ticket—major corporations such as Xerox and IBM recruiting at IU would sometimes hire a Steering Committee member on the spot, solely on Armstrong's recommendation. With rewards like that, Armstrong made sure that only the most dedicated rose to the top. Though new Steering Committee members were named during race week, Armstrong's selection process began several months before. He would quietly monitor students' work during the not-so-glamorous times, making sure they did a fair share of the grunt work that went into Little 500 planning. On occasion he would come across a student during race week claiming he or she was primed for his approval, despite little work in prior months. Armstrong would stay firm in his method and pass over such students, even though it often meant taking an angry phone call from parents wanting to know why their child was being denied one of IU's most cherished student appointments.

The opportunities for leadership did grow, however, as the number of Little 500 committees ballooned. In 1953 there were a dozen committees: administration/records, bike control, coed sponsors, correspondence, general arrangements, prizes, programs, publicity/promotion, rules/regulations, set-up, tickets, and timing/scoring. Each at-large Student Foundation member joined one of the committees, and each committee had a chairperson. The next-best thing to a seat on the Steering Committee was a chairmanship, and the number of those increased

as Armstrong and the students expanded the scope of the weekend. By 1955 the number of committees had doubled to 24, thanks to the addition of new segments dedicated mostly to riders and publicity of the race. The latter was given particularly close attention, as separate publicity/promotion committees were created for the student newspaper, the campus news bureau, radio outlets, and television. In the mid-1950s subsidiary events were added to the weekend, such as the Little 500 Variety Show and Mini 500, and those were also given separate committees. A potential problem could have occurred if the Student Foundation membership didn't grow along with the race, but like much of the Little 500's charmed early history, this problem never developed. Students flocked to the Student Foundation: In 1953 there were 71 at-large members, and five years later there were more than 200. Its membership increased nearly 300 percent while the undergraduate population grew only 20 percent during that time. And the growth was only beginning.

For the 1954 Little 500, Armstrong made the first major alteration to the race itself since 1951 by breaking off the Foundation's relationship with Schwinn. Wilcox had negotiated the original agreement with Schwinn, and through 1953 the Foundation still paid wholesale cost for bicycles. U.S. Rubber Company of Indianapolis had provided tires free of charge for those early years, and one of their reps tipped off Armstrong to the fact that other companies were looking for a piece of the hot Little 500 pie. The Cleveland Welding Company of Cleveland, Ohio, was one company with a bike division, and Armstrong paid them a visit. Delighted at the chance to be part of the Little 500, the company's president negotiated a deal with the Foundation to provide Roadmaster brand bicycles and parts free of charge in exchange for promotional consideration (with perhaps the greatest free advertising coming with the traditional call to the riders, "Mount Your Roadmaster Bicycles," a variation of the Indianapolis 500's "Gentlemen, Start Your Engines"). The relationship has never ended, with Roadmaster providing new bicycles every year (old bicycles were and are used for practice and qualifying). Schwinn officials soon regretted losing their ties to the high-profile race, and later offered Armstrong anything he wanted, free of charge. Other bicycle companies did the same, but Armstrong and the Student Foundation

THE INDIANA DAILY STUDENT

SIGMA NU WINS '500'; TACKS SLOW PACE

Tacks Mar Race

One of the oddest incidents in Little 500 history occurred in 1954, when pranksters nearly wiped out the race by pouring tacks on the Memorial Stadium cinders. Officials did their best to pick up as many of the tacks as possible (here they are combing a particularly dangerous area in the third turn), but dozens of flat tires were all but unavoidable. Even after winning, the Sigma Nus found a tack in their bicycle. The culprits were never found.

stuck with the Roadmaster, even as its parent company changed from Cleveland Welding Company to American Machine and Foundry (AMF) to its present parent, the Brunswick Corporation.

Surely, when the Cleveland Welding Company president negotiated the equipment deal with the Foundation, he had a vision of the Roadmaster bicycles speeding around the track in a record-setting Little 500 thriller. About the only part of that vision that came to fruition in 1954 was the record-setting. Pranksters got to the Tenth Street Stadium cinders before the riders on race day and spilled hundreds of half-inch carpet tacks on the southeast turn of the track, causing a flat tire epi-

demic. Seventy flats stalled teams throughout the day, leaving student workers scrambling for spare tires and officials scratching their heads in what *Sports Illustrated* called "one of the sports oddities of the year." Twice during the race the caution flag was flown for multiple laps while volunteers picked tacks off the turn, and at lap 125 the race was nearly called off due to a lack of spare tires at the track and downtown (where students quickly exhausted local stores' tire inventories). In the end the results reflected the long day at the stadium, as the winning team of Sigma Nu crossed the line in a record slow time of 2:45.35—and discovered a tack in its front tire. The culprits of the "great tack mystery" were never found,

and starting the following year the Foundation took security measures to curtail future "oddities."

While the tacks were no more than a temporary issue (a few more were found and caused trouble in 1955, even after a giant magnet was circled around the track), the winning performance of the Sigma Nu fraternity was an important sign of the future in Little 500 competition. In the three previous races, Sigma Nu failed to qualify once and finished 17th and 13th, but in 1954 the fraternity built a formidable team. During the 1953–54 school year the Sigma Nu men were having a new house built on North Jordan Avenue, and in the meantime lived in a temporary housing unit on Third Street, not far from the Chatterbox restaurant. Serving up food there was a 24-year-old freshman named Ralph Martin, attending IU on the G.I. Bill. Sigma Nu members ate there often and talked to Martin, and they soon found out that he had amateur cycling experience. A native of New York, Martin was a former western New York junior champion in the under–16 division, and as a high school senior had raced in the national junior championships. The fraternity members liked him and his credentials, and they asked him to pledge and ride Little 500. He joined teammates Joe Magers, Richard Silcox, and Fred Mercer, who came to IU on a track scholarship but pulled ligaments and switched to cycling. Mercer made the transition well and brought the entire team to his hometown of Evansville to train over Easter break on the Evansville Bosse High School cinder track. As with the 1953 North Hall Friars, the out-of-town training paid off on race day, as the Sigma Nus hung around the front all day, then outlasted the field in the final 20 laps. With kisses from the "Sweetheart" McGuire Sisters, it was official—an IU fraternity had finally won the Little 500.

One of the Little 500's greatest assets in its formative years was its inherent unpredictability. An abundance of teams entered qualifications every spring, and not just because the students were curious about the young event and wanted to avoid having their housing unit left out, but because the event appeared *winnable*. The bicycles and the cinders had a beautiful way of creating an even playing field, and even the smallest housing unit had reason to believe it could beat a mighty fraternity or anyone else on campus. A little athleticism and training helped, but with the exception of Bob Moore in 1951 no top team of the race's first four years had a truly dominating, invincible member. Consequently, every team could dream of Little 500 success.

In 1955 a record 57 teams attended April qualifications, including one newcomer from off the beaten path. South Cottage Grove fell under the "residence hall" category, but its men didn't have a home quite like the average dorm residents. They were the co-op students, the ones whose parents didn't have the resources to foot the traditional room and board bills. Their home, at the corner of 13th Street and Indiana Avenue northwest of campus, consisted of a pair of outdated World War II barracks that had so far avoided the wrecking ball. About 36 students lived in each unit, where everyone pitched in with cleaning and fended for their own meals. Freshman Ronald David was the quintessential South Cottage Grove man: he attended IU on a gymnastics scholarship, but he held down multiple jobs to get by, working as a campus policeman, at a restaurant, and as a vendor at football games. "We didn't consider ourselves part of the dorm system," David said, but that didn't mean his building passed on the biggest campus event of the spring. David met Alan Dusendschon, Gene Hindenlang, and Richard Myers, and they formed the first South Cottage Grove team. None of them had Little 500 experience, and though just having a team and an alternate was an accomplishment in itself, dreams of more were very much alive.

South Cottage Grove successfully qualified 14th for the race, a good starting position but not one that generated any serious attention from veteran teams or local media. That was probably an advantage, as the men went about their training uninterrupted and ignored. Like many top teams, the Grovers rode around town during the day, but like no one

A team from one of the campus's smallest housing units, South Cottage Grove, shocked the field by winning the 1955 race. The dorm had no Little 500 history, and the four riders (left to right, Gene Hindenlang, Richard Myers, Ronald David and Alan Dusendschon) were all underclassmen, but weeks of training during the day and late at night put them ahead of all the older, more seasoned teams.

else they would sneak onto the University School track late at night to ride on the cinders and practice exchanges. The fact that there were no lights didn't dissuade them.

Not since South Hall in the race's first year had an all-rookie team won a Little 500, but on May 14, 1955, South Cottage Grove did just that. The feat grew more impressive over time—the next winning newcomer wouldn't come until 29 years later. The win wasn't flashy, as SCG didn't hold the lead until the race's mid-point and then held off a strong ride

from the West Hall Trojans. The race was also far from record-setting, as the winning time was eight minutes slower than 1953's tack-free race (thanks to new chain-tread tires that were safer, but slower). The campus and media didn't know quite how to react—"when we won, you could hear people saying 'where's South Cottage Grove?'" David said—but the winners cared little. In the early years of the Little 500, champions could still come from unknown places.

3. Rise of the Greek Empire

Growing out of its infancy, the Little 500 soon became more than a bicycle exhibition, but a quest for supremacy among IU's most competitive society—the greeks. For most housing units in the early 1950s, simply fielding a bike team and successfully qualifying was sufficient, and finishing well was a nice bonus. However, as the decade progressed, the Little 500 weekend evolved into a battleground not just for bike teams, but for social status. Nowhere on campus was this more evident than in the crowded IU greek system, where being known as "the best" at anything meant standing above the rank and file on Third Street, Tenth Street, and Jordan Avenue. For a fraternity, the spoils of winning the high-profile Little 500 went beyond bragging rights, a first-place trophy, and lavish rider awards—winning brought respect in the system, a priceless selling point for luring new members, and, perhaps the most treasured entity, admiration from sororities (who, as coed sponsors, preferred winners to socialize with and cheer for on race day). Under Bill Armstrong's leadership, the Student Foundation not only maintained the race's competitive level but also created a festival-like atmosphere. Within such a setting, it was little coincidence that the fraternity houses with the best teams in May often had the most fun.

In the early 1950s the fraternities battled amongst each other for greek supremacy, but annually came up short in the running for the top prize. The powers from South and North Halls won championships in the event's first three years, and not until 1954 and 1956 did the top fraternity double as the overall race winner. Phi Gamma Delta (nicknamed Phi Gams in the 1950s, then more commonly known as Fijis in later years) fielded the top team in 1956, winning the first of many titles in what was an especially bizarre Little 500 season. April's qualifications were postponed one week due to heavy winds and snow flurries, and when they finally were held the experienced Sigma Nus took the pole with a record-setting 2:33.4 run on their *third* attempt—a gutsy performance when one slip-up could have meant not making the field at all. Compared to the polesitters the Phi Gams were an unknown commodity, as veteran Bud Mangles teamed with three race rookies in Joe Abatie, Jim Cusick, and Tom Herendeen. But like other successful teams of previous years, the team made up for its lack of track knowledge with heavy road training. The miles paid off at the race's midpoint, when the Phi Gams passed the flat-tire-plagued defending champion South Cottage Grove squad and built close to a one-minute lead. That lead proved important

With a win in the 1956 dust-filled Little 500, Phi Gamma Delta started a long-standing greek domination of the event (from left to right, Joe Abatie, Bud Mangles, President Herman B Wells, Jim Cusick and Tom Herendeen).

at lap 147, when the Phi Gams were penalized one lap for an illegal exchange. In winning the race the fraternity team had to ride 201 laps (not until 1964 did a penalty box and timed punishments replace lap penalties), but in the end still crossed the line well ahead of second-place Dodds House.

A record crowd of 14,020 attended the 1956 race, but hardly under ideal conditions. Eighty-plus-degree temperatures, unusually warm for mid-May, beat down upon the dry cinder track. When the 33-bicycle cavalcade got up to speed, it created a considerable dust storm. The Student Foundation workers hosed down straightaways at various points

throughout the race, but that did little to help the competitors, many of whom held cloths over their faces while riding. Track dust carried into the stands and added to spectators' discomfort, sending so many fans to the Indiana Memorial Union showers after the race that water pressure in the building dropped to zero.

The Phi Gam victory in the heat-drenched sixth Little 500 marked the end of one era and the beginning of another. While Sigma Nu's 1954 win kept the unorganized teams at bay for one year, the '56 Phi Gam triumph would ultimately keep non-greek teams out of the winner's circle for 28 years. A fraternity monopoly was underway, along with a new concept of team construction. In the early years top teams excelled by out-training the competition, like the Phi Gams, but after 1956 many of the leading fraternities initiated more of a hands-on approach to team building. With the growing race spectacle and competition on fraternity row, houses became desperate for a leg up, for a way to ensure that their team would be at the front on race day. If the race could conceivably be won on the roads prior to May, fraternities thought, maybe the race could be won even before that. Maybe—with the right personnel. After all, greeks prided themselves on finding the right men for membership, leadership, and scholarship, so why couldn't they also find the right men for the campus's main event? The era of ready-made teams was about to step to the forefront of the Little 500 landscape.

The practice of IU underclassmen making the transition from the dorm to the frat house was not uncommon, as roughly a quarter to a third of the male student population made it annually. Greek member-recruiting traditions held firm year after year, as organizations would seek out new faces to best fit in with the current at-large membership. Some houses generally attracted athletic types, while others attracted a more academic membership. Others might be regarded as having none of either. But as the 1950s wore on, a new group of young students entered the fraternity-rushing arena with a new feather in their caps—"experienced Little 500 rider." For a team, the benefits of adding such a race-tested rider showed both in-house and out. Publicly, the addition meant instant respectability in the Little 500 community and the media. Privately, an old rider in a new setting could mean fresh ideas, confidence, and a renewed sense of enthusiasm among members in a unit. Race

history showed it had happened before, when Russ Keller moved from the South Hall Buccaneers to North Hall in 1952. He not only brought his own skills but also the knowledge of what it took be a champion, and the Friars of 1952 and '53 immediately caught on and won. Fraternities decided to bank on history repeating itself.

On fraternity row, Sigma Nu became the first team to successfully lure, and eventually win with, riders who paid their Little 500 dues on other teams. The "Snus" won in 1954 without riders from old teams but with in-house talent and Ralph Martin, the New York junior champion. Starting in 1955, however, the roster changed. Clarence Doninger, a versatile athlete who played on IU freshman baseball and basketball teams and rode Little 500 for the pole-starting, fourth-finishing 1954 North Hall Barons, joined the Sigma Nu team. Cut from Branch McCracken's basketball team as a sophomore (though he would return as a senior on the 1957 Big Ten championship team), Doninger was deeply disappointed but not to the point of transferring out of Bloomington. Instead he answered the call of the Sigma Nu men, who offered an immediate spot on their bike team as incentive for his pledging. The fraternity knew he was an Evansville native, as was Fred Mercer, an active member and veteran of the '54 team, and the hometown connection sealed the deal for Doninger (who today still remains close to home, serving as IU's athletic director).

Sigma Nu finished sixth in the 1955 race, riding with just three men after a pre-race accident sidelined junior veteran Richard Silcox with a broken collarbone. For the 1956 Little 500 Silcox returned, along with Doninger and Mercer, and their fourth rider again came from the well of dorm veterans. Jerry Ruff, an integral member of the 1952–53 North Hall Friars champs, was another Evansville guy (Doninger and Ruff had attended the same high school), and he joined the fraternity after returning from the Korean War. With Ruff the pole-winning Sigma Nus represented an amazing collection of talent with a dream-team resumé. Combined, the 1956 Sigma Nu foursome brought experience from eight prior races (including four wins and two poles) with three different teams (Sigma Nu, North Hall Friars, and North Hall Barons). Only Doninger did not have a win under his belt, at least in the Little 500. Campus politics were kinder to him, and in April 1956, he won the race for IU student body president.

One month later Doninger became the first and only president to ride in a Little 500, but race day proved less successful than election day. In the "dust bowl" race Sigma Nu was not a serious contender in the latter stages, and ended up fifth behind the winning Phi Gams, Dodds House, South Cottage Grove, and Delta Chi. Despite all their talent, on race day the Sigma Nu riders couldn't overcome a problem unique to the early Little 500s—the "one bike" rule. This rule stated that teams could only use one bicycle during the race, which meant trouble if you had mechanical problems (like South Hall in 1951) or had a team with both short and tall riders. The latter circumstance tormented Sigma Nu, as Ruff stood only five-feet-eight, while Doninger was six feet tall, and Silcox and Mercer were closer to six-feet-four. The bicycle seat had to be kept low enough to accommodate Ruff, which meant cramping the taller men. In later years teams would be allowed to use another bike to help such inequalities, but in 1956 the rules did nothing to help Sigma Nu. The restrictive seat height was a factor in Sigma Nu's fifth-place performance, a disappointing showing for a group that Doninger claims was the best of his riding career—a career that included a winning team in 1957. He almost didn't ride that year, as he pondered quitting after the 1956 disappointment, but a new face on the team kept him around for his senior season.

The new face was Hilary "Moose" Walterhouse, a rider whose Little 500 lineage stretched back to the 1951 inaugural race and a fourth-place finish on the Rogers East V team. "He was easily [Rogers'] best rider, and outside Bob Moore and maybe Russ Keller, he was the best rider in the first race," said Ruff, who would get to know Walterhouse all too well during his North Hall Friar days. In 1952 Walterhouse's Rogers team took the pole position and finished second, running hard with Ruff's Friars all day. Ruff never forgot the talented and imposing, yet very well-liked Moose (a high school nickname that stuck), and vigorously recruited him when he returned to school after military service. Walterhouse embraced the offer but couldn't accept the financial responsibilities of greek life, so Sigma Nu made him an unprecedented proposition—free room and board in exchange for his riding talent.

For the third time in as many years, Sigma Nu had gone outside the house to find new riding talent, and with Walterhouse in 1957 a winning formula finally came to life. Moose and Doninger brought superior

The Sigma Nu fraternity blazed a trail for future greek powers with their aggressive recruiting of dorm riders. Its 1957 winning team included former dorm veterans Clarence Doninger (left) and Hilary "Moose" Walterhouse (with Little 500 Sweetheart Jill Corey), along with 1954 winner Joe Magers (second from right) and Armin "Bud" Olsen.

No other dormitory in the 1950s could boast a better Little 500 record than Dodds House, whose men held a close-knit relationship conducive to retaining quality teams year after year. Its 1956 and 1957 teams finished second in the races (and won pole position in 1957, which clearly was a source of pride to the dorm), but would lose some of its best riders to greek houses in subsequent years.

talent and motivation, Joseph Magers returned from the 1954 winners, and Armin "Bud" Olsen rounded out the Ruff-coached team, which trained in Florida over spring break. In the race Sigma Nu spent much of the day pursuing the Dodds House pole team, finally moving into the lead on lap 169, when Dodds dropped its bike on an exchange. Doninger rode the final 15 laps, crossing the line in a record 2:19.56. Sigma Nu's ardent pursuit of riding talent had finally added up to a second Little 500

victory, while forever changing the way many fraternities would approach the race.

Notable in its second-place finish in 1957, for the second consecutive year, was the Dodds House dormitory team. Sitting less than one lap's distance from Memorial Stadium, on the northwest corner of what would later be known as Wright Quad, the men of Dodds maintained a love for the Little 500 unparalleled in the residence hall system. In the first seven years of the event only six teams had appeared in every race, and of those six only Dodds was non-greek. But in its own way Dodds was akin to a fraternity, only without the letters, private residences, and rituals. It had a close-knit membership, with many of its residents spending their entire college careers at the corner of Tenth Street and Jordan Avenue. Consequently, like a fraternity, those who graduated as Dodds men often stayed in touch with each other and kept abreast of the unit's activities long after their departure. All these characteristics helped keep a steady flow of quality bicyclists and teams, which since the Little 500's inception had been quite respectable. The Dodds "Gargoyles" finished no lower than 12th every year except 1953, and in 1956 and 1957 became the second team ever (joining the 1953 and '54 Acacia team) to post two second-place finishes in a row.

In 1956 the Dodds men hung a banner outside their house boldly predicting a Little 500 victory, and they might have gotten it had it not been for the surprising Phi Gamma Deltas. One year later the Dodds team stepped into the spotlight as favorites, even ahead of the experienced Sigma Nus. At the 1957 qualifications they unveiled an alternative exchange technique, which involved riders hopping off the side of the bike instead of off the rear (the 1951 South Hall method that had been adopted by most other teams). Though more complex and difficult to perfect, the technique made for much faster exchanges when done right and at speed. Team manager Bob Finehout created the then-unusual method (later embraced by others), and his team showed it off on qual day with an unheard-of 2-minute, 28-second attempt, beating the previous record by five seconds and coming in seven seconds ahead of the second-qualifying team.

Equally impressive that day was the performance of one individual Dodds member, Karl Napper. During every Little 500 qualifications individual lap times were recorded along with team times, and in 1957 Napper turned in a 33.7 second lap. "I had some skills that weren't prevalent then," he said. Indeed—his time set a record nearly two seconds faster than the old record set by the North Hall Barons' Wilson Hubbell in 1956. However, for all the speed and talent on the Dodds team, which included veterans Bob Dillard and Jim Law plus freshman Dave Nolan, it wasn't enough to overcome one failed exchange and

Sigma Nu. Napper believes his team rode more than 200 laps and that scorers lost count and denied Dodds the title, but no evidence exists to support such a claim. Later he and Law would become Little 500 champions in 1958, but not for Dodds House.

The Phi Kappa Psi fraternity also qualified for each of the first seven races, but only had moderate success on race day. Four top tens and no finishes lower than 14th represented a steady effort, but the Phi Psi membership pined for something more. Sigma Nu had raised the bar for greek performance in the Little 500 with its two wins, and the Phi Gamma Delta and Acacia teams were establishing themselves as perennial favorites (from 1953 to 1957, one of the two finished in the top four each year), leaving the rest of the greek population to grasp at whatever pieces were left of the Little 500 pie. The Phi Psi house was, by its own admission, a little crazy, but for the 1958 race its leaders became crazy like foxes. Taking a page out of Sigma Nu's book, Phi Psi hit the unorganized rider market in late 1957 to search for riders who they hoped would anchor their first championship team.

Any pursuit of top dorm talent in 1957 virtually started and finished at the Dodds House front door. The Dodds team had finished second with only one senior, which meant the majority of the team was ripe for picking—especially the supersonic Karl Napper. Sigma Nu took a shot at recruiting him but, according to Clarence Doninger, Napper made a bad impression by bluntly asking for compensation. (Napper denies making such a request.) Phi Kappa Psi, however, had an edge in the Dodds sweepstakes through Jim Law, Napper's teammate and fellow Dodds man. Law had been a Phi Psi at Wabash College, and said he began visiting the IU chapter when the Dodds team "was beginning to unravel" after frustrating back-to-back second-place finishes and the graduation of team captain and leader Bob Dillard. Law could move into the Phi Psi house without having to suffer the rigors of pledgeship again, and members enticed the anti-greek Napper with a similar offer—join the fraternity, ride for the bike team, and be spared the house-cleaning and other pledge duties. "My pledgeship was a farce," admitted Napper, who along with Law and sophomore Dave Nolan, left Dodds for Third Street and the greek system in 1958.

To complement the Dodds veterans, Phi Psi called on a few of its

more athletic members to round out the 1958 team. Lewis Cook and Lou Sharp were two of a handful of IU varsity swimmers in the house, and their skills in the pool translated well to the track. Sharp was a muscular sprinter, Cook a lean backstroker from the hills of San Francisco. Together Lew and Lou incorporated tenets of IU coach Doc Counsilman's swim training, such as interval exercises and pulse rate monitoring, into bike training for the race. The coach, never exactly thrilled to see his swimmers risk injury on two-wheelers, helped them anyway. Napper listened intently to his new teammates' ideas and added bicycling tips he had gathered through outside competitions the previous summer. Altogether, the 1958 Phi Psi team was way ahead of the pack in training for the race. While many teams were holding their heaviest workouts two weeks before the race, the Phi Psis were in the middle of their "taper and shave" period, a swimming technique that called for less strenuous workouts prior to major events.

On race day 1958 the Phi Psi chapter received instant payback for its recruiting efforts, as the multi-talented foursome outsmarted the competition. If strength and conditioning put Phi Psi in the front of the field, Napper's innovative strategies kept them there. His plan called for the team's fourth rider to start the race, instead of the traditional first and fastest rider, and ride just a couple laps before sprinting hard for a lap and exchanging. Upon exchanging, the next rider would catch up to the lead, sprint out again and exchange. In no time Phi Psi held the lead even when it slowed for exchanges, and within the first 20 laps had put the field one full lap down. Then, for the rest of the day, the Phi Psis did the cycling equivalent of resting—they drafted. Napper had learned that by riding directly behind a competitor, he could ride just as fast with a fraction of the work. "Nobody understood the benefits of sitting on a wheel [in 1958], everyone just rode a fixed number of laps and let the results fall where they did," said Napper. But his teammates understood perfectly, taking all drama out of the race by maintaining a sometimes multiple-lap lead and simply drafting off other decent teams en route to a new record time of 2:17.23.

Like Sigma Nu, Phi Kappa Psi had built a winning team with some recruiting savvy. But unlike Sigma Nu, Phi Psi would fall under scrutiny for its success. In 1957, the Student Foundation did not see Sigma Nu as truly threatening the structure of the race, as the team had been building for a few years prior to its second victory. But Phi Psi had become all but unstoppable overnight, and the powers behind the Little 500 saw the makings of what they perceived as a possible problem—a team with endless winning in its future. With six different teams winning the first eight races, the Student Foundation took pride in the parity of its event and was prepared to stand in the way of threats to such equality. Academic requirements had been added in 1956, ordering participants to be full-time undergraduates, thus ensuring students weren't majoring in Little 500. With academic standards in place, the Student Foundation turned to tinkering with rider eligibility rules following the 1958 Phi Psi march to victory.

As a fifth-year senior with only three races to his name, Napper had expected to be able to defend his title the following year as other past champions with eligibility had. But Napper was not just any previous champion. In one year's time he not only switched teams and won, but introduced a whole new style of racing to the Little 500, drawing a great deal of attention to himself in the process. His outside racing triumphs were well known in the Little 500 community, impressive to other riders but nerve-wracking to Armstrong and his student leaders. In 1959 they were quite convinced Napper's boys would repeat 1958's runaway, so they aimed their legislative powers right at Napper. He had participated in Little 500s from 1956 to 1958, and also qualified with the 1955 Dodds team. Little 500 regulations said qualifying but not riding in a given year would not mean losing a year of eligibility—unless your name was Karl Napper. An exception was made to the rule and Napper was ousted from future Little 500 competition, though ironically he was named to the 1958–59 Student Foundation Steering Committee. "That was to keep me quiet," he said, "though I didn't make that much of a fuss."

Napper didn't have to, as his Phi Psis got the last laugh with back-to-back wins in 1959 and 1960, despite Student Foundation attempts to derail their rise to the top. What eluded the Student Foundation was that fraternities recruiting top riders weren't only trying to secure immediate success, but often future success as well. When Russ Keller moved from South Hall to North Hall in 1952 he engineered and rode on a winning team, and that team continued his legacy in 1953 after his riding days were over. Napper was the same kind of figure—skilled, dedicated, and likable enough in the house to help breed a new generation of riders. "He was known in the house as the 'Big M'—'The Big Machine,'" said Dave Atha, who rode for Phi Psi in 1959 and 1960. "What Karl gave to Phi Psi was an ethic and a devotion I feel certain has been unequaled since." The Student Foundation could keep Napper off the track, but not from becoming the heart and soul of the first three-peat Little 500 champion.

One rider, Lew Cook, returned from the 1958 team for the 1959 race, and Phi Psi added another outsider in Jerry Swisher (formerly of the North Hall Barons) and developed two riders from its own ranks in Atha and Jim Roy. Winning in 1959 wasn't quite as easy as the year before, as

For Little 500 riders, the trackside pits were home during a race. Coed sponsors would help design their respective teams' pits (papier-mâché designs such as this one in 1956 (above) were popular in early years, then replaced by painted pit boards), then the riders would arrive and customize their areas with everything from stationary bikes to even mattresses and makeshift canopies. For many years after the race, an infield pool (opposite) helped riders cool off after a long day's work.

Phi Psi won by "only" 21 seconds over Sigma Alpha Epsilon in a time seven minutes slower than 1958. The 1960 championship team had an easier run to the title, winning from the pole and defeating SAE by 50 seconds. "We drafted off them for 50 laps at a time, and they'd get frustrated," said Cook, who displayed the Phi Psi free spirit in each winning race by wearing pink-framed sunglasses. He and Atha were returning riders in 1960, and rookies Don Leedy and John Odusch (another IU swimmer) rounded out the team. (A testament to Phi Psi's depth and internal competition was that veterans Roy and Swisher didn't make the 1960 squad.) A total of eight different riders competed for Phi Psi during the three-year run, and each one credited Napper for creating the winning aura that surrounded the team. Even after graduating and while attending medical school in Indianapolis, he visited often to check up on the teams and lend racing advice. And his own amazing bicycling career continued: Napper missed a trip to Rome and the 1960 Summer Olympics by half a wheel at the U.S. Olympic Trials, but in 1964 he reached the pinnacle of the sport in winning the National Road Racing Championship.

Of all the riders Napper pulled into the Phi Psi dynasty, none left a bigger mark on Little 500 history than a skinny kid he met on the road in 1958. While riding around town during the fall of that year, on a sophisticated lightweight, derailleur-equipped cycle, he spotted a rider in the distance pedaling away on one of the common bikes of the day, a balloon-tired "bomber." His name was Dave Blase, and on that day Napper trailed him for a while and found it difficult to catch up. He wouldn't be the only one.

Growing up in Speedway, Indiana, Dave Blase had one of those childhoods destined for ridicule. Quiet and without noticeable physical or athletic gifts, he was often the kid off on his own at the playground or picked last in a sandlot ballgame. His social progress was slow, as he spent more time pursuing academics than eligible teenage females at the drive-in. He further isolated himself by avoiding the pop music culture, instead preferring classical music. Overall he was a well-behaved child, strong in his morals and values, but even his parents wondered about his reclusive nature. His personality hadn't changed upon arriving at IU in 1957, which made it all the more surprising when Gene Sriver, the athletics chairman of Rollins House, asked Blase if he was interested in trying out for the unit's 1958 Little 500 team.

Unable to come up with a quick excuse, the lanky, unimposing, and uninterested Blase first accepted the invitation from the tall, muscular Sriver—then proceeded to hide in a bathroom stall on the day of his tryout. Not taking "no" for an answer, Sriver confronted Blase at dinner that night and suggested the next day for a ride. Figuring he couldn't run away all semester, Blase gave in and rode the next day. Though not spectacular, he earned a spot on the team. Riding as a freshman in the big event proved rather daunting—Rollins qualified 27th and finished 18th in 1958—but Blase drew inspiration from the competitive and individual nature of the sport.

That summer Blase dedicated full-time energy to bicycling, and at the beginning of the 1958–59 school year met Napper, whom he called "God on wheels." Blase was flattered that a rider of Napper's ability would even acknowledge his existence, much less talk to him and ride with him, as Napper did for the rest of the school year. But Napper had no peer when it came to judging talent, and he knew Blase was something special. Blase trained with Napper and the Phi Psi team even while riding in the Little 500 for Rollins House in 1959, where he took on a heavy workload of 96 laps en route to a tenth-place finish. The day after the race Blase formally announced his intention to join Phi Psi, pledging as a junior for the 1959–60 school year. The fraternity had found another outside force to continue its dynasty.

Bill Armstrong and the Student Foundation, however, had seen enough. In 1960 the Phi Psis were gunning for three in a row, and though the race continued to be popular with fans, dormitories felt the fraternity stranglehold and stayed away from entering teams in the event. From the race's inception until 1957, a minimum of 47 teams had showed up each year for qualifications, but in 1958 the numbers started to fall. Forty teams made qual attempts in 1958, 42 in 1959, and in 1960 an all-time low of 35. Fraternity participation remained high and unaffected, but the Little 500 was losing ground with the dorm teams, which had enough trouble fielding competent foursomes without the greeks invading their ranks and taking away the best riders. Blase's former team was a prime example—Rollins House had fielded teams each year from 1955 to 1959,

Just minutes after the finish of many early Little 500 races, the Indiana Daily Student *had an Extra edition out, literally "hot off the presses" and in the hands of fans and winners (such as the 1961 Acacia team). During a race, reporters in the press box would phone in results to the newspaper's offices in Ernie Pyle Hall, where production would be underway. With a photo from the race's opening laps and much of the text already laid out, only a few short paragraphs and a banner headline were needed to complete the issue, which was then printed at Ernie Pyle Hall and quickly delivered to the stadium.*

but died when Blase left for Phi Psi. The Student Foundation couldn't ignore such a trend, and prior to the 1960 race it enacted a new rule forcing riders to sit out one year when changing housing organizations.

At the time the rule primarily targeted Blase, and he paid Armstrong a personal visit to find out why. "I had him sit in my chair, and see it from my perspective," Armstrong said. The dwindling number of teams was clear, and Blase understood and went along with the rule for 1960. Ultimately, the new rule failed to break up the streak as the Student Foundation had hoped it would—Phi Psi won anyway. (The rule did stay on the books, however, and a similar version still exists today.) So the Steering Committee went back to work in the fall of 1960 to come up with another plan to keep Blase off the track, believing that with him Phi Psi would have no trouble winning its fourth straight and further damaging Little 500 competition.

Having exhausted all chances to ban Blase for his team allegiances, the Student Foundation examined his off-campus cycling history. Between 1959 and 1960 Blase had participated in various outside cycling events, from the 1959 Midwest Championships (which he won) to Olympic and Pan-American Games trials. For the Student Foundation, red flags went up, and its members passed yet another Blase-specific rule, deeming that "any person riding in an outside cycling event will not be eligible to ride in the Little 500 unless the other event is sanctioned by the Steering Committee." The fact that Blase had participated in these events well before the rule was ever thought of didn't factor into the decision. (Interestingly, the Committee's president at the time was Frank McKinney of Sigma Alpha Epsilon, a fraternity that had finished third-third-second during the Phi Psi reign and badly wanted to get to the top.) Blase was outraged at the *ex post facto* standard. "I was the only one they were aiming this at, and everybody on campus knew it," he said. The *Daily Student* wrote multiple editorials on the ruling, stating "no team should be cheated from entering its top riders just because it has won previous Little 500 races" and that Blase was far from the "professional" competitor the Student Foundation made him out to be. Disgusted and depressed, Blase saw his grades plunge, and he left IU at the end of the fall 1960 semester. For a year he stayed home in Indianapolis, taking classes and studying medicine, though returning to Bloomington on weekends to catch up with Phi Psi friends and ride.

In the 1961 Little 500 Blase could only watch as his Phi Psi team turned in a third-place finish behind Acacia and Phi Gamma Delta. Past champions Leedy, Odusch, and Roy returned for Phi Psi, but Acacia had an equally if not more talented team. Acacia also had the field's top individual rider, Dave Brown, who was in the third year of a brilliant four-year Little 500 career that would include an unprecedented three years of fastest-lap honors at qualifications. Phi Psi did, however, win the first annual Sportsmanship Cup, awarded by, of all people, the Student Foundation Steering Committee. Race turnout that year continued its downward spiral, as only 33 teams attempted qualifying—one of which wasn't even a campus team. (Normal College of Indianapolis successfully petitioned for entry, on the grounds of being an IU branch school, and became the only out-of-town team to ever participate.) Such low entry figures came as no surprise, since the Phi Psi monopoly had not yet officially ended, but on race day the teams who did compete received a boost with Acacia's win. (Also during the race Kappa Sigma got another kind of boost—from an illegal oxygen tank in its pit, resulting in a three-lap penalty.) The once invincible Phi Psi fraternity team had been humbled, at least for one year.

Blase returned to IU for the 1962 spring semester to complete his classwork and take one more shot at Little 500 glory. The rule that kept him out of the 1961 edition had served its purpose and was eliminated, clearing the way for his return. He came back to Bloomington as the same top-notch cyclist he was prior to leaving, but he also carried a new look and personality. While studying at home he met a few Italian doctors and picked up some of their mannerisms and language. He also began following the top European bicyclists of the day and emulating them by growing his hair long—an uncommon look for 1962. And though cycling heroes Felice Gimondi and Eddy Merckx probably didn't sing arias from operas while they pedaled, Blase did, creating a completely new identity that helped him break away from the reclusive, silent Blase who lived away from the bicycle. Off the wheels, however, he remained socially inept. One day that spring he returned to Phi Psi from a long ride and passed the neighboring Kappa Kappa Gamma sorority house, where two women were relaxing on a porch swing. Intrigued by this foreign exchange–like student, they asked him how his training was going. Blase

proceeded to give the ladies a technically detailed answer about just that, then excused himself to go home. Later a Phi Psi brother had to explain to him that the women didn't really care about his ride—they wanted to get to know *him*. "I couldn't think that anybody of that gender could have the least bit of interest in striking up a conversation with me," he said.

For the 1962 race Blase was motivated and focused, even while the rest of the Phi Psi team was in disarray. A lack of drive plagued many riders, who had finally come back down to earth in 1961 and were not ready to train their way back to the top. So Blase took the team into his hands, answering the fraternity president's questions about what the heck was going on with the team. "We'll win," Blase assured him—even if he had to ride the whole thing himself. And there was no doubt about his ability to do just that, as he proved a week before the race. The team staged a practice race in which Blase rode alone while the other three Phi Psis tried to lap him. There was indeed lapping every seventh lap, but it was Blase putting the laps on the other three riders. Working off other teams' practicing riders, Blase drafted and passed constantly. By himself, he pedaled at a frenetic pace clocked by teammates as faster than any previous Little 500. His epic ride went on for 120 laps, until the sun set on the track. And when it did, other teams applauded Blase's amazing individual performance. It came as little surprise to Little 500 followers when Phi Kappa Psi won the race the following week, although the margin of victory was just nine seconds over Sigma Alpha Epsilon. Just as he had planned, Blase carried the team with 139 laps—the most ever at that time for one man on a winning team.

In the overall picture of Little 500 competition, the 1962 race represented a rebirth of sorts. After the few years of declining team interest, 1962's qualifications attracted 39 teams—still a relatively low number, but the best since 1959. And after the controversial 1961 ruling, which for the first time singled out one rider for his ability, the 1962 race was a welcome sight. In it, that same rider was allowed back on the track, taking the heat off race organizers. The Phi Psis' win with Blase was expected, but the fact that he didn't lap the field silly as he had done in practice returned credibility to the race. The Little 500 was an event in which a superstar rider could participate and win, yet still get a run for his money and even be vulnerable to uncertainty (Blase was involved in a minor accident early in the race). Plus, the superstar of 1962 was graduating,

The Little
500

After two years of riding for Rollins House and two years of sitting out the Little 500 under suspiciously new Student Foundation eligibility rules, Dave Blase (in sunglasses) finally got a chance to ride for his Phi Kappa Psi fraternity in 1962. The results were worth the wait for him and the team, as his talents were on display for 139 laps in his house's fourth win in five years.

and the team that had won four of the last five races appeared to finally be coming down from the mountaintop. Other teams and riders readied themselves to step in and claim some of the precious Little 500 glory.

Over the next 10 years, from 1963 to 1972, a new era of strong competition with parity took hold. During this 10-race span seven different teams won, five of which had never experienced a Little 500 win in the prior dozen races. All were fraternities, most of which contained one star rider with a good supporting cast, and each year a different team won, with no repeat champions. Attendance figures bore out the continuing popularity of the race and its new unpredictability, with records set annually from 1963 to 1967 and an average gate of 22,000 over the entire period. For sheer competition and the unexpected, 1963–72 were the Little 500's glory years.

The first team to step to the forefront in this period was, somewhat appropriately, Sigma Alpha Epsilon. Throughout the first 12 years of Little 500 history no other team was the bridesmaid as often as SAE. Their riders finished second behind South Hall in 1951, then second three more times behind the Phi Psi winners of 1959, 1960, and 1962. The closest finish of the four was in 1962, when SAE finished just nine seconds behind, but at least its riders never considered that close finish to be an opportunity lost. "We didn't have the gas to beat [Phi Psi]. They were the better team," SAE rider Bob Bolyard admitted. But with chief competitor Blase out of the picture for 1963, SAE wasted no time displacing Phi Psi as the new favorites. At quals the Bolyard-led team (Bob rode while older brother and IU basketball star Tom coached) set a new record with a 2:24.12 attempt, and on May 11 came out on top in the fastest, most suspenseful Little 500 yet.

Warm and clear skies greeted a record crowd of 19,858 at Tenth Street Stadium on race day 1963 (formerly Memorial Stadium, the Little 500 home became more commonly known as Tenth Street Stadium after the new Memorial Stadium was dedicated in October 1960), and they were treated to a showdown between the top two qualifying teams, SAE and Alpha Tau Omega. ATO, which had participated in every Little 500 prior to '63, fielded its best team ever, anchored by freshman rider Larry Marks and adventurous junior Eddie Doerr. Over spring break Doerr rode his bike 850 miles from IU to Monticello, Florida, while the rest of the team trailed in a car. SAE's foursome included veterans Bolyard and Ron Blue and a pair of varsity athletes—hoopster Dave Porter and swimmer Claude Thompson. These talented teams battled from the start, as Bolyard rode the first 52 laps for SAE, primarily against ATO's Marks. Teammates alternated in throughout the day for both squads, but at the end of the race Bolyard and Marks were left together again to run for the title. Coming to the line on lap 199, SAE nearly killed its title shot when coach Tom Bolyard signaled to his little brother that there were three laps to go. Luckily Bob Bolyard saw the white flag being waved and realized he couldn't wait three laps to start his sprint. He crossed the finish line one second ahead of Marks, capping off the first true sprint-to-the-finish ending in race history and clocking in at a new record time of 2:17.04 (21.89 miles per hour). The payoff wasn't too shabby, either— SAE riders received portable televisions, bikes, jackets, tie tacks, lighters, tickets to the Little 500 Variety Show and the Indianapolis 500, and, most importantly, the winner's trophy that had eluded them so many times before.

Unlike SAE, Beta Theta Pi spent its early Little 500 history on the fringes of the field rather than among the leaders. From 1951 to 1961 the Betas had only two top–10 finishes in eight starts, hardly imposing figures to the upper-echelon teams. Those fortunes began to change in 1962, when a young rider named Brock Blosser edged his way onto the fraternity team. Growing up in Warsaw, Indiana, he had some experience with bicycles, riding on Saturday nights at a stock-car racetrack. A friend suggested trying out for the Little 500, which he did during his first year at IU. His mentor was a Beta senior and top IU swimmer named Bill Barton, who had pedaled for the house's 1961 fifth-place team. Barton introduced Blosser to swim-training regimens, which he put to use in the '62 race (finishing seventh), and over the rest of his racing career. In 1963 the Betas continued to improve and finished fifth, but come 1964 Blosser stood as the only returning veteran and faced the task of breaking in three Little 500 rookies. Phil Goddard, Steve Taylor, and James McEwen all had athletic backgrounds (McEwen was a high school swim champion in Canada) but no bicycling experience. The fraternity compensated for the lack of seasoning with heavy training.

"We had kind of a surprise factor going for us," said Blosser of his 1964 Betas, who by qualifying 10th didn't immediately give top teams like SAE, Acacia, and the Phi Gams reason to worry. Though disappointed by the qual result, Blosser believed having the No. 10 on the racing jerseys would help his team "hide" a little from the single-digit-adorned frontrunners. At the race, however, the Betas couldn't hide from anyone. Their conditioning paid off early and often, helping them dash ahead of everyone all the way to the end, seven seconds ahead of SAE. In the end the combination of the experienced Blosser and three rookies proved to be not a hindrance, but a valuable asset. "They didn't realize they were supposed to lose," Blosser said, giving the most credit to lone senior McEwen for keeping the team focused and loose. (On the winner's stand, the gregarious McEwen made small talk with Little 500 Sweetheart and popular record-

Tightly-aligned packs of riders, the trademark of present-day Little 500 racing, were few and far between in the race's first few decades (1964 pictured). Most participants maneuvered about more on their own than by "drafting" off other teams.

ing artist Molly Bee. She asked McEwen for a date later that evening, but he declined in favor of recovering from the day's race. He says, half-jokingly, that the decision still haunts him.) McEwen's influence was felt even more after his graduation, as the core of Blosser-Taylor-Goddard returned to take pole in 1965, only to finish seventh in the race. "That element Jamie brought was missing," Blosser said. But regardless of those results, the Beta team had already claimed its piece of Little 500 success, clinging to the back of the four-year veteran Blosser, one of the top riders of the 1960s.

Following the SAE and Beta first-time triumphs, the 1965 and 1966 Little 500s again featured record crowds and fast times, not to mention the return to the winners' stand of the top two teams in the event's first decade and a half.

Of all the Little 500 teams that raced the first 15 years, none had a better overall record than Phi Gamma Delta. While the Fijis didn't have as many wins as some teams (such as Phi Psi, Sigma Nu, or North Hall), or even as many second-place finishes (see SAE), they did have their own distinctive achievement—14 races, 14 top tens. Through 1965, the fraternity had yet to finish lower than ninth, or even *start* lower than ninth. Much like their Third Street neighbors, Acacia (who owned 13 top tens in 14 races from 1951 to 1965), Fiji took pride in developing talent from within its ranks and mastering the finer points of Little 500 competition, such as bicycle exchanges. The latter represented the key to qualifying well, and every year Fiji did just that with its usual solid core of riders. About the only element Fiji lacked year in and year out was a touch of luck to take to the line.

For the 1965 Fijis, luck struck on lap 175. The team was occupying its familiar spot in the lead group, along with Alpha Tau Omega, SAE, and the Phi Psis. A moment later, Fiji pulled away for good. An ATO rider plowed into a race worker in turn one who was helping a downed rider, and while the rest of the group avoided that scene Fiji soared way out in front, never looking back. The foursome of Jerry Bradley, Steve Powell, John Konowitz, and Alan Abbott exchanged riders every two laps over the last 25 laps of the race, a unique approach that never allowed the chasers back into any realistic chase. Had the men botched any exchanges the plan would have surely backfired, but such mistakes were

While setting a record in 1966, team No. 10 Phi Kappa Psi pedaled around one interesting obstacle—an unmanned Zeta Beta Tau bicycle. Actually, its rider fell moments before this picture was taken, but, amazingly, the bike continued forward.

The Little
500

rare for Fiji. The final margin over second-place (again) SAE was 41 seconds, the time of 2:17.18 the second-fastest ever.

Phi Kappa Psi bettered that mark and set a new record of 2:16.51 the following year. In previous winning seasons Phi Psi teams had been anchored by former top dorm riders like Dave Blase and Karl Napper or talented varsity swimmers like Lew Cook and Lou Sharp, but in 1966 the team had both in the person of Terry Townsend. After riding for two years on the Edmondson II dormitory team, where he recorded two top–10 finishes in 1962 and 1963, Townsend joined several other IU swimmers at Phi Kappa Psi. Having already known some of the house's members through swimming, Townsend wasn't the typical recruit-for-Little 500 pledge, but the fraternity did know the newcomer brought talent from not only the pool but the racetrack. Townsend sat out the 1964 race under the rider transfer rule, but arrived ready to ride in 1965. Teammate Ken Frost remembered him as "the Dave Blase of our team," which meant speed and endurance of the highest level. Those skills showed on race day, as he handled half the Phi Psi's laps en route to a 48-second win over Sigma Phi Epsilon. In 1960 Little 500 riders began voting on All-Stars for the year, with six elected men receiving the honor, along with every member of the winning team. Townsend won the honor his freshman and sophomore years with Edmondson and his junior and senior years with Phi Psi, becoming the first four-year All-Star.

Fiji and Phi Psi duplicated their winning efforts again in 1967 and 1968, but this time under very different circumstances. In these years the seemingly invincible Little 500 dodged a pair of potentially devastating events, one directly affecting the outcome of the competition and the other nearly destroying the race before it even started.

Methods used for timing and scoring teams in the race largely stayed the same through the early years, as a small army of volunteers in the press box handled the duties. Each team had two timing/scoring representatives, one coming from the team and the other usually from the university faculty. One person was responsible for timing each individual lap, while the other wrote the lap time down on a card. During the race all cards would be collected and recorded again by timing/scoring officials on a computer, and the leaders were monitored through the lap times. Because there was not always a cluster of lead teams riding together, the lap times would frequently be called upon to identify the leaders at various points of the race. Overall the system fared well, but Armstrong and the Student Foundation recognized the difficulty in keeping track of the 33 teams, not to mention the inherent dangers of having a human element in the process. In any year mistakes could have been made, and in 1967 mistakes were made, wreaking havoc with two "winning" teams.

The pole team for the May 13 race was Phi Kappa Theta, a small fraternity whose Little 500 history only dated to 1962. Though the Phi Kaps had a pair of veterans in Bill Hoelker (a 1966 All-Star) and Jack Wehner, a mid-race accident involving a rookie teammate put the team one lap down and dashed any hopes of winning. But by the end of the race, the lost lap had somehow been made up, at least according to scorers. Hoelker was shown the white flag on lap 199 and, of course, didn't stop to ask *why*. Instead he frantically pedaled for the finish, just ahead of Fiji rider Gerald Danielson. The Fiji men thought they were in the lead in the closing laps and planned on getting Danielson off at 199 to let another rider take it home, but were forced into calling a quick audible after seeing the Phi Kaps recognized as the leader. Danielson had to stay on to try to catch Hoelker, but he came up short. Phi Kappa Theta was declared the winner.

"For 24 hours, we were happy," recalled Wehner of the moments following the race. His team received the winning trophy and kisses from sweetheart Claudia Martin, while the Fijis collected second-place honors and a quick trip home. "We felt like we just had our guts ripped out," said Fiji rookie Scott Ricke. "It was like getting cheated out of Victory Lane at Indy and having to go back to the garage." Fiji filed a protest with the Student Foundation before leaving, claiming what several other teams and many fans believed to be true—the leading team at the end was not Phi Kappa Theta. After a review later in the day, the Student Foundation agreed. A Fiji coach was notified at the house, and the word was spread. Ricke found out while he lay in bed depressed, and teammate Steve Powell found out about his second win at the Little 500 Variety Show. Phi Kappa Theta was informed of the decision on Sunday morning, when Armstrong called the team into his office. Student Foundation Assistant Director Curt Simic made the official announcement on the incident, explaining that the Phi Kaps' scorers had inadvertently written the team's score for lap 174 on the lap 175 card, which led officials to believe Phi

FIJIS FINISH FIRST – WIN '500'

Phi Kappa Theta ends up No. 5, not No. 1; Phi Delts, SAE's, ATO's 2nd, 3rd, and 4th

'Record and colorful' describe crowd and race

In 1967 the Phi Kappa Theta fraternity was a short-lived Little 500 champion, thanks to a bizarre scoring snafu which had the team listed as completing 200 laps when it actually had only ridden 199. The team (standing at right) was honored as the winners on the victory stand (with President Elvis Stahr, Sweetheart Claudia Martin and Bill Armstrong), but dropped to fifth the next day, when it was announced that Phi Gamma Delta was the true winner.

Kappa Theta was on the lead lap at the end, therefore receiving the white and checkered flags. In reality Phi Kappa Theta had only completed 199 laps. Revised scoring bumped the team down to fifth place, and Fiji rose to the top for its second win in three years. To prevent such embarrassing mishaps from occurring again, the Student Foundation adopted an old Indianapolis 500 system of lap flip-cards for each team, which were added to the outside of the press box and flipped for each team on every pass of the oval, giving spectators and riders an official account of every team's performance. As for the Phi Kaps, Wehner insisted that the stripped title wasn't devastating to the house's morale, and that the '68 performance did help them recruit new members. But the fraternity would only participate in three more races after 1968, finishing lower each year from 1969 to 1971, before disappearing from the Little 500 landscape entirely and, not long after that, disappearing from campus as well for some 20 years.

The Little 500

While the Little 500 moved merrily along through the late 1960s, even through bizarre incidents such as the 1967 scoring snafu, the same could not be said for race relations at the university. Black students on the Bloomington campus were never great in number, but their collective voice grew louder in 1968 as they fought to eliminate discriminatory practices at IU. On a Saturday in late March, some 250 black students staged a sit-in on IU President Elvis Stahr's lawn, calling for the abolition of a stagnant committee Stahr had formed earlier that year to fight discrimination on campus. The black students wanted to replace the president's committee with one composed of and elected by black students and faculty, and they got it after well-organized peaceful protests.

One month later the black students turned their attention to the IU greek system and the Little 500. From a racing standpoint, prior to 1968 black students rarely were involved in the event. The traditionally black fraternity Alpha Phi Alpha fielded teams in three of the first four races, and all-black teams from North Maple Hall competed in 1956 and 1957. Only one of those five, the 1956 Maple team, finished in the top 15. The mostly white fraternities comprised the majority of the fields year after year, and in 1968 black students targeted those organizations and the "national acceptance clauses" that many had in their national charters. Such clauses permitted any member of one fraternity's chapter to "blackball," or keep out, a pledge in any other chapter. Black students saw racism written all over the clauses, and though they admitted no interest in actually integrating the fraternities, they demanded IU fraternity chapters sign waivers denouncing the clauses.

To get their point across, 50 black students began a sit-in the Friday night prior to race day in the infield of Tenth Street Stadium. "The declared bigots will not ride on Saturday, or nobody will ride on Saturday," the group said in a statement. Some of the protesters wore helmets and carried lead pipes. Representatives from student government and the Interfraternity Council moved quickly to assemble signatures from the fraternities in question by 1 P.M. Saturday, the start time of the race. Heavy rain, not the protesters, forced postponement of the May 11 race, which caused enough of a headache for the Foundation and IU, but an even greater problem remained to be resolved. The protesters remained at the stadium, awaiting signatures or proof from 24 fraternities that the national acceptance clauses either didn't exist in their charters or that the clauses, if present, would be void at the IU campus. Twenty fraternities quickly met the demands late Friday, and three more followed suit Saturday. But one fraternity, Phi Delta Theta, did not sign the petition as it originally read. On its signed copy, presented to the protesters at 2 A.M. Sunday, Phi Delt crossed out the portion concerning discriminatory clauses, saying only that its national chapter was in the process of abolishing such a clause. The protesters didn't accept the revised statement, and immediately called for the removal of Phi Delta Theta from the race.

At 6 A.M. Sunday morning, the student leaders who had largely worked on their own to resolve the conflict called in President Stahr. In an emergency meeting with the students and members of the IU Faculty Council, it was determined Stahr would request Phi Delt to step aside from competing in the Little 500. Not willing to jeopardize the race any further, the fraternity's president quietly removed his team in light of the president's request.

At 9 A.M., Stahr met the remaining protesters at the track (some left Saturday) and notified them that he had removed Phi Delta Theta. After 38 hours at the stadium, the last of the protesters went home.

The race proceeded as planned Sunday afternoon, after Student Foundation workers frantically prepared the track following the rains and the protesters, some of whom left their mark in the form of wooden stakes hammered into the cinders. Despite the one-day delay, the usual throng of 20,000-plus filled the stands. Thirty-two teams competed, as the 10th-qualifying Phi Delts were not replaced in the field. (It was not

Black students targeted the Little 500 in 1968 while voicing their complaints over greek membership clauses. The race was clearly the best forum to make themselves heard, as it was the centerpiece of the greek calendar. Only a handful of black teams competed over the first 18 races—Alpha Phi Alpha fraternity in 1951, '52, and '54, and Maple Hall North in 1956 and, pictured, '57.

the first year the race ran without its customary 33 teams. Ironically, in 1960 Phi Delta Theta also missed the race, after earning a social suspension due to a vandalism incident at a local cemetery.) By virtue of qualifying times, the 1968 race looked as if it would be one of the most competitive ever, as only 10 seconds separated the pole-sitting Sigma Nus from the 33rd-qualifying Tau Kappa Epsilon fraternity team. Qualifying indeed had been a true competition in itself, with 51 teams appearing, the highest number since 1957. But Sunday afternoon belonged to the sixth-qualifying Phi Kappa Psis, who got a lap on the field early in the

race, held a 41-second lead at 100 laps and were never threatened in a record effort of 2:12.51. The foursome of Dave Kienlen, Steve Gluff, Alan Ogden, and David Shaw didn't include any swimmers, as Phi Psi had in its other winning teams, but it did have a swimmer for a coach in Kevin Berry, a 1964 Olympic gold medalist for Australia in the 200 butterfly. On race day Berry had prepared to match wits with a fellow swimmer/ bike coach, Charlie Hickcox of Phi Delta Theta, who would win four Olympic swimming medals that summer. The entire Phi Psi team sympathized with Hickcox and especially the absent riders, and in tribute to them passed their winning bike through the Phi Delta Theta fan section after winning. "It wasn't a defiant move in terms of the racial thing," Ogden explained. "It was to acknowledge those four guys, who had spent a lot of time working out and didn't get to ride."

The long-term effects of the 1968 protest are debatable, as the IU campus continued to battle important racial issues from its minority student population and greek system. Stahr, however, bore the heaviest burden at the time, having publicly taken responsibility for removing Phi Delta Theta. In a *Daily Student* article reflecting on the incident one year later in 1969, it was mentioned that "rumors spread throughout Indiana that state officials and members of the Board of Trustees were dissatisfied with Stahr's handling of events," and "many wanted to take a hard line against the black students for 'attempting disruption.'" Stahr announced his retirement after six years in office less than one month after the 1968 Little 500, on June 8, citing "presidential fatigue." Perhaps much of the fatigue, literally and figuratively, came from the long race weekend.

Compared to the prior year the 1969 Little 500 weekend appeared tame, though it still gave the Student Foundation a few scares. An ongoing student boycott against increased fees affected class attendance all over campus, but to the Foundation's relief the weekend's events went on as planned—though not before Mother Nature made her nearly annual race visit. Tornado warnings pushed the race's start time back to 3 P.M., and the still unstable skies kept a few spectators away. Attendance numbered 18,000—a good turnout, though the smallest crowd in seven years. On the track, Alpha Tau Omega scored its first-ever title, following a string of strong finishes (only Sigma Alpha Epsilon matched ATO's feat of top-ten finishes in every race from 1962 to 1968). ATO had the race's

In addition to the black protesters in 1968, other students used the Little 500 as a place to voice their concerns about campus and social issues. Pictured here are students against the Vietnam War picketing outside the fences of Tenth Street Stadium in 1970.

newest superstar in Carlo Logan, who as a sophomore in 1969 rode a 34.02-second fast lap in qualifying—the best since qualifications had been moved to Tenth Street Stadium in 1964. Logan's breakaway speed was called upon most of the day and especially on the final lap, as he held off a returned Phi Delta Theta team (pole winners in 1969 after sitting out in 1968) to take the checkered flag. Two years later he duplicated the feat in another ATO victory, but under very different conditions. Instead of tornado warnings and stiff winds, the Logan-led team raced under calmer skies, and the race times reflected the discrepancies over the two years. ATO's first victory in 1969 clocked in at 2:27.45, a full 15 minutes slower than the record pace of 1968. But in 1971, ATO paced a much faster contest, finishing in another new record time of 2:12.19.

After his winning effort as a senior in 1971 Logan was elected into the Little 500 Hall of Fame, a mecca of Little 500 excellence hatched by the Student Foundation in 1970 to help commemorate the 20th running of the race. Its charter class (selected by a committee of Student Foundation members and Little 500 alums) included 24 riders from the first 19 races, from first-race heroes Bob Moore and Russ Keller to mid-'60s stars Terry Townsend and Steve Powell. Each charter member had either won a championship or raced on three or four top non-winning teams (except Bill Snapp of Phi Delta Theta, who somehow managed to slip through the eligibility cracks and ride in *five* races from 1954 to 1958). After the 1970 race, the Hall grew by one or two members each year (somewhat like the Major League Baseball Hall of Fame, which the Little 500's was patterned after), elected by their peers at the annual Little 500 post-race banquet. The Class of 1970, announced the following year at a Hall of Fame brunch, included Curt Simic, the former Dodds House rider, Student Foundation Steering Committee president and assistant director, and Tom Battle of Sigma Phi Epsilon.

Growing up in nearby Columbus, Indiana, Tom Battle had heard about the Little 500 before enrolling at IU. Before selecting the Bloomington campus the bright, young three-sport athlete interviewed with a few Ivy League schools, including Yale, where football coach John Pont showed interest in bringing him eastward. (Pont's efforts failed, though he did end up at the same school as Battle when he accepted the head coach's job at IU.) Big Ten football was a little out of Battle's range at IU, as he stood 6-foot-4 but was not especially bulky, so he joined the club soccer team (coached by another up-and-comer in Hoosier athletics, Jerry Yeagley). He had joined the Sigma Phi Epsilon fraternity, one of the campus's growing greek houses, and in 1967 he rode for the first time in the Little 500. The Sig Eps had little significant history in the race, but began putting together good teams just prior to Battle's arrival.

With Battle the Sig Eps became a team to be watched, and not always for their talent. Instead, Sigma Phi Epsilon was a team with an entertaining penchant for drama. During Battle's first three years of riding, from 1967 to 1969, his team made every qualifying day a marathon. Though qualifying proved to be very much a pressure-filled affair, with many teams gunning for the 33 spots, it was quite rare for the talented teams to take more than two tries at making the field. Except for Sigma Phi Epsilon— it needed three tries every year, waiting until the last stressful minute to make the race and assure a pleasant spring social season for its members. By 1970 the Sig Eps' qualifying travails became a joke at the Student Foundation, as prior to qualifying that year Bill Armstrong and Student Foundation Director Jerry Tardy asked them how long they planned to keep race officials at the track. Only this time the team got it right, posting a successful run early that stood up all day and won the pole.

Sigma Phi Epsilon also had a knack for finding trouble on race day, which in Little 500 parlance usually meant wrecks. In 1968 multiple accidents kept Sig Ep from making a charge at the runaway Phi Psis, despite a 132-lap effort from Battle, and the team finished third. In 1969 Battle went down on the 83rd lap while in the lead, separating his shoulder and further hurting what was already a banged-up team. Though he miraculously (or foolishly, it could be argued) returned later in the race to ride, Sig Ep was long out of the running and finished 13th. In 1970 the team finally got the end result right with a win, though that, too, included the usual trail of tears. Battle was involved in two accidents, and teammates Bob Henderson and

Mark Wade went down one time each, but solid race strategy bailed them out. All day the team looked for mismatches on the track, putting Battle on the bike when other teams were resting their top riders, which allowed Battle to put the field a lap down on several occasions. With that edge the accidents were bearable. Though the Sig Eps had the race well in hand by the last few miles, they put the icing on the cake with a unique maneuver on the pursuing Sigma Nus. On the track Battle signaled his pit for an exchange, one he didn't intend to make, and trailed the Sigma Nu rider right up to the pit area. Race officials called a 10-second penalty on Sigma Nu for blocking the Sig Ep exchange, despite the exchange being no more than a decoy on Battle's part. After four years of close calls and more personal contact with the stadium cinders than perhaps any Hall of Famer before him, Battle crossed the finish line a winner and gave the fraternity its first win.

The last fraternity team to secure its piece of Little 500 history during the 1963–72 parity era was Kappa Sigma, another house on the fringes of the racing and greek scenes. Bob Kirkwood, a four-year Kappa Sig rider from 1971 to 1974 and Hall of Famer, admitted the fraternity didn't excel at many activities, including the campus bike-fest. But like ATO and the Sig Eps, other second-tier teams in the Little 500 hierarchy, Kappa Sigma recorded a period of memorable performances, including a one-of-a-kind win in 1972. After taking the pole position only to finish seventh in 1971, Kappa Sigma returned with a well-conditioned foursome anxious to take on another new group on the block, Delta Chi. Kirkwood and Bob Shanteau, lifelong friends from Logansport, Indiana, were Kappa Sigma's returning veterans, joined by rookies Steve Drayna and David Emenhiser. Race day strategy unfolded well for Kappa Sig at the start, with three riders splitting track duties until lap 78, when persistent rains pushed the surface to its safety limit. For the first time in history, the race was stopped cold and moved to Sunday. On the restart, eight teams near the lead drew lots for position in a single-file

The Sigma Phi Epsilon fraternity team made a habit out of making life difficult for itself in the Little 500, through qualifying travails and race-day troubles. Hall-of-Fame rider Tom Battle suffered in 1969 with a separated shoulder sustained in an accident, but celebrated in 1970 after winning despite two accidents (Battle has sunglasses on forehead, celebrating in infield pool with Tim Branigan, coach Wally McOuat, manager Dick Fess and Mark Wade).

start at lap 79. Kappa Sigma drew the 8th spot and resumed its strategy of the previous day to get a lap up on the field. The plan worked until lap 180, when the Delta Chi team caught up. Delta Chi superstar Eddy Van Guyse, expected by many to be in a sprint to the finish, surprisingly exchanged at lap 196, leaving Bob Kirkwood to stay in the lead for good and bring home the win. In the pits the team cracked open a cooler of champagne, which had accompanied the team for a few years in anticipation of a winning moment, one that finally arrived on April 30, 1972.

Much as Sigma Alpha Epsilon's win in 1963 ultimately marked the beginning of a period where many teams shared in race wins, Kappa Sigma's win in 1972 would be looked back upon as the end to the period. Just as the Phi Kappa Psi fraternity had won nearly every race from 1958 to 1962, Kappa Sigma's chief rival in 1972, Delta Chi, was about to begin the same sort of reign—only its would be even longer in duration. The face of the Little 500 competition was about to change again.

4. The World's Greatest College Weekend

The ever-increasing crowds and heightened campus interest in the Little 500 did not completely come from the many great bicyclists and bike teams that passed through the Memorial Stadium gates during the first 20 years of the race. What was in 1951 just a three-hour Saturday afternoon curiosity had evolved into an entire weekend of entertainment. Situated where it was on the university calendar—in early May just before final exams—the Little 500 weekend was a perfect time for students to enjoy one last hurrah of partying and socializing. By the mid-50s, even the words "Little Five" took on a double meaning to students. It wasn't just a bike race anymore, but a packed weekend of activities.

Students first led the way in planning subsidiary activities. Beginning in 1951 the Theta Chi fraternity hosted an annual "Bicycle Bounce" in its front yard, open to everyone. Three years later the Men's Quad started a dorm dance called the "Sprocket Hop." Starting in 1954, the Acacia fraternity held its "Ice Cream Social," a very popular event that promised "Distinguished Dippers" (IU administrators, deans, and often President Wells) serving thousands of scoops of ice cream. Sororities also created events, as the Delta Gamma and Kappa Alpha Theta sororities held an annual showdown in their "Little Little 500," a balancing duel involving hard-boiled eggs, spoons, and a little bicycling. To the winner of that hotly contested event went, naturally, an eggbeater.

Not long after Bill Armstrong replaced Howdy Wilcox as Executive Director of the Foundation/Student Foundation in late 1952, more Student Foundation–sponsored events began to enter the Little 500 scene. Once convinced the Little 500 was a worthy endeavor, Armstrong began thinking of new ways to entertain students and guests—all in the name of generating goodwill, scholarship funds, and, he hoped, more donations to the Foundation. Like the students, Armstrong viewed the bike race as just one element of a potentially huge weekend. What was at first termed "The Greatest Collegiate Bicycle Race in the World" was about to become, with additional fanfare and activities, "The World's Greatest College Weekend."

Armstrong's first order of business was to introduce a new tradition—the "Little 500 Sweetheart." Beginning with Lu Ann Simms in 1953, the Sweetheart was, as the cliché goes, "more than a pretty face." It

Among the popular activities that filled the 1950s Little 500 weekends was the "Little Little 500," an annual egg-skills showdown between the Delta Gamma and Kappa Alpha Theta sororities. In 1954 Delta Gamma won and took home the eggbeater, presented by Bill Armstrong (left) and Dean of Students Col. R.L. Shoemaker.

was no accident that the Sweetheart was front-and-center at all Little 500–related gatherings, especially around the stadium. The weekend could have had its own student queen, much like the ballyhooed fall Homecoming queen, but having a famous "pretty face" added a higher degree of luster to the weekend. Race fans enjoyed seeing a celebrity roam the grounds during the day, and riders lucky enough to win the race and smooch the Sweetheart earned the envy of everyone and usually a story to tell and retell. Armstrong took great pride in lining up the Sweethearts, calling on connections in the entertainment industry for young singers/entertainers such as Simms, the McGuire Sisters, the Burton Sisters, Denise Lor, and Jill Corey. Later in the 1950s, Armstrong traveled to Atlantic City to talk to Miss America Pageant coordinators and lure a few of their glamorous champions, and from that visit came some of the Sweethearts of the early 1960s, such as Miss Americas Mary Ann Mobley and Lynda Lee Mead.

Soon after the introduction of the Little 500 Sweetheart, Armstrong introduced his next idea, again involving celebrities. With thousands of fans arriving in town for the bicycle race, Armstrong wondered how he could keep the crowds around and entertained in the evening after the competition. Instead of another sporting event, Armstrong envisioned an indoor show, featuring multiple performers with various talents. "Variety shows," as they were known, were extremely popular in early 1950s television, with programs such as *Your Show of Shows*, *Texaco Star Theater*, and *The Ed Sullivan Show*. Armstrong landed many of the same guests from those programs and, with an occasional dash of campus talent tossed in, created what would be known as the "Little 500 Variety Show." Its 1955 debut featured band leader Horace Heidt and his 50-person "Swift Show Wagon," presenting their show titled "The American Way." Heidt himself embodied the variety show concept, as his aptly named "wagon" traveled from state to state each week, finding the best local talent for an NBC show which ran for 10 months in 1955. On May 14 of that year, the Swift Show Wagon came to Bloomington and was a hit at the IU Auditorium. Armstrong had found his Saturday night savior, and another Little 500 institution was born.

On the same weekend the Variety Show debuted, another major event came to life. Until 1955 women were largely excluded from the

The Little 500

Bill Armstrong's first move in expanding the scope of the Little 500 weekend was to invite a yearly "Little 500 Sweetheart," specifically an attractive young woman from the entertainment industry. To him, the addition of such a known person would add class to the weekend and credibility in the media. The first Sweetheart was Lu Ann Simms in 1953 (pictured singing at the Theta Chi Bicycle Bounce), and in 1954 Armstrong brought in three Sweethearts, the McGuire Sisters.

Little 500 landscape, except in the subservient role of coed sponsor to the men's bicycle teams. They could be found decorating bike team pits, designing uniforms, and cheering on the men, but with the exception of the two-sorority "Little Little 500" (which ran until 1959), there was no event that showcased female students. But two members of the Pi Beta Phi sorority had an idea, proposing to Armstrong a diminutive version of the bicycle race—a tricycle race, or "Miniature 500." Like its big brother, the proposed race would involve four-person teams sharing one cycle

and would run Friday evening, the day before the Little 500. Armstrong liked the idea and especially liked having another event for the expanding Student Foundation's members to devote energies to, so he accepted the proposal.

For its first running in 1955, the "Minny" shared one trait all too familiar to its companion bicycle race—vulnerability to weather. The race was to be held in the street on the south end of the Auditorium, on a straight-line course. Riders were to pedal from one end to the other,

The first Mini 500 was planned to be an outdoor event, on a straight-line course, but rain in 1955 altered those plans. Moving inside, Armstrong and Student Foundation President Jim Fitzpatrick came up with a tight, oval-shaped course for the tricyclists. Its sharp turns (negotiated by a Kappa Delta rider during a 1960s Mini) are still the trademark of the event today.

with exchanges to teammates along the way. For spectators, bleachers were installed up and down one side of the straightaway. The plan was solid—until the rains came late Thursday. Fortunately, Armstrong and Steering Committee President Jim Fitzpatrick had a backup plan. They had reserved the Wildermuth Fieldhouse for Friday evening as a substitute locale, and they visited there early Friday morning with the IU athletic equipment manager to turn the outdoor event into an indoor one. The straight-line course would have to be scrapped because of the tighter surroundings, so the men created an oval-shaped route. In the dirt of the Fieldhouse they sketched three tracks, each with long straightaways and tight turns. On those routes three teams would race simultaneously in heats, with the winners advancing. One rider would start in the middle of a straightaway, ride her tricycle around a curve and halfway down the opposite straight before exchanging to a teammate. The team-

mate would then ride the rest of that straight, make the far turn, and come back on the first straight. Another rider would be there for an exchange, and one more identical lap would be completed for a total of two laps. Like the men's race, fouls would be issued for riding the trike improperly (standing on it or not keeping both feet on pedals), illegal exchanges, and riding out of bounds.

Friday evening's Miniature 500 went off without any further problems and with typical Little 500 flair. Wilbur Shaw's wife, Catherine, emceed the event, and her young son Bill drove the "pace car," a pedal-powered miniature Austin-Healey. Twenty-nine teams with 116 women participated in the single-elimination format, riding tricycles furnished by American Machine and Foundry, the same company that supplied the Roadmaster bicycles. Judging the competition were Jim Dils, Jack Kern, Bill Mann, Fred Mercer, Bill Snapp, and Steve Snyder, six of the year's best Little 500 riders. The Kappa Kappa Gamma sorority won the inaugural affair, beating the founding Pi Beta Phis in the championship heat. Like high-finishing bike teams, the Mini 500 finalists also received prizes, though not exactly televisions and Indy 500 tickets. Kappa Kappa Gamma's riders won cashmere sweaters, while the second-place Pi Phis received hosiery cases. Another hotly contested competition was the "best-dressed" award, won by the Sycamore Hall women. They won argyle knee socks.

Perhaps nothing else exhibited the charmed life the Little 500 led in the late 1950s and 1960s more than the success of the Friday night tricycle race. If the Little 500 bicycle race was primarily an athletic event with a little showmanship, the Mini 500 was mostly show with just a little athleticism. The distinctly female event played to near-overflowing crowds during its stay at the Wildermuth Fieldhouse from 1955 to 1961 and later the New Fieldhouse from 1962 to 1971 (the Student Foundation never considered racing outside again after 1955). It evolved into much more than just a race, taking on pomp and circumstance all its own, with pre-race pageantry that even eclipsed the bicycle race's. Much like the Little 500's celebrity pace cars, the Mini 500 had celebrity bikes: a large circus-like model pedaled by the Student Foundation Steering Committee president and a carriage-equipped bike with which the Little 500's fastest-lap qualifier pedaled around the Little 500 Sweetheart. Teams continued to dress in elaborate costumes, and before the race

constructed floats celebrating the Mini theme of the year. These always played off the word "mini," and included "Mini Gras," "Around the World in Mini Ways," and "Minilympics" (during the Vietnam era some teams improvised even further and came up with "Ho Chi Mini"). The awards for best parade float and best-dressed team were almost as coveted as the actual race awards, and Mini fans never dared arrive late and miss the spectacle. As the crowds approached 10,000 in the 1960s, Armstrong and his crew annually ran out of bleacher space and had to spread paper over the dirt floor to accommodate more fans. Tickets were even *scalped* outside the doors, and often Armstrong spent more time outside the arena than inside, making sure all the high-ranking-but-ticketless IU administrators got in for the not-to-be-missed Mini 500.

Despite the 1955 addition of the Variety Show and Mini 500, Armstrong and the Student Foundation still found space for more activities. In 1958 the Golf Jamboree was added as a Friday morning activity. The idea of adding a golf tourney came about rather easily, with the combination of the IU Golf Course opening for business and an increasing adult interest in Little 500 weekend. Armstrong, a golf nut himself, saw the Jamboree as a vehicle for financial sponsors, faculty, and alumni to have some fun of their own as participants, not just spectators. Over the years the tournament proper developed a devoted following, and others would come to see the celebrity golfers Armstrong arranged to have on hand. Much as he did for the Variety Show (thanks in part to an era in which celebrities and professional athletes were easily accessible), Armstrong called on some of the country's top golfers to come and entertain fans with clinics and demonstrations, including Patty Berg, Art Wall, Jimmy Demaret, and Sam Snead.

While the Variety Show was the Saturday night fixture, another show was hatched in 1960 for Friday night—the Little 500 Extravaganza. Originally created to help celebrate the 10th Little 500 weekend, the Extravaganza thrived and survived through 1973 as a show featuring top musical talent. The first Extravaganza showcased the Four Lads at the Woodlawn tennis courts in the heart of campus, and other memorable shows featured the Kingsmen in 1965 and Chicago in 1970.

With the Extravaganza in place, Armstrong's vision of a full and complete weekend of activities came into focus. In 1963, for example, a

Much of the success of the Mini in its prime was due to the magnitude of its spectacle. Each year's event would have a theme playing off the word "Mini," such as "Minilympics" in 1968, opposite, and the arena would be decorated to fit the theme. The popular pre-race parade included floats featuring the year's theme (such as a Geisha depiction in 1967, when the theme was "Around the World in Mini Ways"), though some teams occasionally improvised (as did Willkie's "Ho Chi Mini," also in 1967).

Crowds at the flashy Mini reached nearly 10,000 in the 1960s (pictured: a rafters view from 1967), leading to scalped tickets and a few headaches among Student Foundation officials, who seemingly could never find enough extra seats to accommodate the masses.

The Little
500

At its heart, the Mini was still a competition among women's housing units—and a fierce one at that. Teams raced in heats of three at a time, and the single-elimination nature of the event added high drama and tension. To be on top at the end and receive a crown and congratulations from IU dignitaries was, for the women, comparable to winning the Little 500 (pictured are the 1963 Oak Hall winners, along with IU President Elvis Stahr and Chancellor Herman B Wells).

student (after a day of classes, of course) could have spent Friday evening at the Mini and then the Extravaganza, spent Saturday at the track, attended the Variety Show, had ice cream at Acacia, and then perhaps gone to the Sprocket Hop at Wright Quad or one of the countless other student gatherings. A friend of the IU Foundation could have a slightly different, though equally full weekend, with visits to the Golf Jamboree and the Saturday morning Cream and Crimson football game (added in 1963 by Armstrong, 22 years after he founded the game as a student).

There was truly something for everyone, with the bicycle race at the center of it all.

Through the first nine years of the Variety Show, from 1955 to 1963, there was no lack of star power at the Auditorium, with Connie Francis, Andy Williams, the Smothers Brothers, and native son Hoagy Carmichael appearing as headliners at the annual gala. But there was one star Bill Armstrong wanted more at the Little 500 weekend than any other. He

LITTLE 500 — It's Beyond Belief!

Join CHARLIE BROWN and his friends at the WORLD'S GREATEST COLLEGE WEEKEND!

FRIDAY

Golf Jamboree—I.U. Golf Course—8:00 a.m.

The Miniature—Fieldhouse—8:00 p.m.

Bicycle Bounce—Theta Chi House—9:00 p.m.

SATURDAY

Little, Little 500—8th and Woodlawn—10:00 a.m.

The Race—I.U. Stadium—1:00 p.m.

Variety Show—I.U. Auditorium—8:00 p.m.

Ice Cream Social—Acacia House—9:00 p.m.

Sprocket Hop—Men's Quad—9:00 p.m.

SEE YOU AT LITTLE 500 WEEKEND!

wanted the King of Comedy, the man who entertained millions, from veterans in the fields of battle with his USO shows to families at home with his television specials. Armstrong, always thinking big, wanted Bob Hope. Luring him to Bloomington would be arguably his greatest Little 500–related achievement.

"I was determined to get him. He was the hottest thing you could have," Armstrong said. Making a personal crusade out of landing *the* big act of the day, he traveled to Hope's North Hollywood, California, home

in early 1963 to personally ask for the star's attendance. Armstrong ignored the warnings of Hope's manager, who warned that his boss could be moody when approached for such an appearance. The manager turned out to be quite right, as initially Hope rebuffed Armstrong's request, saying that IU couldn't be anywhere near as great as advertised, and that the school up the road in West Lafayette was better. Armstrong, undaunted, continued his sales pitch for the school and the weekend, and finally Hope expressed a glimmer of interest. The 1963 race week-

The Little
500

The incomparable Little 500 Variety Show brought some of the country's biggest names in entertainment to Bloomington, and many attended the race prior to their Saturday night performances. In 1961 the hip Pat Boone (driving) visited, along with Sweetheart Joanie Summers (rear).

Opposite: in 1958, "Peants" cartoonist Charles Schultz donated a drawing of his Little 500 team to be used by the Student Foundation for advertising.

end wouldn't fit into his schedule, Hope said, but he told Armstrong to call him in January 1964.

It was no coincidence that the May 9, 1964, Little 500 set an attendance record of 23,790, with almost 4,000 more fans than the previous best. In addition to the great weather and another great race, there was a buzz in the air as fans anxiously awaited the evening's entertainment and the most anticipated Variety Show ever. Bob Hope was in town. Armstrong had followed Hope's orders to call him four months earlier, and Hope agreed to do two Saturday night performances for $30,000. Several previous Variety Shows had two installments, usually both sell-outs, so Armstrong was pleased to get two shows out of Hope—that is, until the ticket deluge came. The Student Foundation took ticket requests through the mail and in no time had enough to fill *six* programs at the IU Auditorium. Armstrong got his man on the phone again and pleaded for two Sunday performances. Hope agreed, offering to do two more shows for no additional cost.

Hope didn't disappoint. The weekend's four shows were a roaring success, with Hope and three good supporting acts in singer/comic Molly Bee and musical groups the Lettermen and the Four Lads. Hope's trademark ad-libbing and timely humor won over the crowd, and he sprinkled in new material at each performance. He also amazed Armstrong with his down-to-earth demeanor and un-Hollywood-like demands, such as asking Armstrong what the Student Foundation wanted from his act and advising him that hand-and-foot service throughout the weekend would not be necessary, as long as some time was made for his beloved golf game. The way Hope dealt with his own payment was also unique. Armstrong stopped by his dressing room between the first and second Saturday night shows with a check for $30,000. Hope tore it up, lecturing Armstrong that performers should never be paid until all shows are done. As it turned out, Hope didn't request the money even after he was through, instead asking Armstrong if he could come back the following year. "I didn't know when I've had a better time doing a show, or when I've met so many wonderful people all in one weekend," Hope told the *Indiana Daily Student,* bidding farewell to his hosts.

And so it began, a relationship between the biggest name in showbiz and the World's Greatest College Weekend. Hope did indeed return in 1965, playing to four more full houses at the Auditorium. He continued

More than anyone else, Bill Armstrong yearned to have Bob Hope play at a Little 500 Variety Show. Hope's highly-anticipated first appearance in 1964 delighted fans with four sold-out Auditorium shows, and he was so impressed with the event and its following, he returned four more times (pictured in 1965 at Tenth Street Stadium, with WFIU radio reporter Marilyn Feigenbaum).

to be so impressed with the university and the Little 500 program that he donated his appearance fee to the Foundation for a scholarship fund in his name. Always enjoying the outdoor stage, Hope expressed interest in playing at the new Memorial Stadium, which he did to a crowd of more than 25,000 in 1967. He returned to IU again in the fall of 1971 for an Assembly Hall dedication show with singer Petula Clark and 18,000 fans. Hope played the 1975 Variety Show in conjunction with the Little 500's 25th anniversary and returned two years later for his final IU appearance, performing at the ripe young age of 74. Collectively, he performed at five Variety Shows and never accepted a penny for any of them. "He always liked a clean-cut, polite crowd," Armstrong said. "He was really impressed with the students of Indiana University." Hope was equally im-

pressed with Armstrong, and through the years he invited him to many of his television show tapings, from Hollywood to New York City to the Kennedy Center, maintaining a friendship with the man who wouldn't take no for an answer back in 1963.

Boosted by popular events like the Bob Hope Variety Shows and the beloved Mini, the Little 500 weekend sailed through the 1960s with spectacular success. As a result, Armstrong and the Student Foundation faced the pleasant, though at times difficult, dilemma of having to find work for the increasing number of students joining the organization. From 1955 to 1965, the Student Foundation's at-large membership swelled from 100 to 564 (student enrollment also increased over that

span, but at a much slower clip). Fortunately, the weekend's activities grew over the same period, creating new committees and work for the members. When taking into account every aspect of the weekend, the student involvement statistics were staggering—in 1965 it was estimated that one out of every four undergraduates was actively involved in the weekend planning, not only as Student Foundation members but as bike riders, trike riders, coaches, ticket vendors, or Mini parade float builders. With the undergraduate population at just over 13,700, that translated into more than 3,000 students involved.

The overall atmosphere of fun and work all circled back to the bicycling and the riders that were at the core of the Little 500 experience. Champion riders and teams were lauded extensively in the early years of the race, but even more so as the weekend expanded. Consequently, more fans visited the stadium. Crossing the finish line only represented the start of the festivities for a winning foursome. After the podium kiss from the Sweetheart came the rest of the evening's activities, where the winners would serve as honored guests. At the Variety Show they would be announced and brought on stage, usually to be congratulated again by the leading ladies on hand. Banner newspaper headlines would hail the victors, and the title of "Little 500 champion" would follow the rider for the rest of his IU days. One particular rider, Ken Frost of the 1966 Phi Psi winning team, uniquely experienced the transition from average Joe to immortal. "In 1964 I was an All-American [swimmer] and not known at all," he said. "But winning the bike race made you an instant campus hero."

But even as the event cruised along at the peak of its popularity, skeptics began to wonder how long the Little 500 would last at such a high-octane level. A 1964 *Daily Student* editorial stated that "the IU Foundation, to put it simply, has created a monster." While "ingenuity and a spirit of fun were the hallmark of the early races," the critique noted, the 1960s version had become "a slick, professional spectacular put on by a hand-picked clique of the cream of the campus elite." Such a statement wasn't untrue, as the race's chief organizing body, the Student Foundation Steering Committee, had grown into a greek-heavy group that many students yearned to be a part of every year (though competition for spots on the committee existed in the early days as well). And calling the production "slick" was probably an understatement, with

all the money the Foundation poured into promoting and putting on the event. Evidence of tremendous expense could be seen everywhere, from the big-name performers to the massive supplies of Little 500–logoed merchandise, including matching T-shirts for all Student Foundation members and Little 500 matchbooks and napkins. The Foundation never disclosed exactly how much money was put into the affair, but estimates in the tens of thousands of dollars likely were accurate. Though the tremendous masses of paying spectators at events helped pay the expenses and leave enough extra money for the working student scholarships, some wondered how long it would be until the bubble burst. The *Daily Student* editorial pointed out how the campus's traditional Fall Carnival weekend died at the hands of IU officials who believed too much time, money, and energy was being allotted to one weekend, and asked whether the same fate awaited the giant Little 500.

The skeptics were proven wrong. By the end of the decade even more students turned to the Student Foundation for extracurricular action, and more activities were piled onto the weeks leading up to the already-crowded race weekend program to create even more work opportunities and, for the rest of the campus, more recreation. A fashion/style show debuted in 1969, featuring student models clothed in outfits made by home economics students and local retailers. Though this enjoyed a loyal following (supported greatly by community merchants, it lasted through 1983), it didn't include a great number of students, especially when compared to another event that began one year before: the Little 500 Regatta.

Armstrong felt the need for yet another participation-oriented event in the late 1960s to accommodate his expanding membership and appease the active student body, and in 1968 he introduced a completely new function for those needs. Unlike the other main Little 500–related sideshow, this one would take to the *water*, not to wheels. A regatta was born. For the 33 qualifying bike teams' housing units and coed sponsors, a paddleboat race was created at nearby Lake Monroe on the weekend before Little 500. Armstrong figured the housing units would enjoy an event that had competition without cycling, and like so many other events he kicked off, he was right on the money with the Regatta. Almost overnight it became a major gathering like the cycling events, with high

For the ever-expanding Student Foundation membership and a student body that couldn't get enough Little 500–related fun, a Regatta debuted in 1968 at Lake Monroe one week before the race. Paddleboat (shown in 1968) and, later, canoe races gave hundreds of students chances for competition, and thousands more a chance to visit the lakeshores and relax. But unlike the other main participatory sidebar event, the Mini, the Regatta would ultimately not survive the test of time.

participation and skyrocketing attendance. Housing units without bike teams were allowed to enter regatta teams after the first year, and the fields increased to 50-plus teams in two disciplines, coed paddleboat and women's canoe. Thousands of students made the trip to the lakeshores to watch the competition (held at Lake Monroe in 1968 and 1974–78, and from 1969 to 1973 at Lake Lemon), catch some occasional sun, and listen to music (bands, too, came during a few years, sometimes playing on pontoon boats in the middle of the lake). With new events like the Regatta the range of the Little 500 kingdom extended even past its own single weekend, taking more of students' time and energy and making an even greater mark on the campus calendar.

The great mark would fade, however. Many of the new events kicked off in the years between 1955–1969 would soon become victims of their own success, as the makeup of campus changed and students took new approaches to "fun" on Little 500 weekend. (A weekend which, also, would in 1972 begin to fall in April rather than May, as IU changed its academic calendar. The April weekends ultimately would bring weather concerns and time constraints for the Little 500 family of activities, since race week would only be a few weeks after the spring holiday.) The bicycling would go on, strong as always, but the complete weekend that everyone came to know would begin to come down to earth in the 1970s.

The Little
500

5. The Dynasty

The Little 500, counted on through the years by many fraternities for fun and camaraderie, took on a new role in the late 1960s and into the 1970s—lifesaver of a dying brotherhood. As a high-profile campus event, the weekend was already many things to many people: for administrators, the diverse events showed off the university in its most positive light, bringing students together in spirits of competition, recreation, and fund-raising. For Student Foundation members, Little 500 represented the ultimate campus leadership and work opportunity. And for the average student group, most notably fraternities and sororities, the Little 500 merely brought a festive atmosphere to the end of a school year. Overall, the Little 500 served to entertain more than anything else. But as it matured from its adolescence to "tradition" status, it was called upon by one organization to serve as a savior. The results were unlike anything previously seen in race history.

Though greeks largely dominated the Little 500 through its first two decades, not all fraternities shared equally in the mastery. A total of nine different fraternities won races through 1972, but with the many greek triumphs came a few greek tragedies. There was Phi Delta Theta, twice the bridesmaids and twice barred from competition due to circumstances completely unrelated to cycling. There was Phi Kappa Theta, hailed as champions on the winners' stand only to be found one lap short upon further review. Then there were also teams such as Delta Tau Delta, Kappa Delta Rho, and Zeta Beta Tau, perennial participants that never found race-day success.

And then there was Delta Chi, a fraternity on life-support both on and off the track. From 1954 to 1964 its teams didn't miss a single Little 500, respectably competing and even posting five top–10 finishes. But from 1965 to 1968 it failed to qualify in three of four races, an embarrassing streak at a time when most fraternity teams made the field with little or no trouble. Missing out on a berth in the race was especially costly to greek houses, who often counted on Little 500 weekend to be the pinnacle of the spring social season. Greek membership drives also frequently touted Little 500 success, and failing to qualify meant lagging behind in the quest for new pledges, the lifeblood of any fraternity.

As the president of Delta Chi in 1968–69, Steve Reisinger looked around his 106 North Jordan Avenue house and felt the time for an upheaval had arrived. The chapter was generally believed to be the smallest of the 33 fraternities on campus at the time in terms of manpower, with only a small fraction of the 75 to 100 members most IU fraternities boasted. That in itself was cause for concern in terms of the house's ability to survive, but there were also doubts about the fraternity's activities, or lack thereof. It was not a standout social power, wasn't strong in intramurals, and didn't exactly boast a knockout house grade point average. Though blaming such maladies solely on the lack of good showings in recent Little 500s might have been oversimplifying matters, Reisinger took a long, hard look at Delta Chi's situation and decided that the only way to return the fraternity to distinction on campus would be to turn around its cycling program. In short, his fraternity would rebuild in an unprecedented fashion—on two wheels.

The road to rebuilding for Reisinger and Delta Chi began with a letter from an alumnus working in a Chicago-area bank. He had read articles about a young phenom named Eddy Van Guyse, who was winning Illinois state cycling championships and making noise on the national scene while still in high school—and who just happened to be working part-time in the same bank. Though Van Guyse was preparing to attend the University of Illinois, he listened to the alum's description of the Little 500 and, intrigued, accepted an invitation to attend the 1968 qualifications at IU with Reisinger. It was an unforgettable day. "I was totally in awe to see the numbers of people who got into this thing called 'qualifications,'" said Van Guyse, who was born in Belgium but grew up in Chicago. "I was in awe to see a campus where bicycle riders were heroes." It was an atmosphere 180 degrees different from suburban Chicago, where Van Guyse would train in the streets and be either taunted or unnoticed. Returning home after the weekend, he told his parents all about the race and announced his change of heart. He wanted to pledge Delta Chi and ride in the Little 500. The first piece of Reisinger's grand scheme had fallen into place.

Not surprisingly, the addition of Van Guyse to Delta Chi rocked the Little 500 community, which in recent years had seen the race prosper but largely remain unchanged. In the eyes of top teams, a relative no-name team had recruited a foreigner to take over matters and thwart the balance of power. "People thought Delta Chi had brought in someone off the boat, a non-English speaker," said Van Guyse, laughing. At one point he was even summoned to the IU Student Foundation offices, where he had to prove to officials that he was indeed an American and an active student, not a hired hand for Delta Chi. Judging from the 1969 race, however, many riders probably still found something illegal in the addition of Van Guyse, as he single-handedly turned around his team's fortunes. In qualifying, the fraternity placed eighth, its highest starting spot since 1956, and on race day the team finished 10th, no small feat considering Van Guyse rode the majority of the team's laps in the windstorm that was the 1969 Little 500. "It was a remarkable performance," Reisinger recalled. In Little 500 racing circles from that point on, Van Guyse was no longer a no-name, his team no longer an unknown.

As valuable as the freshman Van Guyse immediately became as a rider, he proved to be even more valuable as an advisor and teacher. Steve Reisinger and his younger brother Randy (who arrived at IU in the fall of 1968, in the same pledge class as Van Guyse), were both non-riders themselves and, according to Van Guyse, "didn't know beans about bicycle racing," but were determined to learn everything they could about the sport. Together, the trio of Van Guyse and the Reisingers traveled around the Midwest to other top amateur events of all kinds, from road races to velodrome events, and the education grew. "They were like two sponges, soaking everything up," Van Guyse said. "They asked a million questions, I gave a million answers, and they took it all in."

One of the lessons the Reisingers learned early on in their bicycling education was that having a Little 500 rider serve double-duty as rider and coach was impractical. Upon arriving at Delta Chi Van Guyse was expected to serve as the main rider and coach, but after his first year the Reisinger brothers stepped in and took over full coaching responsibilities—a rare luxury for a young team. While almost every team employed help from former riders or team alternates in the pits on race day, usually only the top fraternities and a few strong dorm teams had full-time coaches. But the Reisingers planned on becoming one of those top teams in a hurry, and their cycling know-how soon became so extensive that coaching, developing, and motivating riders became their passion and, eventually, a major thorn in the side of their competition.

The road to rebuilding for Delta Chi began with Eddy Van Guyse, an Illinois state champion with national cycling aspirations. He was invaluable as a cycling advisor to his fellow Delta Chis, not to mention the anchor on its teams of 1969–72 (pictured riding in 1972, he has the four stars on helmet).

In 1970, its second year of rebuilding, Delta Chi continued to improve and demand the attention of greek rivals. Another nationally ranked rider and junior champion, Mark Cassady, joined the Delta Chi contingent, giving the team an extra workhorse to complement Van Guyse. Cassady and Van Guyse were good friends, and at a race sponsored by the Amateur Bicycle League of America (ABLA, later changed to the USCF, for United States Cycling Federation), Cassady met the Reisingers and agreed to come to IU and ride. Delta Chi's new one-two punch displayed its strength at qualifications, as the team surprised everyone—even itself—with a pole-position run. However, race day wasn't as successful, as the team suffered an early wreck, lost a lap, and never quite caught up to the Tom Battle–led Sigma Phi Epsilon team. Still, the 1970 race marked a milestone day for the fraternity, when Van Guyse beat Dodds House's future Hall-of-Famer Mike Howard at the line for second place, the team's highest finish ever. "We would have liked to win, but we were happy with how far we had come," Steve Reisinger said.

Though its Little 500 rebuilding process progressed well through the first couple years, Delta Chi still struggled as an organization. During the 1969–70 school year the university stepped in and evicted the fraternity from its Jordan Avenue residence, putting the wrecking ball to the dilapidated structure soon after. The members were able to stay together, renting an abandoned house on Third Street near the corner of Third and Jordan, but according to Steve Reisinger, only 15 members remained by the end of the 1970–71 school year. As a result, one week after the 1971 race (in which Van Guyse flipped over his bike in a mid-race crash and broke three ribs, yet continued riding in a 15th-place effort), the chapter learned that Delta Chi alumni were planning to shut down the operation entirely. Falling back again on the Little 500 as a means to stay afloat, the remaining Delta Chi members sold their alumni on the fact that Van Guyse had one more year of race eligibility, and therefore perhaps one more shot at a victory.

After three years of re-establishing the Delta Chi name in Little 500 circles, the fraternity came back in 1972 with its strongest team yet and, for the first time, entertained reasonable thoughts of winning. For the first time Van Guyse would have experience all around him in the pits, as a stellar supporting cast of experienced cyclists assembled. Returning from Delta Chi's 1971 squad was Mike Dayton, a seasoned amateur, his older brother Steve, and a new addition to the team—senior Steve Schaefer, a former Briscoe dorm rider. Steve Dayton, a transfer student from Purdue (racing in what would be his only Little 500), was the reigning national road racing champion. That triumph came on a 100-mile road course, so his endurance for a 50-mile team event was unquestioned. On paper, at least, the team appeared to be the finest ever assembled for a Little 500. The first evidence of Delta Chi's strengths emerged at qualifications, as Van Guyse posted the fastest lap and the team the fastest overall attempt—2:28.37 in *snow*. "We would have broken every four-lap record that existed [under good conditions]," Van Guyse said. Just about every other team in the field conceded victory to Delta Chi in the newspapers leading up to the race, one team even going so far as to claim that only "an act of God" would keep the powerhouse foursome out of the winner's circle.

Surely enough, an act of God came on April 29, 1972. "We knew we had the best four riders, and our goal was to make life miserable for the other teams," explained Van Guyse on the race-day plan. "It went like clockwork until the rain." Race rules stated that after 101 laps were completed, the white flag could be shown and the race ended early in the event of inclement weather. So as the rain progressed Van Guyse pedaled his hardest in hopes of getting that far and taking an early checkered flag. His wishes fell short, as only 78 laps could be completed under fair conditions. Sunday, Delta Chi was unable to pick up where it left off the prior day, due to the surging Kappa Sigmas and a very sick Van Guyse, who had slept all of 15 minutes the night before after a dinner that didn't agree. The team tried to keep Van Guyse's illness a secret from the field, but when the Kappa Sigmas noticed the star was sidelined, they attacked and pulled away. The sick senior did put in one heroic set at the end of the race, closing the gap with the leaders before exchanging to Steve Dayton for a sprint finish, only to watch an appropriate ending to the all-around, bad-luck weekend. Dayton and the Reisingers miscommunicated over when the white flag would be shown, resulting in Dayton being woefully out of position for the sprint. It took a heroic effort on Dayton's part in the last lap just to secure second place, but that wasn't enough to mask the Delta Chi disappointment.

Van Guyse cried after the race, having worked so hard for four years only to come up short on his last try with a team expected to do so much.

Sitting on the pole in 1972 and hailed as the undisputed favorites, Delta Chi appeared destined to notch its first title. An opposing team said that only "an act of God" could stop the fraternity from winning, a prediction that proved true. Rains made life miserable for the entire field, and on the Sunday restart Delta Chi was not the same team, opening the door for Kappa Sigma to win its first Little 500.

But his place in Little 500 history was secure, with three All-Star appointments from 1970 to 1972 and a Hall of Fame induction. He continued to ride competitively after his IU career, but nothing ever compared. "Of my whole racing experience, wherever I've been, I've never walked into an arena where I almost felt like a gladiator," he said. "There's nothing like it."

Despite coming up short in the 1972 race, the fraternity prospered from all the attention its team generated in the time leading up to the 500, and it was able to stay on solid ground as an organization. Its place on campus was even more secure after the 1973 event, when the bike team generated even more attention and, finally, backed it up with a win. This time, all the attention and advanced billing favoring Delta Chi swirled around a young Olympian who brought his skills to IU and helped to further push the envelope of Little 500 competition.

The Reisingers feared that Delta Chi's rebuilding efforts on the track would fall apart after 1972 with the loss of Van Guyse, Schaefer, and Steve Dayton, but their intense inspections of outside cycling paid dividends yet again with an Indianapolis kid named Wayne Stetina. "We had been observing Wayne for several years, and we thought he'd be an excellent Little 500 rider," Steve Reisinger said. Stetina had been riding seemingly since birth, coming from a bicycle-crazed family, and in the summer of 1972 left home to compete in the Olympics in Munich as an 18-year-old, defying critics who thought him too young to compete on the world stage. The Reisingers made an offer to Stetina to join and ride for Delta Chi, but he was noncommittal prior to the Games. Upon coming back, however (his team finished 14th out of 35 in Munich), he had made up his mind. "I'm going to go to IU and ride for Delta Chi," Stetina proclaimed at the stateside airport to a throng of reporters and news crews. As a teenage Olympian he had become a sort of media darling, and his bold announcement was big news for the intramural bicycling event.

"Stetina was the best rider that ever was or ever will be on that track," Kappa Sigma's Bob Kirkwood said of the man to beat in 1973. "He had physical strength, the mental strength and the international experience." While Delta Chi was somewhat humbled in the knowledge that even with the best team a Little 500 win was never a lock, as was the case with its '72 team, it couldn't help but like the chances for victory with

such a talented newcomer. Starting from the fifth spot on race day (Dodds House sat on the pole), Stetina logged the first 66 laps for his team, putting them in first place. If that was the first good sign of things to come, the second sign came a little later when Stetina pulled an amazing recovery out of a potentially dangerous situation. A major accident had developed right after he began his second set, and he hit a downed rider directly in front of him. After *cartwheeling in mid-air* and somehow avoiding serious injury, Stetina maneuvered back around to his pit to exchange riders and bikes. The incident cost the team nearly one full lap to the field, but Stetina managed to get it back all by himself. On the final lap of the race—his 144th lap of the afternoon—he held off Kappa Sigma's Bob Shanteau for Delta Chi's first Little 500 victory. Kirkwood simply called it "a superhuman effort."

When Stetina crossed the finish line, Delta Chi's rebuilding officially became complete. Compared to the many fraternity teams who had won before them, what distinguished Delta Chi's first five teams, and especially its winning team of 1973, was its high concentration of riders who brought outside skills to the Little 500 track. With the exception of 1969, when Van Guyse rode as a freshman and as the first rider of the team's revival, each Delta Chi team included two or more seasoned amateurs. Even when such amateurs rode as Little 500 rookies, their cycling endurance and savvy shone at least as brightly as those of opposing riders who had several years of Little 500 racing under their belts. Of 1973's foursome, technically three men participated as Little 500 rookies, with only Mike Dayton serving as the Little 500 veteran. Stetina and Mark Dayton (younger brother of Mike and Steve) were first-time Little Fivers, but that description belied their talents—Stetina, for example, logged 10,000 miles in his training for the '72 Olympics, a number which the *Daily Student* estimated as five times the amount of miles the average Little 500 *team* would put in for one race. The team's fourth member, Roger

Accidents were, and are, an ever-present danger in Little 500 racing, and the worst ones often leave a tangled mess of bicycles and bodies. In this 1974 accident, Dan Chase of Sigma Chi is tumbling over a felled Theta Chi rider, and Jeff Campbell of Beta Theta Pi (15) is about to do the exact same thing.

The Little 500

Delta Chi finally broke through with back-to-back wins in 1973 and '74, fielding teams built around Wayne Stetina, considered by many to be the finest Little 500 rider of all time. Stetina arrived in Bloomington after competing in the 1972 Summer Olympics as an 18-year-old, rode the bulk of Delta Chi's laps in the two winning years, then left the Little 500 racing scene after 1974 to continue training full-time for various national and international competitions.

Antoniu, was the only rider developed from within the current membership. Through such in-house development or through recruiting of dormitory-based Little 500 riders was how many successful Little 500 teams of the past built their winners, but Delta Chi and the Reisingers also looked for talent from the amateur ranks. It was a formula that would win again, but also fall under intense scrutiny from the race's governing body, the Student Foundation.

The months leading up to the 1973 race represented a microcosm of how most of the rest of the decade would progress for Delta Chi—winning races while fighting the system. A clash between the organization and the Student Foundation was inevitable, with Delta Chi's overnight influx of talent and the subsequent whispers from others in the Little 500 public that perhaps something was unfair. First came the questions about Van Guyse's background in 1969, which were answered, and then came more issues raised about other Delta Chi recruits. After Steve Dayton rode in 1972, having transferred from Purdue to IU just for the spring semester, the Student Foundation added a new twist to its years-old transfer rules. A rider would have to be affiliated with his team starting in the fall, as coming over from another school the same semester as the race would not be allowed. Delta Chi immediately challenged the rule in 1973 with two of its newest riders, Mark Dayton and Garry Rybar. Dayton had graduated early from Southport High near Indianapolis to come to IU and get an early start in the music school, but when he came out for the bike team a Student Foundation Steering Committee member who had also attended Southport raised questions over how Dayton managed to graduate early. At first, the Student Foundation ruled him ineligible for the 1973 race, but overturned the decision on an appeal from Delta Chi, who cited Dayton's transfer was different in that it wasn't from another college, but from high school. As for Rybar, he had transferred from Purdue for the spring semester as Steve Dayton had, and couldn't get around the transfer rule.

Rybar, who arrived at IU as yet another link of the Indianapolis amateur rider chain, was, however, eligible to ride in 1974. Stetina and Mark Dayton returned, along with rookie Mike Alexander, forming another confident blockbuster team hungry for another win. Such confidence started at the top with the Reisinger brothers, who claimed to have finally developed the winning approach to Little 500 racing. Though Steve Reisinger remains mum on details of the strategy even 20 years later, it was common knowledge that Delta Chi's strengths included a combination of solid personnel and a keen sense of when and how to use each member, not to mention a thorough knowledge of opponents' strengths and methods. Talent-wise the fraternity was almost always tops in the field, but the intangibles the coaches brought to the equation made the team almost unstoppable.

Such was the case in 1974, a Little 500 season filled with new track records but again ruled by Delta Chi. For 1974, the Roadmaster bicycle received a substantial makeover, with a lighter frame, a larger gear ratio, and a thinner profile. The result was a bike much more maneuverable and conducive to speed. In qualifications, both the individual fastest lap and team records fell, with Bob Kirkwood running a 32.34-second lap and Sigma Alpha Epsilon a 2-minute, 22.43-second qualifying run. Delta Chi qualified second, just eight-hundredths of a second behind SAE, then on race day obliterated the previous track record of 2:12.19 (22.69 mph, by Alpha Tau Omega in 1971) by nearly two and a half minutes with a 2:09.48 time (23.11 mph). The time itself wasn't an earth-shattering feat with the improved bikes, but the gusto with which Delta Chi went after the title was most impressive. "We set out to demoralize everybody, to take the spirit out of competition," Mark Dayton explained. "That race couldn't have gone any better for us." The team got out of the gate quick, then all day watched for other teams' exchanges. When other teams switched riders Delta Chi pushed the pace of the pack, effectively leaving behind the stragglers. Such aggressiveness coupled with flat-out speed added up to a two-lap cushion. Victory was such a foregone conclusion that Stetina took his time on the last couple laps to wave to the fans and still won by a half mile.

While Delta Chi's 1974 performance surprised no one, it infuriated many teams. One year of being overmatched was one thing, two years in a row was quite another. "If we ride a perfect race and Delta Chi does the same, we'll finish second," said Dodds House's Howard in the *Daily Student* before the race. Also in the paper were the thoughts of another team's coach, who compared Stetina riding in Little 500 to Mark Spitz swimming IU intramurals. Such sharp critiques finally reached the Student Foundation, where some other touchy issues were already being examined.

For the first time in 1973, the IU Foundation failed to make a profit from the Little 500 weekend. After many years of weekends jam-packed with activities and grandeur, some of the sideshows and other expenses were starting to wear on the bottom line. In keeping with the mission of Little 500, scholarships continued to be awarded to students in 1973, but the funds had to come from Foundation coffers. As a result, Student Foundation Director Jerry Tardy set out to tighten the Little 500 budget. Eliminated were some of the frills, such as the hundreds of T-shirts for the Student Foundation membership, and entertainment, like the Little 500 Extravaganza. The event was not holding its own in terms of attendance or star power, though this was not necessarily organizers' fault—landing big-name talent had become all but impossible due to skyrocketing appearance fees, and the Student Foundation couldn't foot the bill anymore.

Such adjustments had no effect on the Little 500 race. Coming up on its 25th birthday, it remained on firm ground as a drawing card, with high attendance and a loyal following on campus and even throughout the state, occasionally being broadcast on television (in 1971 the race was televised by an Indianapolis station, WTTV). But with the long-standing greek dominance and the recent stranglehold Delta Chi put on the contest, competitive issues were coming into question. Teams vying for the 33 qualifying spots remained plentiful, with 50 to 60 coming out for quals each year, usually with an equal number of fraternity and residence hall entries. But in the race greek teams always outnumbered dorm teams, sometimes by as many as two to one. These were becoming simply the Little 500 facts of life. A 1973 study in the *Daily Student* brought to light the reality of expenses in racing, for everything from bikes to clothing to the spring break trips teams counted on, and the fact that fraternities on average had much more money available for such expenses. The highest fraternity budgets exceeded $1,000, figures that dorm teams couldn't dream of reaching. The Student Foundation had no authority to regulate teams' spending to make it fairer for lesser-endowed groups to compete, but it could regulate the types of riders involved. To them, teams having money and better resources was one thing, but having almost professional-level members was becoming quite another.

With that reasoning, Wayne Stetina's days as a Little 500 rider came to an end. Delta Chi's two wins, and especially his efforts in riding 144 laps in 1973 and 92 laps in 1974, forced the Student Foundation into action. A rule was enacted in 1975 that prohibited prospective Little 500 riders from competing in ABLA races between March 1 and race day. Just as with Phi Kappa Psi and Dave Blase in the early 1960s, there was a fear that one rider and his team could make a mockery of the competition. Blase, however, returned when a rule about outside riding was lifted. Stetina didn't. He carried a full schedule of races outside Bloomington, and with Pan American Games and Olympic trials on the horizon elected not to take off two months solely to ride in Little 500. (Rules prohibiting

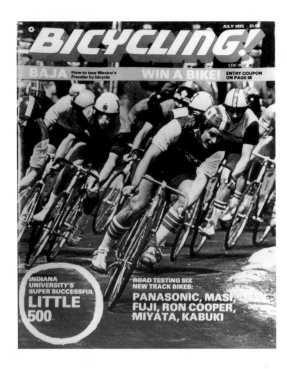

Little 500 participants from riding in top-level events continued to remain in various forms, and consequently kept two of Stetina's younger brothers, Dale and Joel, from riding in later years.)

The 1975 race moved along without him, and the Delta Chi winning streak fell. Not having Stetina on the track did hurt, but the fraternity had built such a roster of talent that it could still field an all-veteran team. Rybar, Mark Dayton, Alexander, and Antoniu made up the squad, and started the 1975 race from the pole. However, any hopes at a third consecutive victory were dashed early, as the team was assessed a 10-second penalty at lap 47 for advancing under a yellow flag. The Phi Gamma Delta team, anchored by talented freshman Jay Allardt, pulled away while Delta Chi sat in the penalty box, opening up a three-quarter lap lead that was never seriously threatened. In winning the Fijis completed a record achievement of their own, moving from 23rd to first in just one year's time, the largest one-year turnaround ever for a winner. As for the victorious freshman Allardt, only after the race did he fully realize the magnitude of the feat, when he got to stand on the Variety Show stage with his teammates and Bob Hope.

Angered by losing but not torn apart as a team, Delta Chi returned in 1976 with the same foursome it had the previous year, and set out to take back the crown from Fiji. Riding in his fourth race was Mark Dayton, who like many previous Delta Chis had become quite the amateur star in his own right, with Indiana state road racing and 1000-meter championship wins in 1975 and 1976, respectively. At qualifications for the 1976 Little 500, Dayton added to his list of individual accolades with a record single lap of 32.08 seconds, helping the team cruise to a record attempt of 2:20.9. Phi Gamma Delta qualified second, setting up the race-day showdown.

Skilled coaching paid off for Delta Chi in the race (held on a Monday for the first time after a weekend of rain), as the Reisingers picked apart the Fiji strategy. "We thought that Fiji would try to make us make the first exchange, so we put Rybar on [to start the race] and told him to stay out until they exchanged," Steve Reisinger said. It took some 60 laps, but Rybar successfully outlasted Fiji. From then on the race was largely a cat-and-mouse between the two teams, but Delta Chi's depth made the difference at the end, when Dayton and Allardt raced for the finish.

Allardt had to ride more than half his team's laps during the race to stay in the hunt, while Dayton was completely fresh for the sprint. Riding his team's final leg for the first time in his career, Dayton couldn't be touched, opening up a lead going into the final lap before pedaling the last lap in 31.2 seconds to take the checkered flag.

Delta Chi notched back-to-back wins again in 1977, with another triumph from the pole position. Rybar and Alexander returned as senior fourth-year riders (Rybar was a fifth-year senior, after being held out of the race in 1973), along with two senior rookies in Rob Brown and Jeff Pollum. The team's win resembled its performance from the year before, with Rybar riding a prolonged set at the beginning of the race to give his team a lead. That advantage held up all day until a sprint finish, in which Rybar edged the perennially competent Phi Psis by two seconds. About the only difference between the 1976 and 1977 races was how the '77 team benefited from an overall faster race, and clocked a record-breaking time of 2:09.46. The new record was two seconds better than the mighty 1974 team's.

The 1977 race did not go off without conflict, however. Another controversial ruling from IUSF affected the status of not only a Delta Chi rider, but a total of 20 riders who registered with teams to qualify for the event. Rule "1-f" stated that riders must be enrolled as full-time students in the fall semester prior to the race, a regulation not unlike the one that affected Rybar in 1973. This time the rule was applied to all participants, not just targeted at one house's top riders. Two men ruled out for 1977 included Delta Chi's Greg Silence, who had spent much of the fall semester hospitalized with a heart ailment, and Chi Phi's Ron Platter, who cited financial reasons for his absence. Silence went as far as to seek out legal counsel for his situation, but the Student Foundation didn't budge on the ruling. "I don't say we're right all the time on every ruling we make," Foundation President Bill Armstrong told a reporter. "But when we make one, we have to abide by it." His word remained true during the race, when he spotted Platter riding despite being ruled ineligible. At lap 156, the entire Chi Phi team was disqualified for using the illegal rider, earning them the dubious distinction of being the only team ever tossed out of a Little 500 in mid-race.

Five years after the Little 500 Extravaganza disappeared from the weekend schedule, the Student Foundation lost another sideshow when the popular Regatta met its untimely death. Since its 1968 debut, the waterfest rivaled the Mini 500 trike race as the most popular event outside Little 500, drawing 45,000 spectators over 11 years. The canoe and paddleboat races were fiercely contested each year by both men and women, but the skills needed were, of course, not comparable to the ones needed to maneuver Roadmasters, so over the years some 9,500 students came out to qualify and compete. But the combination of a lakefront atmosphere and students ultimately brought alcohol and other vices, and the off-campus nature of the event left it vulnerable to state police and other officials outside of the usual Student Foundation personnel. In 1978 the crowds were high as usual, with 4,000 paid spectators and estimates of up to 10,000 people crowded around Lake Monroe's Fairfax Beach. In previous years the Indiana Department of Natural Resources (DNR) had recommended that the event not be held at Fairfax Beach due to the large crowds, but the Foundation vowed to control traffic and clean up after the event. The DNR still sent a 19-man contingent of its own conservation officers for the 1978 crowds. The year before it had sent just six to patrol the area. The officers thoroughly monitored the lakefront and especially cars entering the park, and by the end of the day they had charged 31 students with various misdemeanors, mostly illegal possession, transportation, and consumption of alcohol and marijuana. Armstrong thought it was harassment. Even 20 years later, Armstrong described it as "a police state in action," adding that he thought officers came down hard on students to make a statement about the DNR's attitude toward the Regatta.

Armstrong took his complaints about the DNR all the way to the Indiana governor's office in 1978, but he never got an apology. On February 14, 1979, Student Foundation Director Mark Hesemann announced the Regatta would be eliminated from the roster of Little 500 activities, citing not only the conflicts with the DNR, but also the unpredictable weather, difficulty in collecting tickets, and poor conditions of the paddleboats. Staging an aquatic event in Indiana in mid-April did have its obstacles, but nevertheless it was a smash hit and profitable right up to the end—the 1978 edition made $5,000. But the problems with alcohol and authorities were not what the Student Foundation had in mind for Little 500 camaraderie, and therefore the 1978 debacle was widely believed to be the impetus for the Regatta's demise. "In the end, it was so uncomfortable for the spectators as well as the sponsors, it just wasn't worth doing," said Tardy, who in 1979 was Foundation vice president under Armstrong. The Student Foundation attempted to replace the Regatta in 1979 with "A Day at the Forum," a team competition at Tenth Street Stadium with several odd races, including blind tug-of-war and Earthball, which involved pushing a six-foot-high rubber ball down a field over various obstacles. It proved to be a lame substitute and only lasted two years.

What started out as one man's dream of a rebuilt fraternity had blossomed into a full-fledged dynasty, as through 1977 Delta Chi recorded four wins in five years, with the best still yet to come. In less than a decade's time the fraternity progressed from a dilapidated structure at 106 North Jordan to a brand new home at 1100 North Jordan, on a strip of road where many of the most prosperous IU greek organizations were relocating. The fraternity remained relatively small—28 members moved into the new house in the fall of 1976 (according to Steve Hoeferle, a member in the late '70s and long-time coach and aide to the team). Though membership would grow to around 50 later in the decade, it was still much smaller than the big fraternities. "One dorm floor would be more populous than Delta Chi," Hoeferle said. But as a unit Delta Chi had tamed the biggest event on campus, and effectively turned the greek system on its ear, with not just four skilled bike riders but an entire Little 500 support staff. Over half the house's members helped the team in some way, from massaging to bike repairing to cooking and dishwashing on the important spring break training trips. Other teams had good riders and more money, but few could match Delta Chi's complete program and entourage. In its later years, the house had a banner

Following the demise of the Regatta, the Student Foundation tried to replace the popular event with "A Day at the Forum," a team competition featuring out-of-the-ordinary events. Its dirtiest contest involved teams assembling themselves on a pole suspended over a mud pit, and often the results were predictable. As a replacement for the Regatta, the Day at the Forum was nowhere near as well-received, and it lasted only two years, from 1979 to 1980.

The Little 500

hanging in the entrance area of its house, simply asking the members "WHAT HAVE YOU DONE TO WIN LITTLE 500 TODAY?" Most of them could give a good answer anytime.

What sustained Delta Chi's winning tradition more than anything else, and no doubt infuriated everyone out to beat them, was the team's ability to reload after losing talented individual riders. In 1978, Delta Chi suffered a bit of a hiccup in finishing 10th, its lowest finish since the rebuilding began in 1969. With four rookies forced into action after the foursome of 1977 left the riding scene (three had graduated, and senior Rob Brown qualified with the 1978 team but did not ride in the race), the finish was not a complete shock to the house. It knew that those four rookies—Bill Brissman, Chris Gutowsky, Greg Silence, and Al Williams— would all return and play roles in what would be Delta Chi's final runs for glory in its incredible dynasty era.

While Delta Chi, the team of the 1970s, failed to play a major role in the 1978 contest (a botched exchange early in the race and a late wreck sealed its fate), the Little 500's all-time top team recorded its seventh win. Like Delta Chi, Phi Kappa Psi also had an innate ability to reload and continually produce quality teams. When Dodds House failed to qualify in 1977 for the first time ever, Phi Psi stood alone as the only Little 500 team to have qualified for every race—a streak that continues today. And Phi Psi was not just a team that showed up, as in the first 27 races it tallied six wins, 20 top-10s, and not a single finish lower than 16th. If Delta Chi was lightning in a bottle, Phi Psi was more of a steady downpour. In 1978 it was ready to pounce while the defending champs were off stride, as future Phi Psi Hall of Famer Doug Moody edged Sigma Nu and Alpha Epsilon Pi at the finish line.

Down but far from forgotten, Delta Chi returned in 1979 with the hunger to return to the top. It also battled the Student Foundation on yet another eligibility rule, an almost routine occurrence that was starting to spell doom for other teams. In 1977, the team lost a rider to a rule and won anyway, and would do the same in 1979. The newest Little 500 rule, put on the books just weeks before the 1978 qualifications, prohibited riders who had achieved a U.S. Cycling Federation "Category One" or "Category Two" level of ability. For amateurs, a label of "Cat One" designated Olympian-like ability, while "Cat Two" was considered pre-Olym-

pian. By eliminating such riders from Little 500, the Student Foundation believed it could finally return the race to an intramural level of competition. The rule immediately destroyed one promising independent team called the Velo-Men, which finished fifth in its first year as a team in 1977. Its four riders were all rookies—two would be named all-stars in 1977— but three of the four were USCF riders classified under the outlawed categories. The rule killed the team, and it never got a chance to build on its good finish (though in the history books, the Velo-Men went down as the best one-hit wonders ever). Delta Chi freshman Gutowsky also had achieved "Category Two" status prior to the 1978 race, but was allowed to ride after taking a few months off from sanctioned USCF competition. In October 1978, the Student Foundation expanded its original rule to include riders like Gutowsky, saying essentially that riders who were classified as "ones" or "twos" at any time could not ride.

A flabbergasted Gutowsky had to sit out in 1979, while returning vets Brissman, Williams, and Silence and rookie Doug Tate took the reins for Delta Chi and blasted the competition. Leading from lap 60 until the end, the team lapped the field on two occasions and was never threatened as it cruised to a fifth win in seven years. As for Gutowsky, he would return for the 1980 race after an appeal. He took legal counsel and fought his way back, finally being ruled eligible when USCF headquarters in Colorado Springs, Colorado, discovered it had no record of Gutowsky ever being classified as a top-category rider. The Student Foundation went on to eliminate the rule for "Category Two" riders in late 1981, though it would resurface a decade later.

Back in the lineup for 1980, Gutowsky joined returning champs Brissman, Tate, and Williams to create what became another mini-dynasty within the dynasty. In 1980 and 1981, Delta Chi recorded its sixth and seventh wins in spectacular fashion, setting records and taking the suspense out of the race for the overflow crowds and media. A new wave of curious onlookers had converged in Bloomington after the release of the Little 500–inspired film *Breaking Away*, and instead of Hollywood-level dramatic racing they got to witness the Delta Chi machine. In 1980 the fraternity led the race at every 10-lap interval, won by over two full laps and chopped 18 seconds off the previous record. So much for drama.

What differentiated these Delta Chi teams from their predecessors

The Little
500

was how the cycling-savvy names like Stetina and Dayton were gone, replaced by relative unknowns in the cycling community. Brissman and Gutowsky both had solid cycling experience under their belts but did not come to IU as prized recruits of the Reisingers and the Delta Chi system. In fact, both of them first briefly looked at joining Phi Kappa Psi and Phi Gamma Delta, but pledged Delta Chi after a series of conversations and house visits with graduate student and three-time winner Rybar. As for Tate and Williams, neither came to school with any bicycle racing experience. Tate transferred to IU from Iowa's Drake University, and Williams hadn't even planned on going greek when he arrived at IU, but liked the Delta Chi membership and moved in.

The entire team vigorously trained for the race, as did many other top teams. In the Little 500's infancy not all entrants put in mile after mile of work, but as the competition became greater through the years and spots in the race more hotly contested, teams started working out well before the weeks leading up to qualifications. Proof came in many of the 1970s races, where speeds were up and mishaps were relatively few in number (though massive multiple-team spills still occurred from time to time, thanks to the speeds and more aggressive riders all over the track).

(Opposite) The one constant throughout the Delta Chi dynasty was the leadership of Steve and Randy Reisinger, the brothers considered to be the "braintrust" behind the fraternity's success. They were easy to pick out in the pits on race day, with their stopwatches and strategic dossiers (pictured in 1979, Steve Reisinger is wearing the stopwatch and Randy Reisinger is standing below, along with Greg Silence and Doug Tate on the bottom row and Mike Alexander, Steve Hoeferle and Bill Brissman across the top).

In the later years of the Delta Chi dynasty, its teams made up for the lack of Olympic-caliber riders with voracious training year-round, from outdoor winter rides to long hours on rollers at the fraternity house (pictured monitoring the progress of Chris Gutowsky in 1981 is coach Kevin Weaver, with Doug Tate riding behind).

One Delta Chi creation that continues in today's Little 500 circle of activities is Team Pursuit, a race against the clock that tests a team's overall strength. Bill Brissman and Chris Gutowsky helped author the original proposal for the event in 1979, and both helped their team win its first two runnings in 1979 and 1981 (pictured is the 1981 team, from left to right, Doug Tate, Gutowsky, Brissman, and Al Williams).

Delta Chi riders between 1979 and 1981 took great pride in their heavy training and ability to keep it under wraps, as while competition increased many teams watched others' training regimens. "We tried to outtrain everyone else without them knowing it," Brissman said proudly. "Some [teams] went up and down Jordan [Avenue] for the sororities, but we would sneak out the back door." Even with snow on the ground the riders trained outside, exiting the house from the rear and carrying their bikes until out of sight from greek neighbors so as to not make tracks in the snow and reveal their efforts. "We wanted to *way* outtrain everyone else, and we didn't want them to know until we had 2,500 miles under us," Brissman said.

Such fierce training led to not only lopsided results on race day for

Delta Chi completed its amazing run with three consecutive wins from 1979 to 1981. From the final races at Tenth Street Stadium (pictured at right is Bill Brissman, winning under Howdy Wilcox's watch in 1979) to a new Little 500 home (Brissman again took the checkered flag, from Chappie Blackwell in 1980), the team was not seriously challenged in any of the three races. However, though no one would have believed it at the time, 1981 would be the last win in the Delta Chi dynasty era.

Delta Chi, but also to outlandish rumors about its methods. A sometimes-comical twist to the fraternity's achievements in Little 500 came from opposing teams' disbelief in how they could win time and time again without some kind of illegal aid. Words like "steroids" and "tampered bikes" were tossed around in association with the team, all of which Delta Chi firmly denied, but usually with a smile. Team members were flattered at the degree of absurdity the rumors reached, and took every opportunity to share tall tales with the media. In a 1981 front-page feature in the *New York Times* (yes, publicity was that extensive), team members told about how they were supposedly taken care of with free tuition, credit cards, automobiles, and academic help. After a while the team didn't mind the accusations and innuendo, instead deciding to use it as a psychological advantage. After all, if other teams wanted to believe such rumors, they probably weren't thinking as much about beating Delta Chi—not that beating Delta Chi was usually possible anyway.

Few would have believed it at the time, but Delta Chi's April 25, 1981, win at the new Little 500/Soccer Stadium would be its last in what was, and still is, the most dominant period for a team in race history. Brissman, Tate, and Williams rode out on a winning note, while Gutowsky would return for one more year, only to finish second. There would be no powers waiting in the wings to take over, no seasoned cycling studs preparing to make a mark in the Delta Chi annals. As it turned out, some of the problems that nearly doomed the fraternity in the late 1960s nearly doomed it again in the early 1980s, and it would be a while until the team returned to prominence in the Little 500 scene. But that in no way dimmed the brightness of its achievements from 1969 to 1981.

The bottom line compiled by the fraternity looks more remarkable with every passing year. From the starting grid, Delta Chi won five poles and only once failed to make the first three rows in those 13 races. As for the finishes, they are most impressive when observed all at once: 10th, second, fifth, second, first, first, second, first, first, 10th, first, first, first. On an individual basis, six Delta Chis gained induction into the Little 500 Hall of Fame: Van Guyse, Mark Dayton, Rybar, Stetina, Brissman, and Gutowsky (only Phi Psi can equal such a number of Hall of Famers). Such a record speaks volumes, but what was also significant was how, in many ways, Delta Chi changed the way teams approached the Little 500. "We studied that race inside and out—where to ride, how to ride, how to get other teams in trouble and how to keep track of what other teams were doing," Mark Dayton said. "It's amazing, to have started where we did, which was nothing," added Steve Reisinger. "It took us a few years to learn the ropes, but once we learned the formula we were able to crank out winner after winner." Just about every bike team in later years tried to emulate parts of that formula, and some found the winning way for one race. But no men's team has even posted two consecutive wins since the Delta Chi era, much less approached seven in nine years. It's a record that will likely remain as long as bicycles race in Bloomington.

6. Bloomington Goes Hollywood

Peter Yates, standing in the infield as a spectator at the 1979 Little 500, was dumbfounded. Surrounding him was IU at its springtime finest, in the student celebration simply known as the World's Greatest College Weekend. In the stands, for as far as the eye could see, 21,000-plus fans cheered the performances of their classmates, the men on two wheels. Pedaling furiously about the cinder-based track were the competitors, divided into 33 teams to push the limits of speed and courage in a race not for national glory or money, but merely for campus supremacy. It was as beautiful and passionate as its 28 previous installments, but to first-time viewer Yates, the sight was almost disturbing. For the acclaimed director had just finished a masterpiece about the very race he was watching, and a bothersome thought entered his mind—should he have filmed the climactic scenes from his greatest motion picture in the spring and not the summer?

Dave Blase, the Speedway, Indiana, native with a passion for cycling and opera, was riding up a hill and singing his ever-present aria during a weekend training ride in 1962 when he approached another rider. Steve Tesich, struggling up the hill, turned in amazement to see the singing Blase, riding with ease. Exchanging names and greetings, the two men realized they already knew plenty about each other—Blase had heard about the recruitment of Tesich back at the Phi Kappa Psi fraternity house, and Tesich was well aware of the superstar Blase's talents and eccentricities. "I just got to like him enormously," Tesich told the *Daily Student* in 1992. "There was something so liberating that he could go all out with the Italian thing without being embarrassed." The pair became fast friends.

Joining Phi Psi as a freshman, Tesich, originally a wrestler, became a popular member of a house largely inhabited by varsity swimmers. Despite growing up in Yugoslavia and coming to America at age 14 with no English skills, Tesich earned a wrestling scholarship to IU in 1961 and set out to study Slavic literature and languages. By the time he arrived at school Tesich had developed a firm command of English, and frequently employed a playfully sharp tongue on his fraternity brothers. By the end of his freshman year Tesich turned his athletic energies toward cycling and began training with Blase (his fraternity father) and the rest of the

As Phi Kappa Psi fraternity brothers in the early 1960s, Dave Blase (with winners' trophy after a fantastic individual effort in 1962) and Steve Tesich (seated with number 5 on sleeve) became fast friends. Tesich's great admiration for Blase's distinctive character would surface in his first screenplay.

Phi Psis. When Phi Psi won in 1962, Tesich was on the roster as an alternate. In 1963 and 1964 he made the starting foursome and was a two-time all-star.

Blase graduated in 1962 but remained close to the Phi Psis. He continued competitive riding while working as a teacher, and he and Tesich finished one-two in the Indiana 10-mile district championships in 1965. After graduating from IU in 1965, Tesich left Bloomington for New York City to pursue a doctorate in Russian literature at Columbia University. But soon after arriving in the big city, Tesich turned his attention from Russian to English and began playwriting. "As soon as I started learning English," he said, "it was almost as though I had a tuning fork in me that could respond to the language and the country." As a child in Yugoslavia he earned the nickname "Truman" for his frequent boastings about the greatness of America, and he showed some of that patriotism

in his early plays, a few of which appeared on Broadway. In the early 1970s he began work on his first screenplay, again showcasing an optimistic voice and the same Midwestern values he found while living as a teenager in Chicago and a college student in Indiana.

While Tesich was working on the screenplay and writing stage plays for New York's American Play Theatre in 1974, his agent, Sam Cohn, introduced him to acclaimed director Peter Yates. A native Englishman trained in theater at the Royal Academy of Dramatic Arts, Yates first struck gold in the United States with the action-adventure film *Bullitt,* a Steve McQueen classic and one of the top-grossing films of 1968. Though he erred in turning down an offer to direct *The Godfather* (which Francis Ford Coppola later accepted and turned into a masterpiece of American film), Yates continued to direct box office hits, earning him leverage with movie studios to try new, different projects. He first worked with Tesich in 1977 on a play called *The Passing Game,* a story about a basketball star. The collaboration revealed the pair's common interest in sport—Tesich had a cycling background, while Yates had dabbled in auto racing in Great Britain. It was a shared passion that would surface again later—not on stage, but on the big screen.

Tesich's first screenplay, *The Eagle of Naptown,* was the story of an Indianapolis boy with cycling dreams and an obsession with Italian life, living at home before moving out into the world. It was not an autobiographical work nor a piece of fiction—it was a story based on Tesich's college friend, Blase. Shortly after beginning that work, Tesich created another screenplay, titled *The Cutters,* about class conflict in small-town Bloomington between local kids and privileged university students. Yates read both scripts and saw promise in each one, liking the characters of *Cutters* and the visual potential of *Naptown,* but didn't believe either one could stand on its own as a feature film. So he simply asked Tesich to combine the two. "I thought it was the most absurd idea I had ever heard until I tried it," Tesich said, again in a 1992 interview with the *Daily Student.* The result was indeed a viable movie script, and Tesich and Yates saw great potential in it. Already several years in the making, the script would go through a few more drafts before its completion, but the writer and director agreed from the outset that the story would focus on the main characters—the Bloomington locals—and their trials and tribula-

tions, rather than on the bicycling. *Bambino,* as it was called, would be a movie with cycling but not exactly a cycling movie. And, perhaps more than anything else, *Bambino* would be a *Bloomington* movie.

With the help of agent Cohn, Yates, and Tesich successfully pitched the script to 20th Century Fox studios. After the nationwide student unrest years of the late 1960s, major motion picture studios had largely stayed away from college campuses for on-location filming (20th Century Fox's 1972 film *The Paper Chase,* set at Harvard, and Universal's 1978 classic *Animal House,* set at Oregon, were two exceptions), but the light-hearted *Bambino* story reflected the change in the college society—a change studios could be comfortable with. Nowhere in the *Bambino* script were protesting, authority-fighting students; instead the student body was portrayed as playful and content, whether they were throwing a frisbee in front of the campus opera house or supporting fellow class-mates in an athletic event. Twentieth Century Fox liked the storyline and trusted Yates's judgment, recalling his previous hits, and gave the project a green light. Yates agreed to direct the film, and insisted Tesich be allowed to remain at his side throughout the process of scouting locations and filming.

Yates's vision was to have the entire picture filmed on location in Bloomington, and he explained his plan in person to Foundation heads Bill Armstrong and Jerry Tardy. They had heard about potential Little 500–related movies over the years as the race's popularity increased, but never anything like *Bambino.* Written by an IU graduate and Little 500 veteran and based in part on the life of another Little 500 rider, the proposed script sold itself easily to the Foundation and university leaders—even IU President John Ryan cheerfully agreed to play himself. The script would also be brought to the screen by an accomplished director, though for Armstrong, a call to friend Bob Hope's office was needed first to make sure Yates was top-notch. The city equally embraced the project, and the film's cast and crew were given free reign over the town during the shoot, which was scheduled for late summer 1978.

After closing the deals with the studios, Bloomington, and IU to produce the film, Yates turned his attention to casting. Working with a meager budget of just over $2 million, Yates didn't have the funds to lure any major stars, but that suited his plans just fine. For one thing, the main

At the center of the Breaking Away story were four teenagers, unknowns in their hometown of Bloomington. The performances of (from left) Jackie Earle Haley, Dennis Quaid, Daniel Stern and Dennis Christopher were made more realistic by the fact that, at the time, three of the four were relatively unknown actors. Only the 17-year-old Haley had significant exposure, having starred in three Bad News Bears movies.

characters were to be around 19 years old in the movie, so less-experienced, youthful actors would be needed instead of older, perhaps more familiar faces. And more importantly, Yates wanted the audience to not be distracted by a major "star," as that would detract from the story's plotlines of four ordinary, small-town young men. In casting Dennis Christopher, Jackie Earle Haley, Dennis Quaid, and Daniel Stern, Yates filled his requirements.

Though the youngest of the four at 17 years old during filming, Jackie Earle Haley ("Moocher") was easily the most familiar to movie fans, having starred as the wise-cracking outfielder of three *Bad News Bears* films. Stern was a New York stage actor with no experience in films,

but Yates remembered him from a failed audition for *The Passing Game*. The actor and director flew together from New York to California for a rehearsal, and Stern, flying for the first time, stared out the window the entire trip—revealing to Yates the exact kind of innocence he wanted for the "Cyril" character. Unlike Cyril, the "Mike" character would be a little more rough around the edges, and Yates found a match for him in Dennis Quaid, a native Texan just starting out in Hollywood. "We were looking for an ex-football star, somebody who could have been something but was frustrated because he wasn't getting the opportunity," Yates said. "Dennis was fairly angry in those days."

Efforts to cast the leading role, "Dave," gave Yates fits for a while, as

The Little
500

Cast in the roles of Dave's parents were the savvy Barbara Barrie and Paul Dooley. Mrs. Stohler was an optimistic housewife who carried a passport, Mr. Stohler was a cynical used car salesman who loved his son but didn't exactly love his Italian act.

Hart Bochner and Robyn Douglass played secondary roles as the greek IU students Rod and Katherine. Bochner was himself just two weeks out of college when filming began, and the Chicago-native Douglass fit the Midwestern girl part perfectly.

he searched for the right young actor to fit the bill of innocent youth and aspiring Italian cyclist. On a recommendation from fellow director Robert Altman, Yates gave a reading to an unknown named Dennis Christopher, a New York–trained stage actor who had previously appeared in the films *September 30, 1955* (a picture about a group of college kids mourning the death of James Dean, also the film debut of Quaid) and Altman's *A Wedding*. Christopher originally read for the parts of both Cyril and Dave, preferring Cyril, but Yates and Tesich instead preferred his free-spirited portrayal of Dave—a read that was aided by Christopher's heritage. In real life, he was half-Italian.

In addition to the four central figures, the *Bambino* cast included

Dave's parents, a romantic interest, and a cocky college student. For the parents, Yates signed Paul Dooley and Barbara Barrie, two veterans of stage and screen who had played many roles as caring parents and spouses. On a casting call in Chicago, Yates found his leading lady "Katherine" in Robyn Douglass, an actress who had logged time in television commercials and theater but not yet on film. "I thought she had a school-girlish feel to her, yet she looked good and was a good actress," said Yates, also pleased to find a Midwestern girl for the Midwest-based film. "I find there's a certain quality in Chicago, where you get the real fit—you get actors who want to be actors, rather than film stars." To play the part of "Rod," the fraternity man with an eye for women

(Katherine one of them) and scorn for the likes of Dave, Yates cast Californian Hart Bochner, an actor's son, who graduated from the University of California at San Diego two weeks before filming for *Bambino*.

When the film crew arrived in Bloomington in late summer 1978 to begin shooting, they took care of additional casting needs by hiring IU students. For the visually inspiring scene of a man diving 65 feet off a cliff into a quarryhole, for example, the casting directors chose a student and not a stuntman. Students interested in being extras in the film could sign up in the studio's production office on campus, and some got rather prominent roles. Jennifer Mickel, a 17-year-old freshman, signed up and was chosen to be the young female interest of Rod, riding through campus in his sports car and later becoming the center of attention and cause of a brawl in the student commons of the Indiana Memorial Union.

Naturally, when it came time to fill the picture's bicycling roles, Little 500 riders came out to help. For the parts of riders for professional cycling team Cinzano, first admired and later reviled by Italian-wanna-be Dave in the film, the studio made an open casting call in the local newspaper. Dozens of men answered the call, and Yates interviewed them all, but he settled on a tanned and slim 28-year-old teacher from Chicago—Eddy Van Guyse, the Hall of Fame Delta Chi rider of 1969 through 1972. Yates thought he looked Italian, and Van Guyse explained that while he wasn't, he did speak Flemish and Dutch and could do Italian if needed. Van Guyse also volunteered to fill out the Cinzano team with three friends from Chicago, and with Yates's blessing called on Carlos Sintes, John Van de Velde, and Peter Lazarra, all experienced cyclists (though only Lazarra was Italian). In the film, the Cinzano team would be the front-runners in an 80-man road race, and Van Guyse made it clear to Yates and the crew that only seasoned riders could make the race look realistic. Van Guyse also helped cast Dennis Christopher's stunt double by recommending Garry Rybar, another former Delta Chi. Rybar himself had a little experience as an amateur filmmaker and was itching to be a part of the 20th Century Fox production, and it only took one look from Yates and Tesich to land a job. "I had the look [like Christopher], with the blonde hair and the big nose," said Rybar, who would get plenty of work subbing for his Hollywood counterpart, a bicycling novice.

For the climactic Little 500 racing scenes, the Student Foundation pitched in by arranging for more than 100 Little 500 riders, mechanics, and coaches to be on campus for the four-day September 1978 shoot at Tenth Street Stadium. The goal was to re-create a Little 500 race as accurately as possible, and the majority of those participants occupied the pits while some 40 of the real Little 500's top riders performed the actual racing scenes (and were compensated at the rate of $2.65 per hour, from the studio payroll). From the full field of teams, riding on Roadmasters and clad in official Little 500 attire (the jerseys were the same ones used in the 1978 race), to the painted pits and balloons, the Student Foundation pulled off the stadium-sized set to near-perfection. About the only variance from an actual race was in the stands, where the crowd fell well short of capacity. Running ads in the *Daily Student* telling students they could be in the movies, the Foundation had hoped to fill the stadium for Yates and his crew, who had set up scaffolding and cameras high atop the press box and the neighboring library in hopes of obtaining panoramic shots of a packed house. But when only a few thousand spectators showed up, they were forced to improvise. Blazing temperatures discouraged many fans from attending and sitting through the slow pace of movie filming, and only 7,000 entered the stadium during the weekend days instead of the 20,000 fans the Foundation promised the studio. Tardy estimated that no more than 3,000 were in the stands at any given time, and as a result Yates altered his storyboards to work around the smaller crowd. Instead of wide-view camera shots he opted to film only certain sections of the stadium at a time, moving the crowd around when necessary. Later, after the film was completed, Yates saw an authentic Little 500 race in person. At first he regretted not filming the real-life overflow crowds, but knew the angles he used prevented viewers from realizing the stadium was anything less than full.

During his days as an action-adventure filmmaker, Yates's trademark scenes were frantic chase sequences. *Bullitt* featured car chase scenes widely considered as some of the best in movie history, and he drew on those experiences to help create dramatic bicycling footage in *Bambino*. For his mock Little 500, Yates used a cameraman mounted on a motorcycle to get close-up shots of the main characters in action and catch the sights and sounds of a pack of riders negotiating the cinder track. "It was interesting because you were involved with the people and with the character, and also because on a bicycle you show physical effort," Yates

The Little 500

Acclaimed film director Peter Yates befriended Steve Tesich in 1974 and had a guiding hand in Breaking Away from its infancy. He had a very clear idea of what the final product would be and communicated it to the cast and crew at every filming site, from the edge of campus near Kirkwood Avenue and on the used car lot (as Paul Dooley and Dennis Christopher look on) to Tenth Street Stadium, where he did his finest work in creating the climactic racing scenes.

All it took was one look from Yates and Tesich to cast Garry Rybar (left) as Dennis Christopher's stunt double. The three-time Delta Chi Little 500 champion stepped in for the star in the road race and the movie version of the Little 500, as well as the scene on State Road 37 where Dave Stohler drafted off an 18-wheeler.

Former Delta Chi rider and Belgian native Eddy Van Guyse (right) made a strong impression on director Peter Yates at an open casting call for a Cinzano team member, and after landing the part called on three cycling friends from Chicago—from left, Carlos Sintes, John Van de Velde, and Peter Lazzara.

"On a bike, Dennis was real shaky," said Cinzano team portrayer Eddy Van Guyse. Fear was evident in the actor's eyes in this picture, when he took a rare spin on a real bike. In the film, shots of Christopher in the road race are from the waist-up, as he was not riding an actual bicycle but instead a half-bike towed by a car.

said. "It's not just pushing an accelerator down and watching tires." He was most proud of the finishing sequence in his Little 500 race, where the underdog Cutters edged the pole-sitting Sigma Tau Omega team by inches at the finish line. Rybar suggested to Yates that fellow Delta Chi star Bill Brissman stand in for Hart Bochner's character, assuring him that he and Brissman could team up to create a Hollywood finish. The pair took a half-hour of time to practice, then came back and, in one take, created the picture's signature scene. "It was one of the most amazing

moments in film that I've ever known—so amazing you didn't have to edit it," Yates said.

The stadium scenes for the film were recorded first (though seen last by the viewer), and then the crew moved around campus and out into town for the rest of the story. Scouting the Bloomington area with art director Patrizia Von Brandenstein, Yates and Tesich found many areas appealing, from the abandoned limestone quarries (which required

The scene where Dave and Cyril serenade Katherine outside the sorority house also petrified Christopher, but with the help of opera lessons and some liquid calming he was able to complete the shoot over two nights.

sandblasting of graffiti before filming) to an understated home on South Lincoln Street, where Dave Stohler's family lived. (Dave's character, incidentally, was to be named Dave Blase in honor of the Phi Psi legend, but legal issues prevented use of the name. The new name, Dave Stohler, was a combination of Dave Blase and Bob Stohler, the Phi Psi team manager from Tesich's riding days.) The Indiana countryside proved to be a wonderful backdrop for more bicycling footage, from the hills where the road race was held to State Road 37, where Rybar was the star for a day while drafting off a tractor-trailer at 60 miles per hour (which he really did, pedaling a very large gear on his 10-speed). Audiences familiar with the IU campus would revel in the many spots the film showcased, from Memorial Stadium to the Union to the Well House.

Many of the film's stories about the plight of the four "Cutters" were shot at the limestone quarryholes south of town. Shooting was challenging, as is evidenced here by the pontoon boat used by the film crew. Visible on the rock are Jackie Earle Haley (top) and Daniel Stern, and a stand-in for Dennis Quaid is in the water.

Through the many locales Yates and Tesich developed their main character, the young man pretending to be Italian while searching for his own identity. Dennis Christopher gave a standout performance in the role of Dave, aided in several ways by his youth and inexperience. For the nighttime scenes at the Chi Delta Delta sorority house on Third Street (actually the Delta Delta Delta house), where Dave and Cyril were to serenade Katherine, Christopher was terrified at the prospect of singing on camera. The scenes were filmed over two nights, and delays over the first night compounded Christopher's anxiety. Noting the tension in his leading man, Yates calmed Christopher down with a few sips of liquor. "As the evening wore on, I was really a little tipsy and even worried," Christopher said, laughing at the memory. "Fortunately I got through the first night without singing." He completed his singing the next night without incident, and sang quite well thanks to lessons from opera teachers.

Tesich's story about the dreamy Italian wannabe very much resembled the life of his fraternity brother, Blase. As an IU student Blase discovered that by acting a little odd and foreign, people wouldn't judge him by the same standards as they would others. "Instead of being a nerd from Speedway, you're charming and cute," he said. "If you're a little rough around the edges or you don't seem to be as hip or as cool with the ladies, you're not expected to be. You're the Italian bike rider." Just as Blase had used the Italian mask to hide behind in the early 1960s, the film's character used the Italian act to cover his local ties. Blase admits he never courted a beautiful sorority woman while pretending to be someone else, but he related to some of his movie alter ego's actions, such as the moment when Dave retrieved Katherine's book and chased her down to return it—though Blase said he himself would have never had the guts to follow through with pursuing the girl. In the film, however, Dave is brought back to earth by the cutthroat Cinzano team and, while ridding himself of the Italian act, reveals his true identity to Katherine. "My name is Dave Stohler. I made all that other stuff up," the character admits, seen for the first time without his Italian racing apparel. "I was born in Bloomington. I went to Bloomington High. I was the treasurer of the Latin Club. . . . I'm what you call a cutter." At the end of the film the viewer sees Dave as an ordinary American college freshman (but still prone to a little acting, as he befriends a French exchange student). Blase, on the other hand, never really conceded his Italian dreams. He

never had to play the American dating game, as in 1971 he married a Holland native.

The movie's title *Bambino*, an Italian term for an endeared child or loved one, referred to the main character's Italian infatuation. But shortly before filming concluded 20th Century Fox changed the title, fearing audiences might mistake *Bambino* for an Italian picture. Asked to come up with something else, Tesich chose *Breaking Away*. The term held a double meaning for the movie, as a bicycling term (meaning to separate from the pack) and a metaphor for life, referring to his four main characters' maturing and "breaking away" from their youths.

Upon completion, the more appropriately named *Breaking Away* was played in a few cities to gauge audience interest. Armstrong and Tardy accompanied studio officials to a screening in Denver, and the reaction to the film was overwhelming, as the theater's 600 patrons applauded and sang along with the characters. "At first we didn't know what to expect," Tardy said, "but by the end I turned to Bill and said 'I think we've got something here.'" Twentieth Century Fox's people also discovered they had something special, as the responses from Denver and two more sneak previews in New Orleans and Phoenix gave *Breaking Away* the highest test ratings in the studio's history. Encouraged by such enthusiasm from the preview audiences, many of whom likened *Breaking Away* to the 1976 blockbuster *Rocky* because of its underdog-turns-winner plotline, the studio scheduled August 1979 as the nationwide release date for the picture.

Never one to miss out on a terrific public relations opportunity, Armstrong persuaded 20th Century Fox to hold the worldwide premiere

Various on-campus sites for filming included the Indiana Memorial Union cafeteria, where Cyril (with bowling ball) and Mike fought with students; President John Ryan's office (actor John Ashton is on the right), where the Cutters were granted an entry into the Little 500; and the Well House, where Dave came clean with Katherine about his identity and got smacked for it.

The Little
500

of *Breaking Away* in Bloomington during the 1979 Little 500 weekend. Rarely would a film's premiere come four months before its nationwide release, but the opportunity to bring Hollywood glamour to a Saturday night after the Little 500 was too good for the Foundation to pass up. "[The premiere] is Bill Armstrong's Sistine Chapel, his Mona Lisa, his moon landing, his triple crown all rolled into one," said a local reporter. On April 21, 1979, all the stops were pulled out to create a memorable evening for the sold-out Auditorium crowd and the hundreds of other gawkers who simply wanted a glimpse of movie stars. Celebrities, 20th Century Fox officials, and local dignitaries arrived via a parade route from the Union in classic and rare automobiles, stopping at the front entrance of the Auditorium on black-and-white checkered carpet before a dazzling display of lights. (Not all the automobiles worked—the 1929 Model "A" Ford Armstrong rode in died about 100 yards from its destination and was pushed the rest of the way.) Outside, the IU pep band played "Indiana, Our Indiana," while inside Al Cobine's Band (performers at many Little 500 Variety Shows) entertained the arriving crowds. Before the movie began, Tesich was inducted into the Little 500 Hall of Fame and Yates received a Distinguished Service Award from the Foundation, an award only given twice before—to the Chairman of the Board of General Electric and to Bob Hope.

With such an extravagant sendoff, *Breaking Away* debuted in theaters across the country and became one of the top "sleeper" films of 1979, receiving a tremendous word-of-mouth following and critical acclaim from nearly every major media outlet. "You leave the theater very proud that America has both an Indiana and a Hollywood," said *Sports Illustrated*'s Frank Deford. The critics loved the film's scenery and unpretentious characters and savored the easygoing pace of the film—a rare major-studio production that didn't include car chases, overdone violence, profanity, or sex. "Here is a movie so fresh and funny it didn't even need a big budget or a pedigree," said Janet Maslin of the *New York Times*. Ironically, about the only publication to knock *Breaking Away* was the *Daily Student*, which in its review called the film "superficial and trivial," with "severe limitations" and "uninteresting and colorless" characters "the audience cannot become emotionally involved with." In the reviewer's opinion, the movie wouldn't catch on anywhere outside Bloomington.

IU Foundation officials promised 20th Century Fox that some 20,000 spectators would see this sign and help recreate a Little 500, but only a couple thousand came, forcing director Yates to redraw his storyboards and move the crowd around to create the illusion of a packed stadium.

The film not only caught on nationwide, but collected a handful of prestigious honors. It won Best Picture from the National Society of Film Critics, and at the 1979 Academy Awards collected nominations for Best Director, Best Picture, Best Supporting Actress (for Barbara Barrie), and Best Original Score. *Kramer vs. Kramer* came out on top in the running for Best Picture and Best Director, but *Breaking Away* won the Academy Award for Best Original Screenplay—a victory for Steve Tesich and his years of labor. Dennis Christopher earned a nod for Best Actor at the 1980 Golden Globes, and the film won top honors in the musical/comedy category. For a picture made for a pittance with an unfamiliar

The Little
500

A look at the stands in this shot taken during the national anthem of the staged Little 500 shows the relatively meager crowd that attended filming. In the foreground are a few of the familiar real-life Little 500 faces that held small parts in the movie, including Chappie Blackwell (far left at table), Howdy Wilcox, Bill Armstrong and Jim Pauloski (behind right table) and Dave Blase (far right).

20th-C Fox is shooting at IU!

"Bambino" is a full length motion picture being produced in Bloomington. And the Twentieth Century Fox cast and crew invite YOU to participate in the actual filming of a special scene.

You are invited to join two days of shooting at the Tenth Street Stadium, where the excitement will continue from 10am to 6pm on September 9th and 10th.

The scene centers around Indiana University Foundation's Little 500 Bicycle Race. And besides a 33 team race, activities include 20 lap sprint races, a performance by the "Wright Brothers Reunion," and other live entertainment. All you have to do is show up, relax, and have fun!

As an extra bonus, your participation will increase student scholarship funds. Each spectator represents a one dollar donation from 20th Century Fox to the I. U. Foundation. So, let's fill the stadium!

Peter Yates, the director who's best known for "The Deep" and "Bullit," wants to film Bloomington and Indiana University in a natural setting. That's why you're invited to play a part in the movie and promote student scholarship at the same time.

See you there, at the Tenth Street Stadium, September 9th and 10th. Please, NO COOLERS!

✱ Watch the IDS for details. ✱

cast, *Breaking Away* clearly defied the odds. "We never expected [a hit]," Yates said. "You never should. You should get a story you like and do it as well as you can, and if people fall in love with it, that's terrific. But we never expected it."

Of course, the love affair with *Breaking Away* was nowhere more passionate than in Bloomington. "Usually when a movie goes to a town, it leaves it in worse shape," Dennis Christopher said. "I think we left the town in better shape." Long after the celebrities and the cameras departed, the city and university were left with a tremendous sense of civic pride—and a valuable selling tool. Part of the movie studio's contract with IU included giving the university full rights to use the film for school activities, and for the Foundation that meant *Breaking Away* was a virtual license to print money, as the movie was used at out-of-town alumni gatherings for entertainment and fund-raising. (One newspaper writer compared Armstrong taking the movie while on the contribution trail as "a bit like allowing Jack Nicklaus to tee off from the women's tee.") With the movie's help, donations in 1979 soared by over $3 million above figures from the year before. For IU the movie provided publicity no full-color brochure could ever match, and the admissions office gained a highlight reel no other school could match. The city profited in the form of a tourism boom, as the film showed the area as bicycle-friendly and laid-back, and for years the city's tourism slogan was "Break Away to Bloomington." Bloomington Mayor Frank McCloskey even used the movie to win him another term in office, airing radio ads with Yates expressing his appreciation for the Mayor's help during filming. McCloskey's opponent, Howard Young, said McCloskey was unfairly taking credit for the movie, but the ads continued and McCloskey won his bid for re-election.

Dave Stohler of the No. 34 Cutters team crosses the finish line to the cheers of the crowd. Note the cameraman riding on the motorcycle, used to film close-up action.

The Little 500 race began reaping the benefits of *Breaking Away* in 1980, when a swarm of media from across the country visited IU to see the real version of the contest featured in the film. Newspapers from across the country, from the *New York Times* to the *Washington Post* to the Albuquerque, New Mexico, *Journal* sent reporters to cover the event, and camera crews from every Indianapolis network affiliate and stations as far away as Mobile, Alabama, also came to the sold-out event. NBC's *Real People* taped a segment about the Little 500, and that summer ABC signed a three-year contract to televise the race live. Once introduced to the race, some of the media outlets continued attending the race for several more years, allowing publicity about Little 500 to continue to be spread far and wide. To the Little 500's organizers, the Student Foundation, *Breaking Away* was more than a movie about the spring race—it became a lifetime reference point for helping explain the race to outsiders. Asked "what is Little 500?" a Student Foundation member could reply with "have you seen *Breaking Away*?"

After *Breaking Away*, the lives of the participants involved went off in many different directions. Of the principal cast members, Dennis Quaid and Daniel Stern enjoyed the most prolonged success, establishing instantly recognizable identities as stars. Quaid went on to star in dozens of films including *The Right Stuff* and *The Big Easy*, and married fellow film star Meg Ryan, forming one of Hollywood's most star-studded couples. (His first wife, P.J. Soles, played a small part in *Breaking Away* as one of Katherine's sorority sisters.) Stern starred in popular films such as *Diner, City Slickers*, and *Home Alone*, and did voice-overs for the lead character in television's *The Wonder Years*. In the 1990s both Quaid and Stern also dabbled in directing for films and television.

Dennis Christopher's acclaimed performance as Dave Stohler helped him stay busy on the big screen, but never in quite as strong a leading role. Barbara Barrie and Jackie Earle Haley also continued working in theater and television, including a 1980 ill-fated *Breaking Away* television series (filmed not in Bloomington but in Athens, Georgia, it lasted only a few episodes). Robyn Douglass appeared nude in a 1981 issue of *Hustler* magazine and sued the publication and the photographer, claiming the pictures severely damaged her acting career. Her claims proved true—she would go on to appear in just a few obscure

20th Century Fox
and the
Indiana University Foundation
present the premiere of

Breaking Away

All the stops were pulled out for the Breaking Away *premiere on Saturday night, April 21, 1979 at the Auditorium, as all the lights and cameras of a Hollywood premiere were brought to Bloomington—four months before the film's nationwide release.*

The Little
500

Steve Tesich and his Best Screenplay Academy Award, 1979.

films—and the jury awarded her $2 million in damages (later reduced to $600,000 by a judge). Garry Rybar, the former Delta Chi who worked as Dennis Christopher's stunt double, perhaps made the biggest post-*Breaking Away* transformation. In 1986 he underwent a sex change operation and today is known as Nancy Wilson.

In the Little 500, Jerry Tardy continues to drive the Little 500 pace car, as he did for the first time in the fictitious film race. Dave Blase, whose announcer's voice could be heard during the race, still listens to opera religiously and announces Little 500 races for television. He, Howdy Wilcox, and John Ryan still draw annual royalty checks from 20th Century Fox for their speaking roles in the film, though in Ryan's case, his voice never aired—a faulty audio take resulted in his voice being dubbed over.

Peter Yates and Steve Tesich would work as a director/writer team again in two more pictures, but neither came close to the success of their first collaboration. In 1985 Tesich made another cycling-inspired movie called *American Flyers,* a Colorado-set film about two brothers training for a three-day race while dealing with the fact that one has a potentially fatal brain aneurysm. Its bicycling scenes were praised, but critics panned the confusing subplots. On the whole, it wasn't on the level of *Breaking Away,* and the unavoidable comparisons between the two films never helped *American Flyers.*

Of the five films Tesich was involved with after *Breaking Away,* the most acclaimed was 1982's *The World According to Garp,* starring Robin Williams, which Tesich adapted from a John Irving novel. By the late 1980s Tesich returned to his first love, writing plays for the theater, and began expressing a more cynical view of America through his work. Having already achieved a level of financial and professional stability, he was able to work on projects of his own making. One notable product was his last Broadway play, *The Speed of Darkness,* a bleak tale about the contrasting experiences of two Vietnam War veterans. "He thought that America wasn't living up to its potential and the way that it positioned itself as an idealistic country," said Rebecca Tesich, Steve's wife of 16 years, about his mindset during some of his final projects.

Tesich died suddenly July 1, 1996, after suffering a heart attack while vacationing with his family. He was 53. But his place in Bloomington and

IU history was secure with 1979's *Breaking Away,* and for the rest of his life he took a great deal of pride in his Academy Award–winning story, the tale based in part on his free-spirited days as an IU student. "What I first loved about bike racing when I first began ages ago was that it was not a mainstream sport," he said in a 1989 *Bicycling* magazine story titled "Why 'Breaking Away' Succeeded." "My heroes were self-made. There were no coaches, no training centers, and only a handful of sponsors.

Since nobody could expect to make a living by racing, the riders I knew either went to school or had jobs. Training riders were not totally devoted to bike talk. I got to know a lot of riders this way, not just as good sprinters or good climbers, but as people who had ideas different from mine, jobs different from mine, and dreams different from mine.

"When I write, this is what I write about. . . . 'Breaking Away' succeeded because I knew and loved the people I wrote about."

7. A Declaration of Independents

After 30 years of bicycle races and 55 years as an IU landmark, old Memorial Stadium—Tenth Street Stadium to the younger generations—couldn't fight time any longer.

A product of the IU Memorial Fund drive of the early 1920s, Memorial Stadium was erected with a portion of $1.6 million raised to also build a women's dormitory and the Indiana Memorial Union, all of which were considered necessary elements to a complete university campus. Of the three structures, the stadium was likely the most anticipated by donors (mostly students and faculty), and it surely had the most colorful and historical beginnings. The stadium was partially finished around 1924 when workers discovered some disintegration occurring due to excess amounts of sand in the cement mixture, so the only option was to tear it completely down and start over. A different company was hired to finish the job properly, and lawsuits between IU and the original contractors dragged on for several years after the incident.

Sitting on Tenth Street at what was then the northern border of campus, the horseshoe-shaped stadium was officially dedicated November 21, 1925, on Homecoming day. The opponent for the big gridiron showdown was none other than the dreaded in-state rival Purdue Boilermakers, and the highlight of the dedication ceremony was the unveiling of the Old Oaken Bucket, now synonymous with the IU-Purdue football rivalry. After the game a link with an "I" and a "P" was added, as the score was 0–0. Memorial Stadium would continue to host "bucket games" and all other IU home football games through 1959, with the last game coming 34 years to the day after the stadium's dedication, on November 21, 1959. Again the opponent was Purdue, but IU lost 10–7.

The football team was the primary inhabitant of old Memorial Stadium, so when it left after the 1959 season for a new stadium of the same name, the days were numbered for what would from then on be known as Tenth Street Stadium. Signs of aging were evident all over the facility, from broken seats and cracks in the stands to rusted and partially unhinged gates to an overall deteriorating press box. Other IU sports and events left the old stadium for new facilities, including the track team, which began competing at Billy Hayes Track in 1965, but Tenth Street

The Little
500

After 55 years of serving IU, including 30 years of Little 500 races, Tenth Street Stadium bowed out from the campus landscape shortly after the 1980 race (above and right). It was a move long overdue—throughout the 1970s the stadium was criticized by safety officials, and immediately prior to its last race it needed emergency repairs to be safe for an overflow crowd of 23,350.

Stadium was still home to the Little 500. Every spring the stadium welcomed and withstood hundreds of bicyclists and thousands of fans, in what was a very intimate setting for a bicycle race.

For fans, Tenth Street Stadium was a fabulous venue to watch cycling, with seating right up to the edge of the track and good views from higher rows. But for riders, the track was usually unfriendly at best, downright dangerous at worst. Various hazards loomed all around the oval, giving riders something else to worry about besides the competition. For starters, the riding area wasn't very wide, and there was no margin for error on the inside or outside. Riders who ventured too far inside could come perilously close to a four-inch-high curb, and contact meant a sure accident. Bordering much of the outside area was a concrete wall, and not until 1965 were hay bales added to the outside of the turns to cushion wayward falls. The track's turns were unbanked and tight, making maneuverability difficult. Pedaling through the turns was always an exercise in courage, but usually necessary to keep pace in the race.

All in all, it was a most unique facility, but far from immune to wear and tear. By the 1970s, Tenth Street Stadium was already way past its prime, but year after year it was allowed to hang around and host its main event, the Little 500. In 1973 the IU Fire and Safety Department ruled it structurally unsound just weeks before the race, and emergency repairs were required to allow the race to go on. Two years later IU hoped to begin demolition of the stadium, but lacked funding. By the late 1970s the facility simply stood pat and in disrepair, awaiting its fate. "It was an eyesore, and it was falling apart," recalled Terry Clapacs, once the director of physical facilities at IU before rising to vice president of administration (and once a Little 500 rider, for Delta Upsilon in the early 1960s). "We knew we couldn't use it very much longer." Clapacs worked out some figures on the stadium, and calculated that it would cost just under $1 million to fully renovate Tenth Street Stadium (including lights), but only $200,000 to tear it down. With that discovery, the stadium's days were officially numbered. More emergency repairs were needed in the stadium prior to the 1980 race, but by then IU officials had already focused attention elsewhere—on a new Little 500 facility.

At the same time the Foundation and the Student Foundation were discovering the pressing need for a new home for their prized event, the

IU athletic department was trying to find a home for its young, up-and-coming sport, men's soccer. The team had already recorded two Final Four appearances in its first seven seasons at the varsity level through 1979, while playing most home games on a football field. Its coach, Jerry Yeagley, longed for a bona fide soccer stadium.

Yeagley's involvement with IU soccer dated to 1963, when he first arrived on campus as a young faculty member and club soccer coach. Like many of his faculty peers, Yeagley got involved with the hot campus event, the Little 500. "I was shocked at the excitement generated and the enormous amount of interest—I volunteered right away," he said. A couple years later he started dating a young coed named Marilyn Filbrandt, a member of the 1966 Student Foundation Steering Committee. She introduced Yeagley to Bill Armstrong, the Foundation president, former I-Man and all-around IU sports fanatic. Over the next few years Yeagley and Filbrandt would continue to date and later marry, and Armstrong would help Yeagley's soccer program gain varsity status in

Replacing Tenth Street Stadium in 1981 was a $3 million palace for cycling and soccer on the north end of campus, the last piece of the athletic facility puzzle for IU at the time (joining Memorial Stadium, Assembly Hall and the Fieldhouse, seen at top, and Billy Hayes Track, at right). The Little 500/Soccer Stadium (as it was first named) debuted in 1981 somewhat half-completed, with a temporary press box halfway up the main grandstand and auxiliary seats on the south (left) side and all around the track. Still, the stadium packed in 27,412 for the '81 race, and would welcome more in future years. Meanwhile, over time the rest of the IU campus had grown around Tenth Street Stadium, and due to its location and structural condition it was demolished to create an open, natural space. All that was salvaged were two flagposts, its west-end fence (seen at bottom opposite), ticket booths and its north-end opening.

1973. Out of loyalty to Armstrong, Yeagley continued his involvement with Little 500, even serving as assistant starter with longtime starter Chappie Blackwell for a few years. As for the soccer team, which excelled on the field from its first day as varsity, the Little 500 turned out to be a priceless recruiting tool, showing potential stars the spirit of the student body. About the only thing Yeagley couldn't promise recruits in the 1970s was a true soccer arena, as his team played most of its matches on the Astroturf at the giant Memorial Stadium but also practiced and played on fields all over campus. Then came 1979–80, and the search for a new Little 500 home. "It was a natural," Yeagley said of the budding partnership between Little 500 and IU soccer. "We both needed a new place."

Ground was broken in May 1980 for what was to be called, ingeniously, the Little 500/Soccer Stadium. At a cost of $3 million (raised by a Foundation stadium campaign), the new arena would be state of the art for both soccer and cycling. "Bill [Armstrong] was very adamant in wanting to make it the best," Yeagley said. The soccer field was built to regulation size, with lights, so IU could host future NCAA Tournament contests. As a result, the track was longer in the turns and longer overall, 410 meters to be exact, but 14-inch-high banking offset the extra length. On the inside of the 27-foot-wide track would no longer be a dangerous curb like at the Tenth Street track, but a flat draining area that could be pedaled through if necessary. The main grandstand on the north side of the stadium was built to seat 9,000, with room on the south side for 6,000 temporary seats. With auxiliary stands added at the turns, stadium seating capacity was listed at 25,000. High atop the main grandstand would be a two-level press box and VIP area, serviced by an elevator to the ground. And at the east end would be an electronic scoreboard, able to keep track of such soccer minutiae as fouls, corner kicks, and shots, and Little 500 info such as race times, lap counts, and top ten teams.

For Little 500 fans, the brand-new structure was beautiful but somewhat impersonal compared to the cozy confines of Tenth Street Stadium. In the new arena, seating did not come right up to the track, but instead rested several feet back off the cinders to accommodate better spectator flow around the oval. Though many fans would stand at the fence surrounding the track, Little 500 riders who rode in both stadia said it was nothing like having rows of fans right on top of and almost completely around the track. But what might have been lost in atmosphere was more than made up in improved competition, as the banked cinder surface allowed riders to race faster with little worry of the track causing problems. For them, going from Tenth Street Stadium to the new dwelling was akin to moving from a dorm room to a hotel suite.

Delta Chi showed how fast the track was in its inaugural race on April 25, 1981, with its second consecutive runaway win and third straight overall. In 1980 and 1981 the team set records in winning, but the 1981 effort clocked in at 2:05.17, better than four minutes faster than the 1980 old stadium record. The discrepancy worked out to better than a one-mile-per-hour difference, with the faster time clocking 24.40 mph. Not bad for a race that was almost one mile longer than its predecessor, thanks to the 400-meter oval (Tenth Street Stadium's measured 400 yards). Such times would become the rule rather than the exception at the new track, and unlike the Delta Chi–dominated 1970s, a few more teams would get a taste of success.

As for Tenth Street Stadium, it was leveled shortly after its last hurrah in 1980 to make room for an arboretum and pedestrian walkway. While in 1930 it was surrounded by little else at its location north of the heart of campus, by 1980 it *was* the heart of campus. To its immediate east stood the towering main library, while to its north and northwest, across Tenth Street, sat the business school and other academic buildings, dormitories, and numerous IU athletic facilities, including the new Little 500 arena. "[The stadium] was a block to the natural development of campus," Clapacs said. Aesthetically, a centrally located green area would open up the campus much more than an out-of-date, unusable athletic facility, so the Tenth Street Stadium faded from the IU landscape. Fifteen years later, students would find it hard to believe a stadium once stood where a small pond and greenery prosper, but some proof of its existence still remains. The main entrance to the stadium was preserved, as well as two limestone ticket booths, flagpost towers, and the iron fence that marked the west end of the stadium.

The move to a new stadium for 1981 came at a most opportune time for the Student Foundation and the Little 500, as the aftershocks from *Breaking Away* were still being very much felt in the form of overflow attendance and increased publicity. In 1980 more than 23,000 fans packed every nook and cranny of Tenth Street Stadium, to the point that

The Little
500

some 1,000 fans were denied admission, as officials worried about the stadium's ability to hold such a sizable throng, the likes of which had not been seen at the Little 500 since the 1960s. But the new Little 500/Soccer Stadium's main grandstands and auxiliary seating could easily manage such crowds, so 27,412 spectators filed through the turnstiles in 1981, followed by 28,632 in 1982.

Television maintained an interest in Little 500 as well, with central Indiana station WTTV–4 televising the race live for the first time in 1980. Later that year the Student Foundation signed a three-year deal with national network ABC to have parts of the race shown on *Wide World of Sports*, though that contract never came to fruition due to issues concerning exclusive rights to the race. Instead of ABC, the CBS network, which stepped in to air the 1982 race, provided the first national broadcast coverage of Little 500 racing. The network brought a 50-person crew to Bloomington, including Ken Squier, its voice of auto racing, and to accommodate CBS tape-editing needs, the Student Foundation moved the start of the race from 1 P.M. back to 11:30 A.M.

The race CBS cameras would witness that day was a Little 500 classic. It wasn't quite townies-over-college kids, but the storyline was still exciting by race standards. In front of a record crowd the field of 33 rode at an unprecedented pace without a single yellow flag to slow them down. An entire flock of teams, 10 in all, found themselves on the lead lap at the end. And at the finish line, separated by inches, were frontrunners Delta Chi and Phi Delta Theta, two teams who until that moment lived at the opposite ends of the Little 500 hierarchy.

Delta Chi, of course, was the three-time defending champion, the well-oiled machine that the media loved and opponents loathed. Some signs of vulnerability, however, were coming out of the team's camp in the weeks prior to the race. In qualifications Delta Chi fouled twice and took a third attempt, which meant a one-way ticket straight to the bottom of the ladder, if on the ladder at all. Delta Chi did indeed squeeze in at the 28th spot, but faltered again at Team Pursuit, a pre-race event two of its members had created in 1979. Team Pursuit was a team event against the clock, with each foursome riding 15 laps as a cohesive unit, strategically drafting off one another to maintain group speed. Heats of two teams would ride at a time, with the two fastest teams competing in a one-heat final. In 1982 Delta Chi was lapped in its preliminary heat, and for the

The fallout from Breaking Away *was felt at IU for several years after its 1979 release, in the form of a national media invasion at the Little 500. Writers from many major newspapers came to Bloomington along with national television networks, such as CBS in 1982 (cameraman shown recording off turn three), to find out what the real race was all about. They found, as CBS's Brent Musburger said, that the race was all about "no million dollar, no-cut contracts, no agents, just guys giving it all they have—the essence of sport."*

first time failed to win the event. But even with such potential signs of demise, on race day the Chris Gutowsky–led team found itself in a familiar leading role.

Phi Delta Theta, on the other hand, was a fraternity team with a Little 500 history that inspired no one. Since its high-water mark of two second-place finishes in the late 1960s (sandwiched around its disqualification during the black protest weekend of 1968), the Phi Delts only occasionally placed among the top one-third of the field in Little 500 races. But

Delta Chi's bid for an unprecedented fourth Little 500 win came up inches short in 1982, when Jim Mahaffey of Phi Delta Theta (left) edged Chris Gutowsky in a thrilling finish. For Phi Delt, the win was a start to several years of competitive teams, while for Delta Chi the loss signified the end of an era.

starting in 1980 the team's outlook brightened as a few new riders joined the team, anchored by a self-described "misfit and troublemaker" named Jim Mahaffey. In 1981, his second year of riding, the Phi Delts won the pole position only to finish 19th in the race, the worst finish ever for a polesitter. "We partied for three weeks after winning the pole, then got creamed in the race," Mahaffey said. "It was humiliating." With that race, however, the Phi Delt riders learned a lesson about Little 500 racing, namely, that the social and athletic scenes didn't mix prior to race day. For 1982 they would go about their business in a different fashion, and the results turned around their racing reputation.

The sprint finish of 1982 pitted the veterans Gutowsky and Mahaffey against each other, and a changing of the guard ensued. On the final lap Gutowsky held the lead into turn three and looked untouchable, like so many Delta Chi teams before, but the fearless Mahaffey dashed to the outside off the last turn and caught Gutowsky at the line by inches in a record time of 2:03.33. CBS got a dream finish to its race—not to mention some interesting post-race comments from the victors. Working as the color commentator for CBS, former Phi Psi great and movie inspiration Dave Blase complimented Mahaffey, telling him he'd savor the moment for years to come. Mahaffey responded with a line destined for the CBS cutting-room floor—"I probably won't know about this day in two hours 'cause I'll be drunk for a week." Years later, he laughed heartily at the memory. "I was not a shining example of what they wanted to promote," said Mahaffey, who as social chairman of the fraternity stretched his Little 500 victory parties into November of the next school year. "But my mind did skip a week, I promise you."

Mahaffey and the Phi Delts returned strong the next year, qualifying second and finishing second behind a revitalized Acacia team. Until the 1980s, Acacia was a fraternity team that almost never missed a race (only in 1952 did it fail to qualify) but like Phi Delta Theta never turned a lot of heads either. Its first 15 years of racing were outstanding, with annual finishes in the top ten and a win in 1961, but the second 15 years were less impressive, with a few top tens but also several back-of-the-field finishes. In 1982 the house looked to return to its earlier success by taking a more aggressive approach to the race, starting with the addition of new riders and a coach from the ranks of the alumni.

Acacia, a once strong fraternity team in the midst of a rebuilding process, returned to the top in 1983 with its first win in over 20 years. Riding under a do-it-all coach in Tom Schwoegler and an experienced USCF competitor in Jeff Hilligoss (left), Acacia held off the returning champion Phi Delta Thetas and the unpredictable Jim Mahaffey (right), who put in a heroic effort just weeks after a bad accident that left him with a badly torn ear.

Tom Schwoegler had served on the 1975 Student Foundation Steering Committee during his IU days, and kept an off-and-on relationship as coach and advisor for his Acacia fraternity's bike team through the rest of the decade. While working in an Indianapolis bicycle shop during the early 1980s, Schwoegler got to know fellow employee Jeff Hilligoss, an experienced USCF junior cyclist. The two talked about the Little 500, and as Schwoegler explained the race to Hilligoss, he renewed his own interest in the Acacia program. Schwoegler longed to return as Acacia's coach, but only with a promising group of riders. He saw a potential team

anchor in Hilligoss, who had entered IU in the fall of 1981, and talked him into Little 500 competition beginning with the 1982 race. Racing with Hilligoss that year were junior Chris Richardson and two more freshmen, George Grubb and Cary Sierzputowski, both former high school football players. On paper it wasn't a world-beating team, but the Acacia riders had an advantage in Coach Schwoegler, who took care of the countless intangibles of Little 500 such as meetings and bicycle repairs. "He was the kind of coach who simply took care of everything for the riders, so the riders didn't have to worry about organizing much for the race," Hilligoss said. "It took a huge burden off."

Immediately the team concept paid off for Acacia. In the 1982 race the team finished fifth, a substantial improvement from 23rd the year before. And in 1983, during just the second year of the revitalization program, Acacia pulled off a surprising victory. Qualifying in the ninth spot, Acacia benefited from the fact that it wasn't among the list of teams to watch. "Because no one was keying for us, we had the element of surprise," Hilligoss said. (Indeed, the method of coming out of the pack to win wasn't just a cliché—seven times in the 1980s a team won despite qualifying outside the top two rows.) Hilligoss rode 130 of Acacia's laps in 1982, but in 1983 the team achieved a better balance across all four riders, keeping Hilligoss well rested for the final laps. In the sprint finish, Hilligoss made his move on the 199th lap to get some space on Mahaffey, then held on to win with relative ease.

By finishing second Mahaffey completed his own heroic performance, riding three weeks after a horrific accident in practice in which he suffered a badly torn ear. Questionable all the way up to race day, Mahaffey rode nonetheless and left his mark on the race with an incident that for years would be known as "the Mahaffey rule." While under a yellow flag, rookie Chief Steward Mike Howard (a former Dodds rider who is still head official today) warned Mahaffey to hold his position on the track. Some opposing fans cheered the command and booed Mahaffey on his next lap, and he saluted them with a middle finger. Howard slapped him with a 10-second unsportsmanlike conduct penalty, believed to be the first ever for an obscene gesture to the crowd. "I realized I made a mistake two seconds after I did it," Mahaffey said. "In retrospect, it's kind of embarrassing, though a lot of people thought it was pretty funny." One person who found it particularly funny was IU basketball coach Bob Knight, who had a well-known penchant for similar outbursts. He had heard the story from a sportswriting friend and IU Phi Delt supporter named Ritter Collett, and a couple years later was sitting in the Indianapolis airport when Mahaffey recognized the coach and introduced himself. Remembering the story, Knight's face immediately brightened, and he rose to shake Mahaffey's hand and voice his approval.

As usual, the 1983 Little 500 field had a preponderance of greeks, with 22 fraternities among the 33 teams. Such a sizable greek contingent wasn't a surprise in and of itself, except for one greek team that was missing, one that for 13 years had done more than just show up on race day. Delta Chi, only two years removed from its last blockbuster win, had failed to qualify. For 1983, Delta Chi attended quals with one of its youngest teams in years, with three rookies and only one veteran from 1982, Randy Strong. Like the 1982 team, the foursome botched exchanges in its first two qualifying attempts and was forced to take a third and final attempt. Only this time luck didn't go Delta Chi's way, as the attempt was hindered by a steady rain and the time, 2:29.34, came up one-tenth of a second short for the 33rd spot in the field. Delta Chi was out of the 1983 Little 500, sidelined for the first time in 15 years. Months of training had suddenly and unbelievably lost all value, as the team couldn't get past what was usually a routine exercise. "It was a long walk back to the fraternity that day," said Adam Giles, one of the rookies. For the riders it would be not only a long walk but a final one, as that spring would be their last under the roof of the Delta Chi house.

Incredibly, for all the success and notoriety Delta Chi achieved in conquering the Little 500, its internal strength as an organization—both in numbers and character—had never quite reached the level of IU's top fraternities. Gutowsky, the two-time winner for Delta Chi, was the house president during the 1981–82 school year and knew there were major problems. For one weekend each year his fraternity was the biggest on campus, but the rest of the time it was plagued by financial woes and a lack of dependable members to fill its North Jordan Avenue home. The fraternity had unquestionably owned the bicycle race but made few other positive impressions on campus, academically or socially. During his term as president, Gutowsky began taking steps to try to help his fading chapter, and looked to the fraternity's alumni board for assistance. Out-

of-town board members such as Steve and Randy Reisinger, the longtime bike gurus, also recognized the problems and stepped aside from the board to allow some Indiana-based alums to get involved.

The local alumni who took new seats on the board recruited one of their own to serve as a live-in guidance counselor, observing the fraternity on a daily basis to get to the core of the problems. "On the surface, it was a terrific idea," Giles recalled. "But what turned out was that the people who got more and more involved began to approach the house in a personal nature, liking and disliking some members, and they decided that the best way to clean things up would be to remove a core group of people." The core group of people turned out to be, of all people, some members of the bike team. Harboring resentment toward the riders and the perception of Delta Chi as a house living only for the Little 500, the alumni board did not renew the housing contracts of riders Giles and Scott Senese, and a few other members, for the 1983–84 school year. The house that could not afford to lose any more members ultimately kicked out some of its most productive men. During the summer Giles and Senese appealed the board's decision but were denied reinstatement. Fellow rider Randy Strong, not included in the "hit list," left the house voluntarily in a show of support for his teammates, and another rider, Adam Beck (a Delta Chi transfer from Denison University), sided with the bike team instead of the IU chapter.

For the Little 500, Delta Chi had set two long-term goals during its dynasty run: to one day own the race record for most victories, and rise to the top spot in all-time race points. (A cumulative points system had been devised by former Student Foundation member John Greenman in the 1960s and became another source of bragging rights for top teams.) Through 1983 Delta Chi had cracked the top 10 in overall standings but still trailed the leading Phi Psis, and in total victories Delta Chi was also tied with Phi Psi, at seven wins each. But with the stroke of an administrative pen, all immediate hopes of improving those marks were dashed. For three more years after the rider purge, Delta Chi failed to qualify for a Little 500, and not until the 1990s would the fraternity finally return to prominence in the race. The famed Delta Chi "braintrust" also left with the riders in the wake of the housecleaning, opting instead to lend support to the ousted men in a new quest for Little 500 glory, this time as an independent team.

The Little 500

Giles and Strong lived together off campus during the 1983–84 school year and continued riding with Beck and Senese to erase the bad memories of April 1983. Life as a bike team went on basically as it had before, only without the financial and emotional support of a fraternal organization. As qualifying time approached the foursome was ready to compete, only without an official team name. Fortunately Delta Chi Hall of Famers Bill Brissman, Garry Rybar, and Eddy Van Guyse had heard about the new team, and called to lend their support and suggest a name from *Breaking Away,* the film in which all of them had played roles. Playing off the movie, and a little bit off the struggle with Delta Chi, the alums' idea was right on the mark—"Cutters." The riders loved it, and the newest Little 500 independent team was born.

Unburdened by their old fraternity ties and reputation, the Cutters showed up at 1984's April Fools' Day qualification and landed in the 10th spot for the race, showing that their entry was no joke. The riders desperately wanted to prove that the 1983 disappointment was a fluke, and after successfully qualifying they openly entertained thoughts of winning come race day. In their favor was a seemingly wide-open field, with no single standout favorite among the 33 teams. Acacia, the defending champs, returned its core riders but hadn't immediately impressed anyone with its 21st-place qualifying attempt. On the pole for the second consecutive year sat Sigma Chi, but after a 15th-place finish from the pole in 1983 few teams considered it a serious contender. Rounding out the top five qualifiers were Beta Theta Pi, Phi Delta Theta, Rollins House, and Lambda Chi Alpha, and of those four teams only the Phi Delts had recent race-day success. The Cutters, already armed with motivation and talent, appeared to be blessed with a race ripe for a surprise.

The 1984 Little 500 was not aided at the ticket booth by the weather or the calendar, as the Saturday date was rained out, forcing the race to be run on Easter Sunday, April 22. The combination of a holiday and chilly weather added up to a crowd of only 15,321, the lowest for a Little 500 since the 1950s (discounting the 1976 race, which ran on a Monday). But those who did brave the elements at Bill Armstrong Stadium (re-named in the former Foundation director's honor after his 1983 retire-ment) witnessed a Little 500 first, as a team without dorm or greek affiliation won. The savvy Cutters rode an incident-free race and put themselves in a position to win, with Giles on the bike and in the lead group with five laps remaining. Then on the last turn of the last lap, Giles pulled off a finish reminiscent of the Cutters team of *Breaking Away* fame. In the movie, Dennis Christopher's character took a hard inside line off turn four while his competitor faded to the outside, then pedaled through first to the line. Giles did the exact same thing, advancing on the inside of Acacia's Hilligoss and beating out him and Alpha Epsilon Pi's Jim Pollak at the line. (An added ironic twist came with how, in the movie, Delta Chi's Rybar did the actual riding and came in first, while the real-life Cutters won with a former Delta Chi in Giles.)

Never in the previous 33 Little 500s had an independent team won, and only once before had a team won on its first try (discounting 1951, South Cottage Grove pulled off the feat in 1955). In the span of just over two hours on a Sunday afternoon, the Cutters became legendary. It's tough to say how many people supported the Cutters prior to the race's start, as the riders didn't recall having an overflowing fan section, but at the end of the race seemingly thousands of Little 500 fans embraced the Cutters, the team that finally stopped the 28-year greek winning streak. "There was almost a grass-roots groundswell of support," Giles said, adding that a high level of fraternity resentment existed among the newly found supporters. In the days following the race, the phone at Giles's and Strong's apartment rang constantly with calls from well-wishers they didn't even know. Not since a certain fictitious No. 34 team rode on film had a Little 500 victory been so popular, and it wouldn't be the last one for the independent power.

One year later, in 1985, the Cutters still held top billing among Little 500 teams, despite only one veteran returning from the winning four-some. Giles came back to ride as a senior, having achieved what the *Daily Student* called "household-name status" along the way. The picture of Giles crossing the finish line in 1984 with a look of absolute, unrestrained glee was one of the best Little 500 finish photos ever and was reprinted several times in the school paper, including on the cover of its 1985 race preview edition. In addition to that publication Giles was featured in other papers and taped a promotional advertisement for WTTV–4, the broadcasters of the 1985 race. The excess publicity proved justified through the Cutters' performance in the 1985 pre-race season. Even with three rookies the team won pole position in qualifying and set a record in winning the Team Pursuit event. By race day the Cutters were solid favorites, along with the Acacia team. The Cutters had the obvious talent and momentum, and Acacia had by far the most experienced team in the field, with a rare trio of four-year riders in Hilligoss, Grubb, and Sierzputowski. But recent races had been partial to darkhorse teams, and 1985 continued the trend, as Alpha Epsilon Pi rose to the occasion for its first victory.

Prior to the 1980s, AEPi was a fraternity team with only a dozen races to its name and three top-10 finishes, but in 1983 the team's fortunes changed as it added some new blood in freshman Jim Pollak. As a youth Pollak was crippled by a degenerative hip disease and spent two full years on crutches, but by his teen years he had miraculously recovered and excelled in athletics. Upon arriving at IU, Pollak originally planned on going out for the cross-country team, but instead followed a fraternity brother's lead and picked up bicycling. Joining the AEPi team, Pollak was immediately competitive with his veteran teammates and participated in the 1983 Little 500, riding nearly one-third of his team's laps in a fourth-place effort. With that race—and rookie-of-the-year and all-star recognition—Pollak was hooked.

In the Cutters' 1984 breakthrough season Pollak captained Alpha Epsilon Pi to second place, then in 1985 set out to finish one place higher. "I was obsessed with winning," Pollak said. "Every day I told my teammates 'we'll win this race, I promise you'—and they all looked at me like I was crazy." And crazy he probably was—the team had set a general training rule to not ride outside when the temperature dropped below freezing, but Pollak usually broke it. He also altered the team's training to include intervals and indoor sprints on training bikes, and it all paid off at the track. AEPi qualified third, tying its previous high mark set in 1979, and on race day recorded its first win. All Pollak had asked of teammates Sheldon Weiss, Marc Korman, and Tony Checroun was that they help him get to the final laps with the leaders, and from there Pollak closed out the pursuing Acacia, Chi Phi, and Cutters teams.

Pollak returned with the same three teammates in 1986 and found himself in a position to win again in the closing laps, only to come up short. One of the oddities of Little 500s in the early to mid-1980s was how great teams often returned intact after victories but couldn't repeat their success. In a five-year span four Hall of Fame riders and their teams

(Opposite) Upon crossing the finish line first on April 22, 1984, Adam Giles (elated, ahead of Alpha Epsilon Pi, Acacia and Chi Phi) and the Cutters ushered in a new era of Little 500 racing. Though initially made up of cast-offs from the once proud Delta Chi house, the Cutters would flourish for many years as an independent team, working without the traditional strong support and money most top teams enjoyed. In love with either the mystique of the name or the quality of the cycling, or both, fans who had never before been involved with Little 500 lent their support to the Cutters. (Above) These Cutters fans watched the race from St. Paul's Catholic Church on the south side of the stadium.

Following the Delta Chi dynasty, no teams managed to repeat as Little 500 champions. Often, the hero from one year would fall just short another year. In 1985 Jim Pollak of Alpha Epsilon Pi emerged victorious (at right, riding against former Acacia champion Jeff Hilligoss), then in 1986 (below) finished a heartbreaking second to Tony Ceccanese of the Cutters (Pollak is on the far right).

came close but not close enough either one or two years after winning: Gutowsky finished second in '82 to Mahaffey, who finished second in '83 to Hilligoss, who finished second in '85 to Pollak, who finished second in '86 to Jay Polsgrove of the Cutters. Whether it was the new stadium's equal-opportunity track or parity among teams, repeating had become a very difficult proposition.

Without any repeat champions, it was difficult for any one team to lay claim to the "dynasty" title previously held by Delta Chi. But the Cutters team could make the best argument for it, as they added titles in 1986 and 1988. What had started as four former Delta Chis out for vindication turned into a full-fledged cycling factory, one that despite its infancy could match up with any top, long-standing greek power. The Cutters did not have, and would never have, the greek-level financial resources to train teams, but one skill the team had that no fraternity could match was the power to pull in riders from all over campus. Greeks were limited to teams made up of members or, occasionally, recruited riders from other teams, but the Cutters could take on any unaffiliated riders without the greek formalities.

Losing two riders from the 1984 winning team, the remaining Cutters veterans immediately looked to other independent teams for new teammates. Tony Ceccanese and Vince Hoeser were two of the first to jump aboard, joining the Cutters after riding for Avere in 1984, another new independent which had finished a respectable seventh. By 1986 the Cutters' stable of riders had grown even larger, to the point that a Cutters "B" team was created. Qualifying 27th and finishing 23rd in 1986, team Trophy Dash more resembled its nickname "Trophy Crash" (playfully given by their Cutters teammates), but developed riders for future Cutter teams.

On the 1986 Cutters "A" team were Ceccanese, Hoeser, and two newcomers again from other teams. George Carlin came from the independent Cinzano team (its name, like the Cutters', inspired by *Breaking Away*), which finished 15th on its first try in 1985, and Jay Polsgrove came from two different teams. After stints with the Sigma Pi greek team in 1984 and Avere in 1985 (Avere failed to qualify for the race), Polsgrove opted to move to the Cutters, the cream of the independents. "They had a big, mysterious aura about them," Polsgrove said. "I liked them because it was more of a challenge." Riding under the Cutters' support system and rigorous training methods, he believed he had found his best chance to win.

In front of a record 31,908 fans, on a rare warm and pleasant day for a Little 500, the Cutters aura reached a new level. Just days before the race Hoeser broke his collarbone in practice, forcing Polsgrove, Ceccanese, and Carlin to ride the 200 laps as a three-man team. No team had ever won with such a handicap, and only one team, South Cottage Grove in 1955, had won after qualifying 14th, as the Cutters had. With all that against them, the Cutters took the track—and proceeded to win *in record time*. Polsgrove logged most of the extra laps needed in Hoeser's absence, freeing up Ceccanese for the sprint finish with the leading AEPi team. The fraternity had hoped to run away with the '86 race (something no winner had done at the new track), and appeared on the verge of just that with three laps remaining. Sheldon Weiss of AEPi had opened a quarter-lap lead at that point and sped to the pits to exchange to Pollak, who would then hold the lead until the end. At least, that was the plan. Instead, Weiss took too much speed in the exchange and wrecked with Pollak, and by the time Pollak regained control of the bike and took off, the field had reached him. Ceccanese sat on Pollak's wheel and shot around him on the last turn, denying AEPi the repeat and the record time, which instead went to the Cutters (2:01.44, 25.11 mph). "I felt like I had let down the world," said Pollak, who after the finish crumpled in the infield and cried. (Pollak would move on to a bright professional career, which included four world championship appearances and the 1992 Barcelona Olympics.) His team might have indeed lost the race, but the Cutters' three-man performance was more memorable as a heroic winning effort.

Two years later the team won again in a similar manner. Once more, the team raced with just three riders—Polsgrove, Andrew Meister, and John White. Both new to the Cutters, Meister was a freshman with European cycling experience, and White was acquired from the 1987 Posers independent team. The team's fourth rider, Robby Fromin, missed the race with an illness. As in 1986, the 1988 Cutters didn't do themselves any favors at qualifications, placing 20th in the field of 33. The poor starting spot did come back to haunt the team in the race, as it got tied up in an early crash and had to make up ground before riding

What did IU basketball star Steve Alford and Little 500 Hall-of-Famer Jim Pollak have in common in 1986? Both appeared in a Gamma Phi Beta sorority calendar featuring men of IU. Sales of the calendar were discontinued quickly after the discovery that Alford broke an NCAA rule by appearing in it, as under NCAA regulations athletes could not be connected with such products unless approved. Alford wasn't, and the penalty was a one-game suspension. For its part, the Student Foundation had no problem with Pollak's appearance (as, appropriately, Mr. April).

with the leaders. But at the finish Polsgrove again came through, making a move on the backstretch of the last lap to beat Phi Gamma Delta and Phi Delta Theta. The race wasn't contested at speeds as fast as the 1986 race, due to heavy winds and multiple yellow flags, though in the end the same team stood alone at the top.

With the 1988 triumph, the Cutters moved into fourth place on the Little 500's all-time win list. The three teams ahead of them in the standings, Delta Chi, Phi Kappa Psi, and Phi Gamma Delta, had more wins but had taken between 11 and 20 total races to accumulate their first

three. The Cutters had achieved their three in five races—all while operating under an increasingly secretive veil. As the Cutters program grew, its riders cut themselves off from much of the Little 500 atmosphere, shunning many of the pre-race series events and friendly rides with other teams. "We wouldn't ride with anyone else, or let anyone see what we were doing," Polsgrove said. "We tried to mess with people." And it worked on many levels, as come race day usually no one really seemed to know anything about the Cutters. Many fans truly believed the riders were all local kids like the movie Cutters, perhaps just lucky to be at the track, and opposing teams often didn't know how they would operate on race day, underestimating the Cutters on the basis of few pre-race appearances and generally bad qualifying runs. But they learned plenty as the years passed, that the Cutters were more than just another flash-in-the-pan independent.

Ironically, some Cutters influence played into the hands of the 1987 Little 500 winners, the Phi Gamma Deltas. After the Hall of Fame years of Jay Allardt in the late 1970s, the Fijis hadn't made much noise in the Little 500, and in 1985 sunk to an all-time low finish of 28th. For one of the prouder houses on campus, such poor showings in the year's biggest event were unacceptable and embarrassing. But the team's fortunes changed in 1986, when former Cutter Scott Senese began working with his brother Mark, a Fiji. "Scott leaked a lot of the training secrets that Delta Chi and the Cutters had used for years, and that switched our whole philosophy over," Mark Senese said. The fraternity increased the bike team budget to allow for holiday trips, changed training regimens to include more road work like other top teams, and overall turned Little 500 training into a year-round obsession.

Under the tutelage of the former champion Senese, the Fijis quickly returned to the ranks of the race's elite. In their second year of re-dedication to the Little 500 Fiji won, in a manner proving beyond doubt that their new methods were effective. As the Cutters did in 1986 and would do again in 1988, the Fijis rode the race with three riders. But unlike the Cutters' sidelined riders, the injured Fiji, Dave Schmidt, was expected to be the team's workhorse and ride the bulk of the laps. "Without him, we weren't really sure if we were going to be able to pull it off," said Mark Senese, referring not just to winning but to racing at all.

Mark Senese and the Phi Gamma Deltas were all smiles after a surprising win in 1987. Mark's older brother, Scott Senese, was a former Cutter and taught Fiji many of his team's training secrets, and the results paid off in just the second year of what was a rebuilding effort.

Closing out the 1980s in Little 500 racing, appropriately, were two more winning efforts from popular independent teams. The Cutters won for the third time in a five-year span in 1988 (pictured are Jay Polsgrove and Fiji Dave Schmidt), adding to their amazing young history, while in 1989 another upstart independent took the field by storm. Team Cinzano included a motley mix of riders from several teams and was not expected to contend after qualifying 23rd, but rode a perfect race and won—appropriately on the 10th anniversary of the premiere of Breaking Away. No team before or since has won after starting so far back.

He and Jim Strobel were only the second- and third-best riders on the team, while fourth man Tom Herendeen had struggled in practices at the track. But on race day the trio turned in their best performances and gained confidence as the race wore on. On the bike at the end, Senese didn't lead the pack but instead conserved energy while sitting on wheels, and waited until the end to pass Acacia's John Huesing and the Cutters' Polsgrove to win by a bike length and a half. In winning the team made history with its family ties, as Tom Herendeen followed in his father's footsteps as a Fiji winner (Tom Herendeen Sr. had won in 1956) and the Senese brothers became the second brother tandem (along with Delta Chi's Mark and Mike Dayton) to both win races. In the end, Scott Senese had not only helped guide his brother to victory, but also created a new rival for the Cutters in Fiji, much to the chagrin of his former mates. The rivalry remains strong today.

To commemorate the 10th anniversary of the release of *Breaking Away,* the Student Foundation held a reunion over the 1989 race weekend for the movie's alums. Actors Dennis Christopher, Robyn Douglass, and Jackie Earle Haley, among others, returned to Bloomington for a gala party and a glimpse of a Little 500 race in the new stadium. Screenplay writer Steve Tesich was unable to return, but he would have undoubtedly approved of how the race played out, as the two teams born out of his film finished one-two.

Formed in 1985, the Cinzano independent team spent its first four years mostly in the shadow of the Cutters. Finishing 15th, 12th, fifth, and 10th between 1985 and 1988, Cinzano would have been the top independent in any other decade, but with the Cutters coming in fourth, first, fourth, and first over the same span, it was tough to gain recognition. The inaugural Cinzano team had been composed mainly of men from Teter dormitory, and in subsequent years some of its riders would come from other teams. But the Cutters also were always in the market for experi-

enced riders, and Cinzano wasn't immediately able to compete with the popular champions. From its first team in 1985, when George Carlin and John Magro rode one race before jumping over to the Cutters, Cinzano fought a difficult uphill battle in the rider recruitment arena. Not until they could beat the Cutters in recruiting could they beat them in a race.

The pieces finally fell together for Cinzano in 1989, as four seniors came together to ride under the familiar red and blue Cinzano umbrella. Two-year veteran Mike Asher returned and helped assemble a motley crew of riders from other teams. His race-day teammates included Kendall Harnett, a two-year rider from Collins dormitory, Fred Rose, who had participated in 1986 for an independent team named "Joint Venture," and Doug Schmidt, the only one untested in the race, though he had attempted to qualify in 1988. "We knew we were strong, though probably not very intelligent," Harnett recalled. His assessment rang true in the weeks leading up to the race, as Cinzano gave little reason to be considered among the top teams. At Team Pursuit, universally believed by Little 500 riders to be the best test of overall team talent, Cinzano placed 11th out of 20 teams, and at race qualifications only managed a 23rd-place effort after a fouled attempt.

Compared to Cinzano the Cutters had a less experienced team, with veteran John White and three rookies, but as usual still found ways to stay at the top of the heap. They won Team Pursuit and qualified 12th for the race—not a spectacular effort but nevertheless better than 1986 and 1988, where they won anyway. But on race day, before a record crowd of 32,351 (a mark that still stands today and likely will never be touched), the contrasting Cutters and Cinzano teams found themselves neck-and-neck for the title.

In a sort of role reversal, the unknown Cinzano team rode a perfect race, smart and without incidents, while the usually trouble-free Cutters had to fight back from an accident and a creeping (improving track position under yellow) penalty. At the finish the two veterans Asher and White battled along with Acacia rookie sensation Pete Noverr, and Asher won at the line. The Cutters finished second.

With the Cinderella of perhaps all Cinderellas—a 23rd-qualifying independent team—winning, the decade of the 1980s in Little 500 ended on a most fitting note. When *Breaking Away* came out in 1979, its fabricated Little 500 stood out as most unreal by having a non-greek team win. At that time, no one associated with the real-life Little 500 could have rationally pictured such an occurrence. But by the film's 10th anniversary independent teams had taken over the limelight, showing that the great race could be won without fraternity-level support. As the fictitious Cutters provided great drama in winning at the movies, the independent Cutters and Cinzano teams provided fans with some of the most interesting races in history by taking on the traditional powers and beating them in real life. "We pulled in the disenfranchised people," said Harnett of Cinzano, whose fans came from heavy anti-greek areas like Collins dormitory. Those fans finally had legitimate teams to cheer on, and the real winner in the end was the Little 500 itself—especially in 1989, when a record throng and Hollywood audience was treated to a one-two Cinzano and Cutters finish.

8. "Ladies, Mount Your Roadmaster Bicycles"

All the recruiting and all the lobbying finally paid off on a sunny Friday afternoon, April 23, 1988. The day was not unlike any other race day Bill Armstrong Stadium had seen, as a throng of thousands had come out to support friends and strangers riding Roadmasters on the cinder track, but at the same time it was very much unlike any other race. Pioneers and newcomers stood ready to ride, but to many of them a race had already been run and won. Indiana women and the Little 500 were finally coming together—on two wheels.

For the better part of 40 years, the women of IU played only support-ing roles in the story of the "World's Greatest College Weekend." When Howdy Wilcox and his Student Committee first dreamed up the idea for a Little 500, there was no consideration given to how women could get involved in the event. The coed sponsor role, with its jersey-knitting and pit-decorating duties was, at first, the only option for a sorority or resi-dence hall to get involved in the male-oriented event. Two years after the Little 500 began, a new female role was introduced in the form of the celebrity "Sweetheart," furthering women's involvement to include look-ing pretty and kissing the male bicycling heroes.

In 1955 the Mini 500 tricycle race was born, giving IU women their own exclusive, team-oriented activity, but with its flamboyant parades and colorful themes Mini was more of an entertainment vehicle than an athletic spectacle. That's not to say tricycling was easy and that the top teams weren't accomplishing anything, as indeed the frantic pace, tight turns, and quick exchanges of Mini involved a great deal of skill and practice and the winning team each year had to survive many heats and outlast roughly 50 opponents. But those who did excel ended up as footnotes in the story of a Little 500 weekend, and even then often shared the spotlight with winners of such lighthearted Mini contests as "Best Dressed" and "Best Parade Entry." Another example of the imbalance in Little 500 gender roles was on display every year in the Mini when the Student Foundation Steering Committee president took a traditional ride around the arena on an oversized, circus-style bicycle. Every year the rider atop the cycle was male—not until 1979, on the 30th Steering Committee, did a woman serve as president.

Women began making noise in the bicycle race in the early 1970s, at the same time as federal law Title IX was breaking ground for women in athletic pursuits. In 1973 six women set out to enter a Little 500 team, but

Women's first roles in the Little 500 were as coed sponsors for men's bike teams, which in the 1950s meant pit decorating (as the Kappa Alpha Theta women did for Phi Gamma Delta in 1951) and uniform designing (pictured are Pi Beta Phi clothiers with a Sigma Alpha Epsilon rider in 1951). By the end of the 1950s the elaborate pit decorations were replaced by simple, painted wood boards and the jerseys were provided by the Student Foundation, but the coed sponsor role continued among all teams for the first 30 years of Little 500. Today, usually only greek houses share the Little 500 experience with a coed sponsor.

The Little
500

were told by the Student Foundation that they weren't allowed. Never was it specifically written into Little 500 rules that women could not ride, but the Student Foundation took such a stance because it feared the worst. "It is true there is no reason why a woman should not ride in Little 500, but it is equally clear she would not be safe on the track," said a 1972 *Daily Student* editorial in a section evaluating the relevance of Little 500. "Given the torrid feelings of male supremacy on the track, any woman rider would be in serious trouble." Unmoved by the Student Foundation's position, the women filed a complaint with the Bloomington Human Rights Commission. The motion worked, as the HRC issued an emergency order forcing the Foundation to allow the women to ride at qualifications, but in the end a legitimate rule kept them off the track. One of their riders had transferred to IU that semester, and eligibility rules stated that teams couldn't have transfer students. But the seal was finally broken—women could no longer be kept away from Little 500 bicycling.

Over the next few years more women dabbled in Little 500 training, but none made it to the main event. In 1974 a women's team filed an application, but didn't attempt to qualify. In 1975 one women's team had a qualification time but didn't show up, and two other riders trained with men's teams but didn't ride in the race. (Cathy Weber broke her ankle while practicing exchanges with Rollins House, which later failed to qualify, and alternate Mary Brewster quit the 19th-qualifying Cravens B team.) Kathy Cerajeski became the first woman on an active team roster in 1976, with Cravens B, but as an alternate she didn't ride (the four men who did finished 31st).

Women first attempted qualifying in 1979, when a coed team of four women and one man competed. The team of Leigh Parker, Rhonda Pretlow, Jim Studenic, and Robin and Laurie Calland were unsuccessful in their attempt, but weren't overly disappointed considering they were rookies and the qualifying field included a staggering 62 other teams. "It doesn't matter so much," said Robin Calland in a *Daily Student* qualification wrap-up. "Hopefully, we'll open the way for other women, making it easier for them to qualify." Calland's words rang true two years later, as another group of women came out for qualifying as the Little 500's first all-woman team.

"Double Take," as the team was called, was the brainchild of sopho-more Pam Swedeen. After a summer of bicycling between home and work, Swedeen returned to IU and decided to form a bike team. By October she had a foursome, with teammates Carol Marks (whose brother, Dean, had ridden Little 500s for Lambda Chi Alpha), Cindy Alvear (an IU volleyball player), and Bonnie Sullivan. Double Take put in a full spring of training, even traveling to Florida with the Pi Kappa Phi team to ride, but faltered on the April 5, 1981, qualifying day. The team fouled on its first two attempts, then on the third try rode with extra caution to make sure each woman got one official lap for the history books. They did complete the final attempt, but their 2:54.9 time was 19 seconds shy of the 33rd spot. Double Take took a good shot, but the Little 500 race remained an all-male affair.

One of the fears the Student Foundation had when women started expressing interest in Little 500 was that, in turn, men would want to compete with women in the Mini 500 tricycle race. By the early 1980s the Mini was still very much a popular event (though not what it once was in terms of pageantry), drawing around 5,000 fans and full fields of 63 teams annually to Assembly Hall. Through the years the event had relocated from its beginnings in Wildermuth Fieldhouse to the new 17th Street Fieldhouse in 1961 to Assembly Hall in 1972, and added qualifying days to pare down its ever-growing number of entrants. At first, fields were limited to 48 teams, but later expanded to 54 and then, in 1977, 63. Though the Mini was ridiculed by *Daily Student* columnists (one in 1982 called the event "an affront to women of [IU]" and "degrading, insulting and patronizing") and even the Bloomington Faculty Council (in 1984 it issued a resolution urging the Student Foundation to replace the Mini), its cult-like following suited the Little 500 weekend just fine.

However, the Mini 500 fans had known for nearly 30 years changed when IU's men took up three-wheeling. In 1982 the first all-male team competed—a Dodds House outfit named "Jerry's Kids." Qualifying in Hawaiian shirts and baseball caps, the team of Jeff Ball, Dave Boos, Tom Danielson, and Tom Reed annoyed many of their fellow competitors, who thought they were mocking the proceedings. Nonetheless, Jerry's Kids qualified 35th out of the 63 teams and made a good showing in the event, winning two heats before losing in a semifinal round. But the scattered boos that cascaded down from the Assembly Hall crowd made a statement—men weren't going to be welcomed into Mini with open arms.

It was one thing for the women to attempt landing spots in the men's bicycle race, as the playing field was tilted heavily in the men's' favor. Tricycling, on the other hand, was another story—men's teams who took the event seriously could easily qualify, thanks to inherent physical advantages. And once they did that in 1982, it was only a matter of time before the men would be beating the women. "It's always been a woman-dominating sport and it's kind of frustrating that men are coming in to dominate it," said a 1984 female rider to the *Daily Student* prior to the Mini, echoing the majority opinion of the time. "It's just kind of useless if men are gonna start winning." Indeed, men started winning that very year, as a team called Phi Spika Trika, riding for the second consecutive year, won the 1984 pole. That team failed to win the overall event from the pole, advancing to the final heat before losing to champion Kappa Delta, and failed to win over many fans with a banner from supporters that said "women belong in the kitchen, not on trikes."

Male riders made it to the Mini winners' stand in 1985, as a coed team named "Who Knows?" won and made Scott Norton and Eiu Oh not-quite-household names. The team of two men and two women nearly won again in 1986, but were edged out by the all-male McNutt-Dejoya II T.L.W. team of Major Franklin, Tony Goldboss, Jim Paulette, and Jay Smith. In 1987 men again won, as a foursome from McNutt-Crone continued the overhaul of the historically all-women's event. McNutt-Crone was one of a record five all-male teams competing that year, all of whom were loudly booed by fans throughout the evening. If there was one sound Student Foundation officials were unfamiliar with at their events it was malicious booing from spectators toward students, and for 1988

Among the early pioneers of Little 500 cycling was Kathy Cerajeski, who in 1976 became the first woman on an active team roster, serving as an alternate for the 31st-finishing Cravens B dorm team.

The Little
500

Men began invading the traditionally all-women Mini 500 in 1982, and in 1986 an all-men's team won for the first time (McNutt-Dejoya II T.L.W., with riders Tony Goldboss, Jay Smith, Major Franklin and Jim Paulette), frustrating many competitors and angering fans.

they put an end to it by creating separate races for men and women. Not coincidentally, women would receive another break that year—in the two-wheeled division of the Little 500 weekend.

As the 1980s progressed, IU women became more involved in bicycling not only through occasional attempts to make the Little 500 but also through the IU Cycling Club, which arrived on the campus recreational sports scene in 1980. Through the "IUCC" more women formally were introduced to cycling, and after a few years that led to more women becoming interested in Little 500–related riding. In 1984 the Student Foundation didn't offer an exclusive women's event, but it did create women's divisions in Team Pursuit, the five-year-old pre–Little 500 event that tested men's teams' depth and teamwork. Eighteen women's teams participated in the 1984 event, a strong turnout that included sorority,

residence hall, and independent teams. In 1985 another event was added, "Miss-n-Out," a sprint race patterned after an Indianapolis velodrome event called "Hare and Hound." In Miss-n-Out a small group of riders would ride in a pack, alternating sprint laps and rest laps, and on every sprint lap the last rider to cross the start/finish line would be eliminated. After several preliminary heats the top finishers would compete in a championship heat. Like Team Pursuit, Miss-n-Out had separate men's and women's divisions, and 32 women participated in the 1985 premiere.

Through such Little 500 "series events" (as Team Pursuit, Miss-n-Out, and others were collectively known), Debbie Satterfield found just what she was looking for. Already an avid amateur rider outside Bloomington and twice a coach in the men's Little 500, helping out her husband's Read-Curry 4 dorm teams of 1983–84, the series events gave her the chance to organize a campus team of her own. After posting fliers all over campus to recruit riders Satterfield built a formidable team named Stonies, honoring the local stonecutters. In 1987 the Stonies were the preeminent women's team, winning both Team Pursuit and Miss-n-Out. The team which finished second in Miss-n-Out, the "Spokeswomen," was another independent team out of the same mold as the Stonies.

One of the Spokeswomen riders, Jill Janov, exemplified the struggles a dedicated women's rider found at IU. Arriving in Bloomington in the fall of 1984, Janov approached the Student Foundation as a rider looking for competition—and was offered a tricycle. It wasn't the first setback she would face. Going through sorority rush her sophomore year in hopes of joining a financially backed team, she found the IU greek system very cold to prospective cyclists. Selling herself more as a rider than a fun-loving coed (she rode her bike from house to house during rush), many sororities were less than amused. "They weren't interested in hearing [about cycling]," she said. "The girls were more interested in fraternity parties than bike races, especially women's races." Several sororities already had bike teams, but in the mid-1980s generally weren't interested in adding more cycling fanatics. Janov instead pledged the Alpha Epsilon Phi house, which had no team. As a pledge walking around the house in bicycling gear she usually got more long stares than inquiries about riding, but fortunately a fellow Spokeswoman teammate, Sandi Miller, was also in the pledge class. Later, as actives in the house, they would be looked up to by new pledges, a few of whom also decided to pick up cycling.

While competing in the Little 500 series events, riders like Janov and Satterfield began setting their sights on a potential women's main event. The argument they could make for a women's Little 500 was strong, considering that many other schools in the state had women's cycling events. Schools like Franklin College, the University of Indianapolis and DePauw University all had races modeled after IU's Little 500, but unlike the Little 500 theirs had women's divisions. (DePauw, like IU, had a tricycle race for women but killed it in 1975 in favor of a women's bicycle race.) IU was clearly behind the times. Pressing on, the independent women in 1987 distributed fliers at the men's race to gauge the potential appeal of a women's Little 500. The response was impressive, with over 50 women expressing interest in such a race, and it was one of the primary catalysts ultimately leading to a women's Little 500.

The other catalyst in 1987 that led to IU's women securing a permanent place in the Little 500 mainstream came on April 4, when four Kappa Alpha Theta riders attempted to qualify for the men's race. Though not the first feat of its kind, the Theta attempt was more publicized and accepted than attempts from teams such as Double Take in the early 1980s. As an established greek house with a solid reputation on campus, Theta was embraced by the greek-dominated Student Foundation membership and even other men's teams, who in earlier years had been known to treat women's riders with less than complete respect. The foursome of Lee Ann Guzek, Martha Hinkamp, Darci Feick, and Kathy Cleary trained all year on their own but also got help from established teams such as Acacia and Phi Kappa Psi, which lent the Thetas credibility in the race community. "If there were men that didn't like us, we didn't hear it," Guzek said. Support from within the sorority was also positive, another advantage the independent teams didn't always have as they were usually on their own. That's not to say, however, that training was easy—while many fraternity teams had bike rooms in their houses for training and mechanical work, all the Theta house could offer in 1987 was a dark, hot boiler room. But it was better than nothing, and the team did its winter training there. For spring break the Thetas traveled to Florida and practiced exchanges in, of all places, a tomato field. Falling

down in a tomato field, they figured, would be more pleasant than on cinders.

Despite heavy practicing of exchanges, the Thetas' qualifying attempt was marred by poor ones. During the first two attempts, Theta failed to get as far as the third lap, and on the final attempt did post a time but only the 37th best of the day. Again a woman's team fell short in an attempt to make the men's field, and the Student Foundation began to realize that riding in the men's race would never be an option for the many women who were expressing interest in Little 500 competition. For the independent women riders, the failed attempt by Theta probably was a blessing. They watched the bid with mixed emotions, knowing that a successful run by Theta would be great for women in general, but perhaps detrimental to their ultimate goal of a separate women's race.

Once the hoopla of the Theta attempt died down, the meetings began. Phyllis Klotman, Dean of IU's Office of Women's Affairs, joined Satterfield, Janov, and others fighting for the women's race together with Student Foundation officials to hash out the details for what was to be simply known as the "Women's Little 500." (Oddly, for a while the outspoken Theta team opposed the efforts of their peers, claiming that if given a choice between a women's race and a shot at the men's race, they'd take the latter. "I'm not up for a women's race," Guzek said in a September 1987 issue of the *Daily Student*. "I'm not sure how many girls will put in the effort to become competent riders, and I don't want to get hurt doing something a level lower." Later she and her teammates backed off such claims, and embraced the idea of a women's race.) Through the meetings it was established that a women's race would be set up just like the men's, only with 100 laps instead of 200, and would be held on the Friday afternoon of race weekend. On October 7, 1987, the Student Foundation made it official, introducing a women's division of Little 500 racing.

At the time of the announcement the Student Foundation said 22 teams would be in the first race, with one financial sponsor representing the entire field. Delta Faucet was secured as the sponsor, thanks to a little help from the retired Bill Armstrong, who likely gave the company the same successful sales pitch he had used to lure men's team sponsors for 30 years. But the initial estimate of 22 teams proved far below the actual level of interest, as months of recruiting by women's riders in dorms and greek houses produced an amazing 31-team field, the likes of which had

Boldly attempting to qualify for the men's race, the Kappa Alpha Theta foursome of Kathy Cleary, Darci Feick, Lee Ann Guzek and Martha Hinkamp broke new ground in the fight for getting women into the Little 500. But like other first-time teams, the Thetas were plagued by bad exchanges (shown are Martha Hinkamp, left, and Kathy Cleary completing one of the team's good exchanges) and failed in their historic attempt.

never been seen before in the women's series events. There was also a healthy balance among the teams, as 15 greek, 10 independent (including the Stonies, Spokeswomen, and a women's edition of Cinzano), and six dorm teams qualified for the race (though one sorority team, Alpha Chi Omega, would drop out prior to race day). A women's Riders Council was formed to help train the throng of new riders and explain how in time, as Guzek said, "the fun would wear off." However, almost every team stuck with the training and headed for race day, where it wouldn't take long for the reality of a Little 500 to set in.

The afternoon of April 22, 1988, was a sunny one for the estimated 12,000 fans that came to Bill Armstrong Stadium for the inaugural women's Little 500, and what they saw would not exactly be called one of the more competitive races on record. From his infield position, track commentator Dave Blase predicted that the race would be similar to the inaugural men's races, which was a roundabout way of saying it would be largely beginners riding at a slow pace with plenty of accidents. Like many a men's race, the women's race indeed had a massive early pileup that dropped several teams off the pace. Fearing another accident, teams didn't pack up again for the rest of the race, instead riding in a virtual straight line around the track for the last 95 laps, making it hard for riders to work with each other, improve position and monitor their progress in the standings. The latter was especially true for the Kappa Alpha Theta team, the heavy favorite by pole-position qualifying and by birthright, as it had no idea that an all-freshman dorm team was leading the field until it was too late.

A product of the mass recruiting efforts that the Student Foundation and veteran women's riders carried out to fill out the Little 500 field, the southeast campus dorm team named Willkie Sprint had qualified eighth with four freshmen in Kerry Hellmuth, Kirsten Swanson, Amy Tucker, and Louise Elder. For race day the team was outfitted in jerseys similar in color to the Thetas' pole-sitting green (returning from '87 for Theta

were Hinkamp and Guzek, with newcomers Shelly Brundick and Mary Pappas). Late in the race Theta thought it was riding in the lead, but actually Willkie Sprint was ahead in front, unrecognized by the Thetas practically until the white flag was shown to the dorm team and not them. By that time the race was all but decided, and when Swanson crossed the finish line Willkie Sprint reigned as the first women's Little 500 champions (in a time of one hour, ten minutes, and 52 seconds). Ironically, the Thetas' Guzek was probably partly to blame for the winners' strong riding and success—Willkie Sprint was one of the teams she had helped train while serving on Riders Council.

For others in the women's Little 500 circle, the first race was a bittersweet one. Janov cried and got sick as she rode for her Alpha Epsilon Phi sorority team, overwhelmed with excitement at not just finishing fourth, but finally getting to ride in a Little 500. As a senior, it would be her last race. For Satterfield, the experience was a little more bittersweet. Her fight for the women's race lasted the longest, too long by Student Foundation rules. In the spring of 1988 she was a graduate student, and ineligible to ride in the race she has been largely credited with bringing to fruition.

In 1988 and '89 the men's Little 500 crowned consecutive independent champions, a first in the history of the event. The women's Little 500, on the other hand, was dominated by independent teams throughout its early years. After the dorm-based Willkie Sprint won in 1988, independents—powered by many year-round cyclists who rode in USCF and IUCC events—won the next five women's races. Many independents lacked the greek-level funds for equipment and travel, often resorting to T-shirt sales and other fundraisers for cash, but they never lacked the quality personnel needed to win a Little 500. Many independent riders even switched teams regularly, like professional free-agent athletes, in a constant struggle to find an

A better-than-expected turnout of 30 teams participated in the 1988 inaugural women's Little 500, and the faces of many riders showed how physically exhausting yet satisfying the 100-lap journey was. The women were not immune to the dangers of Little 500 racing, as one accident near the start/finish line felled several teams.

energized and experienced unit in a field full of novices. "Nothing is worse than having to constantly motivate people," said Liz Schofer, a top independent for the old Spokeswomen teams and, in 1989, a Little 500 champion. "[We] wanted teams with ambitious riders."

Having moved out of the dorms, the Willkie Sprint riders became the independent Team Sprint in 1989. The team lost Louise Elder from its '88 winning team, but added Mia Middleton and Jennifer Valentine from the eighth-place Notorious independent team. Also from that team were Laura Graziano and Joy Baird, who hooked up with three more riders in Schofer, Melissa Munkwitz, and Catherine LaCrosse to create a new team named Beyond Control. Together, the two teams would alternate finishing 1–2 in 1989 and 1990. In 1989, Team Sprint and Beyond Con-

trol were the only two teams in contention for the title in the closing laps, but Beyond Control held a 15-second lead at lap 96 after a long 19-lap set by Munkwitz and wouldn't be caught (and set a record in winning from the 17th qualifying spot, the lowest ever for a women's champion). Team Sprint would get revenge the following year, winning with just three riders in Middleton, Hellmuth, and Tucker in a race held on the same Saturday as the men's due to rain. While Sigma Nu won on the men's side, ending a two-year greek drought, Team Sprint's win in the women's event was only the second installment in a five-year independent run.

A loss of several riders to graduation killed off the Beyond Control team for 1991, but Munkwitz hooked up with another independent team, Le Pas, which finished fifth in its first race in 1990. For Le Pas, the

Among the many Little 500 personalities in the pits of the 1988 women's race were Kathy Cerajeski, the one-time men's team alternate from 1976 (pictured coaching the Notorious team), and Tom Schwoegler, a former Steering Committee member and coach of the 1983 Acacia winning team. Kappa Alpha Theta's riders chose Schwoegler to work as their coach in 1988, and he's kept the job ever since.

Little 500 was only one of many races it participated in, as the riders were also active in IUCC and USCF Collegiate races. Its top rider, Karen Dunne, was a former IU diver, and on race day she logged the majority of the team's laps as Le Pas won the race in businesslike fashion over pole-sitting Foster-Nirvana and the independent Landsharks. In previous years the women's champions would be honored during the men's race, but Le Pas didn't even stick around for it. Come Saturday they were off to Ohio for another race.

The independent winning streak lasted through 1993 and the Landsharks' back-to-back titles, the first ever in the women's event. Like other independents such as Le Pas, the Landsharks team was founded by dedicated IUCC riders such as Tina Harnett, the sister of 1989 Cinzano men's winner Kendall Harnett (who would coach the team over its first four years). The team finished eighth in its first race in 1990, then rose to third in 1991 with rookie-of-the-year winner Sara Gardner, a sophomore. As a freshman Gardner was proficient not in cycling but in one of the other primary activities of Little 500 weekend—drinking. On Friday night of the 1990 weekend she landed in jail on charges of illegal consumption, possession, and public intoxication. Then on Saturday, she said, she "went back to the dorm for more beer and the men's race." Her mother was unimpressed, and Gardner recalled a firm parental order to "find something more productive to do" over the weekend. So, she talked her mother into buying her a bike.

Gardner knew Harnett from their days at Bloomington South High School, and with a good word from Harnett and Landshark rider Lara Keeley began riding with the team during the 1990–91 school year. After the third-place finish in the 1991 Little 500, Gardner spent the summer traveling with a USCF team that included Le Pas riders Dunne and Munkwitz and Landshark rider Jody Sundt, an experience Gardner credited with helping her build "race smarts." Returning to the Little 500 in 1992 with added confidence, Gardner and teammates Harnett, Keeley, and Andrea Jones found the winning formula—with a little help from other teams' mistakes. The team was leading just past the mid-point of the race, when an accident brought out the yellow flag. An unprecedented five teams near the lead were cited for creeping and given a penalty, and the Landsharks fed off that to build an insurmountable lead

(with the 100-lap format of the women's race, coming back from penalties and accidents was often a difficult, if not impossible task).

Winning proved to be a much more difficult proposition the following year, as Gardner returned to ride without any of her veteran teammates. Focused more on just keeping the team name alive rather than duplicating the 1992 performance, Gardner searched for new teammates. Her search was successful, but Kim Berglund, Julie Schmalz, and Jannine Turner were all rookies, leading Gardner to believe that shooting for a top-10 finish would be more realistic than entertaining thoughts of victory. Not until her coach, Kendall Harnett (who with Tina's victory in 1992 became the only brother-sister winners in Little 500 history), suggested winning did Gardner change her mind. On race day she knew she would have to do most of the work, and ended up doing all that and then some, as on two occasions she made up half-lap deficits to the leaders. With the race still up for grabs going into the final laps, Berglund told Gardner she'd give her a million dollars if she could somehow find the energy to win after already giving a full day's effort. Gardner indeed won at the end, holding off sorority teams Alpha Gamma Delta, Gamma Phi Beta, and the Thetas in a thrilling four-team sprint finish (revealing a higher level of competition in the women's event). She's still waiting for her teammate's money.

Appropriately, when a greek organization finally broke through in 1994 to win the women's Little 500, it was Kappa Alpha Theta standing atop the winner's stand. Its 1987 effort to qualify for the men's race was well known, but so were its struggles in the women's race. Over the first six years Theta annually fielded strong teams, including four polesitters, but never finished first. For 1994 it qualified first for the third consecutive year and won, becoming the first women's team to win with the No. 1 jersey, but not without controversy. Coming into the third turn of the last lap, rivals Alpha Gamma Delta and the Thetas rode neck-and-neck for the title when suddenly the AGD rider, Julie Biros, fell to the cinders—the first time in the history of any Little 500 that a rider in contention went down on the last lap. Biros claimed that the Theta rider, Jocelyn Desmond, had interfered and caused her to fall. A protest filed by AGD was denied by the Student Foundation, but that didn't entirely clear the Thetas, who were never able to completely enjoy their first Little 500 triumph. "We knew [Desmond] didn't do anything," said Julie Beck, a

Comparable to the Cutters in women's Little 500 lore are the independent Landsharks, who in 1992 and 1993 posted the race's first back-to-back titles (pictured in 1993 are Kim Berglund, Julie Schmalz, Jannine Turner and Sara Gardner, with an ESPN reporter). Like the Cutters, the Landsharks found success with talented, well-trained riders participating without a housing unit–level of support.

freshman on the '94 team. "[The protest] was almost like taking away a victory."

The Thetas repeated in 1995 with a much more enjoyable and conventional victory. Beck and Greta Hoetzer, two future Hall of Famers (Hoetzer, a cycling fanatic, pedaled across America in 1998), returned to lead the team over Kappa Kappa Gamma, another rising sorority power. The Kappas sealed their fate in the '95 race when sprinter Gina Murray

exchanged on lap 97 while Hoetzer was in front and at full speed, and three laps proved not enough time to catch up. Murray and her team would redeem themselves in 1996 with a runaway victory in which only one other team, Alpha Chi Omega, finished on the lead lap.

The greek winning streak stopped at three with a win from another rising Little 500 independent, the Roadrunners, at the 10th women's

Appropriately, Kappa Alpha Theta became the first sorority winner in 1994, after years of frustrating high-but-just-short finishes. Four times prior to '94 the team held the pole position but still failed to win, but finally went wire-to-wire on its fifth pole start. With the pressure of not having won firmly off their backs, the Thetas won again in 1995 with a decisive victory over a sorority that would soon win its share of Little 500s, Kappa Kappa Gamma.

race in 1997. Like the Landsharks, the 1993-founded Roadrunners team included top club riders who rode in many other races besides Little 500, giving them a distinct advantage on the Roadmasters. Rounding out the top five, fittingly, were four sorority teams with strong ties to the race's history—Kappa Alpha Theta (pioneers and multiple winners), Phi Mu (one of only four to participate in every race), Alpha Gamma Delta (perennial contenders and two-time runners-up), and Kappa Kappa Gamma (the only other sorority besides Theta to win). Thirty teams in all participated in the '97 race, a testament to the event's strength and

popularity. In many ways, the women's race had evolved even further than the men's race had in its first decade. The women's race, despite a lack of 33-team fields, had just as many if not more competitive teams than the men's—in its first 10 years the women's race had eight different winners, while the men's had six—plus a higher level of skilled riders, as in the 1950s few men rode outside Little 500, but in the 1990s many women competed in other events. To be sure, women had finally found their place in Little 500, not on tricycles but on the cinders.

9. The Price of Popularity

By the beginning of the 1990s, the Student Foundation found itself dealing with an entirely different Little 500 weekend than it had enjoyed at the start of the previous decade. While *Breaking Away* and a new stadium had once given the Student Foundation every reason to continue boasting of Little 500 as "The World's Greatest College Weekend," a rash of problems off the track left the organization and the entire university wondering if its spotlight weekend could survive a severe mid-life crisis.

For the first 30 years of Little 500, entertainment options for the weekend were plentiful. From between star-studded variety shows and concerts to the "sprocket hops" and "ice cream socials," IU students had entertainment options at nearly all hours of the day from Friday to Sunday. Those options, however, began to dwindle in the 1980s as the priorities of students and the Student Foundation began to change. The last true Little 500 Variety Show was in 1981, when entertainer David Letterman and musical group The Spinners performed at the IU Auditorium. It's no small coincidence that by the time Bill Armstrong retired as executive director of the Foundation in 1983, the Variety Show was a memory, as it was mostly his efforts that landed big-name entertainers and mostly his era's students who enjoyed the shows the most. By the end of his 30-year tenure, however, variety shows had become somewhat passé, perhaps most of all on college campuses. At IU, the prime headliners became much more expensive and difficult to land than in the days of Armstrong's personal calls to Bob Hope and others, plus the entertainment choices of students had changed.

During the 1980s music, more than anything else, was the "in" happening among young people, including college students. Rock 'n' roll for years had been a significant part of the college scene, from stadium concerts featuring major recording artists to local bands playing greek houses and campus bars, but the reach of popular music extended even further with the introduction of Music Television—MTV. The cable network gave music fans a new way to enjoy music—through the television screen—and along the way built a reputation as a medium where everything and everyone was "cool." Young people flocked to MTV like birds to a nest, relating to the music, the people, and the message.

With the debut of Music Television—MTV—in the early '80s, college students and all music fans got a new medium for entertainment. In addition to videos MTV was known for its contests and traveling to the "hotspots" for young people. In 1987 and 1988 that included trips to Bloomington for filming of "School's Out Weekend" clips, and among the MTV talent that came along was comedian (and later movie star) Adam Sandler (shown at the 1988 race in the Sigma Phi Epsilon pit). In part because of MTV's influence, the face of the Little 500 weekend would soon change.

MTV established an Indiana tie in the mid-1980s, when it latched on to a rising superstar named John Cougar Mellencamp. The Hoosier rocker's songs sold millions of albums and his videos received substantial air time on MTV, and in 1984 the network staged a creative giveaway where one fan won a pink house (in honor of his late 1983 hit "Pink Houses") near Bloomington's Lake Lemon. Two years later, the network and Mellencamp would team up again, this time over a Little 500 weekend.

At first, MTV and the Little 500 were a perfect match. The Little 500 billed itself as "The World's Greatest College Weekend," and MTV on location from anywhere portrayed itself as a non-stop on-air party. For 1986 the network sponsored "MTV's Ultimate College Weekend with John Cougar Mellencamp" over Little 500 weekend, in conjunction with Mellencamp's last performance on his "Scarecrow" tour, which doubled as the Student Foundation's official "Little 500 Concert." An estimated 43,000 fans filled Memorial Stadium for it, with an additional 10,000 estimated in the parking lots and adjacent streets. From the Student Foundation's standpoint the concert was a big success, as it fit the Saturday night post-race entertainment bill safely for students and outsiders. Impressed with what it saw in 1986, MTV opted to return to Bloomington in 1987 and 1988 to film segments for their "School's Out Weekend" specials, which highlighted parties and activities at various universities.

The Little 500

MTV's first trip to Bloomington, in 1986, was in conjunction with John Cougar Mellencamp's "Scarecrow" tour. His Saturday night show was the official "Little 500 Concert," and one of the single biggest sideshow events in the weekend's history. With 43,000 in the stands and another 10,000 said to be in the parking lots, Mellencamp's show was an overwhelming hit, but unfortunately set a pace that the Student Foundation wouldn't be able to keep up with.

MTV's personalities spent time all over campus and at the race, interviewing various participants and officials (one memorable exchange involved race starter Chappie Blackwell explaining the flags to young comedian Adam Sandler in 1988) while at the same time playing up the entire scene as *the* place to be in the Midwest to party. The Student Foundation loved such publicity at first, but could never have imagined the kind of problems that would eventually come with such a seal of approval from a popular network.

"We underestimated MTV's reach and influence," former Student Foundation Assistant Director Spero Pulos said. Almost overnight, what was once just an IU party weekend became almost a Midwest college student convention, complete with an overabundance of alcohol-fueled mayhem. While some outsiders might have come out of curiosity to see the actual bicycle race and spectacle that was the Little 500, the vast majority came for the other spectacle of the weekend that MTV played up to the hilt—partying. Without question, the Little 500 had plenty of parties through the years all over campus, but those involved mainly IU students celebrating the IU weekend. Some would have run-ins with the law and pay the price, but rarely to the point of mass chaos and property damage. Out-of-town guests, however, were different.

The hot spot for those guests was the off-campus Varsity Villas apartments. Located just across the street from Memorial Stadium on the north end of Bloomington, the Villas complex was one of the largest IU student apartment communities, and among the first ones a visitor driving in from the north would see upon arriving in town. It was an ideal site for partying, with many units spread out over several acres, complete with patios and ample parking for guests, not to mention parking for thousands more in the stadium lots. And with Bill Armstrong Stadium just a short walk away, Varsity Villas was an easy destination for people with no place else to go to congregate after the race.

In 1988, the congregation got out of hand. Bloomington Police Department officers received a call Saturday afternoon, not more than one hour after the Little 500 ended, reporting people firing water balloons with a slingshot into crowds at the Villas. Upon arriving, the police found some 3,000 revelers lined up at the entrance of the complex. To keep the swarm from growing the police halted incoming traffic, but the situation still intensified. As the day turned into night more people

Scenes such as this were all too familiar in 1988 and 1991—arrests at the Varsity Villas apartments. From broad daylight to the early morning hours, revelers would take over the complex and give police and Little 500 officials massive headaches.

gathered in the Villas and more caused trouble, throwing all kinds of objects and tearing down mailboxes and lightposts. One officer got hit in the hand with a flying beer bottle, suffering nerve damage. At 3 A.M. Sunday morning city police called in for reinforcements, including the fire department. Only with a fire truck's hose was order finally restored by 4:30 A.M.

Overall, the arrest counts for the 1988 weekend approached 200, with half of the charged hailing from outside Bloomington. Police and the community realized that the potential of such revelry was just beginning—and would get much worse until preventive measures were taken. Such steps taken for 1989 included closing off Memorial Stadium parking lots and, for the Villas' managers, hiring a security team to keep residents' parties indoors. And the usual police contingent would be out

The Little
500

Indiana Daily Student

22 Pages   25 Cents

Monday, April 25, 1988 Vol. 121 No. 41   Indiana University, Bloomington, IN   © 1988, Indiana Daily Student

Police arrest 5 in Varsity Villas melee

By Terrence O'Hara
Indiana Daily Student

Residents of Varsity Villas, 388 Varsity Lane, use a big slingshot to launch water balloons into the crowd at the complex Saturday.

Campus, city and county law enforcement officers were out in full force Saturday, making a sweep through Varsity Villas in the afternoon in an unsuccessful attempt to disperse Little 500 revelers. Bloomington Police Department officers arrested five people at the complex.

See POLICE, Back page, this section

Shelter helps victim make it on her own

By Sarah A. Mawhorr
Indiana Daily Student

Domestic violence:
An American tradition
Last in a series

See VICTIM, Back page, this section

Ohio administrator named to IU position

By Eric Staats
Indiana Daily Student

See WILSON, Back page, this section

Cutters, Willkie Sprint steal Little 500 gold

Accidents, injuries test riders' stamina

By Mike Stephenson
Indiana Daily Student

Senior Jay Polsgrove of The Cutters rejoices after sprinting to victory in Saturday's Little 500 race.

See WIND, Back page, this section

Team avoids early danger to win first women's crown

By Mike Stephenson
Indiana Daily Student

See FATIGUE, Back page, this section

INSIDE

CAMPUS
IU President Thomas Ehrlich and other University officials plan to meet with representatives of the Black Student Union today to discuss ways to improve racial tensions on campus. PAGE 3

CITY/STATE
General Electric's local refrigerator assembly plant will hire 100 workers to help the company keep up with increasing product demand. PAGE 15

ARTS
Queen Ida Guillory and the Bon Temps Zydeco Band delivered a royal performance filled with Cajun-Creole tunes to weekend concertgoers at Beyond Story. PAGE 22

OUTSIDE

Partly sunny and warmer today. High in the low to middle 60s. Partly cloudy tonight with the low 45 to 50. Mostly cloudy Tuesday with a 40 percent chance of showers. High in the middle to upper 60s.

Arts   17   Comics   3
Campus   3   Opinion   8
City/State   15   Sports
Classifieds   18   World/Nation   7

---

in force, from local and campus police to state excise authorities, all with a slightly more focused eye toward the potential trouble spots such as the Villas.

Thanks to such precautions, the 1989 and 1990 Little 500 weekends were tamer, with lower numbers of arrests and complaints, and no major incidents. A university crackdown against on-campus drinking also proved successful, as big party areas such as greek houses began screening guests and keeping all activities indoors and out of sight of police and patrolling deans (though not all fraternities were successful—in 1990 Alpha Tau Omega and Sigma Phi Epsilon were busted for alcohol violations, and its bike teams were removed from the race). But just when it looked as if the weekend was beginning to return to a sane level, another night of destruction reared up and threatened the future of the Little 500.

The 1991 race weekend was quite cool, temperature-wise, but that didn't keep off-campus partygoers at bay. Early Sunday morning police were called to Varsity Villas to break up yet another mob scene involving hundreds of drunken students' assaults on property. Before the police could arrive one tenant's Cadillac Cimarron had already been flipped 30 feet across a parking lot, other cars had been pounced on and vandalized, and street signs and lightposts were dismantled and bent. Unlike previous years, however, the throng was not easily dispersed by police. "In 1988 people went inside when we came," one officer told the Bloomington *Herald-Times*. "They didn't go inside this year." The apartment complex's hired security couldn't control the violence, and officers equipped with riot gear needed more than an hour to take control of the area. Other incidents were reported at nearby complexes such as Walnut Knolls apartments, where dumpsters and couches were set on fire, and the total arrest figures neared 500, an all-time high.

At the Monroe County Justice Building, the Monday after the weekend turned into what one court reporter called "The World's Greatest College Arraignment." A total of 411 people showed up that day for initial court appearances, almost as many as the previous three years *combined*. Most qualified for a pretrial diversion program, which involved paying a fine and attending alcohol education classes (later years' programs included hard labor such as trash pick-up) in exchange for drop-

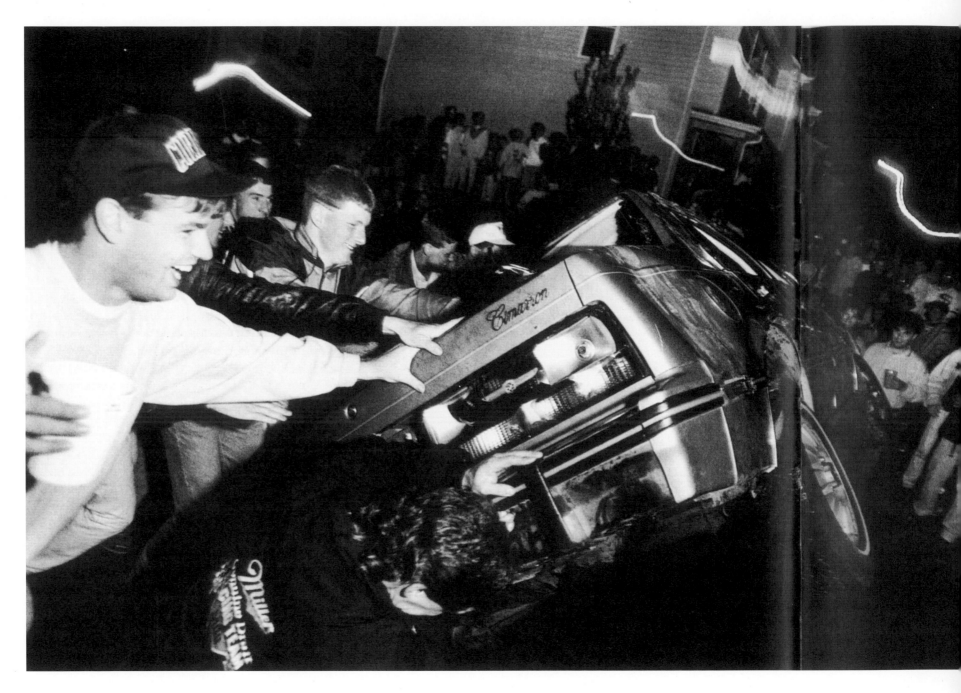

The Little
500

ping of charges. Again, many of the accused were out-of-towners with no ties to IU, with one police officer estimating that 75 percent of all troublesome Little 500 partiers hailed from outside Bloomington.

This time, understandably, everyone had seen enough. Such behavior over a Little 500 weekend was a huge embarrassment for everyone from residents to IU students and administrators—and if anyone needed a reminder of what happened they could pick up a copy of the Monday post-race issue of the *Daily Student,* which featured a five-column, front-page photo of the infamous overturned car episode. The photo was printed at the top of the page above the coverage of the bike races, revealing the prominence partying had taken on in the overall scope of the weekend, and became the lasting symbol of Little 500 destruction. (It also landed the photographer, Richard Schultz, in the middle of a First Amendment dispute. Police demanded he give up some of his pictures so they could identify suspects, and Schultz refused on the basis of press freedom. A judge didn't agree, forcing Schultz to give up the photos, which police used to identify and charge two of the suspects in the car photo. "If I had known it would be so much trouble, I wouldn't have printed it," Schultz said later.) Fueled by such memories, a task force was created.

A group of all parties concerned, including students, faculty, law enforcement, the Dean of Students office, Foundation and Student Foundation officials gathered in the months after the 1991 weekend to discuss options on how to prevent future incidents. "We asked, 'How do we send a message that it's not business as usual?'" said Richard McKaig, Associate Dean of Students in 1991. "Though what happened was bad, it still had the potential to be much, much worse. That couldn't be allowed." The task force initially raised all sorts of suggestions about moving the race—to a weekday or even back to the fall semester to avoid the

Readers of the Monday post-race issue of the Daily Student *in 1991were treated to this infamous photo of Little 500 destruction. The image of the flipped car would stay fresh in the minds of city and university officials for a long time, and the subsequent changes made to the Little 500 weekend were swift and severe.*

crowds—but once convinced the Little 500 was fine in its traditional spot on the calendar, it turned to the questions of how to occupy the starved-for-activity fans. That was normally where the Student Foundation came in, but since 1986 it had not been able to duplicate the success of the Mellencamp concert. In lieu of a big-name act, the Student Foundation created "Little 5 Live" in 1987, held immediately after the men's race at a practice field adjacent to the stadium. That event included several smaller bands, and did attract fans' attention but still left them free at night. Students who still yearned for the nationally known, nighttime show simply satisfied their cravings for action elsewhere—such as in the Varsity Villas.

To be fair, no one would have known for sure if concerts could indeed have prevented the 1988 and 1991 disturbances, but for 1992 the Student Foundation decided to load up the weekend with alternative activities in hopes of occupying the masses. Mellencamp was brought back for another Saturday night show, and a Band Extravaganza was added for late Friday night after the Mini 500. The police, however, opted not to take any chances and instituted a "zero tolerance" policy for the weekend. As Monroe County deputy prosecutor Mary Ellen Diekhoff said in 1993 in the *Daily Student,* "if you've got a beer in your hand and you've taken two sips and an officer sees you, you're going to jail." That was the essence of the policy, and more officers than ever were on hand starting in 1992 to enforce it—full squads of city and county police, state excise, and Indiana State police from as far as Evansville and Gary. The Student Foundation voluntarily paid for the extra police power and tried to distance itself from the party and MTV image with a change of its long-time slogan, opting for the more vanilla "Cycling, Scholarships, Tradition" over "The World's Greatest College Weekend."

The task force's efforts were successful, as the 1992 Little 500 weekend was much calmer and peaceful than 1991's. Police were happy to report that "only" 265 people were arrested, comparing the weekend's problems to those of a regular home football weekend. Light rain and Mellencamp helped relax the Saturday night crowds, and the Villas residents enjoyed a peaceful night with their cars and other property intact. Students, however, had mixed feelings about the increased law presence, specifically denouncing the police helicopter that hovered

Conceding the fact that giant Mellencamp-like shows would not be possible year after year, the Student Foundation created sideshows such as "Little 5 Live" in 1987 (pictured) and a Band Extravaganza to help fill the post-race entertainment needs of fans. Such shows featured many bands but few household names, and as a pacifier for rowdy students the events were never truly successful.

above campus all weekend. Many had to even answer to Mom and Dad, as the task force sent a letter to the parents of all undergraduates explaining the "need for appropriate behavior during the weekend."

Police squads remained at high levels in 1993 and 1994 and the weekends continued to be quieter—not only because of the lack of outsiders but also in part due to an exodus of some IU students. After 1991 some apartment dwellers started leaving town over the weekend for fear of damage to their property, and even in years after order was restored most still found staying away from Bloomington easier than staying home and being watched by the police (another option was to go

to the bars, but Little 500 weekend on Kirkwood Avenue was no picnic either). A *Daily Student* reporter spent Saturday night of the 1994 weekend out with a group of five Bloomington police officers assigned to patrol Walnut Knolls and adjacent apartments (all near the Varsity Villas), and saw no activity at all. Parking lots were empty, courtyards once filled in years past with parties were lifeless, and in one apartment tenants were quietly enjoying sodas and a game of Monopoly. The officers wrote no citations and made no arrests. "I'm ashamed to have gone to this university," one officer joked. The 1991 problems were only three years removed, but felt like ancient history.

The Student Foundation was pleased to see order restored, but the increased regulation of the weekend ended up destroying its bottom line. In 1992 it paid $150,000 for the Mellencamp show and absorbed the costs of the other concerts and the added police power, then got a rude awakening at the turnstiles of the men's Little 500—its main source of revenue—when only 16,411 spectators attended. Before 1991, crowds at or near 30,000 were the norm for the men's event, but the incidents and subsequent task force solutions ultimately drove out some of the race's customers in out-of-town guests and some IU students (bad weather also played a supporting role). The cycling and the post-race parties were never meant to be related, but they were inevitably intertwined when it came to race attendance—Little 500 as "The World's Greatest College Weekend," with national exposure and abundant opportunities for revelry drew the big crowds, but the tempered "Cycling, Scholarships, Tradition" atmosphere couldn't. Student Foundation officials knew they could not tolerate the destruction and community anger in exchange for a large race gate, but consequently realized that with a tamer weekend, the larger crowds were likely gone forever.

Such events as Little 5 Live and the Band Extravaganza were supported and encouraged by the task force as activities to keep the potentially difficult race fans busy, but with the task force's increased police

presence those fans weren't coming anymore anyway. In 1993 the Student Foundation still put on the Band Extravaganza and a Little 500 concert (with the BoDeans and local group The Why Store), and suffered another financial loss on the weekend. Scholarship monies were not affected, as a "rainy day" plan started with proceeds from the super-profitable 1986 Mellencamp show took care of those funds, but the Student Foundation was forced to get out of the concert business in order to sustain the financial viability of its primary events, the bicycle races. Not until they did that and faced the reality of the new Little 500 weekend did they begin making money again in 1995, despite a men's race crowd of 11,672—the lowest in 41 years.

As if the issues with unruly fans and expenses weren't enough for the Student Foundation in the early 1990s, it also had to deal with competition questions in the men's Little 500. In 1989 the Cinzano team pulled off their Cinderella win and in 1990 Sigma Nu returned to the winners' stand for the first time in 33 years, but such triumphs were isolated cases in the overall Little 500 arena. For the most part, the race was becoming increasingly dominated by near–professional caliber riders.

Three races from 1991 to 1993 all featured compelling stories, but mostly involved the same teams. In 1991 Acacia won its third title just two seconds ahead of the Cutters, on the strength of rider Pete Noverr (notable in third was a new team named Team College Life, for which one of its riders, Mike Lantz, rode some 165 laps). The Cutters won their fourth race in nine years in 1992 in blowout fashion, lapping competitors Acacia, Cinzano, and Delta Chi, as anchor Demetri Hubbard heroically rode with a broken scapula suffered in a lap 15 accident. Delta Chi and Cinzano played out the closest finish in race history in 1993, as Todd Hancock edged Ben Sharp by two-tenths of a second at the line (Cinzano protested and the Student Foundation got burned by failing to have photo-finish equipment on hand, but fortu-

Twelve years after the end of its dynasty era, Delta Chi returned to the winners' stand in 1993 with a record eighth Little 500 victory (from left are Christian Reed, Neal Stoeckel, Todd Hancock, Scott Hallberg, Jeff Allman and coach Steve Hoeferle). Starting the race from the pole with a very good team made Delta Chi fans confident—the "1993 Little 500 Champions" shirts were worn by fans underneath other shirts, and when the win was sealed the shirts were revealed.

In winning the 1994 Little 500, Sigma Chi's Randy Spruill made history twice. He gave his fraternity its first ever win, but also became the last USCF-certified "Category Two" rider to win. The Student Foundation enacted a rule outlawing such a class of advanced cyclists, in the process hurting some teams which over time had come to depend on the elite riders. Officials hoped the eligibility ruling would help competition, and ultimately it would indeed.

nately had a conclusive video replay) to put Delta Chi on top in the all-time race win standings with eight.

The common theme throughout the three races was the same group of four teams, as Acacia, Cinzano, Cutters, and Delta Chi each finished in the top four at least twice. Student Foundation officials saw reason for concern, as principal riders such as Noverr, Hubbard, Hancock, and Sharp all brought professional-level riding skills to the event. All were ranked as U.S. Cycling Federation "Category Two" riders, meaning that through many outside races they had displayed near pro-caliber ability. In the Little 500's earlier years such riders also competed and excelled, but for the most part gave the Student Foundation little reason for concern as participation and attendance remained high. But in the late 1980s the number of teams coming out for the race began to slide, down from 50 in 1982 to 39 in 1987 and eventually to an all-time low of 34 in 1992 and 1993. In its salad years the Little 500 could count on dozens of dorm floors from all over campus to enter teams, but those entrants were long gone, survived only by traditional power Dodds House and a few other assorted groups. Even some fraternities were losing interest—in 1992 Beta Theta Pi, participants in 35 of the first 41 races, made news by plainly stating the interest wasn't in the house for a team. Such thoughts from greek teams, long the mainstays of the race, revealed the level of the problem.

Explanations for the drop in participation could be attributed to a number of causes, from the expense of cycling to the same lack of interest that kept fans away in 1992 and 1993, but the Student Foundation believed that the untouchable nature of the top teams was a primary culprit. Few teams would want to ride, organizers thought, if they were destined from the outset to finish behind teams whose members far outdistanced them in ability. If some riders had become strong after years of exclusive Little 500 racing, that was fine to the Student Foundation, but riders who were getting their seasoning from top-level outside races held a distinctly unfair advantage.

For 1994, the Student Foundation went on the offensive in an effort to reverse the trend of the competition. It announced that the '94 race would be the last one in which USCF-certified "Category Two" riders would be allowed to compete, and that starting in 1995 all riders still holding such designations would be ineligible to ride. Predictably, the rider community did not take the news well. "Riders were never going to get behind [the rule], and it's not hard to understand," said Ken Sloo, Student Foundation assistant director from 1993 to 1996. "They thought the Little 500 existed to name the champion riders of IU—not to raise scholarships or leadership opportunities." With all the problems earlier in the decade, the Student Foundation desperately wanted to return the event to an intramural level and focus attention back on the track, and felt that in the long run such a rule would help reach that goal.

At the 1994 race the reasoning for the new rule revealed its validity again as yet another team, Sigma Chi, won the race with a USCF-certified "Category Two" rider in senior Randy Spruill. Only 36 teams attempted to qualify for the race. The Student Foundation was further scarred that year by two rider disputes, as Art Keith of the Cutters and Bryce Zoeller of Sigma Alpha Epsilon sued for the opportunity to ride in the race. (Keith was ruled ineligible due to a high ranking in the National Off-Road Bicycle Association and Zoeller was held out due to his graduate student status.) Both men lost their suits, but not before further soiling the Student Foundation's reputation. In the end, the organization could only cross its fingers for 1995 and hope that its new eligibility rule, once implemented, would bring a change for the better.

Epilogue: The Little 500 at 50

Redemption was sweet for the Student Foundation at the 1995 Men's Little 500, when a six-team sprint finish vindicated its controversial decision to ban the pro-caliber riders. The "Cat Two Rule" eliminated only 12 men, in effect crippling teams such as Cinzano and the Cutters, but also gave other teams a shot at the title. The six in contention at the end in 1995—Acacia, Delta Chi, Dodds House, Phi Delta Theta, Phi Gamma Delta, and Sigma Alpha Epsilon—represented a more healthy balance of recent race powers and teams longing for a return to the top spot. Sprinter Cory Lewis and his Fiji team won the battle, but ultimately the Student Foundation won the war in returning the Little 500 to its intramural roots.

The 1996 race again included several teams in contention in the final laps, with Phi Delta Theta prevailing with a daring strategy. Three of its riders, Mike Krueger, Joel McKay, and Dan Possley, rode two-lap sets over the last eight laps, gradually pulling away from pursuers. A botched exchange at any time would have spelled doom, but the team pulled it off en route to its second Little 500 win. In 1997 the Cutters rejuvenated themselves again, winning a fifth title after a near-photo sprint finish with Fiji. Unlike their independent rivals Cinzano, who failed to ride in 1995 then struggled to finish in the top half of the fields in '96 and '97 after the new rule, the Cutters adjusted and were able to ride as champions without the high-level riders coveted in prior years—just what the Student Foundation had hoped for when it implemented the new eligibility standard.

However, while the rule served its purpose in returning the race to a fairer, amateur-based level, it has yet to boost the number of race entrants or spectators, as organizers had also hoped it might. Indeed, the attendance figures haven't approached 20,000 since the police crackdown of the early 1990s, and the number of men's bike teams registering for the race hasn't exceeded the 34–36 range, making qualifications day much less suspenseful. In some ways, the Little 500 mystique has diminished.

Gone from the present-day Little 500 are the overflow crowds, many of the unique sideshows, and visits from the national media—but also

While the Little 500 weekends of today are different from those of the past, some constants on the track never change: the accidents (this 1991 incident felled 11 riders), the glory (Dave Harstad and his 1995 Fiji brothers celebrating in the infield) and the heartache (in 1989, this Collins rider was down and out).

gone are the IU student bodies of previous generations, namely, the ones that lifted the Little 500 to its greatest heights. Today's Student Foundation directors and students are faced with questions their predecessors never had to answer, questions of how to get more of the campus involved in an event that once had almost *too* many volunteers and participants. "The event should sell itself," laments Student Foundation Assistant Director Mike Foote, a former Dodds House rider who today has the unenviable job of recruiting Little 500 teams. "Either we're not doing things right or there's too much apathy in students."

University administrators prefer not to hear words like "apathy" being used in conjunction with students' lack of interest in the school's activities, but in the case of the Little 500 that word, at least partially, does indeed apply. One major difference between students of today and those of 25-plus years ago is in living patterns, as many current upperclassmen now seek housing off campus, and those students are rarely involved in Student Foundation activities—as is evidenced in the low number of off-campus independent cycling teams (and few teams usually means few fans from those areas). From the 1950s into the 1970s nearly all students lived on campus, either in the dorms or greek houses, and therefore stayed a little more directly connected to university groups like the Student Foundation. Today, the off-campus apartments at Little 500 time are more known as centers of partying than support for the actual event.

However, it should be noted that the Student Foundation has also lost some ground on campus as well. "Diversity" is the buzzword for the turn of the century IU campus, with students from all sorts of backgrounds being involved in an almost infinite number of organizations. To say a student has more opportunities for leadership and personal growth today than just ten years ago is a gross understatement, much less 40 years ago. As a result, today's Student Foundation at-large membership numbers are a fraction of what they once were. The organization continues to boast high levels of participation from greek

students, but greeks are not as prevalent at IU as they once were. Dormitory students also are proving elusive to the Student Foundation, especially in terms of bicycle teams. In the 1980 Little 500, for example, five bicycle teams from Willkie *alone* started the race, along with nine other dorm teams for a total of 14. Fifteen years later, in 1995, there were only three dorm teams. Various reasons cited for the lack of dorm participation have included financial problems, lack of organization among units, and, again, apathy.

Today's Student Foundation yearns to welcome back such teams, and is finding some success by returning the Little 500 to its roots as a bicycling-only event. Student Foundation Director Randy Rogers states, with a hint of pride, that the organization is "out of the music business" and instead focused fully on the participatory activities of Little 500. From a bicycling perspective, students now have more opportunities than ever to develop and use bicycling skills, as the Student Foundation has enlarged its circle of events to include a fall biathlon and an off-road challenge, in addition to the springtime Little 500 "series" events and races. The organization even runs a spring break camp for teams lacking the resources to train out of town over the holiday. Such an emphasis on cycling has even brought in some big national cycling names, such as Lance Armstrong in 1997. He marveled at the speeds achieved on the fixed-gear Roadmasters, and the enthusiasm generated by the supportive fans. And the national media, though not as prevalent on-site as they once were, are still aware of the Little 500 and its unique place in collegiate culture. In 1997 *Sports Illustrated* declared it to be the country's "Greatest Intramural Event."

All in all, the Student Foundation's new focus on cycling appears to be working. The women's race continued its fast growth in 1998 as a record 32 teams entered the 11th Women's Little 500, and its finish was

After nearly 50 years of history, three men stand above all others in Little 500 lore—Bill Armstrong, Dave Blase and Howdy Wilcox (from left to right, in 1980). Wilcox was the inventor, Armstrong was the innovator and Blase was the race's most influential rider, having been the inspiration for the movie that brought worldwide glory to Indiana and the Little 500.

the closest ever, as Kappa Kappa Gamma's Lisa Roessler edged Chi Omega's Lindsey Hawkins at the line by one-tenth of a second. On the men's side Dodds House won, pulling off a feat many had considered impossible in the present-day Little 500 power structure. Not since 1955, when South Cottage Grove won had a residence hall team taken the checkered flag, and it appeared as if the fraternity and independent dominance had no end in sight. But Dodds House was one dorm unit

that had survived the test of time in Little 500, fielding teams in the first 26 races and 46 of 48 races overall, and for 1998 had built one of the best teams in the entire field. The foursome of Jon Foote, Alex Ihnen, Greg O'Brien, and Jonathan Purvis won the pole and the race, in the process exonerating a lifetime of Little 500 demons that had haunted countless Dodds men, from Mike Foote (Jon's brother) to Mike Howard to Curt Simic—all of whom watched with joy from the infield that day.

Among the well-wishers on the winners' stand to congratulate the Dodds men was Bill Armstrong, the longtime Foundation executive director and the Little 500's biggest fan. He remembered better than anyone the years when Dodds House was one of many strong dorm teams gunning for a title, when nearly every IU student supported the event and the Student Foundation with unbridled passion. Through his efforts the Little 500 grew from a bike race to "The World's Greatest College Weekend," with fanfare unlike anything else the university had ever seen. Near the end of his tenure at the Foundation he helped the Little 500 make it to the big screen with *Breaking Away*, and into a new campus home that would bear his name. He had seen, either up front or from a distance, the weekend reach its highest highs and its lowest lows, and no matter what still survive to ride another year. He proudly proclaimed that the race would always go on, even long after he crossed the finish line.

With a visit to Bill Armstrong Stadium, fans today can still catch glimpses of race history in various race personnel. Chappie Blackwell participated in the first Little 500 for Sigma Alpha Epsilon and has been to every race but one since, serving in many of them as assistant or head starter. He'll continue to work as head starter through the 50th men's race in 2000, before handing the flags to his son, Chap Blackwell IV. Easy to spot in the infield are former Dodds House men Mike Howard (at left in above right photo) and Curt Simic (right), two who especially enjoyed Dodds' triumphant 1998 victory. Howard, a Hall-of-Fame rider in the 1970s, has served as the chief steward since 1983, and former rider Simic has served the Foundation and Student Foundation in many capacities, most recently as President of the Foundation. Another former rider and Student Foundation director, Jerry Tardy, today serves as IU Alumni Association Executive Director and still drives the Little 500 pace car, a job he's held since the filming of Breaking Away.

The inherent goals of the Little 500 have remained unchanged for nearly five decades: create strong, productive alumni for the future, and raise scholarship funds for current working students (pictured, the scholarship class of 1973).

(Opposite) In 1998 the Dodds House team won its first Little 500, returning a dorm team to the winner's stand for the first time since 1955. Whether the win will become a catalyst for other dorm teams to build Dodds-like traditions remains to be seen, but for Greg O'Brien (with bike) and his teammates, one day's work exorcised the demons of a half-century of Dodds frustration in the Little 500.

Sadly, that day came on July 17, 1998, when IU and the Little 500 lost its greatest ambassador.

Armstrong was always proudest of the people involved in the Little 500 weekends, and those people remain its legacy as the event moves toward its 50th year and beyond. As a whole, even with some of the recent setbacks and roadblocks, the event's history displays a dazzling trail of achievement. The Little 500 races have welcomed over 12,000 riders, a great many of whom proclaimed the experience as one of the most enjoyable activities of their college lives. Its governing body, the vener-

able Student Foundation, has given thousands more the opportunity to lead and grow as students and, later, become valuable university alumni. And thousands of dollars in scholarship money, the foundation on which the event was started by Howdy Wilcox, continue to be awarded each year. Pedaling into the 21st century and approaching the one million mark in attendance, the spring tradition remains one of Indiana University's most recognizable entities, one that has already seen its early generations' children and will soon see their children.

The Little 500 rides on.

The Little
500

Appendix A: Little 500 Race Results, 1951–1999

The Men's Little 500

(races Saturdays except where noted)

1951
May 12 • Memorial Stadium

1. SOUTH HALL BUCCANEERS
   (2 hours, 38 minutes)
2. Sigma Alpha Epsilon
3. Phi Gamma Delta
4. Rogers East V
5. Lambda Chi Alpha
6. North Hall Friars
7. Zeta Beta Tau
8. Phi Kappa Psi
9. Beta Theta Pi
10. (tie) Phi Delta Theta
        Sigma Pi
12. Dodds House
13. Delta Upsilon
14. Theta Chi
15. Alpha Tau Omega
16. South Hall B
17. Sigma Nu
18. Elliott House
19. North Hall Cavaliers
20. Ferguson House
21. Nichols House
22. Delta Tau Delta
23. Phi Sigma Kappa
24. Rogers West T
25. Acacia
26. Alpha Phi Alpha
27. Kappa Sigma
28. Kappa Delta Rho
29. Pi Lambda Phi
30. Pi Kappa Alpha
31. Parks House
32. Jenkins House
33. Hummer House

1952
May 10 • Memorial Stadium

1. NORTH HALL FRIARS
   (2:26:06)
2. Rogers East V
3. Phi Kappa Psi
4. Phi Delta Theta
5. Alpha Tau Omega
6. Zeta Beta Tau
7. Sigma Chi
8. Kappa Sigma
9. Sigma Pi
10. Dodds House
11. South Hall B
12. Todd House
13. North Hall Cavaliers
14. Rogers East W
15. Pi Kappa Phi
16. Lowe House
17. Rogers West W
18. West Hall III Trojans
19. Hummer House
20. Nichols House
21. Theta Chi
22. North Hall Barons
23. Lambda Chi Alpha
24. Phi Kappa Tau
25. Kappa Delta Rho
26. Alpha Phi Alpha
27. Beta Theta Pi
28. Theta Xi
29. Rogers West V
30. South Hall Buccaneers
31. Sigma Alpha Mu
32. Campbell House
33. Pi Kappa Alpha

1953
May 9 • Memorial Stadium

1. NORTH HALL FRIARS
   (2:28:28)
2. Acacia
3. Sigma Alpha Epsilon
4. Delta Upsilon
5. Phi Kappa Psi
6. Phi Delta Theta
7. Alpha Tau Omega
8. Zeta Beta Tau
9. Phi Gamma Delta
10. Sigma Pi
11. Phi Kappa
12. Phi Sigma Kappa
13. Sigma Nu
14. Kappa Delta Rho
15. West Hall IV
16. West Hall II
17. Pi Kappa Alpha
18. South Hall B
19. Beta Theta Pi
20. Dodds House
21. North Hall Cavaliers
22. Kappa Sigma
23. Lambda Chi Alpha
24. Todd House
25. Delta Tau Delta
26. Rogers East W
27. Lowe House
28. Ruter House
29. Sigma Chi
30. Sigma Phi Epsilon
31. Theta Chi
32. Hummer House
33. Jenkins House

1954
May 8 • Memorial Stadium

1. SIGMA NU
   (2:45:35)
2. Acacia
3. Alpha Tau Omega
4. North Hall Barons
5. Phi Delta Theta
6. Todd House
7. Phi Gamma Delta
8. Delta Chi
9. Dodds House
10. Phi Kappa
11. Sigma Pi
12. North Hall Friars
13. Sigma Alpha Epsilon
14. Phi Kappa Psi
15. Lambda Chi Alpha
16. Alpha Phi Alpha
17. Dunn House
18. Rogers West W
19. Delta Upsilon
20. Theta Chi
21. South Hall B
22. Sigma Chi
23. Kappa Delta Rho
24. Sigma Alpha Mu
25. Beta Theta Pi
26. Zeta Beta Tau
27. Pi Kappa Phi
28. Delta Tau Delta
29. Tau Kappa Epsilon
30. Harding House
31. Jenkins House
32. Phi Sigma Kappa
33. Parks House

1955
May 14 • Memorial Stadium

1. SOUTH COTTAGE GROVE
   (2:36:25)
2. West Hall Trojans
3. Delta Chi
4. Acacia
5. North Hall Barons
6. Sigma Nu
7. Phi Gamma Delta
8. Dodds House
9. Phi Delta Theta
10. Phi Kappa Psi
11. Sigma Pi
12. Rollins House
13. Hickory Hall West
14. Sigma Alpha Epsilon
15. Ruter House
16. Zeta Beta Tau
17. Hickory Hall East
18. Kappa Sigma
19. Kappa Delta Rho
20. Rogers I
21. Phi Kappa
22. Sigma Phi Epsilon
23. Pi Lambda Phi
24. Delta Tau Delta
25. Parks House
26. Alpha Tau Omega
27. West Hall Saints
28. Lambda Chi Alpha
29. Elliott House
30. Sigma Alpha Mu
31. Phi Sigma Kappa
32. Theta Chi
33. Delta Upsilon

1956
May 12 • Memorial Stadium

1. PHI GAMMA DELTA
   (2:31:13)
2. Dodds House
3. South Cottage Grove
4. Delta Chi
5. Sigma Nu

6. North Hall Barons
7. Sigma Pi
8. Acacia
9. Kappa Delta Rho
10. Phi Delta Theta
11. Phi Kappa Psi
12. Delta Upsilon
13. Laurel Hall North
14. Maple Hall North
15. Rollins House
16. Rogers I
17. Sigma Alpha Epsilon
18. Ruter House
19. West Hall II
20. Tau Kappa Epsilon
21. Dunn House
22. West Hall Trojans
23. Kappa Sigma
24. Sigma Chi
25. Alpha Tau Omega
26. Hickory Hall West
27. Parks House
28. Maple Hall South
29. South Hall A
30. Theta Chi
31. Hall House
32. Theta Xi
33. North Hall Cavaliers

1957
May 11 • Memorial Stadium

1. SIGMA NU
   (2:19:56)
2. Dodds House
3. Acacia
4. Phi Delta Theta
5. Delta Chi
6. Phi Gamma Delta
7. Alpha Tau Omega
8. Sigma Pi
9. Ruter House
10. Delta Upsilon
11. South Cottage Grove
12. North Hall Barons
13. Tau Kappa Epsilon
14. Phi Kappa Psi

15. West Hall Saints
16. Kappa Sigma
17. Sigma Chi
18. Rollins House
19. Maple Hall North
20. South Hall Buccaneers
21. Delta Tau Delta
22. Kappa Delta Rho
23. Elliott House
24. Lambda Chi Alpha
25. Todd House
26. Dunn House
27. Zeta Beta Tau
28. Nichols House
29. Hall House
30. West Hall Trojans
31. Sigma Alpha Mu
32. Parks House
33. Theta Xi

1958
May 10 • Memorial Stadium

1. PHI KAPPA PSI
   (2:17:23)
2. Sigma Nu
3. Phi Gamma Delta
4. Delta Upsilon
5. Sigma Alpha Epsilon
6. West Hall II
7. South Cottage Grove
8. Phi Delta Theta
9. Acacia
10. Sigma Pi
11. Chi Phi
12. Alpha Tau Omega
13. Tau Kappa Epsilon
14. South Hall Buccaneers
15. Delta Chi
16. Beta Theta Pi
17. Dodds House
18. Rollins House
19. Kappa Delta Rho
20. Ferguson House
21. North Hall Barons
22. Delta Tau Delta
23. Hickory Hall West

24. Kappa Kappa Psi
25. Kappa Sigma
26. Lambda Chi Alpha
27. Sigma Alpha Mu
28. Rogers V
29. Harding House
30. Zeta Beta Tau
31. Hall House
32. Laurel Hall
33. Ruter House

1959
May 9 • Memorial Stadium

1. PHI KAPPA PSI
   (2:25:02)
2. Sigma Alpha Epsilon
3. Sigma Nu
4. Chi Phi
5. Acacia
6. Phi Gamma Delta
7. Lambda Chi Alpha
8. Ferguson
9. Dodds House
10. Rollins House
11. Phi Delta Theta
12. Pi Kappa Phi
13. Linden Hall West
14. Delta Chi
15. Dunn House
16. Sigma Chi
17. Theta Chi
18. Sigma Phi Epsilon
19. Delta Upsilon
20. South Hall Buccaneers
21. North Hall Friars
22. Beta Theta Pi
23. Alpha Tau Omega
24. Ruter House
25. Todd House
26. Zeta Beta Tau
27. Hickory Hall West
28. Sigma Pi
29. West Hall Trojans
30. Phi Sigma Kappa
31. Delta Tau Delta
32. Kappa Sigma
33. Sigma Alpha Mu

1960
May 14 • Tenth Street Stadium*

1. PHI KAPPA PSI
   (2:21:47)
2. Sigma Alpha Epsilon
3. Lambda Chi Alpha
4. Sigma Nu
5. Phi Gamma Delta
6. Chi Phi
7. Alpha Tau Omega
8. Acacia
9. Dunn House
10. Delta Chi
11. Dodds House
12. Delta Upsilon
13. Sigma Phi Epsilon
14. Campbell House
15. Sigma Chi
16. Beta Theta Pi
17. Towers Center B
18. Forest Hall
19. Pi Kappa Phi
20. Zeta Beta Tau
21. Phi Sigma Kappa
22. Kappa Delta Rho
23. Harding House
24. Ruter House
25. Sigma Pi
26. Ferguson House
27. Sigma Alpha Mu
28. Delta Tau Delta
29. Theta Chi
30. Kappa Sigma
31. Elliott House
32. Lower Linden
Qualified but did not race:
Phi Delta Theta

*Formerly Memorial Stadium, known
as Tenth Street Stadium after
construction of new Memorial Stadium*

1961
May 13 • Tenth Street Stadium

1. ACACIA
   (2:22:16)

2. Phi Gamma Delta
3. Phi Kappa Psi
4. Lambda Chi Alpha
5. Beta Theta Pi
6. Sigma Phi Epsilon
7. Sigma Nu
8. Phi Delta Theta
9. Sigma Alpha Epsilon
10. Dodds House
11. Sigma Chi
12. Chi Phi
13. Zeta Beta Tau
14. Kappa Delta Rho
15. Delta Tau Delta
16. Walnut Hall
17. Stockwell House
18. Kappa Sigma
19. Delta Upsilon
20. Theta Chi
21. Normal College
22. Alpha Tau Omega
23. Laurel Hall
24. Campbell House
25. Forest Hall
26. Dunn House
27. Parks House
28. Delta Chi
29. Tau Kappa Epsilon
30. Alpha Epsilon Pi
31. Maple Hall North
32. Hall House
Qualified but did not race:
Phi Sigma Kappa

1962
May 12 • Tenth Street Stadium

1. PHI KAPPA PSI
   (2:17:26)
2. Sigma Alpha Epsilon
3. Phi Gamma Delta
4. Chi Phi
5. Acacia
6. Alpha Tau Omega
7. Beta Theta Pi
8. Phi Delta Theta
9. Edmondson II
10. Sigma Nu

11. Sigma Phi Epsilon
12. Lambda Chi Alpha
13. Walnut Hall
14. Delta Chi
15. Towers D–2
16. Zeta Beta Tau
17. Delta Tau Delta
18. Laurel Hall
19. Dodds House
20. Kappa Delta Rho
21. Delta Upsilon
22. Kappa Sigma
23. Phi Kappa Tau
24. Ferguson House
25. Sigma Pi
26. Phi Kappa Theta
27. Forest Hall
28. Campbell House
29. Theta Chi
30. Stockwell House
31. Elliott House
32. Sigma Chi
33. Parks House

1963
May 11 • Tenth Street Stadium

1. SIGMA ALPHA EPSILON
   (2:17:04)
2. Alpha Tau Omega
3. Acacia
4. Phi Gamma Delta
5. Beta Theta Pi
6. Dodds House
7. Edmondson II
8. Laurel Hall
9. Phi Kappa Psi
10. Kappa Delta Rho
11. Chi Phi
12. Phi Delta Theta
13. Sigma Nu
14. Sigma Chi
15. Sigma Phi Epsilon
16. Parks House
17. Jenkins House
18. Tau Kappa Epsilon
19. Zeta Beta Tau
20. Forest (Goodbody)

21. Walnut Hall
22. Lambda Chi Alpha
23. Delta Chi
24. Kappa Sigma
25. Delta Tau Delta
26. Edmondson IV
27. Sigma Pi
28. Delta Upsilon
29. Theta Chi
30. Phi Kappa Theta
31. Phi Kappa Tau
32. Martin Hall
33. Hummer House

1964
May 9 • Tenth Street Stadium

1. BETA THETA PI
   (2:22:35)
2. Sigma Alpha Epsilon
3. Phi Gamma Delta
4. Acacia
5. Sigma Nu
6. Alpha Tau Omega
7. Dodds House
8. Parks House
9. Chi Phi
10. Phi Delta Theta
11. Phi Kappa Psi
12. Zeta Beta Tau
13. Jenkinson House
14. Lambda Chi Alpha
15. Sigma Chi
16. Delta Upsilon
17. Delta Chi
18. Theta Chi
19. Walnut Hall
20. Kappa Delta Rho
21. Phi Kappa Tau
22. Tau Kappa Epsilon
23. Delta Tau Delta
24. Shea
25. Cravens A
26. Sigma Phi Epsilon
27. Sigma Alpha Mu
28. Phi Sigma Kappa
29. Ferguson House
30. Kappa Sigma

31. Dunn House
32. Todd House
33. Alpha Epsilon Pi

1965
May 8 • Tenth Street Stadium

1. PHI GAMMA DELTA
   (2:17:18)
2. Sigma Alpha Epsilon
3. Alpha Tau Omega
4. Phi Kappa Psi
5. Sigma Nu
6. Phi Delta Theta
7. Beta Theta Pi
8. Kappa Delta Rho
9. Sigma Phi Epsilon
10. Delta Upsilon
11. Laurel/Walnut
12. Ruter/Jenkins
13. Willkie Co-op
14. Wissler II
15. Acacia
16. Phi Sigma Kappa
17. Delta Tau Delta
18. Tau Kappa Epsilon
19. Jenkinson House
20. Dodds House
21. Lambda Chi Alpha
22. Martin III
23. Pi Kappa Alpha
24. McNutt
25. Kappa Sigma
26. Theta Chi
27. Hummer House
28. Phi Kappa Theta
29. Elliott/Lowe
30. Zeta Beta Tau
31. Alpha Epsilon Pi
32. Todd House
33. Ferguson House

1966
May 14 • Tenth Street Stadium

1. PHI KAPPA PSI
   (2:16:51)
2. Sigma Phi Epsilon

3. Sigma Nu
4. Alpha Tau Omega
5. Phi Gamma Delta
6. Theta Chi
7. Sigma Alpha Epsilon
8. Sigma Chi
9. Delta Upsilon
10. McNutt
11. Beta Theta Pi
12. Kappa Delta Rho
13. Phi Kappa Theta
14. Tau Kappa Epsilon
15. Acacia
16. Chi Phi
17. Lambda Chi Alpha
18. Sigma Alpha Mu
19. Phi Sigma Kappa
20. Martin III
21. Delta Tau Delta
22. Phi Kappa Tau
23. Delta Chi
24. Willkie Co-op
25. Briscoe
26. Sigma Pi
27. Edmondson II
28. Hummer House
29. Dodds House
30. Kappa Sigma
31. Zeta Beta Tau
32. Cravens A
33. Pi Kappa Phi

1967
May 13 • Tenth Street Stadium

1. PHI GAMMA DELTA
   (2:15:36)
2. Phi Delta Theta
3. Sigma Alpha Epsilon
4. Alpha Tau Omega
5. Phi Kappa Theta
6. Sigma Chi
7. Sigma Phi Epsilon
8. Phi Kappa Psi
9. Theta Chi
10. Kappa Sigma
11. Sigma Nu
12. Dodds House

13. Acacia
14. Delta Upsilon
15. Kappa Delta Rho
16. Lambda Chi Alpha
17. Chi Phi
18. Sigma Pi
19. Delta Tau Delta
20. Stew-Bums
21. Briscoe I
22. Beta Theta Pi
23. Magee III
24. Tau Kappa Epsilon
25. Zeta Beta Tau
26. Cravens C
27. Phi Epsilon Pi
28. Martin III
29. Ferguson House
30. Edmondson II
31. Willkie Co-op
32. Edmondson IV
33. Alpha Epsilon Pi

1968
May 12 (Sun.) • Tenth Street Stadium

1. PHI KAPPA PSI
    (2:12:51)
2. Delta Upsilon
3. Sigma Phi Epsilon
4. Alpha Tau Omega
5. Sigma Alpha Mu
6. Acacia
7. Kappa Sigma
8. Sigma Alpha Epsilon
9. Phi Kappa Theta
10. Phi Gamma Delta
11. Theta Chi
12. Cravens C
13. Sigma Nu
14. Dodds House
15. Pi Kappa Alpha
16. Lambda Chi Alpha
17. Willkie
18. Magee II
19. Kappa Delta Rho
20. Beta Theta Pi
21. Phi Kappa Tau

22. Phi Epsilon Pi
23. Wissler IV
24. Martin III
25. Hummer House
26. Zeta Beta Tau
27. Pi Kappa Phi
28. Chi Phi
29. McNutt
30. Tau Kappa Epsilon
31. Sigma Chi
32. Willkie Co-op
Qualified but did not race:
Phi Delta Theta

1969
May 10 • Tenth Street Stadium

1. ALPHA TAU OMEGA
    (2:27:45)
2. Phi Delta Theta
3. Dodds House
4. Beta Theta Pi
5. Kappa Sigma
6. Delta Upsilon
7. Acacia
8. Sigma Nu
9. Briscoe
10. Delta Chi
11. Kappa Delta Rho
12. Wissler IV
13. Sigma Phi Epsilon
14. Phi Kappa Psi
15. Sigma Alpha Epsilon
16. Delta Tau Delta
17. Theta Chi
18. Pi Kappa Alpha
19. Phi Kappa Theta
20. Phi Kappa Tau
21. Sigma Alpha Mu
22. Phi Gamma Delta
23. Sigma Chi
24. Cravens C
25. Zeta Beta Tau
26. Willkie
27. Martin III
28. Theta Xi
29. McNutt
30. Sigma Pi

31. Alpha Epsilon Pi
32. Tau Kappa Epsilon
33. Shea II

1970
May 9 • Tenth Street Stadium

1. SIGMA PHI EPSILON
    (2:15:56)
2. Delta Chi
3. Dodds House
4. Alpha Tau Omega
5. Sigma Nu
6. Martin III
7. Sigma Alpha Epsilon
8. Briscoe
9. Theta Chi
10. Delta Tau Delta
11. Kappa Sigma
12. Lambda Chi Alpha
13. Sigma Chi
14. Phi Gamma Delta
15. Acacia
16. Phi Kappa Psi
17. Pi Kappa Alpha
18. Phi Delta Theta
19. Alpha Sigma Phi
20. Beta Theta Pi
21. Sigma Pi
22. Magee II
23. Phi Kappa Theta
24. Cravens C
25. Crone House
26. Zeta Beta Tau
27. Willkie South VII
28. Chi Phi
29. Dewey
30. Shea III
31. Evans Scholars
32. Shea II
33. Sigma Alpha Mu

1971
May 8 • Tenth Street Stadium

1. ALPHA TAU OMEGA
    (2:12:19)

2. Acacia
3. Theta Chi
4. Phi Gamma Delta
5. Delta Chi
6. Phi Delta Theta
7. Kappa Sigma
8. Sigma Nu
9. Dodds House
10. Sigma Chi
11. Phi Kappa Psi
12. Martin III
13. Sigma Phi Epsilon
14. Delta Upsilon
15. Pi Kappa Alpha
16. Delta Tau Delta
17. Dewey
18. Delta Sigma Pi
19. Briscoe
20. Beta Theta Pi
21. Sigma Alpha Epsilon
22. Willkie South VI
23. Sigma Alpha Mu
24. Theta Xi
25. Willkie IV/XI
26. Sigma Pi
27. Evans Scholars
28. Teter
29. Lambda Chi Alpha
30. Crone House
31. Pi Kappa Phi
32. Magee II
33. Bryan

1972
April 29–30 • Tenth Street Stadium

1. KAPPA SIGMA
    (2:12:06)
2. Delta Chi
3. Sigma Phi Epsilon
4. Sigma Alpha Epsilon
5. Acacia
6. Theta Chi
7. Phi Kappa Psi
8. Delta Upsilon
9. Briscoe V
10. Dodds House
11. Martin III

12. Phi Delta Theta
13. Theta Xi
14. Delta Tau Delta
15. Martin II
16. Sigma Pi
17. Beta Theta Pi
18. (tie) Phi Gamma Delta
    Sigma Chi
20. Crone House
21. Alpha Tau Omega
22. Pi Kappa Alpha
23. Parks House
24. Shea Ground
25. Cravens B
26. Alpha Sigma Phi
27. Sigma Nu
28. Pi Kappa Phi
29. Alpha Epsilon Pi
30. Evans Scholars
31. Sigma Alpha Mu
32. Kappa Delta Rho
33. Funky's

1973
April 28 • Tenth Street Stadium

1. DELTA CHI
    (2:18:41)
2. Kappa Sigma
3. Theta Chi
4. Briscoe
5. Phi Gamma Delta
6. Acacia
7. Dodds House
8. Phi Kappa Psi
9. Sigma Alpha Epsilon
10. Sigma Nu
11. Sigma Chi
12. Pi Kappa Phi
13. Theta Xi
14. Phi Delta Theta
15. Sigma Phi Epsilon
16. Martin III
17. Lambda Chi Alpha
18. Sigma Pi
19. Delta Tau Delta
20. Evans Scholars
21. Shea III

22. Delta Upsilon
23. Pi Kappa Alpha
24. Shea II
25. Alpha Epsilon Pi
26. Martin II
27. Cravens B
28. Beta Theta Pi
29. Alpha Tau Omega
30. Bordner NW
31. Wissler IV
32. Willkie South III
33. Cyclotrons

1974
April 27 • Tenth Street Stadium

1. DELTA CHI
   (2:09:48)
2. Kappa Sigma
3. Phi Kappa Psi
4. Martin V
5. Alpha Tau Omega
6. Dodds House
7. Sigma Alpha Epsilon
8. Sigma Chi
9. Sigma Nu
10. Shea II
11. Cravens B
12. Acacia
13. Sigma Phi Epsilon
14. Sigma Pi
15. Theta Chi
16. Pi Kappa Phi
17. Lambda Chi Alpha
18. Shea III
19. Theta Xi
20. Evans Scholars
21. Wissler V
22. Phi Delta Theta
23. Phi Gamma Delta
24. Beta Theta Pi
25. Delta Tau Delta
26. Delta Upsilon
27. Willkie South VI
28. Rollins House
29. Willkie South III
30. Magee I
31. Willkie South X

32. Read
33. Crone House

1975
April 26 • Tenth Street Stadium

1. PHI GAMMA DELTA
   (2:14:00)
2. Delta Chi
3. Dodds House
4. Phi Kappa Psi
5. Delta Tau Delta
6. Kappa Sigma
7. Wissler V
8. Sigma Nu
9. Theta Chi
10. Delta Upsilon
11. Sigma Alpha Epsilon
12. Shea II
13. Beta Theta Pi
14. Sigma Pi
15. Phi Delta Theta
16. Acacia
17. Martin III
18. Alpha Tau Omega
19. Cravens B
20. Hummer Co-op
21. Evans Scholars
22. Read
23. Delgado Ground
24. Willkie South III
25. Theta Xi
26. Boisen IV
27. Jenkinson Ground
28. Chi Phi
29. Magee I
30. Pi Kappa Phi
31. Kappa Delta Rho
32. Willkie South X
33. Alpha Epsilon Pi

1976
April 26 (Mon.) • Tenth Street Stadium

1. DELTA CHI
   (2:10:21)
2. Phi Gamma Delta

3. Delta Tau Delta
4. Sigma Chi
5. Sigma Nu
6. Phi Kappa Psi
7. Sigma Phi Epsilon
8. Acacia
9. Theta Xi
10. Sigma Alpha Epsilon
11. Phi Delta Theta
12. Beta Theta Pi
13. (tie) Kappa Sigma
       Alpha Epsilon Pi
15. Dodds House
16. Theta Chi
17. Rollins House
18. Martin II
19. Pi Kappa Phi
20. Magee I
21. Lambda Chi Alpha
22. Martin III
23. Parks/Shea II
24. Kappa Delta Rho
25. Delta Upsilon
26. Wissler V
27. Chi Phi
28. Alpha Sigma Phi
29. Evans Scholars
30. Boisen IV
31. Cravens B
32. Nichols House
33. Sigma Pi

1977
April 30 • Tenth Street Stadium

1. DELTA CHI
   (2:09:46)
2. Phi Kappa Psi
3. Phi Gamma Delta
4. Sigma Phi Epsilon
5. Velo-Men
6. Sigma Alpha Epsilon
7. Alpha Epsilon Pi
8. Willkie South III
9. Evans Scholars
10. Phi Delta Theta
11. Sigma Chi
12. Parks House

13. Martin III
14. Kappa Sigma
15. Tau Kappa Epsilon
16. Rollins House
17. Sigma Pi
18. Nichols House
19. Theta Xi
20. Theta Chi
21. Pi Kappa Alpha
22. Delta Tau Delta
23. Beta Theta Pi
24. Alpha Sigma Phi
25. Martin II
26. Acacia
27. Kappa Delta Rho
28. Magee I
29. Shea III
30. Jenkins House
31. Signa Phi Nothing
32. Jenkinson II

Disqualified: Chi Phi

1978
April 22 • Tenth Street Stadium

1. PHI KAPPA PSI
   (2:12:12)
2. Sigma Nu
3. Pi Kappa Phi
4. Alpha Epsilon Phi
5. Sigma Phi Epsilon
6. Dodds House
7. Sigma Chi
8. Kappa Sigma
9. Phi Gamma Delta
10. Delta Chi
11. Theta Chi
12. Sigma Pi
13. Lambda Chi Alpha
14. Delta Tau Delta
15. Tau Kappa Epsilon
16. (tie) Evans Scholars
       Alpha Sigma Phi
18. (tie) Acacia
       Hummer House
20. Nichols House
21. Beta Theta Pi

22. Willkie South Suite
23. Elkin II
24. Alpha Tau Omega
25. Rollins House
26. Phi Delta Theta
27. (tie) Pi Kappa Alpha
       Willkie South III
29. Magee I
30. Martin III
31. Wissler V
32. Willkie South X
33. Kappa Delta Rho

1979
April 21 • Tenth Street Stadium

1. DELTA CHI
   (2:10:06)
2. Kappa Sigma
3. Jenkins
4. Sigma Phi Epsilon
5. Sigma Alpha Epsilon
6. Sigma Chi
7. Alpha Epsilon Pi
8. Alpha Sigma Phi
9. Pi Kappa Phi
10. Theta Chi
11. Beta Theta Pi
12. Willkie South Suite
13. Dodds House
14. Wissler V
15. Willkie South III
16. Phi Kappa Psi
17. Hummer House
18. Rollins House
19. Mass Riders
20. Delta Tau Delta
21. Cravens B
22. Delgado Ground
23. Pi Kappa Alpha
24. Lambda Chi Alpha
25. Delta Upsilon
26. Willkie South V
27. Alpha Tau Omega
28. Tau Kappa Epsilon
29. Acacia
30. Willkie South X
31. Chi Phi

32. Martin III
33. Wissler 3

1980
April 26 • Tenth Street Stadium

1. DELTA CHI
   (2:09:28)
2. Pi Kappa Phi
3. Wissler V
4. Phi Gamma Delta
5. Willkie South III
6. Chi Phi
7. Sigma Alpha Epsilon
8. Dodds House
9. Sigma Nu
10. Alpha Tau Omega
11. Acacia
12. Sigma Chi
13. Pi Kappa Alpha
14. Phi Delta Theta
15. Beta Theta Pi
16. Jenkins House
17. Phi Kappa Psi
18. Sigma Phi Epsilon
19. Willkie South VII
20. Shea III
21. Alpha Epsilon Pi
22. Kappa Sigma
23. Willkie South X
24. Theta Chi
25. Martin III
26. Cravens A
27. Blitzkriegers
28. Crone House
29. Willkie South V
30. Nichols House
31. Delta Upsilon
32. Willkie South IV
33. Parks House

1981
April 25 • Little 500/Soccer Stadium

1. DELTA CHI
   (2:05:17)

2. Chi Phi
3. Willkie
4. Alpha Tau Omega
5. Phi Kappa Psi
6. Alpha Epsilon Pi
7. Phi Gamma Delta
8. Sigma Alpha Epsilon
9. Blitzkriegers
10. Wissler V
11. Sigma Phi Epsilon
12. Jenkins House
13. Dodds House
14. Rollins House
15. Theta Chi
16. Sigma Chi
17. Sigma Nu
18. Alpha Sigma Phi
19. Phi Delta Theta
20. Evans Scholars
21. Wissler II/Wissler III
22. Kappa Sigma
23. Acacia
24. Delta Tau Delta
25. Parks House
26. Curry II
27. Tau Kappa Epsilon
28. Pi Kappa Phi
29. Boisen I
30. Sigma Pi
31. Nichols House
32. Pi Kappa Alpha
33. Hummer House

1982
April 24 • Little 500/Soccer Stadium

1. PHI DELTA THETA
   (2:03:33)
2. Delta Chi
3. Kappa Sigma
4. Beta Theta Pi
5. Acacia
6. Phi Gamma Delta
7. Alpha Tau Omega
8. Sigma Chi
9. (tie) Hummer House
   Sigma Phi Epsilon

11. Albatross
12. Phi Kappa Psi
13. Delta Tau Delta
14. Parks House
15. Sigma Alpha Epsilon
16. Willkie
17. Chi Phi
18. Alpha Epsilon Pi
19. Rollins House
20. Dodds House
21. Theta Chi
22. Curry II
23. Wissler II/Wissler III
24. Martin II
25. Jenkins House
26. Lambda Chi Alpha
27. Boisen I
28. Pi Kappa Phi
29. Tau Kappa Epsilon
30. Sigma Pi
31. Willkie South IV
32. Pi Kappa Alpha
33. Nichols House

1983
April 23 • Bill Armstrong Stadium*

1. ACACIA
   (2:08:10)
2. Phi Delta Theta
3. Phi Kappa Psi
4. Alpha Epsilon Pi
5. Alpha Tau Omega
6. Willkie
7. Sigma Phi Epsilon
8. Chi Phi
9. Sigma Alpha Epsilon
10. Jenkins House
11. Kappa Sigma
12. Sigma Pi
13. Phi Gamma Delta
14. Rollins House
15. Sigma Chi
16. Parks House
17. Delta Tau Delta
18. Dodds House
19. Lambda Chi Alpha
20. Delta Upsilon

21. Alpha Sigma Phi
22. Beta Theta Pi
23. Tau Kappa Epsilon
24. Hummer House
25. Sigma Alpha Mu
26. Sigma Nu
27. Blitzkriegers
28. Martin III
29. Team Anything
30. Zeta Beta Tau
31. Nichols House
32. Curry IV
33. Pi Kappa Phi

Little 500/Soccer Stadium renamed Bill Armstrong Stadium, April 22, 1983

1984
April 22 • Bill Armstrong Stadium

1. CUTTERS
   (2:09:44)
2. Alpha Epsilon Pi
3. Acacia
4. Chi Phi
5. Beta Theta Pi
6. Phi Gamma Delta
7. Avere
8. Jenkins House
9. Alpha Tau Omega
10. Lambda Chi Alpha
11. Phi Kappa Psi
12. Phi Delta Theta
13. Delta Tau Delta
14. Sigma Nu
15. Rollins House
16. Delta Upsilon
17. Sigma Pi
18. Kappa Sigma
19. Sigma Chi
20. Curry IV
21. Sigma Phi Epsilon
22. Wissler V
23. Dodds House
24. Sigma Alpha Epsilon
25. Alpha Sigma Phi
26. Nichols House

27. Pi Kappa Alpha
28. Curry II
29. Cosmic Debris
30. Evans Scholars
31. Collins
32. Kappa Delta Rho
33. Spokesmen

1985
April 20 • Bill Armstrong Stadium

1. ALPHA EPSILON PI
   (2:05:13)
2. Acacia
3. Chi Phi
4. Cutters
5. Rollins House
6. Pi Kappa Alpha
7. Phi Kappa Psi
8. Phi Delta Theta
9. Alpha Tau Omega
10. Sigma Alpha Epsilon
11. Latecomers
12. Delta Tau Delta
13. Sigma Phi Epsilon
14. Collins
15. Cinzano
16. Kappa Sigma
17. Sigma Nu
18. Nichols House
19. Theta Chi
20. Curry IV
21. Dodds House
22. Lambda Chi Alpha
23. Beta Theta Pi
24. Sigma Chi
25. Thompson V
26. Delta Upsilon
27. McNutt
28. Phi Gamma Delta
29. Evans Scholars
30. Alpha Sigma Phi
31. Pi Kappa Phi
32. Sigma Alpha Mu
33. Beck II

The Little 500

1986
April 26 • Bill Armstrong Stadium

1. CUTTERS
   (2:01:44)
2. Alpha Epsilon Pi
3. Phi Kappa Psi
4. Phi Delta Theta
5. Chi Phi
6. Lambda Chi Alpha
7. Acacia
8. Evans Scholars
9. Collins
10. Delta Tau Delta
11. Phi Gamma Delta
12. Cinzano
13. Pi Kappa Alpha
14. Alpha Tau Omega
15. Kappa Sigma
16. Sigma Nu
17. Sigma Chi
18. Sigma Phi Epsilon
19. Theta Chi
20. Sigma Alpha Epsilon
21. Delta Upsilon
22. Americana
23. Trophy Dash
24. Read
25. Sigma Alpha Mu
26. Sigma Pi
27. Kappa Delta Rho
28. Nichols House
29. Beck II
30. Joint Venture
31. Curry V
32. Alpha Sigma Phi
33. Pi Kappa Phi

1987
April 25 • Bill Armstrong Stadium

1. PHI GAMMA DELTA
   (2:03:57)
2. Acacia
3. Sigma Phi Epsilon
4. Cutters
5. Cinzano
6. Chi Phi
7. Phi Delta Theta
8. Posers
9. Sigma Alpha Mu
10. Sigma Alpha Epsilon
11. Delta Chi
12. Theta Chi
13. Americana
14. Alpha Tau Omega
15. Delta Tau Delta
16. Sigma Nu
17. Phi Kappa Psi
18. Collins
19. Pi Kappa Alpha
20. Joint Venture
21. Sigma Pi
22. Parks
23. Curry V
24. Teter
25. Evans Scholars
26. Zeta Beta Tau
27. Kappa Sigma
28. Dodds House
29. Wright
30. Beach Riders
31. Beck II
32. Kappa Delta Rho
33. Flying High

1988
April 23 • Bill Armstrong Stadium

1. CUTTERS
   (2:07:30)
2. Phi Gamma Delta
3. Phi Delta Theta
4. Lambda Chi Alpha
5. Alpha Epsilon Pi
6. Pi Kappa Alpha
7. Collins
8. Sigma Alpha Epsilon
9. Americana
10. Cinzano
11. Sigma Alpha Mu
12. Delta Tau Delta
13. Sigma Nu
14. Teter

15. Beach Riders
16. Beta Theta Pi
17. Evans Scholars
18. Alpha Tau Omega
19. Acacia
20. Posers
21. Sigma Chi
22. Foster
23. Sigma Phi Epsilon
24. Kappa Sigma
25. Dodds House
26. Theta Chi
27. Chi Phi
28. Phi Kappa Psi
29. Alpha Sigma Phi
30. Delta Upsilon
31. Delta Chi
32. Sigma Pi
33. Phi Kappa Tau

1989
April 22 • Bill Armstrong Stadium

1. CINZANO
   (2:02:12)
2. Cutters
3. Acacia
4. Teter
5. Sigma Alpha Mu
6. Phi Gamma Delta
7. Phi Delta Theta
8. Americana
9. Phi Kappa Psi
10. Sigma Nu
11. Pi Kappa Alpha
12. Kappa Sigma
13. Delta Tau Delta
14. Dodds House
15. Beta Theta Pi
16. Foster
17. Sigma Chi
18. Sigma Alpha Epsilon
19. Alpha Epsilon Pi
20. Theta Chi
21. Big Red Wave
22. Pi Kappa Phi
23. Delta Chi
24. Evans Scholars

25. Sigma Phi Epsilon
26. Zeta Beta Tau
27. Posers
28. Delta Upsilon
29. Sigma Pi
30. Collins
31. Chi Phi
32. Phi Kappa Tau
33. Read

1990
April 21 • Bill Armstrong Stadium

1. SIGMA NU
   (2:04:49)
2. Acacia
3. Cutters
4. Sigma Chi
5. Phi Gamma Delta
6. Teter
7. Phi Delta Theta
8. Alpha Sigma Phi
9. Foster
10. Pi Kappa Phi
11. Sigma Alpha Mu
12. Sigma Pi
13. Beta Theta Pi
14. Lambda Chi Alpha
15. Delta Upsilon
16. Sigma Alpha Epsilon
17. Pi Kappa Alpha
18. Evans Scholars
19. Phi Kappa Tau
20. Delta Tau Delta
21. Cinzano
22. Phi Kappa Psi
23. Zeta Beta Tau
24. Kappa Sigma
25. Theta Chi
26. Americana
27. Ashton
28. Willkie
29. Alpha Epsilon Pi
30. Collins
31. Dodds House
Qualified but did not race: Alpha
Tau Omega, Sigma Phi Epsilon

1991
April 20 • Bill Armstrong Stadium

1. ACACIA
   (2:04:17)
2. Cutters
3. Team College Life
4. Phi Kappa Psi
5. Sigma Nu
6. Phi Delta Theta
7. Delta Upsilon
8. Phi Gamma Delta
9. Sigma Chi
10. Pi Kappa Alpha
11. Alpha Epsilon Pi
12. Cinzano
13. Sigma Alpha Epsilon
14. Foster
15. Theta Chi
16. Phi Kappa Tau
17. Alpha Tau Omega
18. Evans Scholars
19. Beta Theta Pi
20. Delta Chi
21. Willkie
22. Sigma Pi
23. Team Funk
24. Lambda Chi Alpha
25. Dodds House
26. Delta Tau Delta
27. Chi Phi
28. Pi Kappa Phi
29. McNutt
30. Kappa Sigma
31. Sigma Alpha Mu
32. Sigma Phi Epsilon
33. Team Independence

1992
April 25 • Bill Armstrong Stadium

1. CUTTERS
   (2:05:53)
2. Acacia
3. Cinzano
4. Delta Chi
5. Delta Upsilon

6. Phi Gamma Delta
7. Theta Chi
8. Pi Kappa Alpha
9. Sigma Chi
10. Team College Life
11. Dodds House
12. Alpha Epsilon Pi
13. Phi Kappa Psi
14. Pi Kappa Phi
15. Phi Delta Theta
16. Sigma Alpha Epsilon
17. Delta Tau Delta
18. McNutt
19. Lambda Chi Alpha
20. Phi Kappa Tau
21. Kappa Sigma
22. Willkie/Read
23. Alpha Sigma Phi
24. Evans Scholars
25. Sigma Pi
26. Chi Phi
27. Ashton
28. Tau Kappa Epsilon
29. Sigma Phi Epsilon
30. Zeta Beta Tau
31. Foster
32. Sigma Alpha Mu
33. I.M.O. Major Taylor

1993
April 17 • Bill Armstrong Stadium

1. DELTA CHI
   (2:06:17)
2. Cinzano
3. Pi Kappa Alpha
4. Sigma Alpha Epsilon
5. Cutters
6. Sigma Nu
7. Delta Upsilon
8. Delta Tau Delta
9. Pi Kappa Phi
10. Acacia
11. Sigma Chi
12. Theta Chi
13. Phi Kappa Psi
14. Team College Life

15. Phi Gamma Delta
16. Ashton
17. Foster
18. Sigma Alpha Mu/Delta Sigma Pi
19. Phi Delta Theta
20. Dodds House
21. TFAT
22. Tau Kappa Epsilon
23. Collins
24. Lambda Chi Alpha
25. Alpha Epsilon Pi
26. Evans Scholars
27. Chi Phi
28. Zeta Beta Tau
29. McNutt
30. Sigma Pi
31. Sigma Phi Epsilon
32. Kappa Delta Rho
33. Beta Theta Pi

1994
April 16 • Bill Armstrong Stadium

1. SIGMA CHI
   (2:11:06)
2. Cutters
3. Delta Chi
4. Cinzano
5. Phi Gamma Delta
6. Pi Kappa Alpha
7. Phi Kappa Psi
8. Phi Delta Theta
9. Acacia
10. Dodds House
11. Team College Life
12. Pi Kappa Phi
13. Delta Upsilon
14. Lambda Chi Alpha
15. Sigma Alpha Epsilon
16. Sigma Nu
17. Sigma Phi Epsilon
18. Collins
19. Ashton
20. Alpha Epsilon Pi
21. Beta Theta Pi
22. Delta Tau Delta

23. Human Wheels
24. McNutt
25. Wright
26. Team Last Chance
27. Theta Chi
28. Read
29. Alpha Sigma Phi
30. Sammy & Co.
31. Kappa Sigma
32. Sigma Pi
33. Zeta Beta Tau

1995
April 22 • Bill Armstrong Stadium

1. PHI GAMMA DELTA
   (2:08:45)
2. Acacia
3. Sigma Alpha Epsilon
4. Dodds House
5. Delta Chi
6. Phi Delta Theta
7. Sigma Nu
8. Beta Theta Pi
9. Lambda Chi Alpha
10. Sigma Chi
11. Cutters
12. TFAT
13. Sigma Phi Epsilon
14. Phi Kappa Psi
15. Pi Kappa Phi
16. Delta Upsilon
17. Phi Kappa Alpha
18. Collins/Ashton/Teter
19. Delta Tau Delta
20. Theta Chi
21. Team College Life
22. Sigma Alpha Mu
23. Wright
24. Alpha Epsilon Pi
25. Delta Sigma Pi
26. Kappa Sigma
27. Human Wheels
28. Alpha Tau Omega
29. Zeta Beta Tau
30. Alpha Phi Omega
31. Alpha Sigma Phi

32. Kappa Delta Rho
33. Phi Kappa Theta

1996
April 20 • Bill Armstrong Stadium

1. PHI DELTA THETA
   (2:08:58)
2. Sigma Chi
3. Phi Gamma Delta
4. Delta Chi
5. Acacia
6. Sigma Nu
7. Cutters
8. Dodds House
9. Theta Chi
10. Pneuma
11. Beta Theta Pi
12. Cinzano
13. McNutt
14. Sigma Phi Epsilon
15. Pi Kappa Phi
16. Delta Tau Delta
17. Phi Kappa Psi
18. Pi Kappa Alpha
19. Lambda Chi Alpha
20. Sigma Alpha Epsilon
21. Willkie
22. Sigma Alpha Mu
23. Alpha Epsilon Pi
24. Sigma Pi
25. Collins
26. Wright
27. Team College Life
28. TFAT
29. Alpha Sigma Phi
30. Chi Phi
31. Mezcla
32. Briscoe
33. Alpha Tau Omega

1997
April 26 • Bill Armstrong Stadium

1. CUTTERS
   (2:05:27)
2. Phi Gamma Delta

3. Delta Chi
4. Dodds House
5. Sigma Chi
6. Sigma Nu
7. Acacia
8. Phi Delta Theta
9. Sigma Alpha Epsilon
10. Beta Theta Pi
11. Cinzano
12. Pi Kappa Phi
13. Pi Kappa Alpha
14. Sigma Phi Epsilon
15. Theta Chi
16. Wright
17. Delta Upsilon
18. Delta Tau Delta
19. Phi Kappa Psi
20. Lambda Chi Alpha
21. Chi Phi
22. Pneuma
23. Mezcla
24. Alpha Tau Omega
25. Collins
26. Army ROTC
27. Kappa Sigma
28. South Cottage Grove
29. Sigma Pi
30. Evans Scholars
31. Zeta Beta Tau
32. McNutt
33. Alpha Sigma Phi

1998
April 25 • Bill Armstrong Stadium

1. DODDS HOUSE
   (2:06:26)
2. Cutters
3. Sigma Alpha Epsilon
4. Beta Theta Pi
5. Phi Gamma Delta
6. Acacia
7. Sigma Phi Epsilon
8. Sigma Nu
9. Lambda Chi Alpha
10. Pi Kappa Phi
11. Phi Kappa Psi

12. Mezcla
13. Pi Kappa Alpha
14. Chi Phi
15. Delta Tau Delta
16. Alta
17. Alpha Sigma Phi
18. Delta Chi
19. Collins
20. Alpha Epsilon Pi
21. Cinzano
22. Sigma Chi
23. Wright
24. Sigma Pi
25. Delta Upsilon
26. Region Crew
27. Alpha Tau Omega
28. Forest
29. Delta Sigma Pi
30. Teter
31. Phi Sigma Kappa
32. Sigma Alpha Mu
Qualified but did not race: Theta Chi

1999
April 24 • Bill Armstrong Stadium

1. Sigma Phi Epsilon
2. Phi Gamma Delta
3. Chi Phi
4. Acacia
5. Dodds House
6. Theta Chi
7. Phi Delta Theta
8. Cutters
9. Sigma Chi
10. Delta Chi
11. Sigma Alpha Epsilon
12. Delta Tau Delta
13. Team Dotson
14. Beta Theta Pi
15. Phi Kappa Psi
16. Collins Cycling
17. Alpha Chi Sigma
18. Lambda Chi Alpha
19. Sigma Nu
20. Pi Kappa Phi

21. Alpha Tau Omega
22. Delta Upsilon
23. Fratello
24. Teter
25. Alta
26. Cinzano
27. Wright Cycling
28. Hickory
29. Evans Scholars
30. Kappa Sigma
31. Delta Sigma Pi (Men)
32. Alpha Sigma Phi
33. Alpha Phi Omega (Men)

The Women's Little 500

(races Fridays except where noted)

1988
April 22 • Bill Armstrong Stadium

1. WILLKIE SPRINT
   (1:10:52)
2. Kappa Alpha Theta
3. Delta Delta Delta
4. Alpha Epsilon Phi
5. Notorious
6. Wright
7. Delta Zeta
8. Stonies
9. Delta Gamma
10. Sigma Kappa
11. Collins
12. Alpha Phi
13. Kappa Delta
14. Ambassadors
15. Cinzano
16. Foster
17. Alpha Xi Delta
18. Zeta Tau Alpha
19. Alpha Omicron Pi
20. Alpha Delta Pi
21. Alpha Gamma Delta
22. Briscoe
23. Phi Mu
24. Cinquencento

25. Spokeswomen
26. Windsprint
27. Forest
28. Eureka
29. Copacetic
30. Wild Thing
Qualified but did not race:
Alpha Chi Omega

1989
April 21 • Bill Armstrong Stadium

1. BEYOND CONTROL
   (1:06:58)
2. Team Sprint
3. Delta Gamma
4. Kappa Alpha Theta
5. Foster
6. Alpha Delta Pi
7. Alpha Epsilon Phi
8. Alpha Xi Delta
9. Wright
10. Delta Zeta
11. Collins
12. Sigma Delta Tau
13. Alpha Phi
14. Willkie
15. Kappa Delta
16. Delta Delta Delta
17. De Novo
18. Chi Omega
19. Genuine Draft
20. Phi Mu
21. Kappa Kappa Gamma
22. Read
23. Briscoe
24. Teter
25. Pi Beta Phi
26. Gamma Phi Beta
27. Alpha Omicron Pi

1990
April 21 (Sat.) • Bill Armstrong Stadium

1. TEAM SPRINT
   (1:09:51)

2. Beyond Control
3. Kappa Alpha Theta
4. Foster
5. Le Pas
6. Delta Zeta
7. Kappa Kappa Gamma
8. Landsharks
9. Revolution
10. Wright
11. Willkie/Read
12. Alpha Delta Pi
13. Alpha Phi
14. Off The Back
15. Kappa Delta
16. Alpha Xi Delta
17. Sigma Delta Tau
18. Gamma Phi Beta
19. Alpha Omicron Pi
20. Sigma Kappa
21. Alpha Epsilon Phi
22. Forest
23. Collins
24. Alpha Gamma Delta
25. Chi Omega
26. Phi Mu

1991
April 19 • Bill Armstrong Stadium

1. LE PAS
   (1:08:43)
2. Foster
3. Landsharks
4. Delta Gamma
5. Team Sprint
6. Kappa Alpha Theta
7. Delta Zeta
8. Revolution
9. Alpha Delta Pi
10. Zeta Tau Alpha
11. Alpha Phi
12. Collins
13. Read
14. Kappa Kappa Gamma
15. Phi Mu
16. Gamma Phi Beta
17. Forest
18. Willkie

19. Alpha Omicron Pi
20. Alpha Xi Delta
21. Alpha Gamma Delta

1992
April 24 • Bill Armstrong Stadium

1. LANDSHARKS
   (1:11:25)
2. Kappa Alpha Theta
3. Delta Gamma
4. Alpha Delta Pi
5. Forest
6. Willkie
7. Delta Zeta
8. Kappa Delta
9. Read
10. Alpha Gamma Delta
11. Zeta Tau Alpha
12. Gamma Phi Beta
13. Kappa Kappa Gamma
14. Team Brio
15. Foster
16. Alpha Phi
17. Alpha Omicron Pi
18. Phi Mu
19. Wright
20. Sigma Sigma Sigma
21. Sigma Delta Tau
22. Collins
23. Alpha Epsilon Phi
24. Delta Delta Delta
25. Alpha Sigma Alpha
26. Sigma Kappa

1993
April 16 • Bill Armstrong Stadium

1. LANDSHARKS
   (1:16:48)
2. Alpha Gamma Delta
3. Gamma Phi Beta
4. Kappa Alpha Theta
5. Delta Gamma
6. Alpha Sigma Alpha
7. Alpha Phi
8. Roadrunners

9. Alpha Omicron Pi
10. Willkie
11. Alpha Chi Omega
12. Zeta Tau Alpha
13. Kappa Delta
14. Delta Zeta
15. Forest
16. Phi Mu
17. Delta Delta Delta
18. Kappa Kappa Gamma
19. Collins
20. Wright
21. Sigma Sigma Sigma
22. McNutt
23. Alpha Delta Pi
24. Sigma Kappa

1994
April 15 • Bill Armstrong Stadium

1. KAPPA ALPHA THETA
   (1:13:09)
2. Alpha Gamma Delta
3. Roadrunners
4. Alpha Chi Omega
5. Gamma Phi Beta
6. Delta Delta Delta
7. Alpha Phi
8. Kappa Kappa Gamma
9. Wright
10. Landsharks
11. Alpha Omicron Pi
12. Delta Zeta
13. Kappa Delta
14. Zeta Tau Alpha
15. Team College Life
16. Phi Mu
17. Delta Sigma Pi
18. Willkie
19. McNutt
20. Collins
21. Alpha Delta Pi

22. Alpha Epsilon Phi
23. Chi Omega
24. Human Wheels
25. Alpha Xi Delta

1995
April 21 • Bill Armstrong Stadium

1. KAPPA ALPHA THETA
   (1:12:16)
2. Kappa Kappa Gamma
3. Gamma Phi Beta
4. Alpha Gamma Delta
5. Landsharks
6. Delta Zeta
7. Team College Life
8. Zeta Tau Alpha
9. Wright
10. Pi Beta Phi
11. Alpha Chi Omega
12. Roadrunners
13. Delta Gamma
14. Forest
15. Delta Delta Delta
16. Kappa Delta
17. Phi Mu
18. Alpha Xi Delta
19. Sigma Delta Tau
20. Alpha Phi
21. Chi Omega
22. Delta Sigma Pi

1996
April 19 • Bill Armstrong Stadium

1. KAPPA KAPPA GAMMA
   (1:12:12)
2. Alpha Chi Omega
3. Roadrunners
4. Kappa Alpha Theta
5. Landsharks
6. Alpha Gamma Delta

7. Delta Gamma
8. Wright
9. Teter
10. Delta Zeta
11. Kappa Delta
12. Alpha Phi
13. Team Unique
14. Zeta Tau Alpha
15. Alpha Xi Delta
16. Pi Beta Phi
17. Gamma Phi Beta
18. Phi Mu
19. Alpha Delta Pi
20. Sigma Delta Tau
21. Delta Delta Delta
22. Delta Sigma Pi
23. Alpha Phi Omega

1997
April 25 • Bill Armstrong Stadium

1. ROADRUNNERS
   (1:09:58)
2. Kappa Alpha Theta
3. Phi Mu
4. Alpha Gamma Delta
5. Kappa Kappa Gamma
6. Delta Gamma
7. Alpha Chi Omega
8. Landsharks
9. Alpha Delta Pi
10. Gamma Phi Beta
11. Alpha Xi Delta
12. Pi Beta Phi
13. Kappa Delta
14. Chi Omega
15. Wright
16. Briscoe
17. Delta Zeta
18. Team Z
19. Collins
20. Alpha Phi

21. Delta Delta Delta
22. Sigma Delta Tau
23. Mezcla
24. Foster
25. Teter
26. Zeta Tau Alpha
27. Alpha Kappa Psi
28. Tortues
29. Alpha Phi Omega
30. Alpha Epsilon Phi

1998
April 24 • Bill Armstrong Stadium

1. KAPPA KAPPA GAMMA
   (1:09:35)
2. Chi Omega
3. Kappa Alpha Theta
4. Alpha Chi Omega
5. Landsharks
6. Roadrunners
7. Alpha Gamma Delta
8. Phi Mu
9. Delta Gamma
10. Wright
11. Pi Beta Phi
12. Vayu
13. Team Elite
14. Team College Life
15. Perigee
16. Delta Zeta
17. Alpha Phi Omega
18. Alpha Xi Delta
19. Delta Delta Delta
20. Alpha Phi
21. Sigma Delta Tau
22. Zeta Tau Alpha
23. Alpha Kappa Psi
24. Oz
25. Backdraft
26. Delta Sigma Pi
27. Army ROTC

28. Alpha Delta Pi
29. Teter
30. Foster
31. Briscoe
32. Alpha Chi Sigma

1999
April 23 • Bill Armstrong Stadium

1. Kappa Kappa Gamma
2. Kappa Alpha Theta
3. Alpha Delta Pi
4. Phi Mu
5. Pi Beta Phi
6. Team Athena
7. Chi Omega
8. Roadrunners
9. Alpha Phi
10. Gamma Phi Beta
11. Oz
12. Cycledelics
13. Delta Delta Delta
14. Alpha Xi Delta
15. ConFuoco
16. Delta Zeta
17. Forest
18. Landsharks
19. Vayu
20. Alpha Chi Omega
21. Delta Gamma
22. McNutt Cycling
23. Alpha Phi Omega (Women)
24. Alpha Gamma Delta
25. Team College Life
26. Briscoe Blaze
27. Zeta Tau Alpha
28. Kappa Delta
29. Delta Sigma Pi (Women)
30. Foster 4ce
31. Super Teter
32. Teter Cycling

The Little
500

Appendix B: Comprehensive Rider Index

The following appendix is a directory of Little 500 riders from 1951 to 1999, compiled from IU Student Foundation records. Though the directory is intended solely for actual race participants, several teams' listings may include coaches and/or alternate riders, owing to a lack of official race-day records from some years.

Men's Little 500

1951

1. South Hall Buccaneers
Russ Keller
Bob Moore
John Skomp
Glen Wilson

2. Sigma Alpha Epsilon
Chapman Blackwell
Jim Blozie
Tony Hill
Jack Slingsby

3. Phi Gamma Delta
Bruce Klopfenstein
Bill McLaughlin
Ray Nicholson
Dale Vieau

4. Rogers East V
Stan Dusseau
Robert Kaley
Melvin Parker
Hilary Walterhouse

5. Lambda Chi Alpha
Dick Fegley
Newell Hall
Gene Miller
Paul Wolfram

6. North Hall Friars
Sandy Franklin
David Johnson
Maurice Kiser
Jerry Ruff

7. Zeta Beta Tau
Irving Bright
Jerry Gould
Donald Simon
Jack Zipperman

8. Phi Kappa Psi
Don Button
Bob Carlton
Herb Hand
Jim Jay

9. Beta Theta Pi
Bob Conlon
Dick Hall
Jerry Hubbart
Dick Schweinsberger

10. (tie) Phi Delta Theta
Jack Alexander
David Aver
Wilbur Dremstedt
Phil Snyder

10. (tie) Sigma Pi
Don Holstein
Charles Myers
Herb Parsons
Phil Parsons

12. Dodds House
Robert Beres
Claude Fattore
Thomas O'Rourke
Robert Primavera

13. Delta Upsilon
Bill Bear
Robert Bergdal
Larry Cutner
Martin Kinney

14. Theta Chi
Frank Barnhart
Bob Bork
Coleman LaMaster
Dick Woltman

15. Alpha Tau Omega
Fred Eberly
Dan Hermann
Jim McBride
Fred Stassel

16. South Hall B
Dick DeFreeuw
Don Gugel
Bob Howes
Tom Stankus

17. Sigma Nu
Jim Benz
Jerry Van Ooyen
Jim Way
D. Wilder

18. Elliott House
Dick Garretson
Jim Huff
Ross Michel
Jim Platis

19. North Hall Cavaliers
Tom Lantz
Guy Pellegrinelli
Jack Sellers
Don Willman

20. Ferguson House
Dee Castetter
Larry Hoffman
Tom Keyes
Glenn Mitchell

21. Nichols House
Donald Crabill
Raymond Cutler
A.A. Tuley
Raymond Wrede

22. Delta Tau Delta
Don Henkel
Glen Kastner
Al Linneman
John Wolfe

23. Phi Sigma Kappa
Edwin Corns
William Freitag
Cecil Mellinger
John Peterson

24. Rogers West T
Walt Backus
Glenn Emery
Richard Freeman
Larry Fromhart

25. Acacia
Gene Bockstahler
Tom Haynes
Charles Koger
Vernon Martin

26. Alpha Phi Alpha
Frank Hayes
Jesse Hayes
William Lee
Eugene Taylor

27. Kappa Sigma
Richard Godare
Robert Inserra
Jack Joel
Jay Lang

28. Kappa Delta Rho
Pete Carthinos
Ronald Hinding
Larry Smith
Donald Stroud

29. Pi Lambda Phi
Bob Bartick
Harold Cohen
Al Goldstein
Harold Morrison

30. Pi Kappa Alpha
Ned Bowman
Ken Lemons
Dick Mudge
Strother Whitfield

31. Parks House
Bill Meyers
Jack Primich
Lawrence Scott
Tim Goshern

32. Jenkins House
Don Beaver
Ervin Darling
Bill Palvas
Jim Parent

33. Hummer House
Martin Ball
Leon Bendit
Frank Hayes
Royce Truex

1952

1. North Hall Friars
Sandy Franklin
Russ Keller

Jerry Ruff
Gene Strause

2. Rogers East V
Clif DuBrueil
Bob Kaley
Harry Klein
Joe Konoski
Hilary Walterhouse

3. Phi Kappa Psi
Tom Butler
Don Button
Bob Carlton
Tom Glidden
Bill Romey
Bill Wainscott

4. Phi Delta Theta
Robert Curry
Wilbur Dremstedt
Jerry Lewis
Carl Litten
Dan Newman
A. Davis Tuley

5. Alpha Tau Omega
Dick DeFreeuw
Fred Fouts
Richard Goff
Don Henry
John Shaffer
Fred Stassel

6. Zeta Beta Tau
Ben Behr
Irving Bright, Jr.
Charles Cohen
Don Lozou
Don Simon
Jack Zipperman

7. Sigma Chi
Jerry Ellis
Dwight Parker
Frank Unversaw
Bob Weigel
Robert Williams II
Robert J. Williams

8. Kappa Sigma
John Blackmon
James Bruce
Conrad Burton
James Metcalf
Ronald Taylor
Stuart Templeton

9. Sigma Pi
Don Domenic
John Moenning
John Myers
Herb Parsons
Phil Parsons
Charles Thompson

10. Dodds House
Claude Fattore
Frank Jose
William Knipe
Robert Primavera
Richard Urbauer
Gordon Venderipe

11. South Hall B
Benton Colglazier
Milton Leontiades
Bill Schlundt
Burke Scott
John Wood

12. Todd House
Herb Abramson
Bill Braunlin
Darwin Eshelman

Bill Forney
Bob Knoll
Dave Krevitz

13. North Hall Cavaliers
Jim Crow
Tom Delph
Vern Roudebush
Jack Sellers
Mike Warren
Art Wright

14. Rogers East W
Ray Dunkin
Victor Furiga
Robert Jackson
Jim Kamicar
Les Kun
Ray Moore

15. Pi Kappa Phi
John DeNora
Tom Keyes
Glenn LeMasters
Charles Perschon
Dale Walsh
Gordon Weaver

16. Lowe House
Tom Foy
Gordon Franke
Eddy Kreienbrink
Dick Simko
Bob Vinson
Roger Woods

17. Rogers West W
Stan Dusseau
Don Horan
Jerry Lenertz
Ed Matthews
Hayward Reynolds
William Shadburne

18. West Hall III Trojans
Lenny Cohen
Steward Duetsch
Bruce Kullen
Ken Lucas
Gene Thweat

19. Hummer House
John Anderson
Dan Bauman
Eddie Effinger
Bob Ewbank
Chester Kmak
Joe Thomas

20. Nichols House
Dick Ashburner
Larry Fromhart
Larry Ikerd
Owen Nowlin
Robert Tallman
Raymond Wrede

21. Theta Chi
J.C. Addison
Tom Boone
Jack Frushour
Jack Hume
Jack Schwartz

22. North Hall Barons
Bob Borst
Bob Gillman
Max Graeber
Bill Holland
Dick Pile
John Thornton

23. Lambda Chi Alpha
Howard Breedlove
Charles Castle
Don Green
Newell Hall

Robert Howard
John Lynge

24. Phi Kappa Tau
Frank Bauer
Gilbert Barnes
Ralph Crume
Tom Marshall
Ralph Sheets

25. Kappa Delta Rho
Don Foster
Ron Hinding
W. Gene James
Stan Solomon
Heath Strachon
Don Stroud

26. Alpha Phi Alpha
Cleofus Adams
Raphael Hardwick
Frank Hayes
George Hayes
Cordell Olive
Donald Suggs

27. Beta Theta Pi
Dave Bailey
Richard Barnhart
John Bartkiewiez
Ed DeHority
Dick Hall
Jerry Meadows

28. Theta Xi
Mac Carroll
Ervin Darling
Tom Harders
Tom Lambert
Al Rullman

29. Rogers West V
Bruce Cowen

Bob Katter
Willfred Merkle
George Owczarazak
Don Wold
Bob Wright

30. South Hall Buccaneers
Don Erickson
Bob Fisher
Russ Holloway
Leon Kelleher
Don McClarney
Paul Stone

31. Sigma Alpha Mu
Dick Berger
Monroe Cutler
Mel Ein
Ed Frank
Harry Meyer
Sidney Rothstein

32. Campbell House
George Fipp
Oscar Frenzel III
Len Gherardi
Kenneth Hanson
Ronald Havard
Jack McCartt

33. Pi Kappa Alpha
Ned Bowman
Richard Dolnics
William Eskew
William Peach
Strother Whitfield
Frank Wilkens

1953

1. North Hall Friars
Leonard Border
Jerry Ruff

Robert Sedam
Gene Strause

2. Acacia
Ronald Beckman
Rodney Brandes
Gorman Burton
John DeRome
Russell Judd
Charles Mann

3. Sigma Alpha Epsilon
George Beck
Chapman Blackwell
Walter Colbath
Robert Evans
Peter Gillis
Donald Summers

4. Delta Upsilon
Donald Bissell
Larry Cutner
James Eades
David Fletcher
Charles Pancol
Larry Reinking

5. Phi Kappa Psi
Fred Agnew
Holmes Carlton
Bruce Collins
Paul Knowles
Dave Newell
James Snyder

6. Phi Delta Theta
Jack Conley
Wilbur Dremstedt
Charles Robert Ellis
Jerry Lewis
Dan William Newman
A.A. Tuley

7. Alpha Tau Omega
Richard DeFreeuw
Fred Fouts
John Shaffer
Paul Stohr
Richard White
Jerry Young

8. Zeta Beta Tau
Stephen Bayer
Ben Behr
James Bergsman
Irv Bright
Don Lozow
Lenny Pryweller

9. Phi Gamma Delta
Bruce Breneman
Bruce Klopfenstein
Theodore Moorman
Roger Olivieri
Richard Riely
Luther Thweatt

10. Sigma Pi
Earl Bailey
David Donovan
Donald Holstein
Robert Isenogle
John Moenning
Phillip Parsons

11. Phi Kappa
Hank Anderson
Vince Daniels
Paul Hanas
James Lakatos
Patrick Lind
Norman Pictor

12. Phi Sigma Kappa
Paul Burch, Jr.
James Dekter
Richard Drake

Carrdon Hawkins
Thomas May
John Zavacky

13. Sigma Nu
Reid Crosby
Robert Garrigus
Fred Mercer
William Sparks
Allan Stoner
Samuel Stoner

14. Kappa Delta Rho
Ozzie Baumgartner
Donald Foster
Eugene Hill
Ronald Hinding
Stanley Malkamus
Frank Pisacreta

15. West Hall IV
Roland Dungy
Richard Jordan
John May
Jerry Puls
Joe Rich
Phillip Saliga

16. West Hall II
Stewart Deutsch
Aldo Facca
Jack Herider
John Isenbarger
Joseph Kublinec
Narlon Littell

17. Pi Kappa Alpha
W. Glenn Emery
James Griffin
Robert Howes
Robert Lau
Bernard Rekus
Earl Slingsby

18. South Hall B
James Davis
Milton Leontiades
Joe Orear
James Phipps
Burke Scott
L. Wayne Sigman

19. Beta Theta Pi
John Davies
Scott Hall
George Heighway, Jr.
David Schooley
Joseph Thomas, Jr.
John Van Osdol

20. Dodds House
Thomas Callahan
Brian Davies
Robert Ewald
Bill Kanipe
Ronald Petrovich
Richard Urbauer

21. North Hall Cavaliers
James Collins
John Gallagher
Keith Gettelfinger
David Kaufman
Jerome Montgomery
Roland Snearly

22. Kappa Sigma
John Blackmon
James Bruce
James Donovan
Jack Kollker
Thomas O'Donnell
George Rian

23. Lambda Chi Alpha
Bill Allman
Michael Dague
Wayne Ethridge

Carl Gilpin
W.G. Neiderauer, Jr.
Charles Wilkinson

24. Todd House
William Carley
Darwin Eshelman
William Forney
James Hughes
Arnold Samuel
Nicholas Sangalis

25. Delta Tau Delta
Gordon Curry
Don Hooker
Glen Kastner
Denny Krick
Richard Lawson
Steve Smith

26. Rogers East W
Gordon Belt
Ferrell Bennett
Bill Dallas
Jack Irey
Christian Sharp
Bob Wertz

27. Lowe House
Ronald Beiswanger
Cole Chalmer
Nick Cserevits
Jack Dunfee
Richard Dusseau
William Ryckman

28. Ruter House
Jim Bonvallet
Richard Ellenwood
Burton Johnson
Jack Learly
James Stone
Stewart Witt

29. Sigma Chi
Hap Eggers
Jerry Ellis
Darroll French
Tom Graves
Robert Williams
Clifford Williamson

30. Sigma Phi Epsilon
George Brake
John Carris
Donald Gage
Rex Linville
Harold McClary
Allan Thomas

31. Theta Chi
Tom Boone
Ed Conrey
Don Jung
Wess Stoppenhagen
John Vajner
Jack Wieneke

32. Hummer House
John Angerson
Daniel Bauman
John Cluver
John Gentile
John Pentergrass
Earl Stahl

33. Jenkins House
Bob Denari
Don Jacobs
Bob Skoronski
Frank Skoronski
Ralph Taylor
Bob Woolpert

1954

1. Sigma Nu
Joseph Magers
Ralph Martin
Fred Mercer
Richard Silcox

2. Acacia
George Branam
John DeRome
Russell Judd
Bill Mann
Gary Osborne
Dave Porter

3. Alpha Tau Omega
Fred Fouts
Ron Johnson
Jim Seeright
John Shafer
Gene White
Jerry Young

4. North Hall Barons
Dwain Bass
Clarence Doninger
Ted Fody
Bill Godfrey
Mike Hriso
Bob Wruble

5. Phi Delta Theta
Jack Conley
Jerry Lewis
Frank Martin
Dan Newman
Phil Rash
Bill Snapp

6. Todd House
Dean Blank
John Crismore
Jerry Larson
Kenneth Richardson
Ronald Wagner

7. Phi Gamma Delta
Bruce Brenneman
Jimmy Dils
Howard Fisher
Gene Thweatt
Charles Williams
Richard Williams

8. Delta Chi
Dick Anthony
Jim Bose
Ralph Cundiff
William Edwards
John Hooning
Robert Killian

9. Dodds House
Wayne Dell
Robert Dillard
Fredrick Espie
James Jenkins
William Mount
Richard Munn

10. Phi Kappa
Vincent Daniels
Mike Danko
John Kosin
Joe Mikula
Norm Pictor
Chuck Ramage

11. Sigma Pi
Jim Collins
Bob Hansen

Keith Isenogle
Glenn Meyer
Bob Miser
John Moenning

12. North Hall Friars
Ronald Martin
Dave Romerhaus
Bob Sedam
Gus Sjoholm
Gene Strause
John Thornton

13. Sigma Alpha Epsilon
C. G. Balch
George Beck
Gordon Elsner
Robert Evans
Peter Gillis
Rod Perkins

14. Phi Kappa Psi
Bob Carlton
Joe Dupler
Jack Hand
Mac Marks
Jim Sellegren
Steve Snyder

15. Lambda Chi Alpha
Paul Damm
Jim Laswell
Todd Moravec
Dick Nierman
David Schaaf
Bob Smith

16. Alpha Phi Alpha
Richard Bradley
Marvin Davis
Raphael Hardwick
Robert Jackson

Robert Short
Tom Wright

17. Dunn House
Mark Harper
Robert Luzadder
Harvy Naffer
James Phipps
Thomas Rea
William Shinn

18. Rogers West W
Gorden Belt
Ferrell Bennett
Gary McDonnell
Harry Schaefer

19. Delta Upsilon
Don Bissell
John Custer
James Eades
Tom Kilpatrick
Larry Reinking
Jim Vanek

20. Theta Chi
Fred Adams
Darryl Harris
Kenny Lewis
Dick Shelly
Rex Stinson
Jack Wieneke

21. South Hall B
David Bone
Phil Corbin
Hiram Cushenberry
William Forney
Milton Leontiades
Bob Masterson

22. Sigma Chi
Eugene Day
Tom Hilligoss
Paul McCoy
Tom Payne
Chuck Smith
Bob Williams

23. Kappa Delta Rho
Ozzie Baumgartner
Don Foster
Carter Hall
Ron Hinding
Glenn Kanning
Paul Muckenfuss

24. Sigma Alpha Mu
Sheldon Breskow
Jerry Dann
Paul Gelman
Louis Mervis
James Mossler
Neil Sanaler

25. Beta Theta Pi
John Davies
Jim Evans
Larry Jones
Jim LaBrash
Dave Schooley
Al Willardo

26. Zeta Beta Tau
Steve Bayer
Ben Behr
Irv Bright
Ed Hollander
John Mormal
Bob Whitson

27. Pi Kappa Phi
Julian Blackerby

Richard Boyle
Harlan Christie
Burdell Sell
Gordon Weaver
James Witek

28. Delta Tau Delta
R. E. Bussell
Charles Gannon
Roy Haussman
Edward Knoebber
Jack Shaw
Joe Wedding

29. Tau Kappa Epsilon
John Anderson
Jim Bently
Jim Ferrier
Bob Lee
John Schulz

30. Harding House
Paul Beckly
Jim Faller
Al Friend
Jim Hawkins
Paul Shrieve
Robert Trinkle

31. Jenkins House
Herbert Baylis
Joe Bogue
Brad Bomba
Robert Denari
John Fisher
Lee Thurow

32. Phi Sigma Kappa
Jim Dexter
Frank Geiss
Richard Haunton
Ralph Taylor
Joe Young
John Zavacky

33. Parks House
Bob Bistryski
Duane Burnor
Howard Goldberg
Ted Hirsh
Keith Kauble

1955

1. South Cottage Grove
Ronald David
Alan Dusendschon
Gene Hindenlang
Richard Myers

2. West Hall Trojans
James Anderson
Bill Forney
Donald Gant
Kenneth Mettam
Donald Murat
Samuel Trentadue

3. Delta Chi
Spencer Allen
Richard Anthony
James Bose
John Hooning
Robert Killian
George Rafferty

4. Acacia
John DeRome
Jerry Heavilon
Bill Mann
Gary Osborne
Wayne Simon
Dave Weaver

5. North Hall Barons
Dwain Bass
William Edwards
Theodore Fody

James Phipps
Richard Norris
Robert Wruble

6. Sigma Nu
Clarence Doninger
Robert Ganchiff
Ralph Martin
Fred Mercer
Richard Silcox
Bill Sparks

7. Phi Gamma Delta
Robert Barrett
Bruce Breneman
Jimmy Dils
Harold Harrell
Louis Mangels
Gene McGarvey

8. Dodds House
John Bauer
Wayne Dell
Robert Dillard
Ivan Jones
Thomas Litteral
Edward Straub

9. Phi Delta Theta
Jack Conley
Jerry Lewis
Dick Maul
Bill Snapp
Gene Strause
Glen Wilson

10. Phi Kappa Psi
David Brenner
David Carlton
George Gannon
Gene Maddock
Steve Snyder
Richard Wertz

11. Sigma Pi
Jim Collins
Bill Crow
Ray Heiman
Bob Miser
John Moenning
Phil Willsey

12. Rollins House
John Crismore
Leroy Kochert
Gerald Larson
Kenneth Richardson

13. Hickory Hall West
Gordon Belt
Philip Lough
Jim Mather
Gary McDonald
Richard Morris
Harry Schaefer

14. Sigma Alpha Epsilon
Charles Balch
Robert Evans
Dick Fox
Timothy Furlong
Homer Groves
Rod Perkins

15. Ruter House
Remo Cataldi
Lawrence Cellini, Jr.
Calvin Cheesbrough
Larry Hanley
Florian Latek
Lewis Mayer

16. Zeta Beta Tau
Stephen Bayer
Daniel Dorman
Donald Grande
Ed Hollander, Jr.
James Kuhn
Bob Whitson

17. Hickory Hall East
Tom Arnold
John Farquhar, Jr.
William Fencken
Charles Johnson
Gerald Laswell
Scott Mahon

18. Kappa Sigma
Donald Fiege
Ned Kerr
Peter O'Malley
Donald Scott
Robert Study
John Weddle

19. Kappa Delta Rho
Ozzie Baumgartner
Emery Coon
George Holland
Wayne Moore
Stan Rice
Don Taylor

20. Rogers I
Douglas Bennett
Wayne Hickman
Walter King, Jr.
Warren Meyer
Jerry Pearson
Noel Showers

21. Phi Kappa
John Drabeck
Eugene Drost
John Eichorst
Lester Govert
Norman Pictor
Paul Tretter

22. Sigma Phi Epsilon
John Caris
Ronald Chitwood
Donald Gage

Keith Gettelfinger
Richard Motz
Richard Sutton

23. Pi Lambda Phi
Donald Dorfman
Clark Feldman
Henry Hanau
Leslie Turbowitz
Donald Tusk
Harmon Zacune

24. Delta Tau Delta
Arnold Brock
Thomas Cassidy
Charles Eickman
Jerry Ford
Ed Knoebber
Bob Thompson

25. Parks House
Herbert Baylis, Jr.
Gene Fowler
Richard Gayde, Jr.
Walter Harris
Norman Koselke
Robert Pierce

26. Alpha Tau Omega
Fred Fouts
Thomas Ritchie
Jim Seeright
Paul Stohr
Gene White
Jerry Young

27. West Hall Saints
Leland Ayer
Ronald Brown
Joe Hilton
Ben Hobbs
Marvin Mishkin
Billy Ross Moore

28. Lambda Chi Alpha
Si Burgher
Clarence Dawson
James Laswell
John Ramsey
Charles Rawlings
Karl Schneider

29. Elliott House
Richard Clester
James Hassett
Wilson Hurrell
Stuart Murphy
Arnold Samuel
Thomas Weddle

30. Sigma Alpha Mu
Jerrold Alberts
Sheldon Breskow
Jack Klausner
Robert Kling
Jerry Kursban
James Mossler

31. Phi Sigma Kappa
George Alsip
Frank Geiss
Bob Hardy
Dick Haunton
Bob Parente
Joe Young

32. Theta Chi
Thomas Ferverda
Robert McIlarth
Richard Shelly
Rex Stinson
Jack Wellman

33. Delta Upsilon
James Alling
Wallace Ansburg
Ray Ball

James Conley
Norman Komorowski
Larry Reinking

1956

1. Phi Gamma Delta
Joseph Abatie
James Cusick
Thomas Herendeen
Louis Mangles

2. Dodds House
Wayne Dell
Robert Dillard
Jim Law
Karl Napper
Douglas Shue
Jerry Wright

3. South Cottage Grove
Charles Anderson
Alan Dusendschon
Stanley Hedges
Aram Kalfaian
Richard Myers
Robert Watkins

4. Delta Chi
R. Spencer Allen
James Anthony
Joe Kamman
Robert Killian
Ted McFall
George Rafferty

5. Sigma Nu
Daryl Beaman
Clarence Doninger
Fred Mercer
Jerald Ruff
Richard Silcox
Robert Wruble

6. North Hall Barons
Theodore Fody
Curtis Hare
Wilson Hubbell
Robert Kring
Phillip Lough
Ronald St. Martin

7. Sigma Pi
Ronald Lee Barnhart
Ronald David
Lloyd Emerson
William Irmscher
Robert Miser
Noel Wiley

8. Acacia
Dwain Bass
David Dale
Ghassan Omary
Gary Osborne
Bob Townsend
Jim Wright

9. Kappa Delta Rho
Lorrenz Gugel
George Holland
Minot Schuman
Eldin Versteeg
Larry Wood

10. Phi Delta Theta
Gil Berry
Gale Conley
Carl Golightly
Joe Gordon Hagee
James Kneisley
Bill Snapp

11. Phi Kappa Psi
Charles Mack
Joe Schaub
Jerry Schofield
James Snyder

Richard Wertz
Hans Wuelfing

12. Delta Upsilon
Larry Admire
Jerry Horney
Burnie Maurek
William Miller
Michael Pack
Brad Poling

13. Laurel Hall North
Henry Bach
Bill Henke
John Konzen
Elmer Macke
Thomas McCarthy
Richard McPherson

14. Maple Hall North
Dennis Goldman
James Hurst
Gene Matovich
William Sobat

15. Rollins House
Neil Anderson
John Crismore
Leroy Kochert
Ronald Maris
John Patrick Sanders

16. Rogers I
Wayne Breck
J. D. Clemmons
George Martin
Charles Newstrom
Joe Puckett
Tom White

17. Sigma Alpha Epsilon
Arne Andre
Charles Batch

Thomas Gorman
Homer Groves
Bob King
Rod Perkins

18. Ruter House
David Beldus
Lawrence Cellini
Michael Halus
Florian Latex
James Oliver
George Snay

19. West Hall II
John Black
Robert Cook
Jack Halton
Michael Padula
Lawton Shank
Richard Williams

20. Tau Kappa Epsilon
Richard Carson
Larry Kocal
Bob Lee
Bob Massengill
Virgil Scudder
Larry Stookey

21. Dunn House
David Dersch
John Jackson
John Lerch
Phil Pffenbarger
Thomas Rader
Bill Shinn

22. West Hall Trojans
Jim Anderson
Kenneth Papp
Donald Pickens
Paul Rider
Wayne Sigman
Tom Williams

23. Kappa Sigma
Robert Bruce
John Cravens
Joseph Lull Fox
Russell Kuehl II
Charles Levenhagen
John Wilhoite

24. Sigma Chi
Dick Albershardt
Larry Carter
Tom Egan
William Pomp
Peter Reibel
David Wood

25. Alpha Tau Omega
Brad Laycock
John Reid
Jim Rogge
Clyde Rountree
Bruce Smith
Jerry Young

26. Hickory Hall West
Jerry Kotlarz
Dave Mather
Nicholas Pappas
Charles Ray
Robert Spudic
Wayne Terry

27. Parks House
Bill Engel
Walt Harris
Woody Jones
Jan McCrory
Joe Saladino
Jerry Svetanoff

28. Maple Hall South
Bob Hicks
Dale Humen

Gene Pelizzoni
Roger Tillman

29. South Hall A
Joe Asch
John Hedge
Bob Koene
John Laurence
Harold Rothman
Charles Winslow

30. Theta Chi
Dick Bohnenkamp
Ron Borcherding
Tom Byrum
Bob Mings
Dick Shelly
Jerry Spinler

31. Hall House
Bob Bloecker
Fred Dressel
Dick Kendall
Clem Periolat
Buz Zimmerman

32. Theta Xi
Alan Coplen
Larry Johnson
Lee Judd
Donald Melnik
Fred Rodeman

33. North Hall Cavaliers
James Ellis
DeWitt Jackson
Richard Osburn
Morris Phillips
Ray Reynolds
Burton Sweeton

1957

1. Sigma Nu
Clarence Doninger
Joseph Magers
Armin Olsen
Hilary Walterhouse

2. Dodds House
Robert Dillard
Jim Law
Karl Napper
Dave Nolan

3. Acacia
David Bass
David Dale
Kenton Hartman
Gary Osborne
G. William Phillips
Robert Townsend

4. Phi Delta Theta
John Black
Joe Hagee
Larry Kennedy
Philip Klinger
Jim Kneisley
Bill Snapp

5. Delta Chi
Laurie Cellini
Bob Killian
George Rafferty
Fred Redeker
Dave Whitsell
Max Wilson

6. Phi Gamma Delta
Robert Byrne, Jr.
Harold Harrell
Tom Herendeen
Louis Mangels

Peter Ohremskey
Jack Scott

7. Alpha Tau Omega
Donald Feldkamp
Paul Hendricks
William Hohlt
James McFadden
John Reid
William Snyder

8. Sigma Pi
George Buckingham
Ronald David
Dennis Dewey
Jack Douberteen
Lloyd Emerson
Vic Russell

9. Ruter House
David Beldus
Allen Kolb
Thomas Miller
John Odle
Gary Robbins
Lawrence Smith

10. Delta Upsilon
Dale Bakehorn
Brad Poling
Donald Scott
Donald Weaver
Robert Winkler

11. South Cottage Grove
Abdul Amoria
Leo Boeglin
Richard Myers
George Snay
Bob Watkins
Richard Wright

12. North Hall Barons
Homer Altevogt
John Beyler
Barry Dunn
Frank Hubbell
Phil Lough
Robert Witham

13. Tau Kappa Epsilon
Richard Carson
Ted Lagerwall
Kenneth Lakes
Robert Massengill
John Pearson
Gerald Preusz

14. Phi Kappa Psi
Bill Canter
Dave Carlton
Lewis Cook, Jr.
Thomas Lord
Ronald Pullen
Richard Wertz

15. West Hall Saints
Cort Carrington
Ralph Jones
Edward Latour
Marvin Mishkin
Philip Wilkinson
Jerry Zonker

16. Kappa Sigma
Kurt Carlisle
George Cook
John Cravens
Charles Levenhagen
Paul Showalter
John Wilhoite

17. Sigma Chi
Vedder Broker
Charles Culver
Robert Fesler

Michael Halus
Robertson Kenner
William Pomp

18. Rollins House
Neil Anderson
Darrell Blanton
William Hutto, Jr.
Ron Maris
Gerald Pennock
Eugene Striver

19. Maple Hall North
John Berdis
Phillip Legge, Jr.
Donald Moon
Robert Sadenwater
James Wendell
Paul Youngs

20. South Hall Buccaneers
Avery Carmack
James Davis
Bill Helms
Dick Hori
Robert Preston
Frank Simko

21. Delta Tau Delta
Don Brodie
Charles Eickman
Gene Kalina
Wayne Tencate
Dave Warnimont
Michael Wiest

22. Kappa Delta Rho
Robert Ake
Richard Holmes
Weldon Leimer
Glenn Schowe
Minot Schuman
James Wilson

23. Elliott House
Robert Armstrong
Charles Chapman
Chuck Heal
Dale Kline
Earl Pontius
Dave Pringle

24. Lambda Chi Alpha
Joseph Doninger
James Fletcher
Kenneth Himsel
Frederick Lotze
Thomas Potter
Charles Rawlings

25. Todd House
Doug Abrams
John Gillaspy
Ron Gottschalk
Max Mohler
Gordon Rosenau
Ron Wagner

26. Dunn House
James Aaron
Alan Burt
John Jackson
Dave Kirchoff
Clifford Maesaka
Don Meyer

27. Zeta Beta Tau
Daniel Dorman
Gene Douglis
Dean Glasel
Micah Ross
Moe Silverman
Philip Weinstein

28. Nichols House
Mike Burkett
Jack Chamberlin
James Gibbs

Frank Langford
John Liesenfelt
Harold Southard

29. Hall House
Robert Bloecker
Fred Dressel
Richard Elward
Jerry Pitcher
Jerry Turner

30. West Hall Trojans
James Anderson
John Auld
Bill Cavanaugh
Robert Huggins
James Stout
Axel R. Zinkovich

31. Sigma Alpha Mu
Jerry Alberts
George Feldman
Bob Forman
Kenneth Goldberg
Art Samuel
Bunny Soloman

32. Parks House
Roger Fortna
Walter Harris
Charles Hayes
James Pierazek
Robert Winstead

33. Theta Xi
Jerry Hinds
Don Melnik
Dick Monroe
Bill Rudolph
Jerry Svenenoff
Ron Tsychia

1958

1. Phi Kappa Psi
Lew Cook
Jim Law
Karl Napper
Lou Sharp

2. Sigma Nu
Dick Fox
Dave Grebe
Wilson Hubbell
Joe Magers
Chuck Thulin
Hilary Walterhouse

3. Phi Gamma Delta
John Ashman
Dave Eitman
John Fechtman
Jerry Tardy
Steve White
Jerry Wright

4. Delta Upsilon
Dale Bakehorn
Jan Gardner
Charles Locke
Don Massey
Brad Poling
Don Weaver

5. Sigma Alpha Epsilon
Kent Combs
Bill Givens
Tom Kendrick
Dick Kremp
Dick Leonard
Dave Thulin

6. West Hall
Bill Barton

Dick Beaver
Jerry Miki
Ken Peters
Bill Zirzow

7. South Cottage Grove
David Nawrocki
Bob Watkins
Fred Wehrly
Darwin Wilkeson
Jerry Wright
Richard Wright

8. Phi Delta Theta
John Black
Jim Burrell
Gale Conley
Joe Hagee
Bill Snapp
Bernie Vacendak

9. Acacia
Dave Dale
Kent Hartman
Cal Kemp
Phil Lough
Bill Phillips
Bob Townsend

10. Sigma Pi
George Buckingham
Ron David
Jack Douberteen
Bud Emerson
Stan Holdeman
Donald Williams

11. Chi Phi
Dave Beldus
Dick Clause
Dave Engel
Jim Gibbs
Don Meyer

12. Alpha Tau Omega
John Gregg
Bill Hohlt
Mike Huffman
Jay Lewis
John Reid
Bill Snyder

13. Tau Kappa Epsilon
Dick Carson
Alan Griffith
Ken Lakes
Mike Liste
Bob Massengill
Gerald Preusz

14. South Hall Buccaneers
Don Ball
Jack Boehm
Avery Carmack
Dick Faires
Dick Hori

15. Delta Chi
Jim Bruner
Max Mohler
Floyd Romack
Fred Redeker
Dave Wilson
Jerry Winkler

16. Beta Theta Pi
Dave Arvin
Jack Benedix
Richard Chalfant
Steve Filipowski
Richard Myers
William Pugh

17. Dodds House
Tony Bourdon
Tom Gollmer
Paul Oakes

Doug Shue
Pete Spurbeck
Ed Vondrak

18. Rollins House
Dave Blase
Ron Maris
Sherrill Miller
Max Mykrantz
Larry Rabb
Gene Sriver

19. Kappa Delta Rho
Wallace Fosnight
Wendall Ham
Jack Hetherington
Delano Newkirk
Minot Schuman

20. Ferguson House
Peter Brown
Don Harle
Marty Lovett
Deane Malaker
David Payne
Tom Woehler

21. North Hall Barons
Wade Altevogt
John Beyler
Walter Chase
Kelly Kellstron
William Silcox
Gerard Swisher

22. Delta Tau Delta
Don Brodie
Chuck Eickman
Jerry Ford
Dewain Lightfoot
Russ Smith
Mer Studor

23. Hickory West
Tom Arnold
Dennis Berdis
Jim Hurst
Dave Miller
Nick Pappas
Dick Servies

24. Kappa Kappa Psi
Larry Coon
Dave Ison
Joe Jupin
Don McClough
Ken Schubert
Walt Wilson

25. Kappa Sigma
George Carey
John Cravens
Harrison Davis
Charles Levenhagen
Bob Perna
Richard Turnak

26. Lambda Chi Alpha
Dave Deeg
Ken Himsel
Chuck Jones
Keith Kauble
Chuck Rawlings
John Schram

27. Sigma Alpha Mu
Jerry Alberts
Mark Himelstein
Stan Neimark
Dave Rothberg
Art Samuel
Alan Sherman

28. Rogers V
Shrichand Bajaj
Edward Neblett

Jack Swart
George Tillson
George Tolhurst
Marion Wingard

29. Harding House
George Benhke
Terry Conley
Fred Dressel
Bryan Lenahan
Jim Metcalfe
Morris Phillips

30. Zeta Beta Tau
Peter Eisenberg
Mel Goldstein
Bob Karlsberg
Rich Lees
Harry Sax
Phil Weinstein

31. Hall House
Bob Bloecker
Gary Hayes
Ed Hiatt
Mike Kopernik
Jim Krieger
Ray Peterson

32. Laurel Hall
Richard Angle
James Babb
Robert Gecowets
Robert Hill
Michael Lopez

33. Ruter House
John Green
Alan Kold
John Odle
Tom Miller
Ron Robbin
Jerry Werling

1959

1. Phi Kappa Psi
Dave Atha
Lew Cook
Jim Roy
Jerry Swisher

2. Sigma Alpha Epsilon
Mac Crosbie
Lloyd Hyde
Dick Kremp
Dick Leonard
Jim McFrye
Dave Thulin

3. Sigma Nu
Gary Long
Joe Magers
Bud Olsen
Ron Paskins
Charles Wible
Bob Wilkinson

4. Chi Phi
Tom Cook
Jim Gibbs
Ed Kesl
Don Meyer
Kenny Simpson

5. Acacia
Joe Abrell
Dave Brown
Bill Carbon
John Odle
Bob Townsend

6. Phi Gamma Delta
Cliff Burns
John Fechtman
Hayes Hatfield

Jerry Tardy
Steve White
Jerry Wright

7. Lambda Chi Alpha
Larry Eaton
Richard Engle
Chuck Jones
Keith Kauble
Dick Marshall
Bob Wilson

8. Ferguson Hall
Ted Brown
Jim Downs
Don Hall
Rex Killian
Gordon Pavey
David Payne

9. Dodds House
John Reed
Keith Ritter
Harry Ross
Terry Schriefer
Pete Spurbeck
Steve Sucre

10. Rollins House
Dave Blase
Bill Bucklin
George Huffman
Dick Kelly
Sherill Miller
Jerry Smith

11. Phi Delta Theta
Gale Conley
Richard Day
William Learmoth
Steve Wesner
Edward Willis

12. Pi Kappa Phi
Don Lee
John Maroni
Rod Ruckriegle
Art Savich
Bob Williamson

13. Linden Hall West
Gary Brown
Grayson Carter
Myron Curry
Mike Smith
Richard Wright

14. Delta Chi
Jack Ingle
Fred Settina
Dan Tankersley
Cal White
Dave Wilson

15. Dunn House
Mike Boze
Richard Brown
Tom King
Dave Piser
Paul Pomeroy
Tom Thompson

16. Sigma Chi
Bob Baechle
Vedder Brocker
Frank Cox
Bob Denham
John Lane
Tom Twiss

17. Theta Chi
Bob Dyson
John Marynall
Bob Miller
Bob Pollock

Larry Ruff
Larry Zimmerman

18. Sigma Phi Epsilon
Phil Achton
Don Barr
Jack Boehm
Dave Brewer
Max Martin
Ernie Miller

19. Delta Upsilon
Dale Bakehorn
Bruce Black
Tom Burkhart
Mike Elliot
Jim Hardin
Carl Schmidt

20. South Hall Buccaneers
John Burkel
Avery Carmack
Ron Hallberg
Dick Hori
Bob Phillips

21. North Hall Friars
Joe Corey
Darwin Herbst
Ben Lesniak
John Mutka
Dick Wiehe

22. Beta Theta Pi
Tom Althauser
Dave Arvin
Steve Filipowski
Mick McClurgh
Bill Pugh

23. Alpha Tau Omega
John Bell
Bob Francis

Mike Huffman
Tom Lower
Don Pebworth

24. Ruter House
Harry Benson
Al Kolb
Neil Lantz
Dennis Murihill
Gordon Sims
Tom Steininger

25. Todd House
Doug Abrams
Jerry Harms
Jack Mathena
Dick Mattick
Ron Reas

26. Zeta Beta Tau
Gene Douglis
Al Fetter
Joe Goldberg
Danny Lightman
Harry Sax
Les Tankel

27. Hickory Hall West
Denny Berdis
Joe Janusonis
Gerard Lahmann
Frank Tinsley
Rom Tsuchiya

28. Sigma Pi
Bill Brattain
Lynn Gaylord
Joe Jupin
Mel Richards
Don Seeley

29. West Hall Trojans
Wally Bachir

Bill Cavanaugh
Elliott Harris
Doug Miki
Fred Rounds

30. Phi Sigma Kappa
Gus Duehmig
Ted Marshitz
Wally Pascale
Art Schneider
Todd Wolfrum

31. Delta Tau Delta
Jack Boges
Tom Drehobl
Dave Hedge
Nick Hill
Dewain Lightfoot
Russell Smith

32. Kappa Sigma
Harrison Davis
Jim Davis
Dave Dietz
Pete Griffin
Dick Jennings
John Wilhoite

33. Sigma Alpha Mu
George Feldman
Harold Kessler
Larry Olshan
Dave Rothberg
Don Stern

1960

1. Phi Kappa Psi
Dave Atha
Lew Cook
Don Leedy
John Odusch

2. Sigma Alpha Epsilon
Mac Crosbie
Karl Hagman
Lloyd Hyde
Dave Porter
Dave Thulin

3. Lambda Chi Alpha
Fred Cuppy
Dick Engle
Hank Hudson
Charles Jones
Jack Lehman
Ron Roemer

4. Sigma Nu
Tom Fruechtenicht
Jeff Landrum
Gary Long
Dave Rogers
George Waters
Charles Wible

5. Phi Gamma Delta
Dick Ashenfelter
Mike Ayers
Jeff Coulter
John Fechtman
Ron Gardner
Jerry Tardy

6. Chi Phi
Don Meyer
Ron Miller
Bob Neff
Harry Ross
Ken Simpson

7. Alpha Tau Omega
Steve Collins
Bevo Francis
Tom Klaer
Dave Lindzy
Dave Reng

8. Acacia
Joe Abrell
Mike Albright
Bill Brown
Dave Brown
Bill Carbon
Lonnie Woods

9. Dunn House
Paul Pomeroy
Larry Joe Shields
Leon Stoller
William Trapmann

10. Delta Chi
Bob Fiorini
Jim Flockencier
Gary Hayes
Keith Johnson
Dan Tankersley
Dave Wilson

11. Dodds House
Jeff Graves
Lynn McQuern
Errol Rayle
Curt Simic
Bill Weaverling
Emil Weber

12. Delta Upsilon
Jim Drew
Jan Gardner
Don Maskee
Mike Mellinger
Sam Smith

13. Sigma Phi Epsilon
Jack Boehm
Tom Hopkins
George Szabo
Tom Szabo

14. Campbell House
Larry Alyea
Jim Mahler
Dave Payne
Paul Steward

15. Sigma Chi
Bob Baechle
Jim Harris
Brian M. Jones
Noel Loftin
Pete Palmer
Dave Smith

16. Beta Theta Pi
John Beerbower
Bud Campbell
Mick McClurg
Steve Smith

17. Towers Center B
Jim Hawk
Bob Highfield
Terry Jenkins
Tom Pinder
Larry Strait

18. Forest Hall
Tom Carlile
Avery Carmack
Bob Carter
Charlie Ver
Wendell Tucker

19. Pi Kappa Phi
Bill Bucklin
Fred Lamb
Jack Maroni
Bill Putorti
Art Savich
Bob Williamson

20. Zeta Beta Tau
Jay Fienberg
Don Lee
Elliot Levin
Mickey Monroe
Harry Sax

21. Phi Sigma Kappa
Rich Chentnik
Dick Galich
Don Henry
Jim Herbenar
Mike Vietti

22. Kappa Delta Rho
Ken Beckley
Denny Koehlinger
Gary Long
Dick Meyer
Jim Noveroske
Ed Spray

23. Harding House
Bob Forney
Mike Haag
Stan Hamilton
Bob Sena
Ken Webb

24. Ruter House
Paul Baert
Steve Brown
Ronald Klusman
Gary Miller

25. Sigma Pi
Bob Brough
David Dunn
Mel Richards
Pat Roberts
Paul Schnepf
Phil Thrasher

26. Ferguson House
Ted Brown
Don Buhr
Mike Cashman
Walter Dittrich
Rex Killian
Jerry Judy

27. Sigma Alpha Mu
Mel Anspach
Dave Brandes
Charles Lampel
Abe Ochstein
Larry Simkin
Bunny Solomon

28. Delta Tau Delta
Kenneth Carlin
Stuart Jewell
Gary Pershing
Jerry Rubush
Larry Warren

29. Theta Chi
Maurice Campbell
Larry Contos
John Marynell
Bob Pollack
Douglas Shetterly

30. Kappa Sigma
Tom Burke
George Carey
Jim Davis
Jerry Flener
Jack Ford
Jerry Fritz

31. Elliott House
Fouad Chajai
Jim Grandorf
Russ Hale
Don Muckerheide
Don Schumaker

32. Lower Linden
Gary Brown
Byron Fischer
Dale Tetrault
Chuck Welsh

1961

1. Acacia
Joe Abrell
Dave Brown
Bill Carbon
Denny White

2. Phi Gamma Delta
Jeff Coulter
Charles Davis
Bill LaSalle
Bert Loftman
Paul Pomeroy
Jerry Tardy

3. Phi Kappa Psi
Robert Arnold
Don Leedy
Bob Magdaleno
John Odusch
George Quigley
Bob Stohler

4. Lambda Chi Alpha
Fred Cuppy
Dick Engle
Hank Hudson
John Peters
Dave Phillips
John Spahr

5. Beta Theta Pi
Bill Barton
Robert Eaglesfield
Ed Gustafson
Thomas Highland

John King
Mick McClurg

6. Sigma Phi Epsilon
Jack Boehm
Paul Dubiel
Steve Long
Jerry Niemiec
Bill Saltzman

7. Sigma Nu
Bill Altman
Jerry Bass
Tom Fruechtenicht
Gary Long
Jim Seal
Richard Woosnam

8. Phi Delta Theta
Lloyd Anderson
Dick Beaver
Tom Lindsey
Pete Sintz

9. Sigma Alpha Epsilon
Tom Bolyard
Mac Crosbie
Chuck Hanshaw
Dave Porter
Jim Stewart
Joe Votaw

10. Dodds House
John Georgi
Jim Meyer
Larry Miler
Ken Porter
Max Stinson

11. Sigma Chi
Ed Amos
Jay Carter
Brian Gores
Buck Jones

Art Meng
Ollie Steele

12. Chi Phi
Bob Bransford
George Connell
Tom Cook
Jack Noennig
Tom Rupert
Keith Stackhouse

13. Zeta Beta Tau
John Greenwald
Vlad Mancl
Richard Mantel
Harry Sax
Mike Siegel

14. Kappa Delta Rho
Terry Gorsuch
Dave Kinser
Rex Kirts
Gary Long
James Noveroski
Lawrence Swearingen

15. Delta Tau Delta
Larry Hannah
John Heaton
Fred Hill
Edward Rubush

16. Walnut Hall
Richard Campi
Bill Duerk
Bob Lewis
Ronald Naldi
Val Walters
Don Wittig

17. Stockwell House
Paul Goralski
Steve Henning
Reginald Parsons

Phil Pate
Jery Teller
David Townsend

18. Kappa Sigma
Gary Blackman
Ron Kastner
Ron Pink
Ron Reas

19. Delta Upsilon
Lanny Beach
Barry Hottle
Tom Marvin
Ron Snodgrass

20. Theta Chi
Jack Ashby
Fredrick Buckingham
Roger David
John Marynell
Robert Miller
Dave Oscarson

21. Normal College
Frank Kominowski
Harry Lloyd
Leon Pickens
Charles Spencer

22. Alpha Tau Omega
John Beswick
Larry Junker
John Marosky
Phil Schilling
F. G. Summitt

23. Laurel Hall
Terry Doran
William Hendrey
Jerry Holtrey
Robert Hoops
John Storck

24. Campbell House
Ralph Amos
Bill Claymon
Larry Davis
Dave Lash
Bill Reveley

25. Forest Hall
Don Fekete
Harry L. Powell
Wendall Tucker
Roger Voelker
Dorran Vogler
Darwin Wilkeson

26. Dunn House
Jerry Bremer
Frank Budreck
Ray Malayter
Charles Moll
Jerry Perigo

27. Parks House
John Baker
Jim Coffin
Ed Minczeski
Keith Patrick

28. Delta Chi
Michael Cunningham
Jim Flockencier
Gary Hayes
Bill Logan
Dan Tankersley
Jon Thomas

29. Tau Kappa Epsilon
Larry Armstrong
Dave Kring
Stan Nisevich
Mike Quick
Ed Wilkinson

30. Alpha Epsilon Pi
Joel Congress
Joel Hersch
Jerry Kohn
Norman Pollack

31. Maple Hall North
Mike Franklin
Jerry Goss
Bill Kaster
Paul Snawder
Reggie Stiles

32. Hall House
Tom Barco
Bill Bryan
Bill Martoccia
Homer Shrader
Nelson Steele

1962

1. Phi Kappa Psi
Jim Berry
Dave Blase
Frank Brunell
John Odusch

2. Sigma Alpha Epsilon
Ron Blue
Bob Bolyard
Tom Bolyard
Craig Long
Joe Votaw

3. Phi Gamma Delta
Pete CaJacob
Jeff Coulter
John Konowitz
Bill LaSalle
Dave Perks
Al Plummer

4. Chi Phi
Tom Cook
Ed McClure
Bob Schenk
Ray Snapp
Tom Wilmore

5. Acacia
Dave Brown
Dave Conner
Bruce Farthing
Juris Jansons
Dick Kelly
Denny White

6. Alpha Tau Omega
Mike Ankony
Don Criswell
Ed Doerr
Rick Murray
Bill Nelson
Dave Ring

7. Beta Theta Pi
Bill Barton
Brock Blosser
Dave Eaglesfield
Ed Gustafson
Bob King
John King

8. Phi Delta Theta
Phil Bennett
Denny Dammeyer
Jack Dyer
Craig Koenig
Joe Perdue
Pete Sintz

9. Edmondson II
Mike Fehr
Spike Frederick
Jerry Gerde

Edward Kin
Bob Muehlmann
Terry Townsend

10. Sigma Nu
Ron Guthier
Ed Janney
Tom Johnson
Jim Seal
Emery Spisak
Bill Vogel

11. Sigma Phi Epsilon
Al Balika
Tom Bauer
Tom Edler
Steve Long
Tom Peck
Stu Tuck

12. Lambda Chi Alpha
Dick Carter
Fred Cuppy
Larry Eaton
Hank Hudson
Jack Lehman
Dave Phillips

13. Walnut Hall
Bill Burkett
Glen Kooy
Al Leinback
Bob Lewis
Val Walters
Scott Wood

14. Delta Chi
Jim Banther
Bob Davis
Jim Flockencier
Bill Logan
Dan Tankersley

15. Towers D-2
Tim Banister
Phil Bryant
Jerry Prentice
Henry Salzarulo
Pete Salzarulo
Tom Schoellkopf

16. Zeta Beta Tau
Gary Barrack
Mike Feltman
Bobby Frank
John Greenwald
Harvey Schuchman
Larry Schuchman

17. Delta Tau Delta
Jim Harrison
Stu Jewell
Lee Matthews
Agris Petersons
Dave Reynolds
Jerry Rubush

18. Laurel Hall
Dave Blair
Jack Grinstead
Bill Hendrey
Bob Hunteman
Carl Lundberg
Ron Toppe

19. Dodds House
Jeff Graves
Larry Miller
Dave Morrical
Curt Simic
Max Stinson
Bob Wright

20. Kappa Delta Rho
John Balha
Bill Butz
Gary Long

Tom McClure
Harry Ramsey
Richard Tebik

21. Delta Upsilon
Lanny Beach
Terry Clapacs
Jim Denney
Pat Jenkins
Rudy Rudolph

22. Kappa Sigma
Joe Drozda
George Hass
John McCammon
Chuck Ruckman
Jack Thompson
Dick Wilson

23. Phi Kappa Tau
Mike Edwards
Dave Finney
Dave Ober
Jim Warring
Joe Weidhardt
Dick Whitlow

24. Ferguson House
Ted Brown
Glenn Cardwell
James Houck
William Johnson
Calvin Nigh
Joseph Spradlin

25. Sigma Pi
Bill Carpenter
Don Carswell
John Clark
Steve Gray
Mike Havert
Max Lieberenz

26. Phi Kappa Theta
Ray Dembinski
Dave Kingsbury
Tom Malenshek
Pat Stodola
Carlos Torrela
George Wetzel

27. Forest Hall
Ken Abbott
Bob Keys
Mike Kimberlin
Larry Warner

28. Campbell House
Bill Claymon
Larry Davis
Paul Harkess
Dave Lash
Tom Wheeler

29. Theta Chi
Fred Buckingham
Ron Crick
John Marynell
John Metts
Bob Pollock
Mel Roschelle

30. Stockwell House
John Eichenburger
Tom Gruber
Ivan Jahns
Craig Nelson
Phil Pate
Dave Townsend

31. Elliott House
Bruce Bonner
Max Clay
Bill Cieadlo
Vic Owen
Dave Walsman

32. Sigma Chi
Jay Carter
Lief Hendricksen
Bob Majors
Bob Mason
Art Meng
Jim Vandenbark

33. Parks House
John Baker
Jim Coffin
Jim Horner
Jim Pridgeon
Mike Ruley
Larry Spradlin

1963

1. Sigma Alpha Epsilon
Bob Bolyard
Ron Blue
Dave Porter
Claude Thompson

2. Alpha Tau Omega
Eddie Doerr
Mike Donley
Larry Marks
Mike McCarthy
Richard Murray
Bill Nelson

3. Acacia
Robert Forney
Don Nixon
Vernon Pfaff
George Sigler
Hartman Smith

4. Phi Gamma Delta
Tom Horton
Bill LaSalle

Dave Perks
Al Plummer

5. Beta Theta Pi
Brock Blosser
John King
Steven Mowrer
Phil Oyer

6. Dodds House
Bob Bell
Dean Cooper
Larry Miller
David Morrical
Tom Prebys

7. Edmondson II
Ken Alvares
Ron Alvarez
DeWayne Montgomery
Carl Neuman
Terry Townsend
John Wagner

8. Laurel Hall
Nathaniel Cole
Jack Grinstead
Bruce Haggard
Carl Lundberg
Jim Truho

9. Phi Kappa Psi
Richard Burns
Jim Lukins
Alan Somers
Steve Tesich
Mike Troy

10. Kappa Delta Rho
John Balha
Don Loftus
Tom McGlasson

Harry Ramsey
Rich Tebik

11. Chi Phi
Denny Harrell
Dave Nelson
Bob Schenk
Ron Wiehe
Tom Wilmore

12. Phi Delta Theta
Phil Bennett
Jack Gossard
Tom Graham
Rick Huff
Jack Smart

13. Sigma Nu
Thomas Buecker
Ross Creekmore
Ron Cummings
Bill Jackson
John Olmstead
Philip B. Roby

14. Sigma Chi
Jim Birr
Don Carlson
Tom Hempstead
Art Mang
Ron Roehler
John Roethke

15. Sigma Phi Epsilon
Jim Andrews
Phil Jones
Tom Prall
Mike Wallace

16. Parks House
John B. Baker
Mike Davis

Charles Moll
Steve Strother

17. Jenkins House
Allan Abbott
James Dewalt
Bill Forgey
Bob Hoop
Barratt Patton

18. Tau Kappa Epsilon
Bert Mullins
Stan Nisevich
Jack Sundholm
Ron Swelstad

19. Zeta Beta Tau
Steve Bluestein
Robert Chulock
Mike Freid
John Greenwald
Harvey Schuchman

20. Forest Hall
Jon Brice
Tom Elder
Richard Hollowell
Ed Miesel
Jerry Shurr

21. Walnut Hall
Greg Bogan
Bill Burkett
Gleen Kooy
Val Walters

22. Lambda Chi Alpha
Lee Haak
Hank Hudson
Jerry Miller
Dave Phillips
Leon Pickens
Bruce York

23. Delta Chi
Bill Bally
Jim Banther
Bob Campbell
Chuck Hoover
Steve Johnson
Bill Logan
Chuck Murphy

24. Kappa Sigma
Bill Clark
Joe Drozda
George Hass
Rick Knop
Roger Pink

25. Delta Tau Delta
Stuart Jewell
Agris Petersons
Lonnie Racster
Jerry Rubush
Pat Terry

26. Edmondson IV
Richard Coyle
John Harris
Gary Kruchten
John McIntosh

27. Sigma Pi
Bob Brough
Tom Gill
Max Lieberenz
Tom Keppler
John O'Sullivan, Jr.

28. Delta Upsilon
Jerry Frey
Gary Gardner
Cle Rector
Mike Whittaker

29. Theta Chi
Steve Atkins

Ron Crick
Bruce Kotzan
Ted Prose
Richard Simon

30. Phi Kappa Theta
Roger Beckemeyer
David Debes
John Derheimer
Thomas Malenshek
Walter Roscello

31. Phi Kappa Tau
Steve Allison
Bob Dratwa
Jon Moll
Dave Ober

32. Martin Hall
Jon Abell
David Bikoff
Brownell Payne
Mike Tucker

33. Hummer House
Jerry Abplanalp
Don Burt
Jerry Hunnicutt
Phil McGovern
Steve Tuhy

1964

1. Beta Theta Pi
Brock Blosser
Phil Goddard
James McEwen
Steve Taylor

2. Sigma Alpha Epsilon
Eric Christopherson
Ed Fitzgerald
Ned McCahan

Terry Smith
Claude Thompson

3. Phi Gamma Delta
Jerry Bradley
Pete CaJacob
John Konowitz
Al Plummer

4. Acacia
Dave Cloes
Juris Jansons
Don Nixon
Hartman Smith
Denny White

5. Sigma Nu
Jim Basney
Ross Creekmore
Pete Leininger
Randy Long

6. Alpha Tau Omega
Eddie Doerr
Chris Hornbostel
Larry Marks
Mike McCarthy
John Suhre
Dave Townsend

7. Dodds House
Bob Bell
Bill Forgey
Larry Miller
Tom Prebys

8. Parks House
Tim Brown
Steve Burch
Phil Rohrer
George Woodward

9. Chi Phi
Denny Harrell
Jerry Judjahn
Kent Scherschel
Rick Werling

10. Phi Delta Theta
John Anderson
Mike Bruney
Jack Smart
Dick Ungerer

11. Phi Kappa Psi
Ron Bianco
Richard Burns
Alan Somers
Steve Tesich

12. Zeta Beta Tau
Mike Freid
Bill Friedman
Marc Golden
John Greenwald
Mike Nuemark
Fred Rosenfeld

13. Jenkinson House
Jon Abell
Charles Creasser
Henry Solmer
Bob Walton

14. Lambda Chi Alpha
Harry Lloyd
Jerry Miller
Dave Phillips
John Riggs

15. Sigma Chi
Jay Carter
Dan Hallman
Bill Hunt

Chuck Rhetts
Dick Shortz

16. Delta Upsilon
Barry Hottle
Edward Johnson
Don Simmons
Barc Westerfeld

17. Delta Chi
Bob Boyd
Bob Campbell
Steve Johnson
Bill Logan
Phil Pate
Ken T'Kindt

18. Theta Chi
Harry C. Duckworth
David L. Gallahue
Charles Hoffman
Bruce Kotzan
Jeff Stahl

19. Walnut Hall
Gerald Hartman
Jim Hooper
Don Simmons
Jimmy Weiss

20. Kappa Delta Rho
John Balha
Fred Foushee
Skip Higgins
Don Loftus
Don Miller

21. Phi Kappa Tau
Jim Lesher
Robert Moll
Paul K. Romey
Mike Taylor

22. Tau Kappa Epsilon
Mike Claphan
Dave Kaska
Bert Mullins
Jack Swelstad
Ron Swelstad

23. Delta Tau Delta
Larry Brown
Marvin Hamilton
Lonnie Racster
Bob Thopy

24. Shea
Ron Brehner
George Miller
Ted Orton
Jerry Young

25. Cravens A
Kip Bothwell
Bill Evans
Mike Jagger
Dean Lohmeier

26. Sigma Phi Epsilon
Bill Cavalcanti
Tom Felger
Tom Prall
Mike Wallace

27. Sigma Alpha Mu
Don Adler
Mike Farbman
Clay Lawrence
Dick Tucker

28. Phi Sigma Kappa
Tom Boscher
David Gage
Allen Gibbs
Steve Stafford

29. Ferguson House
Bill Johnson
John Schroer
Terry Silke
Don Tillotson

30. Kappa Sigma
Ben Constable
John Hauschild
John McCammon
Chuck Ruckman

31. Dunn House
Jim Armalavage
Carl Hersh
John Mattix
Gary Townsend

32. Todd House
Ken Ciboch
Ray Mendenhall
Brent Ross
Jerry VanGombos

33. Alpha Epsilon Pi
Howard Kagen
Gene Packer
Michael Schwartz
Andy Ziemelis

1965

1. Phi Gamma Delta
Allan Abbott
Jerry Bradley
John Konowitz
Steve Powell

2. Sigma Alpha Epsilon
Bob Bailey
Eric Christopherson
Morrie Erickson

John Petscher
Sam Yuska

3. Alpha Tau Omega
Jim Gemmer
Larry Glaze
Ivan Jahns
Steve Miller
Bob Springer

4. Phi Kappa Psi
Ken Frost
Fred Schmidt
Steve Tesich
Terry Townsend

5. Sigma Nu
Ed Harper
Jim Leininger
Randy Long
John Olmstead
Chuck Richards
Toby Stone

6. Phi Delta Theta
Rick Juff
Craig Koenig
Roger Thompson
Dick Ungerer

7. Beta Theta Pi
Jim Augsburg
Brock Blosser
Phil Goddard
Steve Taylor

8. Kappa Delta Rho
John Balha
Fred Florjancic
Richard Ham
Dave Lawler
Don Loftus

9. Sigma Phi Epsilon
Malcolm Beckner
Mike McCoun
Rog McKuhen
Bob Romanowsky
Steve Thompson

10. Delta Upsilon
Jim Brunkella
Bryan Moss
Mike Ozment
Tom Whitsett

11. Laurel/Walnut
Greg Bogan
Dennis Kersey
Can McCroskey
Don Simmons

12. Ruter/Jenkins
Bill Bocock
Jon Forgey
Jim Huffer
Bob May
Ken Reiss

13. Willkie Co-op
Frank DeWester
John Heines
Tom Leininger
Delbert Nelson

14. Wissler II
Jim Chandler
Bob Michaels
Dwight Noble
Jerry Young

15. Acacia
Dave Anderson
Barry Forst
George Sigler
Drew Wright

16. Phi Sigma Kappa
Steve Cox
Dave Gage
Dick Peabody
Pete Refakis
Steve Stafford
Bob Stout

17. Delta Tau Delta
Larry Brown
Marvin Hamilton
Gary Kruchen
Tom Roessner
John Warren

18. Tau Kappa Epsilon
Helmut Brugman
Mike Claphan
Jack Hamilton
David Neindorf
Jack Swelstad

19. Jenkinson House
Jon Abell
Bill Carowder
Chris Fulghum
Henry Solmer

20. Dodds House
Bob Bell
Lee Schnell
Bill Searcy
Fred Simic

21. Lambda Chi Alpha
Fred Admaczyk
Tom Kilrain
John Riggs
John Young

22. Martin III
Max Bessler

Arthur Bortolini
Roger Feldhaus
Howard Marvel
Ray Osman

23. Pi Kappa Alpha
Tom Bodkin
Bill Dorcik
Bob Weinheimer
Mike Woods

24. McNutt
John George
Robert Hoop
Stephen Smith
Philip Wiehe

25. Kappa Sigma
Bob Bielewicz
George Brant
George Hass
Chuck Ruckman
Ralf Saunders

26. Theta Chi
Harry Duckworth
Charles Hoffman
Bruce Kotzan
Richard Martin

27. Hummer House
Larry Franklin
Gary Gearhart
Tom Kish
Bob Toffinet
Dean Szabo

28. Phi Kappa Theta
Rick Datzman
Bill Hoelker
Frank Miller
Don Neff

29. Elliott/Lowe
Rick Alden
Ed Burket
Evan Collinsworth
Barney Jaworski
Phil McKean

30. Zeta Beta Tau
Ed Berebitsky
Josh Berman
Mike Freid
Jeff Seaman

31. Alpha Epsilon Pi
Matthew Bud
Steve Herman
Eugene Packer
Steven Seltzer
Andy Ziemelis

32. Todd House
Jay Arnold
Tedd Karnischky
Jim Kryway
Jim Son
Nick Stucky

33. Ferguson House
Doug Fitting
Bill Johnson
Tom Kienitz
Jim Parry

1966

1. Phi Kappa Psi
Ken Frost
Larry Gies
Don Palmer
Terry Townsend

2. Sigma Phi Epsilon
Mike Banser
Malcolm Beckner
Bob Dolan
Mike McCoun
Roger McKuhen
Don Wilson

3. Sigma Nu
Randy Long
Rick Miller
Chuck Richards
Dave Thorne
Dave Wright

4. Alpha Tau Omega
Donn Eley
Louis Gill
Destry Lambert
Jim Knauer
Mike Orr

5. Phi Gamma Delta
Jerry Bradley
Jerry Danielson
Carter Jackson
Steve Powell

6. Theta Chi
Dale Grassmyer
John Hamsley
Charles Hoffman
Bruce Kotzan
Chuck Taylor

7. Sigma Alpha Epsilon
Bob Bailey
Dick Eggers
Morrie Erickson
Steve Harms
Reid Lemasters

8. Sigma Chi
John Barry
Dave Biesemeyer
Don Farquharson
Bill Hamilton
Steve Shoup
Terry Silke

9. Delta Upsilon
Larry Alexander
Jim Brunkella
Ron Fritz
Chris Kirk
Dick Schaub
Tom Whitsitt

10. McNutt
Bill Bocock
William Corbin
Dave Duros
Lynn Olson
Robert May

11. Beta Theta Pi
Steve Conrad
David Diehl
Vane Lashua
David Knall
John Voris

12. Kappa Delta Rho
George Bewley
Fred Florjancic
Wayne Reed
Chuck Robinson
Larry Stout

13. Phi Kappa Theta
Joe Amaral
Rick Dataman
Bill Hoelker
Doug Morrical
Jack Wehner

14. Tau Kappa Epsilon
Helmet Brugman
Russ Cockrum
Dick Flood
Sam Hyde
David Niendorf
Jack Swelstad

15. Acacia
John Curtis
Tom Paskins
George Sigler
Walt Simmons

16. Chi Phi
Todd Hoover
Jerry Judjahn
Don Malcom
Gunnar Richardson
Harry VonTobel

17. Lambda Chi Alpha
Fred Adamczyk
Bob Carter
John Etherton
Steve Luedeman
Ron Roberts

18. Sigma Alpha Mu
Chuck Citrin
Bob Goldberg
Tiby Herman
Peter Kreeger
Bob Malman
Don Scheiber

19. Phi Sigma Kappa
Larry Arany
Jim Benton
Steve Cox
Dick Peabody
Steve Stafford

20. Martin III
Max Bessler
Tom Bodnar
Howard Marvel
Charles Meador

21. Delta Tau Delta
David Gethers
Marvin Hamilton
Don Lee Walker
Rick Wyndham

22. Phi Kappa Tau
Dick Clem
Joe Johnson
Robert Paris
Rick McQueen
Steve Morris

23. Delta Chi
Greg Dunnuck
Paul Howard
Steve Klepfer
Dannie Kline

24. Willkie Co-op
Paul Gielrak
Jim Mathews
Delbert Nelson
David Pund
Dick Schnar
Phil Wuensch

25. Briscoe
Frank DeWester
Michael Retherford
Ken Schaaf
Wilbur Siders

26. Sigma Pi
Bob Alexander
Bob Goodus

Larry Hardesty
John O'Sullivan
John Pawlowski
Grant Williams

27. Edmondson II
Jack Cass
James Euler
Ken Ferguson
Frank O'Brien
Dave Padgett
Joseph Thurston

28. Hummer House
Crash Cargill
Larry Franklin
Jim Maley
Phil Mallatt
Bob Rissing

29. Dodds House
Bob Bell
Thomas Prebys
Lee Schnell
Bill Searcy
Jim Woodall
Steve Woodall

30. Kappa Sigma
Bob Bielewicz
Brian Devaney
Jon Lindemann
Jim Wood

31. Zeta Beta Tau
Ed Berebitsky
Marc Golden
Miles Kauffman
Bruce Natkin
Jeff Weiss

32. Cravens A
Bill Clark

Cliff Culloden
Rich Dawson
Mike Jagger
Lou Kurz
Norman Robinson
Ed Witte

33. Pi Kappa Phi
Don Briscoe
Glen Crosier
John Lemen
Jim McCollough
Mike Nordberg

1967

1. Phi Gamma Delta
Jerry Bradley
Gerry Danielson
Scott Ricke
Steve Powell

2. Phi Delta Theta
Dennis Gettelfinger
Jim O'Neal
Dave Padgett
Jeffrey Raff
Larry Steele

3. Sigma Alpha Epsilon
Bob Bailey
Tom Grier
Reid Lemasters
Bill Price
Vic Thompson

4. Alpha Tau Omega
Jim Kanuer
Destry Lambert
Mike Orr
Bob Springer
Terry Weber

5. Phi Kappa Theta
Jack D'Amato
Bill Hoelker
Greg Martich
William Ptak
Jack Wehner

6. Sigma Chi
John Barry
Dave Biesemeyer
Steve Birr
Mike Cantrell
Dan Daugherty

7. Sigma Phi Epsilon
Tom Battle
Malcolm Beckner
Roger McKuhen
Wally McOuat
Don Wilson

8. Phi Kappa Psi
Jim Babcock
Steve Gluff
Tom Johnston
Dave Kienlen
Tim King
David Shaw

9. Theta Chi
Roger Deckard
John Harlan
Rick Meeks
Chuck Taylor
Phil Wiehe

10. Kappa Sigma
Gary Allen
Mike Bell
Bob Bielewicz
Paul Hoffman

11. Sigma Nu
Phil Darr
Larry Greathouse
Chuck Richards
Al Sandberg

12. Dodds House
Tom Bennett
John Heckman
Morris Kegley
Mark Maxwell
Pete Reynolds

13. Acacia
Jon Forgey
Dan Fowler
Walt Simmons
Bill Van Landingham
Terence Walts

14. Delta Upsilon
Cliff De La Croix
Ron Fritz
Dave Hennon
Gordon Sinning
Tom Whitsitt

15. Kappa Delta Rho
Tom Dingman
Fred Florjancic
Skip Higgins
Jim Williams

16. Lambda Chi Alpha
George Bigg
John Etherton
Mike Greener
Ron Roberts
Ted Smith

17. Chi Phi
Phil King
Jim Miner

Gunnar Richardson
John Smart

18. Sigma Pi
Bob Alexander
Mike Frederick
Donald Hendry
Bob Rockenbaugh

19. Delta Tau Delta
Mike Johns
Jim Meyers
Dallas Mulvaney
Clark Snyder

20. Stew-Bums
Craig Moody
Barrett Patton
Roger Patton
John Snyder
Roy Webb

21. Briscoe I
Mick Garrett
Barry Schuchman
Henry Solmer
Richard Taylor
Tim Wiedman

22. Beta Theta Pi
Larry Combs
Steve Conrad
Bill Elliott
Mark Lanigan
Jim Miller
Rick Reel

23. Magee II
Jim Kain
Don McGinnis
Brian Neville
Jim Rubley
Larry Wilson

24. Tau Kappa Epsilon
John Dillon
Doug Felkins
Mike Hunter
Sam Hyde
Doug Stauch

25. Zeta Beta Tau
Larry Alboher
Neal Cohen
Howie Isaacs
Murray Passo
Gary Saks

26. Cravens C
Byron Baldwin
Jerry Coffman
Paul Goldberg
Wayne Hott
Ernest Smith
Doug Stickell

27. Phi Epsilon Pi
Greg Allen
Darryl Dargitz
John Dickinson
Dave Forman
Steve Gailar

28. Martin 3
Max Bessler
Thomas Bodnar
Steven Franklin
Howard Marvel
Jack McCune

29. Ferguson House
Trigger Dull
Kim Hudson
Dennis Logan
Beau Summers
Cotton Vaughn

30. Edmondson II
Bill Clark
Steve Clayton
Ken Ferguson
Gary Gilstrap
Frank O'Brien

31. Willkie Co-op
Don Bevis
Tom Broyles
Keith Colliver
Jerry Long
Phil Wuensch

32. Wissler IV
Terry Crowe
Randy Hammond
Barney Jaworski
Jim Phillips
Bill Sims

33. Alpha Epsilon Pi
John Erlen
Barry Levin
David Maltzman
Mick Mond
Phil Siegel

1968

1. Phi Kappa Psi
Steve Gluff
Dave Kienlen
Alan Ogden
Dave Shaw

2. Delta Upsilon
Bix Branson
Dean Bruce
Jim Davis
Larry Fagersten
Dennis Kirkman

9. Sigma Phi Epsilon
Tom Battle
Bob Henderson
J. J. Lattak
Wally McOuat
Don Wilson

4. Alpha Tau Omega
Larry Deakyne
Steve Jackson
Carlo Logan
Mike Shepherd

5. Sigma Alpha Mu
Dave Feigenbaum
Burt Jacobs
Russ Samet
Jay Tobias
Steve Weiss

6. Acacia
Mike Andreoli
Kevin Burk
Dan Flowler
Jon Forgey
Tom Hendryz

7. Kappa Sigma
Mike Bell
John Hall
Dick Harmon
Don Perfetto
Dave Riser

8. Sigma Alpha Epsilon
Tom Grier
Reid Lemasters
Steve Richardson
Vic Thompson
Steve Warner

9. Phi Kappa Theta
Joe Amaral
Jack D'Amato
Bill Hoelker
Russ Webb
Jack Wehner

10. Phi Gamma Delta
Ted Bindley
Bill Erdel
Clarke Randall
Mark Rogge
Jim Wilson

11. Theta Chi
Roger Deckard
Dale Grassmyer
John Harlan
Bruce Pennamped
Richard Simon

12. Cravens
Jerry Coffman
Rich Hattendorf
Wayne Hott
John Lutgring
Greg Miles

13. Sigma Nu
Larry Greathouse
Greg Long
Gib Miller
Gene Osborn

14. Dodds House
Carl Bennett
Tom Bennett
Donald Buchanan
Michael Koch
Mark Maxwell

15. Pi Kappa Alpha
Timothy Freeman

Steve Mahoney
Chris Norman
John Sermersheim
Bill Talkington

16. Lambda Chi Alpha
George Bigg
John Etherton
Don Fehd
Jon Lindemann
Ski Schanher

17. Willkie
Dave Bechler
Rob Gohd
Steve Hatfield
Dave Haugk
Maurice Hoffman

18. Magee II
John Brennan
Doug Coffman
Dave Kovas
Don McGinnis
Bryan Neville

19. Kappa Delta Rho
Tim Dingmen
Ray Noppa
Garry O'Neal
Dick Salib
Dave Solan
Jim Williams

20. Beta Theta Pi
Steve Conrad
Greg Friend
Steve Reckley
Steve Reith

21. Phi Kappa Tau
Steve Kafoure
Daivd Layson

Ross Lewton
Dave Simstad
Dennis Talarek

22. Phi Epsilon Pi
Greg Allen
John Dickinson
Steve Gailar
George German
Bill Munse

23. Wissler IV
Randy Hammond
Barney Jaworski
Dan Novreske
Tim Quino
Bill Wilson

24. Martin III
Bentley Austin
Allan Brock
Dick Harruff
Mark Sonntag

25. Hummer House
Martin Glisinski
Mark Hermes
Richard Ison
Chuck Stewart
Jim Tubbs

26. Zeta Beta Tau
Sherm Goldenberg
David Klapper
Rick Linkimer
Murray Passo
Don Simkin

27. Pi Kappa Phi
Paul Bender
Tom Buckley
Rich Hall
Jay Platt
Dan Schantz

28. Chi Phi
Don Allen
Dave Differding
Conrad Hittle
Jim Miner
Ron Richards

29. McNutt
Larry Chrispyn
Jack Graff
Eric Johnson
George Knapp
Bob Rudd

30. Tau Kappa Epsilon
John Dillon
Doug Felkins
Rick Herd
Sam Hyde
Howard Randler

31. Sigma Chi
Dave Biesemeyer
Bill Hamilton
Frank Hamilton
Ken Knue
Dave Rimstidt

32. Willkie Co-op
Al Cartwright
Bob Crain
Roger Glasgow
Mark Lindahl
Jim Mathews

1969

1. Alpha Tau Omega
Carlo Logan
Phil Mugg
Bob Nowak
Mike Orr

2. Phi Delta Theta
Ted Lynch
Bill Moor
Lynn Olsen
Larry Steele

3. Dodds House
Mike Cherry
Mike Howard
Michael Koch
Mike McKnight
John Milner
Jeff Morse

4. Beta Theta Pi
Pat Bender
Jack Call
Art Foley
Tim Hirons
James Reid

5. Kappa Sigma
Mike Bell
Glenn Duncan
Don Perfetto
Dave Risner
Jim Wilson

6. Delta Upsilon
Bix Branson
Jim Davis
Larry Fagersten
Craig Parker
Denny Stalter

7. Acacia
Mike Andreoli
Glen Curtis
Ken Fauth
Dan Fowler
Doug Meyer

8. Sigma Nu
Mark Bailey
Jim Greathouse
Mark Gundy
Gib Miller
Lowell Shank

9. Briscoe
Roger Andes
Paul Logsdon
Don Ramsey
Steve Schaefer
Steve Woodall

10. Delta Chi
Mike Ackerman
Rick Champion
Carl Kowalski
Tim Nussbaum
Eddy Van Guyse

11. Kappa Delta Rho
Robert Gregory
Phil Hadley
Tim Marlow
Robert Moynihan
Gary Pink

12. Wissler IV
James L. Bilinski
Terry Dowty
Dave Hicks
Geoffrey Keller
Mike McCluckie
Bill Royalty

13. Sigma Phi Epsilon
Tom Battle
Bob Henderson
Wally McOuat
Don Wilson

14. Phi Kappa Psi
Steve Bowles
Mark Malangoni
Tim Simmonds
Dave Varner

15. Sigma Alpha Epsilon
Tom Grief
Dave Keckley
Steve Richarson
Vic Thompson
Jim Votaw

16. Delta Tau Delta
John Elliott
Tom Gabe
Bill Murphy
Tom Scott
Steve Smith

17. Theta Chi
Jeff Delaplane
John Harlan
Gary Harper
Bruce Pennamped
Dave Truitt

18. Pi Kappa Alpha
Mike Flanagan
Dave Hawk
John Neil
Tim Rohleder

19. Phi Kappa Theta
Richard Brooks
Michael Clayton
Bob McCree
Fred Wulff
Rick Zientara

20. Phi Kappa Tau
Bill Hadewang
Steve Kofoure
Harold Nefly

Doug Porter
Denny Talarek

21. Sigma Alpha Mu
Dave Feigenbaum
Larry Spivack
Jay Tobias
Steve Weiss
Larry Werbel

22. Phi Gamma Delta
Ted Bindley
John Diekmann
Steve Hockett
Steve Kabisch

23. Sigma Chi
Terry Daugherty
Frank Hamilton
Gene Renuart
Dave Rimstidt
Eric Vincent

24. Cravens C
Greg Bryant
Rich Hattendorf
Fred Herczeg
Eddie Pawlowski
Jamie Thomas

25. Zeta Beta Tau
John Davidson
Mike Friedman
Bik Kowach
David Roskin
Don Simkin

26. Willkie

27. Martin III
John Baldridge
Greg Pool

Mark Sonntag
Ronald Trietsch

28. Theta Xi
Mike Archer
Gary Bell
Bill Bennett
Tim McMahon
Rich Meserve

29. McNutt
Bruce Bohall
Bill Gorrell
George Knapp
Bob Rudd
John Tinder

30. Sigma Pi
Harry Benson
Skip Dayhuff
Dave Dolch
Mike Fredrick
Mike Scott

31. Alpha Epsilon Pi
John Coffman
Alex Csillag
Rob Fogel
Al Frank
Fred Passman
Howard Schwartz

32. Tau Kappa Epsilon
Doug Felkins
Rick Herk
John Rademaker
Dennis Voelker

33. Shea II
Harry Chandler
Doug Guyn
Larry Johnston
Joe Wheeler

1970

1. Sigma Phi Epsilon
Tom Battle
Tim Branigan
Bob Henderson
Mark Wade

2. Delta Chi
Mark Cassady
Bob Jeppson
Don Kail
Carl Kowalski
Eddy Van Guyse

3. Dodds House
Mike Cherry
Richard Felty
Mike Howard
Mike McKnight
Robert Mead

4. Alpha Tau Omega
Mark Brandon
Kevin Fiske
Gerry Kern
Carlo Logan
Tony Miller

5. Sigma Nu
David Abbott
Mark Bailey
Bill Curley
Steve Rogers
David Tabereaux

6. Martin III
Dave Alexander
Greg Pool
Bob Schmelter
Ned Windnagel

7. Sigma Alpha Epsilon
Don Harvey
Jeff Hodge
Dave Keckley
Jim Votaw

8. Briscoe
Jim Kendall
David Mason
Steve Schaefer
Mark Wager
Dale Wendell

9. Theta Chi
John Harlan
Charles Hoffman
Ed Krause
John Nill
Don Rebber

10. Delta Tau Delta
Tom Baas
John Elliott
Frank Franks
Steve Smith

11. Kappa Sigma
Glenn Duncan
Jim Ruckman
Bob Shanteau
Bill Smith
Rick Turley
Jim Wilson

12. Lambda Chi Alpha
Gregg Byrne
Kim Corey
Bill McClure
Stephen Miller
Don Small

13. Sigma Chi
Steve Baker

Frank Hamilton
Tim McKinney
Dave Rimstidt

14. Phi Gamma Delta
Bill Canida
Bob Foster
Harold Luecke
Mike McGee

15. Acacia
Kris Burk
Glen Curtis
Bill Pate
Terry Smith

16. Phi Kappa Psi
Paul Coulis
Bert Dovo
Mark Holmquist
Mark Malangoni
Joe Musser

17. Pi Kappa Alpha
Kevin Cranny
Edward Guion
Steve Higgs
Marty Hughey
Larry McCauley

18. Phi Delta Theta
Ted Lynch
Mike McCroskey
Bill Moor
Rick Small
Ted Lynch

19. Alpha Sigma Phi
Ron Fischer
Jim Gleason
Murray Hall
Jerry Perkins

20. Beta Theta Pi
Pat Bender
Steve Hurley
Mike Morris
Mike Reckley

21. Sigma Pi
Pat Blose
Don Hollinger
Lloyd Mobley
Jon Owen
Roy Wright

22. Magee II
Jeff Foust
David Goralski
Paul Miller
Steve White

23. Phi Kappa Theta
John Clifford
Ron Newton
Erik Wulff
Frederick Wulff
Jack Ziegler

24. Cravens C
Greg Bryant
Paul Goetz
Fred Herczeg
Chuck Holman
Keith Straw

25. Crone House
Bill Bishop
Dusty Godbey
Clark Judge
Scott McManigell
Marti Radecki

26. Zeta Beta Tau
John Davidson

Steve Feiger
Edde Golden
Bik Korach
Scott Sholl
Mark Stolkin

27. Willkie South VII
Jim Arvin
Terry Dowty
Steve Keller
Steve Kirchoff
Jay Rigsby

28. Chi Phi
Ed Ferguson
Steve Lierman
Gary Proud
Tom Smart

29. Dewey
John Etchison
John Hallanger
Tom Schalliol
Dave Schilling
Mike Strong

30. Shea III
David Becker
Tom Bullock
Chris Grabowski
Edward Mathena
Denny Van Houten

31. Evans Scholars
Pierre Drabecki
Johnny Jay Humphrey
Butchie Russell

32. Shea II
Gene Elias
Richard Fisher
Doug Guyn
Ron Koepsel

33. Sigma Alpha Mu
Gary Cohen
Brad Finkle
Terry Waldman

1971

1. Alpha Tau Omega
Mark Brandon
Kevin Fiske
Carlo Logan
Frank Walter

2. Acacia
Kris Burk
Rick McNees
Bill Pate
Leo Savorie
Terry Smith

3. Theta Chi
Chuck Betz
Ken Gray
Ed Krause
Mike Rathert
Rick Robbins

4. Phi Gamma Delta
Bill Canida
Bob Foster
Dave King
Harold Luecke
Warren Meinschein
Tom Templin
Doug Tute
John Wallace

5. Delta Chi
Craig Curless
Mike Dayton
Carl Kowalski
Eddy Van Guyse
Jim Walsh

6. Phi Delta Theta
Rick Canaan
Ward Hey
Jim Koday
Bill Moor
David White

7. Kappa Sigma
Bob Kirkwood
Jim Ruckman
Sam Sample
Bob Shanteau
James Wilson

8. Sigma Nu
Nick Gearhart
Bill Kelley
Jarry Rogers
Jeff Trent
Rick Weisbrod

9. Dodds House
Dave Baer
Mike Howard
Doug Jones
Bob Meade
Steve Moore
Jeff Morse

10. Sigma Chi
Dennis Anderson
Steve Baker
John Hemstreet
Bruce Walters

11. Phi Kappa Psi
Steve Bowles
Denny Bratchel
Peter DeWitt
Bruce Gibson
Mark Malangoni
Tom Stocks
Dave Varner

12. Martin III
Dave Alexander
Matt Buchanan
Greg Pool
Bob Schmelter
Steve Schneider

13. Sigma Phi Epsilon
Jim Ashby
Tom Davis
Chip Owen
Gary Thompson
Mark Wade

14. Delta Upsilon
Bill Cahillane
Jim Cahillane
Bill Donlan
Dave Reynolds
Tom Schallion

15. Pi Kappa Alpha
Jay Hill
Marty Hughey
Larry McCauley
Dave Strohm

16. Delta Tau Delta
Tom Bass
Tom Gabe
Mike McCluckie
Jack Shoaf
Steve Smith

17. Dewey
Kent Biery
Terry Cranert
Mike Strong
Tom Swenson

18. Delta Sigma Pi
Joel Crist

Dave Haugh
Ron Newton
Jay Rigsby
Jerry Schweitzer
Fredrick Wulff

19. Briscoe
Jeff Cheung
James Golden
Jim Kendall
Bob Smith
Dale Wendell

20. Beta Theta Pi
Mike Fagan
Bill Gorrell
Charles McCormick III
Dean Miller
Mike Morris
John Tinder

21. Sigma Alpha Epsilon
Ron Koepsel
Phil McNeeley
Jack Sawrey
Ed Shank

22. Willkie South VI
Charles Bush
Donn Hartzell
Don Kempster
Nick Logan
Dale Mullins

23. Sigma Alpha Mu
Mark Berey
Michael Greenblatt
Bob Hoffman
Rob Kreigshaber
Jeff Perellis
Bob Rubinstein
Bob Shottenstein
Jim Whitman

24. Theta Xi
Roger Hungerfork
Bruce Jennings
Steve LeBeau
Chas Scurr
Mike Woolery

25. Willkie IV/XI
Don Hein
Dave Hohnke
Rick Jones
Mark Penwell
Randy Roberts

26. Sigma Pi
Mike Miller
Dan Ochse
Joe Smucker
Bob Todd
Jack Weiss
Roy Wright

27. Evans Scholars
Tom Chase
Don Habjan
Scoots Herikk
Tim Kuzmiczski
Peter Panarisi

28. Teter
John Brettin
Bob Heyderhoff
Ron Martin
Glenn Medley
Jeffrey Mohamed

29. Lambda Chi Alpha
Al Jancovech
Bill McClure
Stephen Miller
Bob Nickovich
Don Small
Ken Wright

30. Crone House
Dick Goode
Richard Lentz
Dennis Shields
Ed Reinke
Skip Thinnes

31. Pi Kappa Phi
William Hungerford
Joe Keeler
Terry Russell
Mike Schichte
Tom Weitzel

32. Magee II
Paul Bresher
Dave Kingshorn
Randy Roberts
Tom Smith

33. Bryan
Pat Callahan
Joe Demkovich
Terry Ginther
George Knapp
Mike Ratcliff
Mike Thalheimer
Thomas Ster

1972

1. Kappa Sigma
Steve Drayna
Dave Emenhiser
Bob Kirkwood
Bob Shanteau

2. Delta Chi
Mike Dayton
Steve Dayton
Bob Jeppson
Steve Schaefer
Eddy Van Guyse

3. Sigma Phi Epsilon
Terry Cox
Tom Davis
Dennis Dixon
Paul Kilgore
Bob Ruf
Steve Swinehart

4. Sigma Alpha Epsilon
Scott Greene
Ron Koepsel
Mat Miller
Mark Mollelo
Ed Shank
Jim Votaw

5. Acacia
Bob Barlow
Kris Burk
Mark Detroy
Steve Krause
Rick McNees
Scott Swogger

6. Theta Chi
Dennis Checkley
Ken Gray
Ed Krause
Dave Truitt
John Zieg

7. Phi Kappa Psi
Denny Bratchen
Bill Brennen
Pete DeWitt
Bruce Gibson
Tim Kulik
Tim Scheele
Brad Seger

8. Delta Upsilon
Jim Cahillane
Davy Heinze
Jefferson Miller

Dave Reynolds
Bill Rost
Tommy Schalliol
Gene Walden

9. Briscoe V
Jeff Cheung
Jim Kendall
Marjon Roglich
Rich Rusak
Ken Schwarz
Dale Wendall

10. Dodds House
Paul Bresher
Bob Mead
Gale Melick
Lyn Mueller
Denny Speer

11. Martin III
Dave Alexander
Matt Buchanan
Jim Priest
Steve Schneider
Tom Schulthise

12. Phi Delta Theta
Barth Anderson
Scott Etherington
Marc Granson
James Koday
Mike McCrosky
Tom Pykosz

13. Theta Xi
Ernie Califana
Roger Hungerford
Bruce Jennings
David LeBeau
Charles Scurr
Mike Woolery

14. Delta Tau Delta
Tom Baas
George Bray
Tom Gabe
Mike McCluckie
Steve Smith

15. Martin II
John Bauer
Bill Giffrow
Tom Green
Charley Harris
Dan Muchnick

16. Sigma Pi
Dale Arfman
Tom Cummins
Jeff Medlen
Mike Scott
Joe Smucker
Keith Wilking

17. Beta Theta Pi
Joe Juscik
Mike Morris
Mark Pratt
Jim Suenstrop
Flash Wilson

18. (tie) Phi Gamma Delta
Bill Canida
Dave King
Warren Meinschein
Tom Mensch
Rob Rogers

18. (tie) Sigma Chi
Dennis Anderson
Steve Baker
George Hand
Tom Kelley
Jeff Lowe
Michael Rose
Bruce Walters

20. Crone House
Joe Demkovich
George Knapp
Richart Lentz
Jack McCanna
Joe Orr

21. Alpha Tau Omega
Jim Allen
Gary Longuist
Keith Marsden
Chris Miller
George Panco
Frank Walter
Roger Wright

22. Pi Kappa Alpha
Devin Cranny
Mark Homarich
David Strohm
Greg Weinheimer
Tom Zachary

23. Parks House
Marc Buickel
Jim Harrison
Steve Hartman
Bob Linn
Branson Stone
Carl Tobin

24. Shea Ground
Doug Bottorff
Jeff Kolb
Bill Newman
Len Poehler
Tom Singer

25. Cravens B
Stan Arnold
Thom Blackmore
Randy Cauffman
Ross Fraser
Ed Totten
Jerry Whitham

26. Alpha Sigma Phi
Randy Goeglein
Murray Hall
Douglas Merrell
Mike Stemm
Russ Swan

27. Sigma Nu
Dave Cox
Bob McEwen
Kurt Retrum
Ric Retrum
John Shedron

28. Pi Kappa Phi
Philip Pfeifer
James Pruarnik
Gary Schlichte
David Shook
Mark Stevens
Greg Tangalos

29. Alpha Epsilon Pi
Jim Barton
Rick Gardner
Mike Klein
Ed Micon
Howard Schwartz
Barry Zimmerman

30. Evans Scholars
Paul Binder
Jim Burke
Rich James
Mike Marsh

31. Sigma Alpha Mu
Mark Berey
Andy Galdstein
Mike Greenberg
Rob Kreigshaber
Howard Weinreisch
Lee Yosowitz

32. Kappa Delta Rho
Greg Butler
John Faylor
John Gorman
Henry Pataky
Bob Salzarulo
Ed Schmitt
Tom Troutt

33. Funky's
Dan Ballard
Don Ballard
Tom Miller
Bob Nicholls
Mike Reckley

1973

1. Delta Chi
Roger Antoniu
Mark Dayton
Mike Dayton
Wayne Stetina

2. Kappa Sigma
Roger Brown
Bob Kirkwood
Bob Shanteau
Mark Stonecipher
Randy Stouder

3. Theta Chi
Ken Gray
Ed Krouse
Steve Strickler
Gary Walker
John Zigg

4. Briscoe
Jeff Cheung
Dave Fleisher
Jim Kendall
Paul Nacksic

Zane Nevils
Ken Schwarz
Steve Walker

5. Phi Gamma Delta
Bill Canida
Rob Hunt
Pete King
Warren Meinschein
Bill Shonk
Bill Silvey

6. Acacia
Bob Barlow
Kris Burk
Ron Finnigan
Richard Goode
John Jones

7. Dodds House
Paul Bresher
Chuck Gemmer
Paul Hewitt
Ron Martin
Bob Mead
Lyn Mueller
Dave Rubenking
Denny Speer

8. Phi Kappa Psi
Alan Brown
Peter Dewitt
Dave Glover
Phil Sheridan
Tom Stokes

9. Sigma Alpha Epsilon
Scott Greene
Ron Koepsel
Rick Maguire
Maury Monserez
Ed Shank

10. Sigma Nu
Rich Abel
Alan Burns
Kenny Dugan
Nick Gearheart
Louie Mehlig
O. T. Retum

11. Sigma Chi
Dennis Anderson
David Busch
Jim Davis
Kent Davis
Michael Rose
Bruce Walters
Randall Zeller

12. Pi Kappa Phi
Jim Crews
Rich Johnson
George Knapp
Jim Pivarnik
Gary Schichte
Dave Shook

13. Theta Xi
Phil Adams
Ernie Califana
Phil Conn
Gary Davis
Dave de Rox
Roger Hungerford
Dave Pilcher
Charles Scurr

14. Phi Delta Theta
Barth Anderson
Rick Gibbs
Jim Koday
Gary Moor
Tom Pykosz
Alan Smith

15. Sigma Phi Epsilon
Jerry Davis
Dennis Dixin
C. Endicott Enslen
John Jamieson
Paul Kilgore
Gordon McOuat
Boudewyn Wulff

16. Martin III
Dave Alexander
Bob Heyderhoff
Gary Milda
Jim Priest

17. Lambda Chi Alpha
Murray Hall
Brian Hay
Gary Howerton
Irvin Sonne
Tomas Sonne

18. Sigma Pi
Dale Arfman
Tyrell Dudley
Mike Knepper
Tom Lepucki
Jeff Medlen
John Owen
Joe Smucker

19. Delta Tau Delta
Don Ballard
Gregory Ballard
Mikel Eid
Michael McCluckie

20. Evans Scholars
Paul Binder
Jim Burke
Steve Colnitis
Steven Goss
Bob Hermes
Tim Kuzmicz

21. Shea III
Alex Braitman
Bob Hansen
Geoff Giauser
Mark Shertzer

22. Delta Upsilon
Jim Cahillane
J. P. Miller
Tom Schalliol
Mike Strong

23. Pi Kappa Alpha
David Betner
Rick Birnbaun
Jeff Myers
Dave Strohm
Jim Trigger
Tom Zachary

24. Shea II
Bob Buck
Dave Hammer
Dennis Jensen
Paul Wagner

25. Alpha Epsilon Pi
Jim Barton
Rick Gardner
Barry Igdoloff
Steve Langer
Ed Micon
Joel Miller

26. Martin II
John Bauer
Jack Conrad
Bruce Hendrix
Jim Kayden

27. Cravens B
Tom Blackmore
Fred Dudderar

Cary Gore
Kent Templeton
Ed Totten

28. Beta Theta Pi
Jeff Campbell
Tom Campbell
Jim Dougherty
Terry Ginther
Darrell Simone
John Switzer
Joe Teegarden

29. Alpha Tau Omega
John Lipscomb
John Long
Keith Marsden
Steve Price
Ken Shorip
Ron Smith
Frank Walters

30. Bordner NW
Ben Blakley
Brad Lennon
Doug Merrell
George Pevesman

31. Wissler IV
Mike Badnarik
Kenny Durcholz
Matthew Hayman
Tom Ludwig
Pete Mallatt
Bob Nolen
Bill Roberts
Gary Worden

32. Willkie South III
Randy Deane
Rick Hamner
Clifton Payne
Dave Spiner
Bob Steele

33. Cyclotrons
Scott Jeffen
Bob Roberson
Bob Wulpole
Steve Whitecotten

1974

1. Delta Chi
Mike Alexander
Mark Dayton
Gary Rybar
Wayne Stetina

2. Kappa Sigma
Bob Dyer
Bob Kirkwood
Mark Stonecipher
Randy Stouder

3. Phi Kappa Psi
Alan Brown
Dave Glover
Rusty Harrell
Kent Holcomb
Mike Miles
John Miller
Flip Sheridan

4. Martin V
Marc Arce
John Bauer
Bruce Hendrix
Gary Midla
David Robbins

5. Alpha Tau Omega
Pete Cree
Lynn Frye
David Hopkins
Steve Martin
Mike Murrell

Steve Price
Ron Smith
John Spickelmier

6. Dodds House
Jim Gore
Pat Graninger
Ron Martin
Rick McBride
Bob Mead
Lyn Mueller
Dave Rubenking

7. Sigma Alpha Epsilon
Brent Burke
Scott Green
Dave Jackson
Maurice Monserez
Bob Nelson
Ed Shank

8. Sigma Chi
Dennis Anderson
Dan Chase
Robert Ravensberg
Michael Rose
Chris Tucker

9. Sigma Nu
Rick Abel
Steve Conn
John Costello
Kenny Dungeon
Nick Gearheart
Louie Mehlig

10. Shea II
Bob Buck
Kurt Danner
David Hammer
Byron Harris
Mike Hostetler
Richard McAulitte

John Mullikin
Jim Osborn

11. Cravens B
Thom Blackmore
Tim Cookerly
William Davics
Gary Langell
Jeff McReynolds
Neal Puckett
Greg Recker
Ed Totten, Jr.

12. Acacia
Tim Bray
Jim Davis
Dick Goode
John Jones
Mark Smith

13. Sigma Phi Epsilon
Jerry Davis
Dennis Dixon
John Jamieson
Paul Kilgore
Gordon McOuat
Carey Thielemann

14. Sigma Pi
Gary Adams
Dale Arfman
Mac Ford
Spencer Johnson
Tom Lepucki
Doug Middleton
Joe Smucker
Kevin Thompson

15. Theta Chi
Jeff Dixon
Ken Gray
Bob Hazzard
Dave Himebrook
Steve Strickler

Gary Walker
John Zieg

16. Pi Kappa Phi
Jim Crews
Terry Lewis
Chuck Seely
David Shook
Bob Steele

17. Lambda Chi Alpha
Rick Fox
Murray Hall
Robert Hamilton
Rick Mount
Tom Steinert
Mark Todisco

18. Shea III
Timothy Baltz
Alex Braitman
Geoffrey Glaucer
Matew Scherschel
Mark Shertzer

19. Theta Xi
Philip Adams
Andy Clawson
Gary Davis
David Garriott
Dave Martin
Walter Pagel

20. Evans Scholars
Steve Cass
Steve Conitis
Mike Hulse
Rich James
Tim Kuzmicz
Gary Matula

21. Wissler V
Ken Balser

Ken Hicks
Doug Martin
Vic Osecki
Mark Parker
Rod Rowe

22. Phi Delta Theta
Barth Anderson
Jeff Elliott
Rick Gibbs
Mark Koday
Gary Moor
Alan Smith

23. Phi Gamma Delta
Greg Caplinger
Warren Meinschein
Tom Replogle
Rick Schilling
Patrick Smith
Charlie Turk

24. Beta Theta Pi
Dave Babcock
Jeff Campbell
Ed Catlett
Jim Dougherty
Stephen Heidenreid
Keith Matthews

25. Delta Tau Delta
Don Ballard
Greg Ballard
Kent Hill
Don Jones
Dave Montgomery

26. Delta Upsilon
Kirby Moss
Ed Reed
Randy Wilburn
Jerry Wollam

27. Willkie South VI
John Buting
Gerry Dybel
Steven Gammon
Richard Harpenan
John Letts
Jim Pond
Bill Sauter
Phil Sharp
Terry Walter

28. Rollins House
Mark Bolles
Kevin Butterbaugh
Brian Campbell
Sebette Hamill
D. J. McCarty
David Nicholson

29. Willkie South III
Rick Conrad
Vandy Gillespie
Rick Hammer
Kevin Kirk
Larry Lynch
Steve Mallette
Gary Sheridan
Robert Woodling

30. Magee I
Arthur Bess
Donn Detzler
Steve Gorman
Dave Mikulyuk
Thomas Welch

31. Willkie South X
Ray Burkart
Rusty Harris
Tom Nartker
Charlie Steuber

32. Read
Gary Alter

Joe Breidenback
Gregory DeMattia
Jess Holler
Larry Jones
Dan Scott
Mike Stenzinger

33. Crone House
Steve James
Jay Martin
Terry McDermott
Hal Thurston

1975

1. Phi Gamma Delta
Jay Allardt
Eric King
Pete King
Charlie Turk

2. Delta Chi
Mike Alexander
Roger Antoniu
Mark Dayton
Garry Rybar

3. Dodds House
Bob Bray
Rick McBride
Murray Mendenhall
Greg Pruett
Dave Rubenking

4. Phi Kappa Psi
Rusty Harrell
Kent Holcomb
Paul Hotkamp
Howard May
John Miller
Dave Ruoff
Flip Sheridan

5. Delta Tau Delta
Don Jones
Joe Lohmeyer
Dave Montgomery
Shaun Shafer

6. Kappa Sigma
Wils Bell
Roger Brown
Bob Dyer
Yogi Hutsen
Steve Koenig
Butch Welbourn

7. Wissler V
Ken Balser
Dan Gutzweiler
Ken Hicks
Anton Pawlowski
Dave Schapker
George Varga

8. Sigma Nu
Rick Abel
Ron Browning
John Costello
Kevin Eastridge
Mark Nelson

9. Theta Chi
Dennis Checkley
David Himebrook
Warren Hoffman
Steve Strickler
Steven Townsend

10. Delta Upsilon
J. P. Miller
Kirby Moss
Ed Reed
Dan Reynolds

11. Sigma Alpha Epsilon
Brent Burke
Kent Correll
Pete Crumpacker
Dave Jackson

12. Shea II
Dennis Burke
Dan Danner
Kurt Danner
Steve Drayton
Jim Osborn
Phillip Towle

13. Beta Theta Pi
Dave Babcock
Jeff Campbell
Tom Campbell
George Dresbach
Tom Fribley
John Rinne

14. Sigma Pi
Dale Arfman
Andy Bagnell
Spencer Johnson
Tom Lepucki
Doug Middleton
Kevin Thompson

15. Phi Delta Theta
Sam Brubaker
Jeff Elliott
Gary Moor
Alan Smith
Dean Waddington

16. Acacia
Bill Alfke
Henry Baele
Bryan Berkley
Tim Bray
Jim Davis

17. Martin III
Robert Allison II
Marc Arce
Gary Davis
Tom Kruse
Gary Midla
Bill Read

18. Alpha Tau Omega
Bryce Bennett
Peter Cree
Lynn Frye
Bill Kealing
Bill Lindley
Brian Meek

19. Cravens B
John Cookerly
Tim Cookerly
William Davies
Jeff McReynolds
Greg Recker
Ed Totten

20. Hummer Co-Op
Jerry Clark
Tom Glighaut
Gregory Holda
John Hoskam
Leff Long
Paul McMinn

21. Evans Scholars
Steve Colnitis
James Hulse
Gary Matula
John Ply
Greg Urban

22. Read
Gary Alter
T. J. Fountaine
Steve Gammon
Phil Gick

Bruce Hill
Richard Lawson
Doug May
Ken Overton

23. Delgado Ground
Mike Bieganski
Steve Donovan
Ben Mannix
Rob Plankenhorn
Gary Rich
Dan Ritz

24. Willkie South III
David Byrne
Rick Hamner
Larry Lynch
Tom Quandt
Val Swift
Gary Towne
Kim Viera

25. Theta Xi
Kirk Demaree
Dave Garriott
Stan Griner
John Jaques
Mike McDowel

26. Boisen IV
Michael Cole
Dave Debruin
Stan Lower
Greg Sangalis
Randy Sieferd

27. Jenkinson Ground
Ron Greulich
Kevin Knerr
Paul Pinella
Steve Whitecotton

28. Chi Phi
Bill Baker
Alex Braitman
Dave Hillery
Kent Hyslop
Rick Rankin
Kim Scherschel

29. Magee I
Rony Clark
Joe Lawton
Daniel Sposeep
John Vanderkolk
Rudy Vingtris
Tom Welch

30. Pi Kappa Phi
Jim Hunt
John Leonard
Terry Lewis
Gary Schlichte
Tony Schlichte
Mike Shirley

31. Kappa Delta Rho
Mike Avila
Willis Goble, Jr.
Tom Gorman
Bob Holmquist
Mark Jones
Bob Nicholas
Bryan Taylor

32. Willkie South X
Jim Balas
Stan Gering
Bill Herot
Kevin Moore
Tom Nartker
Charlie Stueben

33. Alpha Epsilon Pi
Jim Barton

Steve Langer
Larry Micon
Larry Rosen
Jim Schwarz
Jim Weinberg

1976

1. Delta Chi
Mike Alexander
Roger Antoniu
Mark Dayton
Garry Rybar

2. Phi Gamma Delta
Jay Allardt
Mark McKee
Eric King
Sandy Kunkel
Andy Light
Jay Steele
Charlie Sursa

3. Delta Tau Delta
Mike Eid
Gary Faddis
Don Jones
Dave Montgomery
Shaun Shafer

4. Sigma Chi
Alan Brown
Dan Chase
Bill Draice
Rob Hewes
Jim Kaellner
Dave Ogler
Bob Ravensberg
Chris Tucker

5. Sigma Nu
George Barnett
Kevin Eastridge

Dave Gelhausen
Dan Gutzweiler
Ray Marr
Kevin Stout

6. Phi Kappa Psi
Rusty Harrell
Eddie Hawes
Kent Holcomb
Howard May
Dave Ruoff

7. Sigma Phi Epsilon
Mark Bertram
Dave Criswell
Jeff Kruzawa
Bob Lanham
Rick Meyer
Sergei Traycoff

8. Acacia
Michael Cole
Jim Davis
Tad Huntington
David Parks
Mark Sheppell
Gary Smith

9. Theta Xi
Gary Davis
Kirk Demaree
Bill Demmon
David Garriott
Dave Huston
Bruce Jennings
David Martin

10. Sigma Alpha Epsilon
Brent Burke
Dave Jackson
Chuck Kelderhouse
Greg Kelly
Dave McArdle
Ken Ramsey

11. Phi Delta Theta
Paul Bolin
Jeff Elliott
Jim Etter
Rick Gasper
Jay Hancock
Garry Moor

12. Beta Theta Pi
Jeff Campbell
Tom Campbell
Jack Grummel
William Herst
Kelly Hindman
Kent Lee
John Rinne

13. (tie) Kappa Sigma
Kim Kroll
Mike Hageman
Mark Hart
Scott Peterson
Butch Welburn

13. (tie) Alpha Epsilon Pi
Todd Emoff
Steve Gray
Steve Langer
Larry Micon
Larry Rosen
Louie Star

15. Dodds House
Bob Bray
David King
Rick McBride
Murray Mendenhall
Greg Pruett
Dave Rubenking
Jim Shone
Danny Strickland

16. Theta Chi
Warren Hoffman

Mick Mathews
Jim Miller
Mike Shelby
Steven Townsend
Gary Walker

17. Rollins House
Mark Ayotte
Richard King
Joe Kropp
Jeff Long
Ron Sieller

18. Martin II
Bill Havens
Mark Kozloski
Dave Lynch
Bob Mermelstein
Jeff Morell
Ralph Morgan
Joe Torres

19. Pi Kappa Phi
Gary Ashton
Jim Kaufman
John Leonard
Joe Lingenfelter
Otha Smith

20. Magee I
Tony Clark
Dennis Conard
Perry Harrell
Victor Kelly
Greg Meyer
John Vanderkolk
Rudy Vingris

21. Lambda Chi Alpha
Steve Brock
Bill Fenell
Greg Hines
Robert Kelso
Skip Loge

Patric Overman
Irvin Sonne

22. Martin III
Robert Allison II
Marc Arce
Larry Hodapp
Bill Read
David Trenkner

23. Parks/Shea II
Brad Bertrand
Terry Dawson
Steve Dralryn
Greg Mucha
Ray Paler
Jay Walters

24. Kappa Delta Rho
John Dransfield
Chuck Neidigh
Brent Pope
Kurt Wallenstein

25. Delta Upsilon
Mark Bidwell
Brian Meeks
Kirby Moss
Dan Sposeep

26. Wissler V
Ken Balser
Mark Hallam
Ken Hicks
Kevin Kayes
Anton Pawlowski
Dave Schapker
George Varga

27. Chi Phi
John Baines
Bill Baker
Mike Denson
Kent Hyslop

Edward Leary
Rick Rankin
Kim Scherschel

28. Alpha Sigma Phi
Charles Ellison
Charles Hert
Mike Lake
Donald Pearman
Ken Roslansky

29. Evans Scholars
Drichard Batliner
Patrick Conley
Ron Gentuso
Gary Matula
Glenn Zayner

30. Boisen IV
Stan Lower
Thomas Niccum
Chris Ramsey
Kenny Sanzo
Randy Sieferd
Norman Stroud

31. Cravens B
John Cookerly
Jonathan Fitzner
Ralph Kintzele
Jeff McReynolds
Greg Pickett

32. Nichols House
Ron Engels
Jeff Flatt
Jeff Hannah
Mark Helmond
Jan Hufferd
Pete Iussig

33. Sigma Pi
Terry Atz
Jeff Beck

Alex Einikis
Carl Hawks
Bruce Miller
Doug Suter

1977

1. Delta Chi
Mike Alexander
Rob Brown
Jeff Pollom
Garry Rybar

2. Phi Kappa Psi
Ed Hawes
Stuart Kelly
Howard May
Doug Moody
Dave Ruoff
Bruce Torrance

3. Phi Gamma Delta
Jay Allardt
Jeff Laughlin
Mark McKee
Mike Miller
Mark Needham
John Ohnemus

4. Sigma Phi Epsilon
Wade Berner
Jeff Kurzawa
Joel Ruzich
Jeff Stouhamer
Sergei Traycoff

5. Velo-Men
Greg Brown
David Coar
Steve McClain
Jim Rosa
Hank Schrewker
Lew Siegler

6. Sigma Alpha Epsilon
Dave Barick
Gary Beasley
Brent Burke
John Cottrell
Dave Jackson
Greg Kelly
Dave McArdle
Steve Nix

7. Alpha Epsilon Pi
Mark Elias
Todd Emoff
Stuart Katz
Michael Langer
Jon Mandelbaum
Steve Matzkin
Larry Micon

8. Willkie South III
Dave Atchison
Jim Bohrer
David Byrne
Tom Falkenstein
Bill Gaspelin
Bruce Holder
Brian Jones
Ed Sabis
Gary Towne

9. Evans Scholars
Rock Botliner
Pat Gallagher
Ron Gentuso
Richard Guzowski
Glenn Zayner

10. Phi Delta Theta
Paul Bolin
Jocko Conley
Jeff Elliott
Rick Gasper
Bob Grissom
Dave LaBash

11. Sigma Chi
Alan Brown
Greg Chappell
Dan Chase
Kevin Smith
Dave Straw
Pat True

12. Parks House
Steve Drabyn
Chris Fitzpatrick
Bill Hennings
Robert Lisaius
Greg Mucha

13. Martin III
Robert Allison II
Marc Arce
Stanley Hill
Larry Hodapp
Harry Lewis
David Trenkner

14. Kappa Sigma
Dave Coleman
Joseph Fisher
Mark Hart
Steve Koenig
Roger Theis
David Walden

15. Tau Kappa Epsilon
Michael Baker
Dave Lynch
Carl Maijer
Mark Ogden
Stephen Salmon
Eric Werner

16. Rollins House
Mark Ayotte
Robert Holahan
L. DeWayne Neece

Carl Potenza
Mark Troyer
Christopher Wahl
Ken Williams

17. Sigma Pi
Andy Bagnall
Jeff Beck
Bill Brock
Rob Carstens
Kevin Kayes
Timothy Olsen

18. Nichols House
Terry Beyl
Peter Colovos
Ron Engels
Jeff Flatt
Bruce Hedden
Pete Iussig
Jim Ziemer

19. Theta Xi
Kirk Demaree
Dave Garriott
Michael McDowell
Dave Stankich
Dennis Withered

20. Theta Chi
Steve Dum
Keith Enochs
Greg Hignite
Jim Miller
Tom Rohm
Jim Shoemaker

21. Pi Kappa Alpha
Ed Buis
Steve Ehmke
Bob Greve
Ron Mathews
Greg Meyer

Greg Spudic
Jim Welsh

22. Delta Tau Delta
Gary Gaddis
Dave Howard
Don Jessen
Anton Pawlowski
Jeff Troyer
Tony Wishart

23. Beta Theta Pi
Ted Chase
Steven Ewers
Bill Herst
Craig Heyde
Kelly Hindman
Ralph Mason
John Rinne
Clay Williams

24. Alpha Sigma Phi
Joe Adams
John Chappo
Chuck Ellison
Dave Filbey
Todd Hittinger
Craig Hunter

25. Martin II
Tom Englert
Bill Havens
Bob Mermelstein
Jeff Morell
David Smith
Joe Torres

26. Acacia
Craig Collins
Steve Gilmour
Jamie Pett
William Snow

27. Kappa Delta Rho
Randy Bartholomew
Brad Burton
Matt Kaag
Chuck Neidigh
Lyle Sleeman

28. Magee I
Bruce Clyde
Victor Kelley
James Levine
Tony Rosenberg
Dave Russell
John Vanderkolk

29. Shea III
Gary Bortner
Roger Medina
John Reid
Dennie Rose
Tobin Strupp
John Wardrop

30. Jenkins House
Blaine Case
Jerry Daugherty
Bob Falge
Neil Holbrook
Bob Kushner
Bob LeMay
Charlie Mason

31. Signa Phi Nothing
Jeffrey Dellinger
Dave Purcell
Rod Roebuck
Mark Roseberry

32. Jenkinson II
Don Blackwell
Cabell Cobbs
Brent Goble

Richard Marshall
Bruce McClenahan

1978

1. Phi Kappa Psi
Paul Berg
Tim Cummings
Stewart Kelly
Doug Moody

2. Sigma Nu
Jeff Bolin
John Freistroffer
Gregg Rago
Dave Schapker
Chris Sinn

3. Pi Kappa Phi
Russ Hanning
John Hayden
Jim Kaufman
John Leonard
Jeff Miller
Dennis Rose
Steve Smith
Kenny Van Winkle

4. Alpha Epsilon Pi
Randy Butler
Mike Emoff
Todd Emoff
Larry Hirsch
Mike Langer
Jon Mandelbaum
Larry Micon

5. Sigma Phi Epsilon
Dave Ahearn
Kirk Bayless
Ray Dusman
Jeff Kurzawa

Dave Russell
Peter Wulff

6. Dodds House
Matt Holbert
Jeff Kassing
John Kassing
Rick McBride
Mark Mimms
Jim Shone
Tim Taykowski

7. Sigma Chi
Steve Barth
Alan Brown
Bob Hamilton
Mark Kirkwood
Bill Klaes
Doug Shafer
Dave Straw
Brian Wahl

8. Kappa Sigma
Dave Coleman
Jeff Gerst
Ed Kasper
Steve Koenig
Scott Rosson
Dave Walden

9. Phi Gamma Delta
Dave Evans
Perry Fogelsong
Mike Miller
Mark Needham
Kevin King
Pete Turk

10. Delta Chi
Rob Brown
Garry Rybar
Greg Silence
Doug Tate
Alan Williams

11. Theta Chi
Bruce Blue
Amal Das
Steve Dum
Keith Enochs
Jim Miller
Jerry Muskat
Mike Troyer

12. Sigma Pi
Brian Barton
Rob Carstens
Mitch Chabraja
Bob Harnach
Kevin Kayes
Stephen Korff
Tim Olson

13. Lambda Chi Alpha
Steve Brock
Robert Davee
Wyatt Elmore
Bill Ferrell
Steve Gibson
Dean Marks
Charles Rossen

14. Delta Tau Delta
Mark Bachman
Frank Barth
Gary Gaddis
Craig Halsey
Dave Howard
Anton Pawlowski
Shaun Shafer

15. Tau Kappa Epsilon
Jim Farquharson
Mark Fortune
Dave Lynch
Jim McGuire
Scott Stuart

16. (tie) Evans Scholars
Rich Batliner
Ronald Gentuso
Tony Greiner
Richard Guzowski
Mark Masciola
Stephen Smith

16. (tie) Alpha Sigma Phi
Tom Brown
Dave Filbey
Cary Moorman
Matthew Mullin
Mike Wright

18. (tie) Acacia
Joe Carson
Tod Huntington
Mark Sheppell
Steve Williams

18. (tie) Hummer House
Robert Andrews
Steve Clippert
David Gunderson
Ken Hess
Steve Miller
Joseph Skibek

20. Nichols House
Terry Beyl
Peter Colovos
Joe Denny
Ron Engels
Jeff Flatt
Doug Grant
Jeff Hannah
Mark Helmond
Pete Iussing
David Risley

21. Beta Theta Pi
Ted Chase
Robert Crisci

Steve Ewers
Tom Gaunt
Kelly Heidman
Jay Highley
John Rinne

22. Willkie South Suite
Dave Atchison
George Einterz
Bill Gaspelin
Bruce Holder
George Radakovich
Harry Schlater

23. Elkin II
Scott Barker
Jeff Geisey
Marty Hawkins
Steve Scharf
Warren Sisney
Paul Stern
Steve Strutton
Randy Thompson
Bill Versteeg

24. Alpha Tau Omega
Bob Boeglin
Jim Cordova
Don Fischer
Gary Keyser
Tom Long
Walt Rassel

25. Rollins House
Mark Ayotte
Bob Holahan
Carl Potenza
Dan Powers
Craig Rodgers
David Sanford
William Spitler
Walt Strange
Chris Wahl

26. Phi Delta Theta
Mike Clifton
Rich Gasper
Dave LaBrash
Jack Marshall
Lee Puckett
Jeff Reuter
Joe Walsh

27. (tie) Pi Kappa Alpha
Ed Buis
Steve Ehmke
Ron Mathews
Curt Swan
John Vanderkolk
Neil White

27. (tie) Willkie South III
Tony Albanese
Jim Bohrer
Chris Cruz
Bill Light
Chris Pitts
Doug Pitts
Ed Sabis

29. Magee I
David Canon
Dennis Jacob
Jim Levine
Mike Peek
Tony Rosenberg
Doug Schumacker

30. Martin III
Stanley Hill
Larry Hodapp
Maury Hurwich
Jeff Sedam
Mike Sumers
Dave Trenker
Jeff Ude

31. Wissler V
Frank Battaglia
Jeff Camp
Jeff Cappelli
Tom Dogan
John Grott
Gary Palmer
Bill Quest

32. Willkie South X
Mike Benedict
Bob Broeking
Tony Hunt
Jon Pascolini
Mark Valko
Brad Wilks

33. Kappa Delta Rho
Lance Lahr
Jeff Moeller
Charles Neidigh
Peter Reba
Kurt Wallenstein
Steve Weissert

1979

1. Delta Chi
Bill Brissman
Greg Silence
Doug Tate
Alan Williams

2. Kappa Sigma
Kurt Brown
David Coleman
Steven Dalton
Robert Gibson
Steve Koenig
Steven Willsey

3. Jenkins House
Blayn Cae

Brian Goins
Neil Holbrook
Tom Kearney
Robert LeMay
Brian Pogue
Alan Sankowski
Bill Van Der Pol

4. Sigma Phi Epsilon
J. Mark Bertram
Kevin Harmon
Joseph Kukolla II
Jeff Kurzawa
Thomas Morgan
Randall Staffer
Peter Wulff

5. Sigma Alpha Epsilon
Tim Albright
Dave Draga
Louie Haboush
Jay Jackson
Greg Kelly
Mike Moran
Steve Nix
Jay Phillips

6. Sigma Chi
Alan Brown
Bob Deitch
Bob Hamilton
Mark Kirkwood
John Moenning
Rick Rooney
Doug Shafer
Brian Wahl

7. Alpha Epsilon Pi
Mike Emoff
Dan Fragen
Phil Frank
Jason Levin
Jon Mandelbaum
Bill Mansbach

Rob Mintz
Max Mintzer
Jack Thompson

8. Alpha Sigma Phi
Roy Chisholm
David Filbey
J. Brian Hittinger
Charles Johnson
Brian LaRue
Matthew Mullin

9. Pi Kappa Phi
Mike Baccash
Dave Brown
John Hayden
Jim Kaufman
John Leonard
James Pivarnik
John Rosner
Steve Smith
Jerry Solon
David Teran

10. Theta Chi
Bruce Blue
Timothy Deneen
Steve Dum
Kenneth Free
Jeff Hendren
Jim Millew
Michael Troyer

11. Beta Theta Pi
Dale Albertson
Dave Carlson
Ted Chase
Robert Crisci
Rick Gasaway
Bruce Perry
Ed Scharringhausen
Rob Stiehl
Clay Williams

12. Willkie South Suite
Dave Atchison
George Einertz
Bill Gaspelin
Bruce Holder
George Radkovich
Harvey Schelchter

13. Dodds House
Dave Craig
Dan Dooher
Jeff Greene
Jeff Kassing
John Kassing
Tom Poltras
Tim Taykowski
Stan Vollmer

14. Wissler V
Jeff Camp
John Groff
Gary Palmer
Bill Quest

15. Willkie South III
Tony Albanese
Jim Bohrer
Dean Elliot
John Gaspelin
Jim Oleson
Chris Pitts
Doug Pitts
Ed Sabis

16. Phi Kappa Psi
Paul Berg
Stu Kelly
Doug Moody
Louie Plumlee
Craig Tidwell

17. Hummer House
Steve Baker

Greg Campi
Steve Clippert
Peter Colovos
David Henn
Steve Miller
Gary Retherford
David Treglia
Jim Ziemer

18. Rollins House
Mark Ayotte
Brian Baxter
Stuart Cebovitz
Pat Coughlin
Jeff Long
Chris Montgomery
Tim Olney

19. Mass Riders
David Canon
Jim Levine
Roy Norman
Dave Stankich
Tom Vann
Mike Zoeller

20. Delta Tau Delta
Frank Barth
Brad Bucknam
Gary Gaddis
John Gall, Jr.
Dave Howard
Ted McGrew
Wayne Palmer

21. Cravens B
David Bouwkamp
Patrick Costello
Mike Crouch
Mike Davis
Bruce Fagan
Peter Van der Lugt
David Witzerman

22. Delgado Ground
Dave Bond
Steve Fitzpatrick
Mark Huster
Dave McClanahan
Mike Sherman
Scott Thoas
Sam Thompson
Jeff Tucker

23. Pi Kappa Alpha
Joe Bretz
Steve Ehmke
Ron Mathews
Greg Meyer
Robert Propst
John Vanderkolk

24. Lambda Chi Alpha
Pete Baker
Rick Bohnsack
Robert Davee
Dean Marks
K. Shawn McClarnon
Charles Rossen
Sean St. Clair

25. Delta Upsilon
Mark Bidwell
Jim Hildebranski
John Peat
Dan Reynolds
Dave Schuhler

26. Willkie South V
Robert Andrews
Matt Bromley
Chris Cruz
Greg Gilles
Brett Norman
Brian Radaker
Mike Walz

27. Alpha Tau Omega
Don Albors
Jim Cordova
Grant Gee
Greg Gee
Denny Heller
Tom Long
Bill Spitler

28. Tau Kappa Epsilon
Tom Barkley
Dan Giesecke
Scott Kerjes
Dave Lynch
Jim McGuire
Kris Walker

29. Acacia
Michael Bradash
Joe Carson
Brian Essary
Bob Feigenhauer
Greg Kimmel
Kent MacPherson
Dave Nelson
Peter Toal

30. Willkie South X
Artoro Florcroz
Dave Hoston
Mike Konetzka
Bill Leidecker
Jon Pascolini
Tony Romaski

31. Chi Phi
Mike Brown
Mark Carroll
Peter Gruber
Randy McNutt
Gary Sparks
John Warner

32. Martin III
Tim Commons
Stan Hill
Joseph Hipskind
Dick Kelly
Harry Lewis
Mike Summers
John Watson

33. Wissler III
John Babcock
Jim Egan
Gary Heskett
Larry Neidig
Kevin Spellacy

1980

1. Delta Chi
Bill Brissman
Chris Gutowsky
Doug Tate
Alan Williams

2. Pi Kappa Phi
Mike Baccash
Dan Corcoran
Jay Hargis
John Hayden
Dennis Rose
John Rosner
Steve Smith
Jerry Solon

3. Wissler V
Jeff Camp
John Gratt
John Lynch
Gary Palmer
Bill Quest
John Sami
Steve Shepard

4. Phi Gamma Delta
Mark Effrein
Chip Helm
Kevin King
Michael Miller
Jeffrey Shuman
Mark Weller

5. Willkie South III
Tony Albanese
Dave Atchison
Dean Elliott
John Gaspelin
Chris Pitts
Doug Pitts
Harvey Schleter
Bob Wilson

6. Chi Phi
Tom Brooks
Mark Carroll
Pete Gruber
Rob Jeffers
Kevin Johnson
Randy Ochs
John Warner
Tom Warner

7. Sigma Alpha Epsilon
Tim Albright
Dave Ash
Jeff Jellison
Mike Moran
Dave Zilkowski

8. Dodds House
Dave Craig
Bob Devetski
J. D. Forrest
Matt Holbert
Jeff Kassing
Jim Kiser
Scott Slaughter

9. Sigma Nu
Tom Beam
Chris Clausen
Dave Lucchese
Chris McCray
Dick Peters
Mickey Terrell
Chip Walker
Scott Wolf

10. Alpha Tau Omega
Doug Copley
Jim Cordova
Grant Gee
Greg Gee
Tom Long
Leo Magrini
Chris Proffitt
William Spitler

11. Acacia
Joe Carson
Carl Dankert
Kirk Eggebrecht
Kent MacPherson
Pat McCleary
Peter Toal

12. Sigma Chi
Matthew Cook
Bob Deitch
Bill Drake
Mark Kirkwood
Kris Luhrsen
Mike Scheffer
Brian Wahl

13. Pi Kappa Alpha
Jeff Ansell
Joe Bretz
Edward Buis
Dan Burgason
Steve Ehmke

14. Phi Delta Theta
Mark Berry
Mike Brown
Frank Haig
Jim Mahaffey
Scott Plain
Chris Pluta
Jeff Reuter
Hank Stephan
Marc Williamson

15. Beta Theta Pi
Dave Carlson
Ted Chase
Rob Crisci
Bruce Roach
Rob Stiehl
Clay Williams
Greg Wyant

16. Jenkins House
George Leffler
Robert LeMay
Brian Pogue
Bill Romey
Alan Sankowski
Bil Van Der Pol

17. Phi Kappa Psi
Paul Berg
Doug Moody
Brad Beaman
John Coleman
Joe Gehris
Greg Gilles

18. Sigma Phi Epsilon
Jay Beatty
Jim Edwards
Neal Howe
Rick Johns
Tom Morgan
Jim Said

Randy Stauffer
Bruce Tassell
Dan Weeden

19. Willkie South VII
Brian Fanning
Chris Hubner
Rich Noritake
Rich Reilly
Russ Smith
Brad Taylor
John Waschkies

20. Shea III
Michael Gerdenich
J. P. Hoyer
Stephen Hugus
Dennis Jacob
Chuck Moore
Craig Sieron

21. Alpha Epsilon Pi
Jack Brown
Mike Emoff
Mitchell Emoff
Phillip Frank
Stuart Katz
Jon Mandelbaum
Ken Olan
Rick Yale

22. Kappa Sigma
Scott Bassett
Steve Dalton
John Daly
Ron Eid
David Springer
Steve Willsey

23. Willkie South X
Rick Banasiewicz
Mark Dollinger
Steve Kucharski

Brian Lathrop
Art Morris
Jon Pascolini
Roger Rodich
Allen Ruddick

24. Theta Chi
Bart Book
Glen Garman
Jeff Hendren
Ken Noble
Stan Stansberry
Mike Troyer
Steve Walker
Vaughn Wamsley

25. Martin III
Joe Hipskind
Dick Kelly
John Lennenschmidt
Larry Martin
Todd Midla
Frank Morton

26. Cravens A
Jonathan Buis
Patrick Costello
Jeffrey Harding
John Kincaid
William Martin
Patrick Raftery

27. Blitzkriegers
Douglas Meyer
Chris Montgomery
Dan Powers
Matt Powers
Steve Spencer

28. Crone
Don Cahill
Bob Curts
Mike Duffala

Mark Faulkenberg
Dave Koch
Marty Rogier

29. Willkie South V
Chris Cruz
Bill Gaspelin
Don Grover
Brett Norman
Dave Pioch
Joe Tolbert
Michael Yonks

30. Nichols House
Ken Bergmann
Thomas Butler
Joseph Damann
Greg Jehlik
Mark Kusatzky
Pat McDonald
Steven Owens
Bob Schleter
Stephen Smith

31. Delta Upsilon
James Hildebranski
Garry Karch
Alex Kolumbus
Daniel LaBrash
Edward Marshall

32. Willkie South IV
Steve Caine
Chris Dawson
David Doran
Tim Farney
Phil Marble
Jim Roberts

33. Parks House
Trung Do
Steve Kincaide
Bob Lisaius

Doug Lollar
Brian Smith

1981

1. Delta Chi
Bill Brissman
Chris Gutowsky
Doug Tate
Alan Williams

2. Chi Phi
Cory Campbell
Randy Ochs
Greg Rutzen
John Warner

3. Willkie
Tony Albanese
Mike Boyer
John Gaspelin
Michael Scanlon
Dave Shettleroe
Bob Wilson

4. Alpha Tau Omega
Grant Gee
Leo Magrini
Scott Noss
Ronger Vandergunugten
Brett Westenfelder

5. Phi Kappa Psi
Brad Beaman
Paul Berg
Scott Everrood
Joe Gehris
Greg Gilles
Louie Plumlee

6. Alpha Epsilon Pi
Scott Baruck

Greg Bolotin
Mitch Emoff
Phil Frank
Craig Gutmann
Rich Kolman
Rick Yale

7. Phi Gamma Delta
Mark Effrein
Chip Helni
Kevin King
Matt Milligan
Andy Phila

8. Sigma Alpha Epsilon
Jim Fissinger
Jeff Jellison
Scott Nichols
Jon Pupillo
Ron Repka

9. Blitzkriegers
Pat Coughlin
John Feeney
Chris Montgomery
Tim Olney
Dan Powers
Matt Powers

10. Wissler V
John Grott
James Hixon
Steve Kovich
Gary Palmer
Steve Shepard

11. Sigma Phi Epsilon
Bernie Funke
Jim Kurzawa
Jim Said
John Smith

12. Jenkins House
Tom Kearney
Jeff Pauloski
Brian Pogue
Dave Nabb

13. Dodds House
Jed Barach
Dave Craig
Bob Devetski
Matt Holbert
Jeff Kassing
Dan Murphy
Howard Slaughter
Scott Slaughter

14. Rollins House
Joe Dagnese
Bill Matheson
John Matheson
Carl Scharfe
Steven Spencer

15. Theta Chi
Jeff Ammeron
Chris Breach
Timothy Deneen
Randy Swoboda
Von Wamsley

16. Sigma Chi
Chris Luhrsen
Jack Motors
Greg Oltman
Mike Salerno
Brian Wahl

17. Sigma Nu
Mike Gossman
Dave Lucchese
Dick Peters
Dan Schapker
Ken Stouffel
Mickey Terrell

18. Alpha Sigma Phi
Chris Buls
Tim Graham
Bill Kiszla
Steve Krucharski

19. Phi Delta Theta
Jim Barlow
Tim Kappes
Jim Mahaffey
Glenn Schroeder
Greg Smith

20. Evans Scholars
Rocky Crouch
Tim Ellsworths
Chris Gerardi
Pat Hawkins
Alan Matula
Jack Spartz

21. Wissler II/Wissler III
Phil Guba
Gary Heskett
Dave McKinnley
Jeff Reyeastes

22. Kappa Sigma
Scott Bassett
Bob Gibson
Neil Perron
Craig Richards

23. Acacia
Kirk Eggebrecht
Jack Fogle
Doug Gill
Peter Taol

24. Delta Tau Delta
Bert Harrison
Jeff Howard
Kevin Moyer

Shaun Shaffer
Randy Smock
Andrew Wallace

25. Parks House
Steve Cotter
D. J. Figueroa
Boyd Marts
Tom Miller
Brian Smith
Marc Sparber

26. Curry II
Ernie Blando
Mark McGaha
Chris Mnichowski

27. Tau Kappa Epsilon
Bruce Bales
Bill Borgeson
Jay Brasel
Mike Burns
Eric Diekanes
Dave Lynch

28. Pi Kappa Phi
Mike DeVito
Tom Filipczak
Phil Scheidler
Bob Williams

29. Boisen I
Brian Busby
Brad Czupryn
Carl Swartz
Mark Toljanic

30. Sigma Pi
Steve Crawford
Brian McCormack
John Nierzwicki

Bruce Smalley
Eric Waser

31. Nichols House
Greg Cochran
John Klingelhoffer
Ken Kudrak
John Pleshood
Jim Smutniak

32. Pi Kappa Alpha
Joe Bretz
Steve Finzer
Rich Lind
Bill Nonte
Michael Walz

33. Hummer House
Greg Canpi
Tom Harpring
Dave Kohrman
Joel Seever
Steve Treglia

1982

1. Phi Delta Theta
Tim Kappes
Jim Mahaffey
Glenn Schroeder
Greg Smith

2. Delta Chi
Dave Bond
Chris Gutowsky
Scott Senese
Randy Strong

3. Kappa Sigma
Scott Bassett
Bob Bergren

Bob Gibson
Jeff Pauloski

4. Beta Theta Pi
William Ball
John Bracco
Benjamin Cottingham
Doug Glen
Robert Pugh

5. Acacia
George Grubb
Jeff Hilligoss
Chris Richardson
Cary Sierzputowski

6. Phi Gamma Delta
Mark Effren
Chip Helm
Matt Millikan
Craig Reed
Brian Rundle

7. Alpha Tau Omega
Leo Magrini
Scott Moss
Roger Vandergunugten
Fritz Westenfelder

8. Sigma Chi
Dave Dickson
Tim Farney
Mark Gradison
Tom Kroh
Kris Luhrsen
Tim Palma
Bill Rice
Dan Rose
Mike Shobe
Scott Yancey

9. (tie) Hummer House
Greg Campi

Tom Harpring
Dave Kohrman
Dave Porter
Joel Seever

9. (tie) Sigma Phi Epsilon
Tom Epple
Bernie Funk
Mike Koufos
Dave Maierhofer
John Smith

11. Albatross
Mike Daffala
Steve Fillenwarth
Pat Harmon
Richard Noritake

12. Phi Kappa Psi
Brad Beaman
Steve Dayton
Joe Gehris
Greg Gilles
Dave Shori

13. Delta Tau Delta
Jeff Howard
Scott Kamman
Steve Shearon
Andy Wallace

14. Parks House
Steve Cotter
John Griggs
Greg Luttreil
Boyd Marts
Tom Miller

15. Sigma Alpha Epsilon
Jim Fissinger
Jeff Jellison
Scott Nichols
Ron Repka
Mitch Stuaffer

16. Willkie
Mike Boyer
John Gaspelin
Noel Masters
Brett Norman
Mike Scanlin
Bob Wilson

17. Chi Phi
Cory Campbell
John Garman
Rick Gruber
Randy Ochs

18. Alpha Epsilon Pi
Scott Baruch
Gregg Bolotin
Mitch Emoff
Todd Gordon
Craig Gutmann
Rick Yale

19. Rollins House
Joe Dagnese
Bill Matheson
Carl Scharfe
Brian Walton

20. Dodds House
Jed Barach
Dave Craig
Bob Deuetski
Dan Murphy
David Robertson
Scott Slaughter

21. Theta Chi
Chris Breach
Marq Bresnan
Mike Dum
Vaughn Wamsley

22. Curry II
John Boysen

Tony Emmons
Bruce Johnstone
Mark McGaha
Kelly Minton
Steve Ronske

23. Wissler II/III
Dan Diedrich
Jeffrey Easter
Phil Guba
Dave McKinley
Raja Salaymeh

24. Martin II
Dave Hesting
Derek Lee
Cliff Schumacker
Sheldon Weiss

25. Jenkins House
George Leffler
David Nabb
Brian Pogue
Ed Prosser

26. Lambda Chi Alpha
Mark Aguilar
Greg Beal
Craig Cashow
Doug Hannoy
Bill Hise

27. Boisen I
Joe Burke
Brian Busby
Tim Goggin
Ed Lang
Carl Swartz
Mark Towanic

28. Pi Kappa Phi
Thomas Carr
Paul Hoyden

Phil Scheidler
Dave Shettleroe
Bob Williams

29. Tau Kappa Epsilon
Bruce Bales
Bill Borgeson
Eric Diekans
Steve Mack

30. Sigma Pi
Chris Hansen
Rick Park
Bruce Smalley
Mike Smith
Dave Webb

31. Willkie South IV
Mike Bullock
David Doran
Steven Eller
Rick Kochert

32. Pi Kappa Alpha
Mark Horn
Dave Linville
Sam Moore
Ross Richardson
John White

33. Nichols House
Ken Crandall
Louie Grounds
Steve Hammerstrom
Tom Liddell
Brian Sidor

1983

1. Acacia
George Grubb
Jeff Hilligoss

Chris Richardson
Cary Sierzputowski

2. Phi Delta Theta
Jim Barlow
Ken Crandall
Jim Mahaffey
Glenn Schroeder
Greg Smith

3. Phi Kappa Psi
Brad Beaman
Bob Claycomb
Kent Compton
Steve Dayton
Joe Gheris
Scott Hamilton
Todd Lemmon
Bryan Wilhelm

4. Alpha Epsilon Pi
Gregg Bolotin
Mitch Emoff
Jim Pollak
Marc Korman
Scott Baruch
Art Mandelbaum

5. Alpha Tau Omega
Bob Johnson
Leo Magrini
Scott Moss
Paul Paslaski
Brad Trotten
Roger Veandergenugten
Lou Westenfelder

6. Willkie
Dan Diedrich
Tim McKeon
Raja Salaymeh
Ben Tischler
Bob Wilson

7. Sigma Phi Epsilon
Paul Duwel
Bernie Funk
Kevin Johnson
Pete Korellis
Chris Pruitt
Cary Smith

8. Chi Phi
Gary Campbell
John Garman
Bill McGuire
Dan McNutt
Randall Ochs
Peter Wulff

9. Sigma Alpha Epsilon
Keith Bartley
Jim Fissinger
Tom O'Connell
Dave Repka
Ron Repka
Mitch Stauffer

10. Jenkins House
George Leffler
Dave Nabb
Ed Prosser
Kelly Schwegland

11. Kappa Sigma
Scott Bassett
Bob Bergren
Jeff Pauloski
Tom Schoettle

12. Sigma Pi
John Hannah
Dave Kriozere
Stephen Park
Mike Smith
Dave Tarr
Stephen Tomecek

13. Phi Gamma Delta
Doug Ellmore
Jim Holland
Jeff Johnson
Dan King
Scott Macaland
Mike Mays
Matt Millikan
Jeff Shuman
Don Strobel

14. Rollins House
Bill Dykema
Bill Matheson
Doug Pearson
Carl Scharfe
George Simpson
Brian Walton

15. Sigma Chi
Mark Gradison
Troy Hamilton
Tim Palma
Steve Queisser
Steve Reynolds
Mike Shobe
Scott Yancey

16. Parks House
Stephen Cotter
Scott Eitman
John Griggs
Will Howard
Greg Luttrell
Joe Schneider
Roland Wilson

17. Delta Tau Delta
Rusty Alban
Jim Allen
George Grossardt
Jeff Howard
Chris Van Natta
Andy Wallace

18. Dodds House
Jed Barach
Bob Devetski
Alan Heimlich
Dan Murphy
Howard Slaughter
Kip Tew
Steve Wuertz

19. Lambda Chi Alpha
Mark Aguilar
Craig Coshow
Joe Fitzgerald
Steve Garrett
Bill Hise
Mark Martindill
Steve O'Malley
Bill Palmer

20. Delta Upsilon
Bill Enright
Paul Kluempers
Mike Lockart
Mike Marvel
Jeff Pangburn
Pete Thurin

21. Alpha Sigma Phi
Glenn Barb
Eric Eugene
Kurt Krauter
Steve Kucharski
Kurt Terhar

22. Beta Theta Pi
Al Bodine
Bret Brase
Ben Cottingham
Tim Gavin
Mike Minich
Spero Pulos
Jim Terlizzi

23. Tau Kappa Epsilon
Bruce Bales
Bil Borgeson
Mike Burns
Chuck Combs
Bill Field
Steve Mack

24. Hummer House
John Emkes
Karl Flowers
Eric Hudecek
Dave Kohlman
Steve Kovich
Dave Porter
Steve Sofhauser

25. Sigma Alpha Mu
Jeff Bassock
Mike Berger
Scott Bosner
Howard Feldman
Jim Garfield
Charlie Gottlieb
Mark Siegel
Jim Zellinger

26. Sigma Nu
Steve Davis
Steven Gerrit
Robert Lee
Chris Powers
Mark Shea
Alan Werner

27. Blitzkriegers
David Cowen
Craig Eubank
Joseph Ricciardi
Stephen Spencer

28. Martin III
Matt Didler
Greg Hale

Todd Midla
Doug Olberding
Haskel Weiss

29. Team Anything
Brad Bates
Kevin Beres
Scott Kistler
Bob McKee
Thom Wozniak

30. Zeta Beta Tau
Brad Berish
Greg Dolin
Mitch Goldman
Steve Hoffman
Mike Sandler
Jon Simon

31. Nichols House
Dan Demeter
Louie Grounds
Ron Hendren
Tom Liddell
Sean Phillips
Mark Pogue
Brian Sidor

32. Curry IV
Robert Burstein
Tony Emmons
Dirk Farrell
Michael Satterfield
Daniel Shellenberg

33. Pi Kappa Phi
Rick Blessing
Marty Fender
Mark Kusatzky
Rob Saffrin
Sam Scheidler
Greg Vann
Bob Williams

1984

1. Cutters
Adam Beck
Adam Giles
Scott Senese
Randy Strong

2. Alpha Epsilon Pi
Marc Korman
Art Mandelbaum
Neil Olderman
Jim Pollak
Sheldon Weiss

3. Acacia
George Grubb
Jeff Hilligoss
Cary Sierzputowski
Kevin Weldon

4. Chi Phi
Jeff Barrett
Cory Campbell
John Garman
David Hogsley
Bill McGuire
Tim McNelis
Dan McNutt

5. Beta Theta Pi
Tim Gravin
Dan Hilbrich
John Lugar
Todd May
Rob Mesch
Mike Minich
Spero Pulos

6. Phi Gamma Delta
David Breide
Dan Cusick
Doug Elmore

Jim Holland
Jeff Johnson
Lee Maddox
Ron Wilson

7. Avéré
Tony Ceccanese
Steve Ferklic
Vince Hoeser
Mike Rentio
David Shettleroe
Lou Sowers

8. Jenkins House
John Dreyfuss
Dave Nabb
Ed Prosser
Jon Schwartz
Kelly Schwedland
Tim Spry
Matt Sroboda

9. Alpha Tau Omega
Kerry Cunningham
Steven Diercks
Bob Fields
Bob Johnson
Leo Magrini
Bob Morice
Scott Moss
Paul Paslaski
Brad Trotter

10. Lambda Chi Alpha
Mark Aguilar
Steve Garrett
Jim Griggs
Bill Hise
Bill Palmer

11. Phi Kappa Psi
Steve Dayton
Erick Ellingson
Scott Hamilton

Todd Lemmon
Jon Nagy
John Woodson

12. Phi Delta Theta
Ken Crandall
Tim Kappes
Chris Matzke
Vincent Noone
Steve Smith
Jeff Ulrich

13. Delta Tau Delta
Bob Dunkleu
Mike Edwards
Brian Halloran
Jeff Howard
Scott Kamman
Ted Twinney
Chris Van Natta

14. Sigma Nu

15. Rollins House
Bill Dykema
Brad Jagoe
Doug Pearson
Gregg Rhodes
George Simpson
Brian Walton

16. Delta Upsilon
Ivan Denton
Bill Enright
Paul Kluempers
Mike Lockhart
Pete Thurial

17. Sigma Pi
John Hannah
Chris Hansen
Rick Park
Jay Polsgrove

David Tarr
Steve Tomecek

18. Kappa Sigma
Scott Bassett
John Plenge
Tom Schoettle
Brian Sullivan
Mike Sullivan
Robert Wagner

19. Sigma Chi
Doug Bartol
Greg Edmonds
Mark Gradison
Mike Kay
Jim McGoff
Steve Queisser

20. Curry IV
Rick Broad
Bob Burstein
Dirk Farrell
Mike Kallner
Dan Schnellenberg

21. Sigma Phi Epsilon
Rocke Blair
Chris Bohm
Paul Duwel
Kevin Johnson
Chris Pruitt
Paul Sajben
Carry Smith

22. Wissler V
Steve Buckman
Bob Curts
Mark Dillon
Mark Miller
Mike Phillips
Pat Schellenburg
Dan Schermerhorn
Andy Wezeman

23. Dodds House
Jed Barach
Mark Dunkin
Jim O'Connor
Jim Pruett
David Robertson
David Szentes
Kip Tew

24. Sigma Alpha Epsilon
James Bickley
Pat Cassidy
Matt Hayes
Jim Kiernan
Dave Repka
Mitch Stauffer

25. Alpha Sigma Phi
Eric Born
Mike Brown
John Dehart
David Happel
James Struhs

26. Nichols House
Steve Arnold
Harold Grounds
Ken Hancock
Ronnie Hendren
Joe Hirsch
Sean Phillips
Mark Pogue

27. Pi Kappa Alpha
Mark Beers
Jay Linder
Sam Moore
Craig Pecsenye
Jim Sytniak

28. Curry II
Greg Brown
Wayne Eckerle
Bill Hoke

Mike Miller
Mark Wetekamp

29. Cosmic Debris
David Bushnell
Mike Grossman
Bob Haefke
David Rycerz
Paul Storey

30. Evans Scholars
Kevin Bourke
Joe Farna
Pat Gaughan
Chris Gerardi
Eamonn Killeen

31. Collins
Chris Conner
J. D. Mason
Steve Math
Alias Melius
Greg Sidell
Scott Stinson
David Yufit

32. Kappa Delta Rho
Kevin Banning
Mark Raper
David Waltman
Tom Wheeler

33. Spokesmen
Mike Baird
David Hesting
Bruce Meadows
Cliff Schumacher

1985

1. Alpha Epsilon Pi
Tony Checroun

Marc Korman
Jim Pollak
Sheldon Weiss

2. Acacia
George Grubb
Jeff Hilligoss
Kelly Schwedland
Cary Sierzputowski

3. Chi Phi
Joe Amicucci
Ken Auell
Cory Campbell
Tom Duke
John Garman
Tim McNelis
Dan McNutt

4. Cutters
Tony Ceccanese
Burnett English
Adam Giles
Vince Hoeser
Scott Senese

5. Rollins House
Bill Dykeman
Brak Jugoe
John Kelly
Doug Pearson
George Simpson

6. Pi Kappa Alpha
Mark Beers
Jay Linder
Steve Markham
Mike Niederpruem
Joel Streightiff
Randy Wilson

7. Phi Kappa Psi
Scott Hamilton

Craig Hume
Todd Lemmon
John Woodson

8. Phi Delta Theta
Ken Crandall
Jim Gurbach
Jim Host
Vince Noone
Conrad Smith
Jeff Ulrich

9. Alpha Tau Omega
Steve Diercks
Matt Eskey
Brad Galbraith
Bob Johnson
Leo Magrini
Paul Paslaski
Karl Westenfelder

10. Sigma Alpha Epsilon
Jim Bickley
Mike Haas
Jim Kiernan
Marc Muelle
Donald Scott

11. Latecomers
Steve Cotter
Chris Doran
Scott Eitman
Tim McKeon
Vince Minnick

12. Delta Tau Delta
Bob Craig
Matt Gibbs
Mike Grossman
Scott Joseph
Mitch Mick
Brian Storer
Ted Twinney

13. Sigma Phi Epsilon
Rocke Blair
Chris Bohm
Nidal Masri
Mike Petro
Paul Sajben
Roman Steinberg

14. Collins
Angus Aynsley
John Heichelbech
Kevin Martin
Alius Meilus
Rob Serbent
Ishmael Suarez
Mike Vacirca

15. Cinzano
Hank Ausdenmoore
Greg Brown
George Carlin
John Magro

16. Kappa Sigma
Steve Lains
Tom Schoettle
Jeff Schumaker
Mike Sullivan
Rob Wagner
Jim Wainright

17. Sigma Nu
Andy Cummins
Rob Hancock
Mark Hupfer
Jeff Jensen
Chris Stafford

18. Nichols House
Scott Bacon
Karl Flowers
Ken Hancock
Ron Hendren

Sean Phillips
Mark Pogue

19. Theta Chi
Joe Almon
Jeff Diercks
Jeff Keller
Shawn Mulholland
Matt Perry
Greg Rasmussen
John Reuter

20. Curry IV
Rick Broad
Dirk Farrell
Mike Kauner
Matt O'Donnell
Mike Resener

21. Dodds House
Bob Devetski
Mike Diterese
Jim O'Connor
Barry Pruett
James Pruett
Dave Robertson
Glenn Spiczak
David Szentes

22. Lambda Chi Alpha
Dave Brozmer
Brad Carlson
Tom Davis
Jim Griggs
Buff Palmer
Steve Rupkey
Chet Smith

23. Beta Theta Pi
Tim Gavin
John Lugar
Todd May
Mike Wolfert

24. Sigma Chi
Doug Bartol
John Carter
Mark Gradison
Pete Humbaugh
Karl Queisser
Steve Queisser
Steve Reynolds
Todd Tichenor

25. Thompson V
Mike Bolger
Pat Cogley
Mark Conway
Stu Fleck
Steve Llewellyn
Chris Pajakowski

26. Delta Upsilon
Ivan Denton
Bill Enright
Jeff Hash
Kurt Pfluger

27. McNutt
Dave Bond
Cole Heaston
Jim Mann
Dan Rechner

28. Phi Gamma Delta
Dan Cusick
Dan Effrein
Bruce Eyre
John Fletcher
Chris Jacobs
Jeff Johnson
Mike Smith
John Strobel

29. Evans Scholars
Jeff Collier
Pat Gaughan
Mike Kaiser

Ed Kantor
Eamonn Killeen
Phil LeMaster

30. Alpha Sigma Phi
Mike Brown
Ron Lisch
Rick Otero
Joe Powers

31. Pi Kappa Phi
Rick Blessing
Kevin Cordon
David Davis
Paul Hayden
Lem Lopez
Dan Mikosz

32. Sigma Alpha Mu
Mark Bernstein
Jeff Bramson
Mike Guggenheim
Rich Kaufman
Steve Kleuber
Mark Siegel
Bobby Weiss

33. Beck II
Dave Bradford
Bill Braman
Steve Diedrich
Tom Ryder
Jeff Williams
John Woods

1986

1. Cutters
George Carlin
Tony Ceccanese
Vince Hoeser
Jay Polsgrove

2. Alpha Epsilon Pi
Tony Checroun
Mitch Emoff
Marc Korman
Art Mandelbaum
Jim Pollak
Sheldon Weiss

3. Phi Kappa Psi
Jerry Blanton
Kent Compton
Craig Hume
Todd Lemon

4. Phi Delta Theta
Ken Crandall
Brian Ebeling
Brian Gavett
Dave Holleran
Jim Host
Vince Noone
Dave Pritchett
Conrad Smith

5. Chi Phi
Ken Aull
Cory Campbell
Nick Marshall
Tim McNelis
Dan McNutt

6. Lambda Chi Alpha
Brad Dettmer
Steve Garrett
Jim Griggs
Bill Kring
Kelly McClarnon
Nathan Price
Chet Smith

7. Acacia
John Huesing
Stephen Kominarek
Paul Krackhardt

Edward LaPlante
Kent McDonald

8. Evans Scholars
Jeff Collier
Pat Gaughan
Ed Kantor
Eamonn Killeen
Phil LeMaster
Mike Skirvin
Tom Solon

9. Collins
Angus Aynsley
Glenn Francisco
John Heichelbech
Doug Latham
Kevin Martin
Rob Serbent

10. Delta Tau Delta
Bob Craig
Dave Durochik
Matt Gibbs
Rob Hudson
Kurt Hultberg
Scott Joseph
Brian Storer
Ted Twinney

11. Phi Gamma Delta
Brian Arnett
Chris Jacobs
Jeff Johnson
Dave Schmidt
Mark Senese
Mike Smith
Jim Strobel

12. Cinzano
Hank Ausdenmoore
Greg Brown
Greg Cowen
Cole Heaston

Matt Schuler
Al Trevino

13. Pi Kappa Alpha
David Andrews
David Gasho
Rick Lostutter
Mike Niederpruem
Jim O'Conner
Dave Szentes

14. Alpha Tau Omega
Troy Bradford
Steve Diercks
Brad Galbraith
Scott Hall
Mark Herman
Eric Knipple
Greg Peterson
Karl Westenfelder

15. Kappa Sigma
Dave Gustafson
Dave Harris
Steve Lains
Mike Sullivan
Rob Wagner
Jim Wainwright

16. Sigma Nu
Kevin Cameron
Andy Cummins
Matt Georgi
Bob Hancock
Mark Hupfer
Dave Krahulik
Chris Strafford
Bill Voigt

17. Sigma Chi
Dave Carter
Mark Gradison
Jeff Lundy
Steve Queisser

Steve Reynolds
Boyd Zoccola

18. Sigma Phi Epsilon
Don Birch
Rocke Blair
Nidal Masri
Paul Sajben
Jim Wellington

19. Theta Chi
Joe Almon
Mike Dum
Jim Fleming
Greg Lancelot
Matt Perry
Greg Rasmussen

20. Sigma Alpha Epsilon
Keith Bartley
Mike Haas
Jim Homringhausen
Jim Kiernan
Marc Mueller
Don Scott

21. Delta Upsilon
Ivan Denton
Dave Heller
Jody King
Matt Litzler
Tim Morgan
Hank Reed
Brett Thomas

22. Americana
Pat Cogley
Tim Lewis
Mark Miller
Bill Nihill
Chris Pajakowski
Scott Presley
Pat Shellenberg

23. Trophy Dash
Mike Brauner
Tyler Giles
Rob Green
Brad Jagoe
John Magro

24. Read
Rick Broad
Bob Burstein
Dirk Farrell
Mike Kallner
Matt O'Donnell
Dave Webb

25. Sigma Alpha Mu
Michael Berger
Jeff Bramson
Michael Goldstein
Michael Guggenheim
Adam Klauber
Barry Samuels
Herb Washer

26. Sigma Pi
Thomas Armstrong
David Blades
Ron Harmeyer
Tom Mills
Brian Murphy
Keith Vincent

27. Kappa Delta Rho
James Akin
Mike Mutka
Mike O'Malley
Dave Waltman
Larry Wheeler
Jeff Yarvis

28. Nichols House
Malcolm Fife
Karl Flowers
Ron Hendron

Sean Phillips
Mark Pogue

29. Beck II
Dave Bradford
Bill Braman
Craig Carter
Joe Maher
Bruce Singer
John Woods
Bob Zimmerman

30. Joint Venture
John Osborne
Steve Nuthak
Frederick Rose
Richard Schoff
Elton Slone

31. Curry IV
James Bolander
Graham Fisk
Dave Joseph
Donald Pitzer
Raymond Richie

32. Alpha Sigma Phi
Glen Barb
David Hon
David Leedy
David Nusbaum
Martin Oliver
Rick Otero
Jim Struhs

33. Pi Kappa Phi
Rick Blessing
Kevin Condon
Ed Cyra
Dave Davis
Tim Elfreich
Mike Freshour
Don Mikosz

1987

1. Phi Gamma Delta
Thomas Herendeen
Mark Senese
Jim Strobel

2. Acacia
John Huesing
Stephen Kominiarek
Paul Krackhardt
Edward LaPlants
Kent McDonald

3. Sigma Phi Epsilon
Don Birch
Mike Kallner
Sam Nichol
Mike Petro
Erik Proano
Todd Stallings

4. Cutters
Michael Brauner
Robert Green
Vince Hoeser
John Magro
Jay Polsgrove

5. Cinzano
Mike Asher
Henry Ausdenmore
Cole Heaston
Jeff Ingram
Robert Mackle
Matt Schuler
Al Trevino

6. Chi Phi
Kenneth Aull
John Betzhold
Andrew Lee
Michael Lee

Mark Miller
Mark Spanier

7. Phi Delta Theta
Mark Cline
Ken Crandall
Brian Gavette
David Holleran
David Marcelletti
David Pritchett
Thomas Rothrock

8. Posers
Graham Fisk
John Gatch
Wes Harris
Raymond Richie
Craig Seward
David Webb
John White

9. Sigma Alpha Mu
Michael Goldstein
Michael Guggenheim
Michael Jarvis
Jay Koroff
Andy Markowitz
Ronald Ritzler
Herbert Washer

10. Sigma Alpha Epsilon
Dan DeCraene
James Homrighausen
Rodney Jette
James Kierman
Marc Meuller

11. Delta Chi
David Abrams
Louis Coleo
Gregg Ness
Carl Rommel
Gregg Svoma
Mike Wright

12. Theta Chi
Jay Almon
John Brumm
Nicholas Chareas
Timothy Mazur
Hank Schilling
Nicholas Yetter

13. Americana
Maten Gergenich
Jeffrey Hale
Scott Presley
Terry Roberts
Patrick Schellenberg

14. Alpha Tau Omega
Steven Diercks
Matthew Eskey
Mark Herman
Eric Knipple
David Kotarba
Karl Westenfelder

15. Delta Tau Delta
Mark Fowler
Brian Halloran
Kevvin Halloran
Robert Hudson
Kurt Hultberg
Frederick Miesch
Douglas Tolle

16. Sigma Nu
Andrew Cummins
Mark Hupfer
David Krahulik
Kurt Pershing

17. Phi Kappa Psi
Timothy Davis
Craig Hume
Michael Maasdof
Timothy Madigan
Andrew Parker

Thomas Stemen
Christopher Tirone

18. Collins
Richard Ehlers
David Hamilton
Kendall Harnett
Thomas Richardson
Robert Serbent

19. Pi Kappa Alpha
David Andrews
Bryan Krehnbrink
Rick Lostetter
Michael Niederpruem
David Szentes
Paul Winters

20. Joint Venture
Howard Bruce
John Burnham
Peter Horm
Elton Slone
Richard Thorn

21. Sigma Pi
Thomas Armstrong
Larry Duncan
Mike Hacker
Ronald Harmeyer
Staven Linn
Sean Reidy
Keith Vincent

22. Parks House
John Ames
Scott Eitman
Gregory Salzman
Joe Schnieder
Lee Tezabek

23. Curry V
Sean Davidson
Matt Helman

Scot Lively
Larry Stickler
Kevin Turner

24. Totano
Paul Fowerbaugh
Marc Kase
Lance Latham
James Matheson
Donald Rembert

25. Evans Scholars
John Calto
Jeffrey Collier
Patrick Gaughan
Michael Kaiser
Phillip LeMaster
Randy Rogers

26. Zeta Beta Tau
Steve Bessony
Alan Grossman
Aaron Pearl
Robert Rafelson
Daniel Wofin

27. Kappa Sigma
Max Green
Dave Harris
Douglas Olson
Anthony J. Schoettle
Stuart Reichenbach

28. Dodds House
John Derken
James Pruett
James Saplis
Tim Travis
Michael Whitsell

29. Wright
Robert Cass
David Compton
William Mabry

Corry Owens
Robert Weber

30. Beach Riders
Eric Bray
Gerard Lipinski
John Lundy
Ted Robertson
John Schneider

31. Beck II
David Blank
Dave Bradford
Bill Braham
Steve Diedrich
Joseph Maher
Thomas Ryder
Robert Zimmerman

32. Kappa Delta Rho
James Akin
Mike O'Malley
Mark Raper
Lawrence Wheeler
Jeffrey Yarvis

33. Flying High
Steven Bowman
Edward Broad
William Jones
David Pence

1988

1. Cutters
Andrew Meister
Jay Polsgrove
John White

2. Phi Gamma Delta
Robert Bender
Scott Casey
Jon Grief

Tom Herendeen
David Schmidt

3. Phi Delta Theta
Mark Kline
John Mau
Perry Mayfield
Jeff Pratt
Tom Rothrock
Kris Schneck
Ted Wells

4. Lambda Chi Alpha
Bryan Hite
Gus Hodek
Mitch Johnson
Michael Kern
Chris Pittard

5. Alpha Epsilon Pi
Tony Checroun
Gary Judis
Marc Korman
Stu Mandelbaum
Craig Miller
David Shane
Sheldon Weiss

6. Pi Kappa Alpha
Jason Anderson
Dave Andrews
Aron Dellinger
Rick Lostutter
Mike Niederpruem
Paul Winters

7. Collins
Andrew Adams
Angus Aynsley
David Hamilton
Kendall Harnett
Robert Serbent

8. Sigma Alpha Epsilon
Todd Denkman
Jim Homringhausen
Rod Jette
Marc Mueller

9. Americana
Jeff Hale
Ricardo Otero
Terry Roberts
Mark Runk
Pat Shellenberg

10. Cinzano
Mike Asher
Jeff Ingram
Cole Heaston

11. Sigma Alpha Mu
Michael Goldstein
Herb Washer
Jay Wiczek

12. Delta Tau Delta
Jeff Brim
Kevin Halloran
Brad Harrison
Rob Hudson
Randy Racana
Doug Tolle
Lex Yarion

13. Sigma Nu
Greg Dentino
Dan Gerritzen
David Krahulik
Jack Massad
Kevin McArt
Joe Pekarek
Cam Welles

14. Teter
Jeff Cole

Mark Kase
Jim Matheson
Chip Rembert
Tim Tappan

15. Beach Riders
Eric Bray
Gerard Lipinski
J. T. Lundry
Joe Maher
Ted Robertson

16. Beta Theta Pi
Todd Cress
Bob Gottschalk
Andy Pimlich
Michael Wolfert

17. Evans Scholars
Mike Boyle
John Calto
Jeff Collier
Phil Lemaster
Paul Mammoser
Tom Solon

18. Alpha Tau Omega
Curtis Dean
Aron Hanson
Andrew Lee
Eric Miller
Mark Spanier
Thomas Tobin

19. Acacia
John Huesing
Ed Laplante
Paul Krackhardt
Phil Stephens

20. Posers
Graham Fisk
Wes Harris

John Osborne
Scott Presley
David Webb

21. Sigma Chi
John Carter
Jim Cumming
Mark Gradison
Eric Kellison
Dag Kittlaus
Steve Kosnor
Steve Reynolds

22. Foster
Chad Ashley
Jim Gross
Jeff Heasley
Marc Labovich
Steve Wise

23. Sigma Phi Epsilon
Gary Beyers
Don Birch
Mark Clatt
Eric Proano

24. Kappa Sigma
Tom Armstrong
Mike Hacker
Ron Harmeyer
Sean Kerrigan
Scott Searles
Keith Vincent

25. Dodds House
Mike Asher
Jeff Ingram
Cole Heaston
Craig Seward

26. Theta Chi
Jack Brumm
Dino Falaschetti

Hank Schilling
John Tosick
Nick Yetter

27. Chi Phi
Curtis Dean
Aron Hanson
Andrew Lee
Eric Miller
Mark Spanier
Thomas Tobin

28. Phi Kappa Psi
Jerry Blanton
Kent Compton
Tim Davis
Scott Dziura
Barry Fast
Peter Landgraff
Matt McKenzie

29. Alpha Sigma Phi
Mike Deweese
Curt Johnson
Dave Kendall
Dave Leedy
Glen Szymcak

30. Delta Upsilon
Kevin Caldwell
Bob Childress
Todd Delanger
John Quatroche

31. Delta Chi
John Jones
Eric Long
Colby McCorkel
Bryan Plantenga
Gregg Syoma
Pat Warner
Jeff Wood

32. Sigma Pi
Tom Armstrong
Mike Hacker
Ron Harmeyer
Sean Kerrigan
Scott Searles
Keith Vincent

33. Phi Kappa Tau
Joe Bridwell
Alejandro Caceres
David DeWitt
Dan Polizzi

1989

1. Cinzano
Mike Asher
Kendall Harnett
Fred Rose
Doug Schmidt

2. Cutters
Demetri Hubbard
Tim Legge
Mike Rolfsen
John White

3. Acacia
John Huesing
Peter Noverr
Patrick Riley
Chris Snyder
Phil Stephens

4. Teter
Brian Adams
Jeff Cole
Jonathan Enos
Paul Fowereagh
Mark Kase

Lance Latham
Jim Matheson

5. Sigma Alpha Mu
Danny Glick
Mike Goldstein
Bryan Halpern
Jay Korff
Ron Ritzler
Jason Schneider
Steve Wiczek

6. Phi Gamma Delta
Brent Arnold
Robert Bender
Jerry Cunningham
Mike Franklin
Tim Powers
Todd Ransom
David Schmidt

7. Phi Delta Theta
Kevin Hamernik
Steve Kennedy
John Mau
Jeff Pratt
Kris Schneck
T. D. Smith
John Tirma

8. Americana
Eric Bray
Bruce Duhaime
Jeff Hale
Mark Kern
Scott March
Jerry Roberts
Andrew Strain

9. Phi Kappa Psi
Tim Davis
Peter Landgraff

Todd Larson
Matt McKenzie
Brad Serf

10. Sigma Nu
Dan Gerritlen
Dave Krahulik
Jack Massad
Dave Nedeff
Cary Okmin
Joe Pekarek

11. Pi Kappa Alpha
Jason Anderson
Ron Dellinger
Tim Duever
Rick Lostutter
Brad Martin
Mike Niederpruen
Dave Szentes
Scott Szentes
Paul Winters

12. Kappa Sigma
Jeff Balinao
Ron Kautsky
Greg Lunde
Jeff Reichenback
Anthony Schlette
Leland Wilhoite

13. Delta Tau Delta
Bob Craig
Brad Harrison
Rob Hudson
Paul Kinker
Randy Racana
Doug Tolle

14. Dodds House
Dave Anderson
Lee Baulsen

Alvaro Bellon
Mike Lantz
Rob Oetjen
Glenn Spiczak
Tim Travis
Darrell Whinnery

15. Beta Theta Pi
Craig Cook
Brian Coulter
Rod Fasone
Mark Hurford

16. Foster
Chad Ashley
Sean Black
Bob Gregory
Jeff Heasley
Marc Labovich
Steve Wise

17. Sigma Chi
Joe Cooper
Richard Creedon
Eric Kellison
Mat Plama
John Robinson
Rob Sloan

18. Sigma Alpha Epsilon
Roger Brockman
Jerry Cueller
Steve Grim
Jim Homrighausen
Rod Jette
Chris Nuciforo
Drew Tewksbury

19. Alpha Epsilon Pi
Steve Checroun
Tony Checroun
Adam Fox

Danny Goldberg
Shelby Goldblatt
Adam Hill
Brian Judis
Eliot Schencker
David Shane

20. Theta Chi
Jack Brumm
Captain Carl
Dino Falaschetti
Jon Jafari
Phil Oresik
John Tosik
Nick Yetter

21. Big Red Wave
Wayne Bishop
Joe Dixon
Kame Kaneshiro
Raymond Ripberger

22. Pi Kappa Phi
Tim Bilotta
Drew Elliott
Matt Grueber
Lawrence Liu
Jason Meyer
Dennis Russell

23. Delta Chi
Tom Kirkmeyer
Eric Long
Bryan Plantenga
Gregg Svoma
Pat Warner
Jeff Wood

24. Evans Scholars
Mike Boyle
John Calto
Mike Cleve

Eric Finke
Mike Gitterman
Dave Hrabich
Jeff Janda
Dave Kurzawa

25. Sigma Phi Epsilon
Chris Bifone
Mike Hegstrom
Kyle Jensen
Kurt Koehler
Eric Myers
Erik Proano

26. Zeta Beta Tau
Steve Bessonny
Matt Cohen
Jeph Hirsch
Adam Troner
Danny Wolin

27. Posers
Sean Davidson
Paul McClain
David Webb

28. Delta Upsilon
Todd Belanger
Mark Erceg
Curtis Hart
Matt Kesmodel
Doug Mauter
Roger Peterson
Larry Rodgers

29. Sigma Pi
Mike Hacker
Sean Kerrigan
John Killacky
David Mosley
Sean Reidy
Mike Schwaller
Scott Searles

30. Collins
Mike Cunningham
Colin DuPlantis
Jack Kessler
Kevin Kessler
Chris Spahr

31. Chi Phi
Don Meyer
Eric Miller
Robby Richards
Von Sigler
Mark Spanier
John Tobin

32. Phi Kappa Tau
John Castillo
Darin Engle
Tom Kleyle
Fred Stevens
Scott Teal

33. Read
Tim Austin
Mark Ferguson
Dustin Stamper
Eric Suchecki
Brian Weaver

1990

1. Sigma Nu
Michael Barszcz
Dan Gerritzen
David Nedeff
Joseph Pekarek

2. Acacia
Tim Bochnowski
Peter Noverr
Chris Snyder
Phil Stephens
Jim Swigart

3. Cutters
Robby Fromin
Eric Gullett
Demetri Hubbard
Michael Rolfsen
Brian Weaver

4. Sigma Chi
Joe Cooper
Steve Herbst
Brad Lich
Jim McGoff
Randy Spruill

5. Phi Gamma Delta
Brent Arnold
Mike Cunningham
Mike Franklin
Scott Hunt
Troy Lewis
Tim Power
Rob Pruitt
Todd Ransom

6. Teter
Jeff Cole
Paul Fowerbaugh
Jim Matheson
Chip Rembertini

7. Phi Delta Theta
Alan Barnes
Jeff Beemer
Michael Gerstner
Kevin Hamernik
Stephen Kennedy
John Tibmala

8. Alpha Sigma Phi
Brian Cradick
Ken Johnson
Scott Melchior
Rob Seet
Erik Thompson
Bob Wagoner

9. Foster
Chad Ashley
Bob Gregory
Doc Heasley
Donovan James
Steve Wise

10. Pi Kappa Phi
Tim Bilotta
John Blaylock
Bob Lambert
Lawrence Liu
Joel Spry

11. Sigma Alpha Mu
Danny Foster
Jay Korff
David Levin
Andy Goodman
Ron Ritzler
Brett Safron
Jason Schneider
Steve Wiczek

12. Sigma Pi
Bill Anzelc
Bill Jones
Randy Jones
Sean Kerrigan
Kevin Leone
Marc Schneider

13. Beta Theta Pi
Craig Cook
Todd Cress
Rod Fasone
Mike Kini
Scott Lusk
Pete Rein
Matt Webster

14. Lambda Chi Alpha
Rod Bray
Joe Gooding

Mitch Johnson
Ron Lapp
Ross Paulos

15. Delta Upsilon
Mark Erceg
Derek Fleitz
Donald Grennes
Doug Mauter
Troy Merchhofer
Kevin Perkins
Michael Santoni
Daniel Spiltoro
Perry Stevens
Larry Rodgers

16. Sigma Alpha Epsilon
Jerry Cueller
Mike Geoffrion
Steve Grim
Matt Heller
Chris Nuciforo
Pazo Proano

17. Pi Kappa Alpha
Jason Anderson
Aron Dellinger
Shawn Demarest
Paul Manzano
Todd Schultheis

18. Evans Scholars
Mike Boyle
Mark Cleve
Eric Finker
Dave Kurzawa
Dave Sperry

19. Phi Kappa Tau
Juan Castillo
Darin Engle
Jeff Kawada
Chris Patrick
Phred Stephens

20. Delta Tau Delta
Steve Browning
Bob Edwards
Bing Graig
Brad Harrison
Paul Kinker
Ken Munson
Jim Schuermann
Doug Tolle

21. Cinzano
David Anderson
Mike Asher
Jose de la Cruz
Jonathan Grabill
Donald Hunley
Robert Oetjen
Cary Smith

22. Phi Kappa Psi
Eric Boelter
Peter Landgraff
Matthew McKenzie
Brad Serf
Jeff Sheffield

23. Zeta Beta Tau
Josh Alsberg
Matt Cohen
Jason Golden
Mike Sibell
Adam Troner

24. Kappa Sigma
Brian Hershberger
Ron Kaitsky
Greg Lunde
Jeff Reichenbach
Davey White
Leland Wilhoite

25. Theta Chi
Sean Burke
Bill Jackson

Jon Jafari
Brian McDonald
Chris Rogers
Greg Sayers

26. Americana
Bruce Duhaime
Dave Kendall
Mark Kern
Andrew Strain
Tim Tappan

27. Ashton
William Burke
Joel Cockley
Mike Dodge
Chad Nay
Jason Slatkin

28. Willkie
Roddy Chiong
Aaron Johnson
Kevin Seidehamel
Randy Seidehamel
Rob Silverthorn

29. Alpha Epsilon Pi
Lyle Feigenbaum
Danny Goldberg
Eran Hahn
Paul Harris
Adam Hill
Brian Judis
Richard Meldman

30. Collins
Michael Cunningham
Jamie Hansen
Jack Kessler
Nate Sanders

31. Dodds House
Alvaro Bellon

Phil Davis
Tim Travis
Darrell Whinnery

1991

1. Acacia
Tim Bochnowski
Peter Noverr
Phillip Stephens
Jim Swigart

2. Cutters
Robby Fromin
Eric Gullett
Demetri Hubbard
James Kirkham
Mike Rolfsen

3. Team College Life
Roddy Chiung
John Jones
Michael Lantz
Greg Lew
Steve White

4. Phi Kappa Psi
Kevin Daley
Dan Funk
Scott Jordan
Scott Kauffman
Matt McKenzie
Greg Quackenbush

5. Sigma Nu
John Asbury
Michael Barszcz
Bill Dooley
Dan Gerritzen
David Nedeff
Jason Podvin

6. Phi Delta Theta
Alan Barnes
Dan Bonham
John Gannon
Kevin Hamernik
Stephen Kennedy
Scott Quackenbush

7. Delta Upsilon
Jim Clemo
Mark Erceg
Timothy Hatton
Mike Huss
Will Jones
Troy Menchhofer
Kevin Perkins
Larry Rodgers
Michael Santon
Perry Stephens
Mark Thannert

8. Phi Gamma Delta
Michael Cunningham
Eddie Goodknight
Corey Hansen
Troy Lewis
John Morrison
Timothy Powers
Rob Pruitt

9. Sigma Chi
Rowdy Bryant
Aaron Cho
Steve Herbst
Bryce May
Randy Spruill

10. Pi Kappa Alpha
Jason Anderson
Adam Carter
Aron Dellinger
Brad Walleen

11. Alpha Epsilon Pi
Steve Fineman
Jon Gault
Paul Harris
Adam Hill
Brian Judis
Richard Meldman

12. Cinzano
David Anderson
Chad Burch
Jeffery Cole
Ryan Cole
Jose de la Cruz
Robert Oetjen
Ben Sharp
Cary Smith

13. Sigma Alpha Epsilon
Lane Bloomberg
Matt Daily
Tony Isaacs
Chris Nuciforo
David Ryan

14. Foster
Chad Ashley
Robert Gregory
Doc Heasley
Scott Stephan
Steve Wise

15. Theta Chi
Jon Jafari
Bill Jackson
Brian McDonald
Greg Sayers
John Tosick

16. Phi Kappa Tau
James Breuker
Darin Engle

Stan Gerbig
Welton Harris
Jeffrey Kawuda

17. Alpha Tau Omega
Richard Busch
Chris Fry
Barrett Gardiner
Brian Hefner
Chris Warren

18. Evans Scholars
Mark Cleve
David Deram
Eric Finke
David Kurzawa
Lance Padgett
David Sperry

19. Beta Theta Pi
Craig Cook
Chris Decker
Mark Hurford
Scott Long
Jason Miller
Duke Sturgis

20. Delta Chi
Scott Hallberg
Todd Hancock
Dan Hansen
Pete Lynch
Dan Rowady
Brian Platenza

21. Willkie/Read
Doug Blough
Justin Hazlett
Dennis Lindley
Greg Mueller
Rob Silverthorn
Alex Stafford
Will Weaver

22. Sigma Pi
William Anzele
David Castellanet
Patrick Gifford
Chris Gregson
Randy Jones
Kevin Leone
Andy Stoehr

23. Team Funk
David Ellmers
Greg Lew
Michael Moss
Graham Wink

24. Lambda Chi Alpha
Chris Barthel
Rod Bray
Kevin Keller
Jim Keszei
Ron Lapp
Ross Paulos

25. Dodds House
Al Bellon
Thomas Bondurant
Pete Richardson
John Seelenbinder
Greg Spears
Darrell Whinnery

26. Delta Tau Delta
Robert Edwards
Chris Fontanez
Wade Fulford
Paul Kinker
Ken Munson
Craig Petrusha

27. Chi Phi
Tom Butler
Todd Hodson
Jaime Lopez

Brent Michael
Chris Perkins

28. Pi Kappa Phi
Henry Chou
Chris Cooley
Andrew Elliott
Mike Petro
John Storen
Andrew Wilson

29. McNutt
Daniel Berman
Brian Foster
Rudy Lopez
Eric Schrama
John Williamson

30. Kappa Sigma
Ron Kautsky
Greggie Manson
Jeff Reichenback
Leland Wilhoite

31. Sigma Alpha Mu
Andrew Goodman
Jaime Kosofsky
Daniel Lipson
Brett Safron
Max Andrew Slovis

32. Sigma Phi Epsilon
Barrett Barnes
Brad Browder
Brad Clatt
Erik Foster
John Gaskey
Scott Hudson
Kurt Koehler
Scott Pfafman
Kurt Tillmann

33. Team Independence
Joel Cockley
Michael Dodge
Kevin Leineweber
Nate Sanders

1992

1. Cutters
Eric Gullett
Demetri Hubbard
Art Keith
Jim Kirkham

2. Acacia
Eric Averitt
Rico Riley
Chris Snyder
David Von Allmen

3. Cinzano
David Anderson
Scott Baker
Chad Burch
Eric Harsh
Robert Oetjen
Ben Sharp

4. Delta Chi
Jeff Allman
Scott Hallberg
Todd Hancock
Bryan Plantenga

5. Delta Upsilon
Randy Gianfagna
Tim Hatton
Mike Huss
Allen Krebs
Justin Kurpius
Grant Liston
Perry Stevens
Mark Thannert

6. Phi Gamma Delta
Michael Cunningham
Bob Keedy
Troy Lewis
Rob Pruitt

7. Theta Chi
Steve Colwell
Jon Jafari
Bill Jackson
Brian McDonald
Joe Miller
Greg Sayers

8. Pi Kappa Alpha
Matt Chitwood
Howard Davis
Robert Kapla
Joel Kelly
Todd Schultheis
Brad Walleen

9. Sigma Chi
Eric Altherr
Steve Franklin
Steve Herbst
Sean Jones
Randy Spruill

10. Team College Life
David Bain
John Jones
Alex Oliver
Steve White

11. Dodds House
Tom BonDurant
Mike Foote
Jason Pierce
Rodney Rhodes
Andrew Vasiento
Darryl Whinnery

12. Alpha Epsilon Pi
Jerry Block
Frank Brook
Steve Fimeman
John Gault
Paul Harris
Adam Hilt
Adam Keyser
Richard Meldman
Michael Soter

13. Phi Kappa Psi
David Adler
Dan Funk
Craig Hixon
Scott Kaufman
Nathan Snyder

14. Pi Kappa Phi
Chris Cooley
Todd Gemmer
John Hill
Mike Petrol
John Storen

15. Phi Delta Theta
Tom Beehler
Dan Brackney
Jeff Cearny
Kevin Hamernik
Jeff Schuler
Shawn Spellacey

16. Sigma Alpha Epsilon
Lance Bloomberg
Matt Dailey
Mike Geoffrion
Anthony Isaacs
Chris Nuciforo
Dave Ryan

17. Delta Tau Delta
Judson Brooks
Rob Creeth

Chris Kraft
Ken Munson
Craig Petrusha
Kevin Spang

18. McNutt
Scot Dillman
Nasder Musa
Nathan Schickel
Gregg VanMater
Andy Walton

19. Lambda Chi Alpha
Scott Akers
Chris Barthel
Kevin Keller
Vince Parshall
Scott Mansberger
Joe Goodwin

20. Phi Kappa Tau
James Breuker
Jeff Kawada
Dave Mehring
Fred Stephens
Michael Vaughn

21. Kappa Sigma
Greg Manson
Mike Moss
Brian Schuneman
David White

22. Willkie/Read
Jason Burkhead
Matt Doss
Chad Nay
Greg Mueller
Eric Stonebraker
Jeremiah Wean
Mike Zerega

23. Alpha Sigma Phi
Scott Berg
Jason Blockson
Brian Cradick
Tony Geller
Eric Pratt

24. Evans Scholars
Joe Kimpel
David Sperry
Lance Padgett
Matt Abriani
Eric Finke
David Kurzawa

25. Sigma Pi
Rob Beasley
Matt Hinkle
Randy Jones
Kevin Leone
Sean Newman

26. Chi Phi
Todd Hodson
Jaime Lopez
Quentin Quathamer
Fred Reyna

27. Ashton
Dorian Barnes
Christopher Johnson
Nathan Larimer

28. Tau Kappa Epsilon
Scott Cooper
Scott Davidson
Jason Kleiman
Spencer Mayhew

29. Sigma Phi Epsilon
Scott Calkins
Brad Glotzbach
Mike Oliver
Mike Schini

30. Zeta Beta Tau
Keenan Hauke
Gary Kuhn
Jason Model
Dave Rifkin
Jason Young

31. Foster
Jeff Hessley
Yuri Hoffman
David Purk
Wes Roepke
Scott Stephan

32. Sigma Alpha Mu
Matt Edelheit
Josh Kaufman
Dan Rock
Mark Zucker

33. I.M.O. Major Taylor
Courtney Bishop
Eric Brooks
Jamie Pinder
Greg Taylor

1993

1. Delta Chi
Jeff Allman
Scott Hallberg
Todd Hancock
Neal Stoeckel

2. Cinzano
Scotty Baker
Greg Mueller
Eric Schwartz
Ben Sharp
Roger Stevens

3. Pi Kappa Alpha
Bob Davis

Bob Kapla
Joel Kelly
Chris Tarcynski

4. Sigma Alpha Epsilon
Kurt Adams
Lance Bloomberg
Bill Naas
Chad Ruston
David Ryan

5. Cutters
Bill Brissman
Ryan Cole
Mike Rolfson
Al Williams
Chris Wynn

6. Sigma Nu
Mike Barszcz
Chris Bowden
David Kelley
Russ Seiler
Aaron Spicer
Brent Spicer

7. Delta Upsilon
Randy Gianfagna
Allen Krebs
Justin Kurpius
Grant Liston
Mark Thannert

8. Delta Tau Delta
Judson Brooks
Rob Creeth
Chris Kraft
Craig Petrusha

9. Pi Kappa Phi

10. Acacia
Christopher Eades
Erik Powers
Bryan Riley

11. Sigma Chi
Shawn Humphries
David Perez
Tyler Sparks
Randy Spruill

12. Theta Chi
Steve Colwell
Chuck Linebaugh
Josh Malancuk
Greg Sayers

13. Phi Kappa Psi
Tom Auer
Dan Funk
Craig Hixon
Marcus Mak
Steve Petkovich
Nathan Snyder

14. Team College Life
Chad Lewis
Matt Siemer
Steve White

15. Phi Gamma Delta
Zack Buhner
Jack Clemens
Dave Harstad
Bob Keedy
Cory Lewis
Troy Lewis

16. Ashton
Dorian Barnes
Chris Johnson
Nate Larimer
Simon Watson
Gordon Winter

17. Foster
Charles Dillena
Yuri Hoffman
Dave Purk
Wes Roepke
Doug Showley

18. Sigma Alpha Mu/Delta Sigma Pi
Chris Lohman
Brian Pavers
Dennis Plankar
Chad Satlow

19. Phi Delta Theta
Tullio Asacrelli
Dan Brackney
Jeff Kearny
Jeff Schuler

20. Dodds House
Tom BonDurant
Mike Foote
Rodney Rhodes
John Seelenbinder

21. TFAT
Christopher Bor
Bob Owen
Sam Schad
Stephen Socts

22. Tau Kappa Epsilon
Scott Davidson

Jason Kleiman
Spencer Mayhew
Kent Miller

23. Collins
Regis St. Louis
Jay Weinsharker
Bryan Will

24. Lambda Chi Alpha
Scott Akers
Josh Carter
Mike Keleher
Vince Parshall

25. Alpha Epsilon Pi
Steve Fineman
Brooke Frank
Jon Gault
Dave Katz
Adam Keyser
Matt Schuman
Ryan Woprin

26. Evans Scholars
Matt Abriani
David Kurzawa
Joe Rimpel
David Sperry
Brad Woodson

27. Chi Phi
Brett Brown
Tom Butler
Boban Kecman
Paul White

28. Zeta Beta Tau
Jeff Gerson
Kennan Hauke
Phil Jacobson

Adam Tabak
Jason Youngman

29. McNutt
Shawn Miller
Nasser Muja
Nathan Schickel
Kregg Van Meter

30. Sigma Pi
Andrew Augustine
Dan Burke
Chris Hasselback
Bill Laraway

31. Sigma Phi Epsilon
Rick Austgen
Shawn Gardner
Tim Jester
Matt Manley
Chris Miller
Brian Murphy
Mike Oliver
Jason Stellema

32. Kappa Delta Rho
Monty Cox
Daniel Kahn
Brian Stalder
Dave Wedlock

33. Beta Theta Pi
Britten Hale
Tom Hilbrich
Scott Long
J. C. Stookey

1994

1. Sigma Chi
Shawn Humphries

David Perez
Tyler Sparks
Randy Spruill

2. Cutters
Ryan Calsbeek
Ryan Cole
Todd Myers
Chris Wynn

3. Delta Chi
Jeff Allman
Mark Oldani
Brian Oliger
Neal Stoeckel

4. Cinzano
Scott Baker
Jason Burkehead
Steve Logan
Brad Owens
Jason Pierce
Ben Sharp
Roger Stevens

5. Phi Gamma Delta
Jack Clemens
Dave Harstad
Cory Lewis
Jim Strickland

6. Pi Kappa Alpha
Matt Chitwood
Robert Kapla
Joel Kelly
Chris Tarczynski

7. Phi Kappa Psi
Jeff Culbertson
Craig Hixon
Jason Rahimzadeh
Nathan Snyder

8. Phi Delta Theta
Dan Brackney
Michael Giambarberee
Mike Krueger
Joel McKay
Dan Possley
Dan Vote

9. Acacia
Christopher Eades
Michael Kohn
Erik Powers

10. Dodds House
Dan Dunville
Mike Foote
Mike Kiser
Stephen Mertz

11. Team College Life
Chad Lewis
Matt Siemer
Steve White

12. Pi Kappa Phi
Todd Gemner
Adam Harstein
John Hill
Joe Hummel
Steve Orr
Adam Perler

13. Delta Upsilon
Jeff Bergmann
Chris Johnson
Allen Krebs
Justin Kurpius

14. Lambda Chi Alpha
Scott Frye
Mike Keleher

Vince Parshall
Dane Vanderhaar

15. Sigma Alpha Epsilon
Kurt Adams
Bill Naas
Chad Ruston
Steve Sawa

16. Sigma Nu
Chris Bowden
Justin Herman
Russ Seiler
Brent Spicer
Andy Walton

17. Sigma Phi Epsilon
Todd Engledow
Mike Oliver
Scott Pike
John Schlansker
Cory Winchell

18. Collins
Jay Weinshenker
Bryan Will

19. Ashton
Shane Coats
Nate Larimer
Bob Owen
Sam Schad

20. Alpha Epsilon Pi
Jerry Block
David Katz
Jeff Moss
Louis Okon
Brian Passell
Brian Ratner
Adam Rubin
Matt Schuman
David Sheridan

21. Beta Theta Pi
Deke Faires
Mike Feske
Jason Pilarski
Paul Thoren

22. Delta Tau Delta
Brian Hill
Kyle Hodges
Chris Kraft
Chris Thomas

23. Human Wheels
Brad Burkhalter
Lance Dowden
Brian Hooker
Andy Teed
Chris Tuberty

24. McNutt
Jon Ortman
Nathan Schickel
Boyd Speerschneider

25. Wright
Gary Lucia
Eric Maki
John Seelenbinder
Keith Sullivan

26. Team Last Chance
Jason Monroe
Steve Pejza
Brian Powers

27. Theta Chi
Bil Emhof
Chuck Linebaugh
Kevin Maurer
Greg Wright

28. Read
Jason Deaner

Doug Jett
Josh Johnson
Cormac O'Connor
Daine Smith
James Swinkin

29. Alpha Sigma Phi
Mike Boros
Bill Clarkin
Jeff Geller
Matt Valentine

30. Sammy & Co.
Jud Bishop
Blaise Geddry
Matt Sachs
Kurt Smolek

31. Kappa Sigma
John Craft
Andy Laux
Rick McIlrath
Jim Medley

32. Sigma Pi
Augie Augustine
Mike Degenhart
Shawn Helmer
John Kline
Jim Kottmeyer
Bill Laraway
DeVon Taylor

33. Zeta Beta Tau
John Bloom
Deemah Stalhamer
Adam Tabak

1995

1. Phi Gamma Delta
Mark Edwards
Dave Harstad

Cory Lewis
Jim Lohman

2. Acacia
Justin Fox
Mike Kohn
Erik Powers
Bryan Riley

3. Sigma Alpha Epsilon
Kurt Adams
Bill Naas
Jeff Naas
Steve Sawa

4. Dodds House
Jud Bishop
Mike Foote
Mike Kiser
Steve Mertz

5. Delta Chi
Charles Keiser
George Rambow
Matt Thomas

6. Phi Delta Theta
Dan Brackney
Mike Krueger
Joel McKay
Dan Possley

7. Sigma Nu
Brian Baker
Justin Herman
Russ Seiler
Andy Walton

8. Beta Theta Pi
Kyle Barker
Joe Guido
Thomas Hilbrich
Paul Thoren

9. Lambda Chi Alpha
Josh Carter
Mike Keleher
Scott Mansberger
Vince Parshall

10. Sigma Chi
Shawn Humphries
Matt Langfeldt
Dave Perez
Tyler Sparks

11. Cutters
Ryan Calsbeek
Mark Hoffman
Todd Neville
Aaron Pilling

12. TFAT
Eric Greenwald
Bob Owen
Nathan Schickel
Brian Will

13. Sigma Phi Epsilon
Jason Klavon
Scott Pike
John Schlansker
Cory Winchell

14. Phi Kappa Psi
Kevin Bonning
Jeff Culbertson
Eric Loichle
Jason Rahimzadeh

15. Pi Kappa Phi
Robb Awe
Marcus Droker
Adam Hartstein
Jon Ortman

16. Delta Upsilon
Brian Furuness

David Shock
Matt Sniadecki
Mark Zlatic

17. Pi Kappa Alpha
Chris Barron
Matt Chitwood
Tom Greinke
Bob Woolsey

18. Collins/Ashton/Teter
Paul Fitzgerald
Jeff Halicki
Boyd Speerschneider
Robert Wood

19. Delta Tau Delta
Geoff Andrews
Kyle Hodges
Andy Parrish
Chris Thomas

20. Theta Chi
Mike Chovanec
Bill Emhoff
Justin Folloder
Chuck Linebaugh

21. Team College Life
Scott Frye
Dave Hilbish
Jack Hildreth
Matt Siemer

22. Sigma Alpha Mu
Jeremy Friedman
Matt Sacks
Jared Starr

23. Wright
James Case

Eric Maki
Randy Streator
Keith Sullivan

24. Alpha Epsilon Pi
Jeff Moss
Andy Sandler
Matt Schuman
Dave Sheriden

25. Delta Sigma Pi
Jerry Brawley
Jason James
Brian Soderberg
Ryan Spohn

26. Kappa Sigma
Brian Bishop
John Craft
Bryan Martin
Chris Syderis

27. Human Wheels
Brad Burkhalter
Lance Dowden
Bryan Teed
Chris Tuberty

28. Alpha Tau Omega
Daniel Adamaitis
Bill Noll
Andrew Whitesel
Justin Yanta

29. Zeta Beta Tau
Jay Green
Stuart Nitzkin
Mike Slater
Michael Thomas

30. Alpha Phi Omega
Ross Cadick
Carl Doninger
Sherman Ibarra
Sherwin Ibarra

31. Alpha Sigma Phi
Bill Clarkin
Alex Debonis
Jeff Geller
Brian Thompson

32. Kappa Delta Rho
Scott Frost
Sam McClintock
Keith Toombs

33. Phi Kappa Theta
Mike Doughty
Dan Gerteisen
Anthony Hans
Mike McMinn

1996

1. Phi Delta Theta
Mike Krueger
Joel McKay
Dan Possley
Rob Rhamey

2. Sigma Chi
Karl Bordine
Shawn Humphries
Matt Langfeldt
Tyler Sparks

3. Phi Gamma Delta
Mark Edwards
Cory Lewis
Jim Lohman
David Stagge

4. Delta Chi
Mark Fay
Charles Keiser
Matt Thomas
Jason Wessel

5. Acacia
Gregg Cosgrove
Justin Fox
Michael Kohn
Bryan Riley

6. Sigma Nu
Jason Asper
Brian Baker
Chad Bobe
Phil Thompson

7. Cutters
Mark Hoffman
Greg Krisko
Todd Neville
Ryan Warren

8. Dodds House
Jonathan Foote
Blaise Geddry
Jonathan Purvis
Calvin Wellington

9. Theta Chi
Mike Chovanec
Justin Folloder
Andy Newman
John Wargel

10. Pneuma
Gregory Smith
Tim McNamara
Brett O'Connor
Mark Sniadecki

11. Beta Theta Pi
Kyle Barker
Thomas Hilbrich
Paul Thoren
Ian Zabor

12. Cinzano
Andrew Flynn
Jason E. Pierce
Kevin Sayers
David Wolfe

13. McNutt
Martin Adamczyk
Corey Carrico
Kurt Gensheimer

14. Sigma Phi Epsilon
Todd Engledow
Scott Pike
John Schlansker
Cory Winchell

15. Pi Kappa Phi
Joseph Flores
Jay Morel
Jon Ortman
Adam Perler

16. Delta Tau Delta
Larry Davidson
Kyle Hodges
Steve McLelland
Chris Thomas

17. Phi Kappa Psi
Kevin Bonning
Davin Harpe
Eric Loichle
Jason Rahimzadeh

18. Pi Kappa Alpha
Christopher Barron
Chad Farmer
Thomas Greinke
Robert Sherman

19. Lambda Chi Alpha
Damian Cullom
Jeremy Eaton
Darin Leach
Dane Vander Haar

20. Sigma Alpha Epsilon
Matthew Delks
Jeffrey Naas
Steve Quigley
Steve Sawa

21. Willkie
Brice Alt
Alistair Sponsel
Daniel Stark
Chris Wojtowich

22. Sigma Alpha Mu
Jeremy Friedman
Jared Palmer
Matt Sacks

23. Alpha Epsilon Pi
Robert Greenwald
Louis Okon
Andy Sandler
David Sheriden

24. Sigma Pi
Scott Barnes
Chris Foster
John Kline
John Lane

The Little 500

25. Collins
Corey Dukai
Eric Foldenauer
Ray Hovijitra
Scott Moore

26. Wright
James Case
Gary Lucia
Jason Skelton
Randy Streator

27. Team College Life
Ryan Calhoun
Jeff Halicki
Fred Perry

28. TFAT
Joseph Little
Brian Martino
Cormac O'Connor
Benjamin Rieff

29. Alpha Sigma Phi
Shawn Bowman
Bill Clarkin
Michael Dahman
Jeffrey Geller

30. Chi Phi
Matt Casper
Jonathan Hanley
Matthew Laue
James Vargas

31. Mezcla
Gustavo Chavez
Derrick Espadas
Jerry Gutierrez
Erik Teter

32. Briscoe
Brian Brames
Matthew Freise
Matt Provost
Ben Long

33. Alpha Tau Omega
Dennis Nobles
Brian Penniall
William Sexton

1997

1. Cutters
Sam Gasowski
Aaron Pilling
Casper VanOosten
Chris Wojtowich

2. Phi Gamma Delta
Jon Cornelius
Mark Edwards
Joseph Guido
Jim Lohman

3. Delta Chi
Tony Fay
Charles Keiser
Brian Oliger
Jason Tanner

4. Dodds House
Jon Foote
Alex Ihnen
Greg O'Brien
Jonathan Purvis

5. Sigma Chi
Bill Abel
Karl Bordine
Matt Langfeldt
Craig Skelton

6. Sigma Nu
Jason Asper
Brian Baker
Chad Bobe
Phil Thompson

7. Acacia
Justin Fox
Kurt Gensheimer
Trevis Milton
Scott Noble

8. Phi Delta Theta
Mike Krueger
Brett Lane
Michael Possley
Robert Rhamy

9. Sigma Alpha Epsilon
Matthew Burns
Matthew Delks
Jeffery Naas
Steve Quigley

10. Beta Theta Pi
Ben Ault
Kyle Barker
Thomas Collins
Ian Zabor

11. Cinzano
Robert Adlard
Jeremy Friedman
Keith Leonard
David Wolfe

12. Pi Kappa Phi
Chris Gales
Matthew McAlear
Jon Ortman
Adam Reising

13. Pi Kappa Alpha
Christopher Barron
Chad Farmer
Tom Greinke
Robert Sherman

14. Sigma Phi Epsilon
Chip Drabik
Steven Kopach
Scott Pike
Jett Tackbery

15. Theta Chi
Justin Folloder
Andy Newman
Todd Smith
John Wargel

16. Wright
Gary Lucia
Jason Skelton
Jeremy Sprague
Keith Sullivan

17. Delta Upsilon
James Pennell
Brent Schepper
David Shock

18. Delta Tau Delta
Kyle Hodges
Brent Kaiser
Steven Macelland
Matt Wehby

19. Phi Kappa Psi
Eric Bonning
Kevin Bonning
Davin Harpe
Matthew Infantino

20. Lambda Chi Alpha
David Bender
Damian Cullom
Jeremy Eaton
Matthew Robinson

21. Chi Phi
Matthew Laue
Bob Malinowski
Chris Miller
Steve Papp

22. Pneuma
Scott Mills
Mason Robbins
Dave Shoemaker

23. Mezcla
Ben Abney
Derrick Espadas
Jerry Gutierrez
Erik Teter

24. Alpha Tau Omega
Keith Sexton
Jin Sim
Andrew Whitesel

25. Collins Buccaneers
Stu Bever
Corey Dukai
Eric Foldenauer
Jensen Walker

26. Army ROTC
Jason Beemer
Merv Brott
Nathaniel King
Joseph Lontai

27. Kappa Sigma
Bryan Martin

Eric Pepping
Jared Piper
Grady Sheffield

28. South Cottage Grove
Kyle Bailey
Jeffrey Dunkel
Jason Schwartz
Jason Skolak

29. Sigma Pi
Scott Barnes
Sean Bische
Mallory Knox
Jeffery Seaton

30. Evans Scholars
Matthew Csanyi
Joe Nichols
Ted Nowak
Kevin Thompson

31. Zeta Beta Tau
Adam Berkovits
Jonathan Greenberg
Gary Haymann
Andy Shefsky

32. McNutt
Thomas Jurgensen
Robert Pratt
Jason Storbeck

33. Alpha Sigma Phi
Mike Boros
Zack Hill
David Swaykus

1998

1. Dodds House
Jon Foote

Alex Ihnen
Greg O'Brien
Jonathan Purvis

2. Cutters
Doug Jurs
Aaron Pilling
Greg Spraul
Chris Wojtowich

3. Sigma Alpha Epsilon
Matthew Burns
Matthew Delks
Stephen Quigley
Tom Schmit

4. Beta Theta Pi
Kyle Barker
Thomas Collins
Doug Hughes
Joe Rurode

5. Phi Gamma Delta
Daniel Branam
Jon Cornelius
Joe Guido
Jim Lohman

6. Acacia
Brian Becker
Justin Fox
Kurt Gensheimer
Trevis Milton

7. Sigma Phi Epsilon
Jason Baker
Chip Drabik
Steve Kopach
Jett Tackbery

8. Sigma Nu
Aaron Hays

Derek Lindenschmidt
Branden Miller
Dana Stutzman

9. Lambda Chi Alpha
David Bender
Scott Fast
Josh Geise
Jeff Lane

10. Pi Kappa Phi
Jeff Adams
Chris Gales
Matthew McAlear
Adam Reising

11. Phi Kappa Psi
Michael Finke
Davin Harpe
Matthew Infantino
Nick Valadez

12. Mezcla
Ben Abney
Derrick Espadas
Jerry Gutierrez
Jake Mayer

13. Pi Kappa Alpha
Chad Farmer
Owen Schwartz
Bo Sherman
Jeremy Wise

14. Chi Phi
John Emmetsberger
Bob Malinowski
Chris Miller
Stephen Papp

15. Delta Tau Delta
Sean Gill

Steven McLelland
Michael Stack
Matt Wehby

16. Alta
Michael Davison
Brad Dennis
Michael Israelson
Mitch Rufca

17. Alpha Sigma Phi
Rob Bassett
Jesse Manis
David Swaykus
Eric Williams

18. Delta Chi
Tony Fay
T. J. Schuch
Jason Sonneborn
Jason Tanner

19. Collins
Corey Dukai
Scott Jensen
Drew Marksity
Rob McCrea

20. Alpha Epsilon Pi
Joe Berger
Tom Eidelman
Adam Wachter
Glen Weinberg

21. Cinzano
Nick Lasure
Jason Losey
Thomas Stark
Brian Walton

22. Sigma Chi
Brian Baker

Christian Barnes, Jr.
Neil Bloede
Matt Conrad

23. Wright
Aaron Graff
John Landers
Jason Skelton
Keith Sullivan

24. Sigma Pi
Sean Bische
Chris Foster
Mallory Knox
Jeff Seaton

25. Delta Upsilon
Corey Himrod
Daniel Meadows
James Pennell

26. Region Crew
Andrew Byczko
Anthony Hans
Dennis Merrell
Chris Palazzolo

27. Alpha Tau Omega
Brian Penniall
Daniel Selo
Keith Sexton

28. Forest
Brent Kelly
Jeff Leigh
Ray Podesta

29. Delta Sigma Pi
Dustin Campbell
William Cornerford
Michael Hayashiguchi
Adam White

30. Teter
David Eaton
Adam Gilman
Patrick O'Neil
Christopher Welp

31. Phi Sigma Kappa
Barry Bergling
John Mumbower
Donald Rosenbaum
Bob Smith

32. Sigma Alpha Mu
Joel Aronoff
Dan Bondavalli
Brian Caron
Michael Schimmel

1999

1. Sigma Phi Epsilon
Jason Baker
Steve Kopach
Andy Lupo
Jett Tackbary

2. Phi Gamma Delta
Jon Cornelius
Todd Cornelius
Sam Horton
Anthony Ponce

3. Chi Phi
John Emmetsberger
Kevin Gfell
Bob Malinowski
Chris Miller

4. Acacia
Brian Becker
Kurt Gensheimer
Don Renner
Michael Riley

5. Dodds House
Alex Ihnen
Jonathan Lipnick
Brian Martino
David Warren

6. Theta Chi
Matt Beyer
Todd Eads
Scott Sasse
Todd Smith

7. Phi Delta Theta
Josh Beatty
Jay Fields
Ralph Grimse
Mike Possley

8. Cutters
Brian Mundy
Gregory Ooley
Daniel Stark
Chris Wojtowich

9. Sigma Chi
Neil Bloede
Dan Lehmann
Patrick Mathews
Mitch Rufca

10. Delta Chi
Tony Fay
Jason Pacey
T.J. Schuch
Jason Sonneborn

11. Sigma Alpha Epsilon
Matt Burns
Matt Delks
Roger Nurrenbern
Jason Wier

12. Delta Tau Delta
Ryan Groves
Scott Martyn
Steven McLelland
Michael Stack

13. Team Dotson
Jonathan Carlson
Rob Chelle
Chris Gage
Tony Manna

14. Beta Theta Pi
Tom Collins
Peter Crowe
Thomas Lapp
Trey Wiesjahn

15. Phi Kappa Psi
Michael Finke
Davin Harpe
Matt Infantino
Buzz Miller

16. Collins Cycling
James Boyd
Michael Choinacky
Scott Jensen
Read Pukkila-Worley

17. Alpha Chi Sigma
Chris Jolivette
Andy Moad
Brenton Scott
Scott Whitlock

18. Lambda Chi Alpha
Ryan Birch
Josh Geise
Jeff Lane
Paul Murzyn

19. Sigma Nu
David Bucur
Aaron Hays
Derek Lindenschmidt
Dana Stutzman

20. Pi Kappa Phi
Jamie Belanger
Brian Johnson
Matthew McAlear
Adam Reising

21. Alpha Tau Omega
Jack Caveney
Justin Inabinette
Shawn Monroe
Brian Penniall

22. Delta Upsilon
Jonathan Bassett
Benjamin M. Hasselbring
Daniel Langford
James Pennell

23. Fratello
Jeremy Behler
Dave Emigh
Owen Schwartz
Bo Sherman

24. Teter
Zachary Clark
David Eaton
Chris Welp
Robert Williams

25. Alta
Ryan Bentley
Michael E. Davison
Bradley J. Dennis
Chris Prouty

26. Cinzano
Nick Lasure
Jason Losey
Ray Podesta
Brian Walton

27. Wright Cycling
James M. Choplin
Aaron Graff
Nick Larkin
Christopher Stafford

28. Hickory
Keith Butler
Marc Rendish
Ed Schneider
Michael Tollini

29. Evans Scholars
Dominic J Freiburger
Jeffrey Weingartner
John Wojcik
Chong You

30. Kappa Sigma
David Gerber
David Hawkins
Eric Summa
Bin Sun

31. Delta Sigma Pi (Men)
William Comerford
Michael Hayashiguchi
Chad Rogers
John Wollenburg

32. Alpha Sigma Phi
Fredrick Derheimer
Steven Hale
Jonathan Ratchick
Kirk Winters

33. Alpha Phi Omega (Men)
Brian Harden
Theodore N. Mysliwiec
Matt Pflieger
Jonathan Whitall

Women's Little 500

1988

1. Willkie Sprint
Louise Elder
Kerry Hellmuth
Kirsten Swanson
Amy Tucker

2. Kappa Alpha Theta
Shelly Brundick
Lee Ann Guzek
Martha Hinkamp
Mary Pappas

3. Delta Delta Delta
Heather Balsbaugh
Margi Barry
Meaghan McRaith
Suzi Schoen

4. Alpha Epsilon Phi
Jill Janov
Carrie Lederer
Audrew Manaster
Laura Mandel
Sandi Miller
Heather Ross

5. Notorious
Laura Graziano
Sophia Leongas
Mia Middleton
Joy Raird
Jenifer Valentine

6. Cycledelics
Wendy Blauvelt
Celeste Dolak
Sue Hackett
Susan Rakow
Lisa Young

7. Delta Zeta
Susan Bunch
Kelly Kingsbury
Shelly Lowdermilk
Lisa McConnell
Ashley Tappan
Lisa Treece
Molly Zraik

8. Stonies
Sarah Bohs
Lisa Bough
Kimberly Hunt
Kathy Olsen
Erin Solara
Chris Sotak

9. Alpha Omicron Pi
Jill Clay
Erica Dekko
Lisa DeWinter
Theresa Greco
Julie Mason
Amy Travis

10. Sigma Kappa
Tiffany Bair
Julie DeDomenic
Sherri Thomas

Jennifer Vaughn
Julie Woolington

11. Collins
Karen Coltun
Stacy Knowton
Allyson Knox
Amy Levitin
Julie Riley
Ruth Sidor

12. Alpha Phi
Jenny Barry
Julie Goore
Julie Masciopinto
Christin McElwain
Jennifer Pancner
Amy Prisk
Marla Ragel

13. Kappa Delta
Janene Berra
Tina Doner
Sue Forker
Kathleen Heiney
Kathryn Ziegler

14. Ambassadors
Chris Gardner
Lori Magliola
Michele Mallatt
Margot Mosier

15. Cinzano
Barbara Burke
Kathleen Burke
Marilynn Maher
Michele Roberts
Karen Weinzapfel

16. Foster
Tiana Bartelheim
Alicia Romeo

Lissa Somers
Stephanie Walker

17. Alpha Xi Delta
Michelle Damrell
Karen Falloon
Christine Manske
Michelle Smith

18. Zeta Tau Alpha
Missy Blackford
Kathy Chiu
Kelly Cramer
Val German
Jennifer Haley
Lori Henry
Rachael Riggs
Lauri Schneck

19. Delta Gamma
Whitney Belt
Peggy Filavacek
Lisa McCallum
Sylvia Pollitt

20. Alpha Delta Pi
Robin Kramer
Lori Mickley
Jill Richart
Kathi Pfluger
Lynn Schoner
Wendy Winkeljohn

21. Alpha Gamma Delta
Amy Erwin
Lori Finefrock
Anne Grotefeld
Matty Schooley
Cindy Yarc

22. Briscoe
Diane Cesaroni
Lisa Dever

Jennifer Feeney
Kimberley Pierce

23. Phi Mu
Krissy Ebert
Pam Furst
Michelle Rieman
Paige Snyder
Laura Stith

24. Cinquencento
Cindy Blair
Mary Beth Bolanowsky
Nicole Martins
Kim Risburg

25. Spokeswomen
Lisa Benjamin
Jennifer Ellin
Christine Emde
Johanna Pugh
Elizabeth Schofer

26. Windsprint
Linnea Barker
Brigette Clumb
Karen Gates
Christina Kirchoff
Rayetta Shaw

27. Forest
Alex Bird
Amy Norman
Amy Rose
Susan Towle
Chris Wissel

28. Eureka
Cindy Foster
Kerri Silverman
Julie Watkins

29. Copacetic
Drayer Bott
Angie Hermann
Lori Krause
Mary Shepard
Chris Sotak

30. Wild Thing
Erin Angel
Lori Fisher
Laura Newby
Shea Parker
Nicki Wilkins

1989

1. Beyond Control
Laura Graziano
Catherine Lacrosse
Melissa Munkwitz
Liz Schofer

2. Team Sprint
Kerry Hellmuth
Mia Middleton
Kirsten Swanson
Amy Tucker
Jennifer Valentine

3. Delta Gamma
Jennifer Creed
Suzanne Harmon
Peggy Hlavacek
Julie McDonald
Margaret Wood

4. Kappa Alpha Theta
Michelle Brundick
Cathy Cowman
Kathy Denniston
Martha Hinkamp
Mary Vanmeter

5. Foster
Jen Fincher
Lara Kindschi
Reyna Randall
Alicia Romeo
Jennifer Saunders

6. Alpha Delta Pi
Robin Kramer
Belle Liang
Kathi Pluger
Amy Toy
Wendy Winkeljohn

7. Alpha Epsilon Phi
Jodi Alperstein
Paula Isenberg
Audrey Manaster
Laura Mandel
Julie Wolinsky

8. Alpha Xi Delta
Amy Crowell
Jennifer Daehler
Michelle Damrell
Angela Duntz
Karen Falloon
Susan Sovie

9. Wright
Wendy Blauvelt
Stephanie Hasting
Jessalyn Leyra
Dawn Weller
Stephanie Weller

10. Delta Zeta
Susan Bunch
Christa Esbeck
Jennifer Long
Denise Shelby
Ashley Tappan

11. Collins
Amy Cunningham
Laura Famer
Paula Haney
Jody Sundt

12. Sigma Delta Tau
Barb Cohn
Rosalyn Cooperman
Marnie Franklin

13. Alpha Phi
Annete Caito
Julie Glore
Stephanie Kleine-Ahlbrandt
Jennifer Pancer
Amy Prisk

14. Willkie
Haley Borbush
Monique Lemmon
Mary Nottingham
Jennifer Thomas
Missy Willits

15. Kappa Delta
Angie Burdette
Tina Doner
Sue Forker
Carol Harrison
Karyn Krupinski

16. Delta Delta Delta
Karyn Bartosz
Kelly Burden
Lynne Entzminger
Debbie Hatfield
Julie Schoen
Tracy Troutman

17. De Novo
Paige Baxter
Lisa Ferguson

Anne McLain
Danae Rebel

18. Chi Omega
Gaby Cramer
Chrissy Cullen
Jenny Fraser
Suzanne Hannah
Maureen Sweeney

19. Genuine Draft
Linnea Barker
Julie Boone
Robbin Brewster
Karen Gates
Holly Winklejohn

20. Phi Mu
Betsey Berry
Kristi Collier
Nancy Langdon
Paige Snyder
Lynn Thompson

21. Kappa Kappa Gamma
Cay Mateyko
Tracy Stuart
Maureen Thallemer
Kristin Youngquist

22. Read
Drayer Bott
Sonja Fritzsche
Kimberly Hunt
Jennifer Mitol
Kay Stephens

23. Briscoe
Kim Faulkner
Amy Meneilley
Sandra Soeder
Liz Skramstad

24. Teter
Barbara Burke
Shannon Slark
Anne Lorenz
Kris Marrone
Cindy Santagata

25. Pi Beta Phi
Michelle Bastian
Carla Beatrici
Kent Devine
Elizabeth Hughes

26. Gamma Phi Beta
Melissa Miller
Terry Mohr
Julie Ward
Mandy Wiebe

27. Alpha Omicron Pi
Kelly Ayers
Melissa Clark
Lisa DeWinter
Julie Mason
Amy Travis

1990

1. Team Sprint
Heidi Flobeck
Kerry Hellmuth
Mia Middleton
Amy Tucker

2. Beyond Control
Joy Baird
Laura Graziano
Sue Hackett
Melissa Munkwitz

3. Kappa Alpha Theta
Michelle Brundick

Ellen Buechler
Cathy Cowman
Susie Cvengros

4. Foster
Jennifer Saunders
Lissa Somers
Reyna Randall
Gianna Rosenthal

5. Le Pas
Juli Brown
Stephanie Hasting
Pam Lilak
Gina Nigro
Jennifer Sheehan

6. Delta Zeta
Tara Jackson
Jennifer Long
Elaine Reust
Denise Shelby
Julie Stuffle
Ashley Tappan

7. Kappa Kappa Gamma
Kelly Beck
Anne Karlblom
Theress Pidick
Ashley Puckett
Paula Snow
Kristin Youngquist

8. Landsharks
Paula Haney
Tina Harnett
Stacy Knowlton
Nicole Kramer
Jody Sundt

9. Revolution
Amy Meneilley
Angie Steele

Holly Winkeljohn
Wendy Winkeljohn

10. Wright
Dottie Brown
Kyra Brown
Lara Keeley
Judie Salerno
Alyssa Shelsey

11. Willkie/Read
Sonja Fritzsche
Stephanie Lifflick
Jennifer Postoloff
Deanne Shiroma
Melissa Willits

12. Alpha Delta Pi
Kris Cline
Tracy Haas
Theresa Kneebone
Susan Mattick
Linda Miller
Justyne Scott
Amy Toy

13. Alpha Phi
Andrea Berryman
Annette Caito
Meghan Dolan
Laura Haverty
Holly Hinytzke
Lesley Rigel
Andrea Weir
Molly Wilson

14. Off The Back
Pat Beaty
Randi Senzer
Kristina Sirovica
Sandra Soeder

15. Kappa Delta
Marilyn Brosmer
Windie Burch
Sue Forker
Carol Harrison
Kristen A. Isenberg

16. Alpha Xi Delta
Amy Cromwell
Jennifer Daehler
Michelle Damrell
Robin Levy
Marcy Sedej
Susan Sovie

17. Sigma Delta Tau
Debbie Berman
Barbie Cohn
Rosalyn Cooperman
Dori Rubin

18. Gamma Phi Beta
Tammi Barker
Kezia Endsley
Brigid Fyr
Michelle Manco
Siobhan McCambridge
Terry Mohr
Shannon Monahan
Holly Sillings

19. Alpha Omicron Pi
Alison Clark
Melissa Clark
Elyse Errington
Jen Gordon
Rachel Morse
Amy Travis

20. Sigma Kappa
Drayer Bott
Laura Gerber
Stacey Levins

Jenny Noble
Sherri Thomas
Julie Woolington

21. Alpha Epsilon Phi
Susie Dery
Mindy Grossberg
Debbie Lambert
Audrey Manaster
Alison Schneier

22. Forest
Catherine Dietrich
Vesna Kirincic
Lisa Lock
Nancy Street
Marie Underhill

23. Collins
Amy Cunningham
Rachel Deller
Maureen Kennedy
Lisa McCallister
Becky Swanson

24. Alpha Gamma Delta
Kristin Bauer
Meg Marchese
Amy Waterman
Stephanie Yanta

25. Chi Omega
Chrissy Cullen
Crystal Kjaer
Pam Roush
Christy Sterrett
Barby Webster

26. Phi Mu
Lori Combs
Heather Jones
Elizabeth Joseph

Stefanie Rhuda
Jennifer Thomas

1991

1. Le Pas
Laura Donley
Karen Dunne
Stephanie Hastings
Melissa Munkwitz

2. Foster
Gena Daugherty
Sharon Mermelstein
Reyna Randall
Jennifer Saunders
Lissa Somers

3. Landsharks
Drayer Bott
Sara Gardner
Tina Harnett
Ann Keller
Jody Sundt

4. Delta Gamma
Jen Creed
Jill Ehrensberger
Katie Fleming
Mychel Macapagal
Mari McDonald
Mariana Romano

5. Team Sprint
Laurel Bleich
Laura Gerstenberger
Kerry Hellmuth
Robin Roberts

6. Kappa Alpha Theta
Julie Chickedantz
Cathy Cowman

Maureen Hamburger
Alissa Shelsey

7. Delta Zeta
Tara Jackson
Carrie Johnson
Jennifer Long
Julie Lorey
Robin McWilliams

8. Revolution
Amy Meneilley
Pam Watercutter
Holly Winklejohn

9. Alpha Delta Pi
Kris Cline
Blythe Johnson
Anne Latchford
Jennifer Schmidt
Justyne Scott

10. Zeta Tau Alpha
Maura Brady
Carol Crosby
Jackie Hoehn
Shannon Hoehn
Shannon Kerneck
Brooke Lehmann

11. Alpha Phi
Annette Caito
Kristine DeMoss
Holly Hinytzke
Julie Tyson
Molly Wilson

12. Collins
Brooke Barnes
Maura Fernbacher
Carla Jacobson
Maureen Kennedy

Jenny Reid
Amy Steketee

13. Read
Deana Cammarata
Catherine Dietrich
Nancy Murray
Laura Mulvey
Marie Underhill

14. Kappa Kappa Gamma
Beth Anne Kuzmic
Sallie Moutvic
Mayme Wilhoite
Kristin Youngquist

15. Phi Mu
Mary Draper
Dawn Herbert
Nancy Street
Jen Thomas

16. Gamma Phi Beta
Debbie Causey
Kelly Cook
Michelle Manco
Alison Mulder

17. Forest
Amy Denzinger
Margaret Menge
Kristin Mueller
Emily Reinwald
Elizabeth Siegle

18. Willkie
Heather Burns
Andrea Carbon
Cynthia Davis
Mara Klose
Mary Kay McGinty
Betsy Moehn

19. Alpha Omicron Pi
Jen Gordon
Kim Hart
Rachel Morse
Alison Mura
Jennifer Stewart
Jennifer Sway
Jessica Varley

20. Alpha Xi Delta
Amy Cromwell
Michelle Damrell
Susan Sovie
Tricia Vicere
Melinda Zeller

21. Alpha Gamma Delta
Kristy Abel
Darcy Draeger
Stacy Inglis
Amy Kemp
Debra McClintock

1992

1. Landsharks
Sara Gardner
Tina Harnett
Andrea Jones
Lara Keeley

2. Kappa Alpha Theta
Julie Chickedantz
Megan Coyle
Jocelyn Desmond
Erin Ditto

3. Delta Gamma
Rebecca Brown
Katie Fleming
Michelle Liberatore
Alisa Sheldon
Kristen Stinson

4. Alpha Delta Pi
Natalie Davideneoff
Kris Kline
Anne Latchford
Amy Prochaska
Jennifer Schmidt
Liz Scholman
Justyne Scott

5. Forest
Molly Housman
Jenny Luhman
Elizabeth Roney
Linda Rubright

6. Willkie
Karen Hilton
Millie Jackson
Lauren Staples
Alex Weymouth

7. Delta Zeta
Tara Jackson
Robin McWilliams
Gabrielle Mickels
Marianne Personet

8. Kappa Delta
Missy Dracha
Carol Harrison
Dena Hofer
Kristen Isenberg
Nancy Wine

9. Read
Catherine Dietrich
Sonja Fritzsche
Nancy Murray
Alyssa Solomon

10. Alpha Gamma Delta
Jessica Bowen
Kris Carolick
Jane Crawford

Darcy Draeger
Sarah Fisher
Caren Hirsch
Tracie Morris
Tina Petrello

11. Zeta Tau Alpha
Andrea Bode
Maura Brady
Jackie Hoehn
Kristin Mueller
Janna Smith

12. Gamma Phi Beta
Katie Barnes
Gina Gloe
Peggy Grigus
Alison Mulder
Lesli Smith

13. Kappa Kappa Gamma
Staci Bloomberg
Maile Denbeau
Kristen Schiele
Kristen Youngquist

14. Team Brio
Marnie Puchlyr
Kim Richey
Cheryl Sharpe

15. Foster
Kathy Bennett
Lisa Burger
Stephanie Stern
Heather Zagnit

16. Alpha Phi
Becky Doolittle
Melissa Duffy
Jenn Ruda
Cindy Osborne
Andrea Weir

17. Alpha Omicron Pi
Jean Denious
Amy Hardwick
Kim Hart
Rachel Morse

18. Phi Mu
Mary Draper
Dawn Herbert
Dawn Smith
Jen Thomas

19. Wright
Christy Craig
Cheryl Koch
Yvette Lawsin
Heather Martin
Emily Renwald

20. Sigma Sigma Sigma
Shannon Bell
Jennifer Chapman
Jill Hasser
Lisa Martin
Kimber Tenorio

21. Sigma Delta Tau
Debbie Berman
Ginger Goldman
Laurie Weisberg

22. Collins
Aline Gubrium
Erica Gubrium
Kelly Rymer

23. Alpha Epsilon Phi
Tammy Checroon
Corey Cutter
Tracy Huber

24. Delta Delta Delta
Jenny Day

Debbie Dineglio
Megan Hall
Missy Lomen
Mindy Pashkow
Wendy Walack

25. Alpha Sigma Alpha
Erica Blair
Lara Hazelwood
Dawn McElvain
Laura Naatz
Michelle Ponicki

26. Sigma Kappa
Julie Cardinal
Lisa Fuller
Dena Gregory
Kristie Konieczny

1993

1. Landsharks
Kim Berglund
Sara Gardner
Julie Schmalz
Jannine Turner

2. Alpha Gamma Delta
Julie Biros
Jane Crawford
Meg Gallmeyer
Tracie Morris
Elizabeth Roney

3. Gamma Phi Beta
Mandy Evans
Peggy Grigus
Kristi McNally
Allison Mulder

4. Kappa Alpha Theta
Julie Chickedantz
Megan Coyle
Maria Gemskie
Greta Hoetzer
Chrissy Magrini
Danielle Tucker

5. Delta Gamma
Katie Fleming
Robby Fromin
Maureen Manion
Alisa Sheldon
Shannon Smith
Kristen Stinson

6. Alpha Sigma Alpha
Adrienne Morgan
Laura Naatz
Jennifer Richard
Kim Smith

7. Alpha Phi
Becky Doolittle
Melissa Duffy
Cindy Osborne
Andrea Weir

8. Roadrunners
Kathy Bennett
Betsy Moehn
Tina Schmidt

9. Alpha Omicron Pi
Becki Bakir
Jean Denious
Jenny Luhman
Gaylee Morgan
Rachel Morse
Kristina Weaver

10. Willkie
Cynthia Beuoy
Michelle Boydston
Elizabeth Gibson
Angie Songstad

11. Alpha Chi Omega
Lisa Brown
Charlie McClary
Marnie Puchyr
Kathleen Randall
Stephanie Ward

12. Zeta Tau Alpha
Michelle Foutz
Becky Lengerich
Patricia Martinez
Kristen Mueller

13. Kappa Delta
Kathy Arnold
Erin Conrad
Missy Dracka
Kristy Garrigan
Katie Gill

14. Delta Zeta
Holly Andrews
Heather Hardin
Robin McWilliams
Gabrielle Michels
Rachel Schultz

15. Forest
Robbyn Forry
Biddy Hubman
Amber Striker

16. Phi Mu
Kendra Byvoets
Julie Cwik

Mary Draper
Jill Laffer
Tonya Loscalzo
Nancy Stasica

17. Delta Delta Delta
Jill Allsop
Kerry Foley
Megan Hall
Staci Murphy
Mindy Pashkow

18. Kappa Kappa Gamma
Becky Barnhart
Mandy Beck
Staci Bloomberg
Christina Hunn
Suzy Linskey
Sarah Schmidt

19. Collins
Aline Gubrium
Carmen Palmer-Leahy
Pai-Ling Yin

20. Wright
Cheryl Koch
Patti Olson
Stacy Uliana
Heather Williams

21. Sigma Sigma Sigma
Jennifer Collins
Lisa Martin
Alaine Sperbeck
Kimber Tenorio
Melanie Walton

22. McNutt
Ashley Vance
Nikki Yarbrough
Heather Zagnit

23. Alpha Delta Pi
Patricia Caskey
Natalie Davidenkoff
Elizabeth Shulman
Becky Stark

24. Sigma Kappa
Angie Boyd
Katrin Cisne
Lisa Fuller
Deana Gregory
Erin Smith

1994

1. Kappa Alpha Theta
Julie Beck
Jocelyn Desmond
Greta Hoetzer
Chrissy Magrini

2. Alpha Gamma Delta
Julie Biros
Meg Gallmeyer
Tracie Morris
Sheri Sprau
Amy Wolford

3. Roadrunners
Kathy Bennett
Karen Dunne
Betsy Moehn
Tina Schmidt
Alyssa Solomon

4. Alpha Chi Omega
Lisa Braun
Trisha Hipskind
Mernie Puchyr
Stephanie Ward

5. Gamma Phi Beta
Kelly Canull
Mandy Evans
Peggy Grigus
Cindy Irvin
Kristi McNally

6. Delta Delta Delta
Jill Allsop
Kerry Foley
Megan Hall
Katie McCaffrey

7. Alpha Phi
Becky Doolittle
Amy Grose
Cindy Osborne
Jenni Smart
Mo Weber

8. Kappa Kappa Gamma
Staci Bloomberg
Cathy Hardwick
Gina Murray
Michelle Reynolds
Kristin Youngquist

9. Wright
Jody Foss
Biddy Hubman
Amy Kellerman
Cheryl Koch
Hanna Sarnow

10. Landsharks
Jacky Armstrong
Allison Burholder
Tina Harnett
Kristen Mahot
Julie Schmalz

11. Alpha Omicron Pi
Amy Christiansen
Callie Kunkler
Jenny Luhman
Nicole Peters
Kristina Weaver

12. Delta Zeta
Holly Andrews
Allison Bradbury
Emily Summers
Julie Rosenberg

13. Kappa Delta
Jill Byus
Lisa Cibelli
Melissa Dracka
Kristy Garrigan
Katie Gill

14. Zeta Tau Alpha
Kris Kilburn
Becky Lengerich
Michelle LeVeque
Kristen Mueller
Stacia Spurling

15. Team College Life
Tonya Diehm
Shannon Long
Nicole Tucker

16. Phi Mu
Kendra Byvoets
Heather Gerges
Amanda Guillermo
Michelle Moore

17. Delta Sigma Pi
Erica Fenstermaker
Jenny Hatch
Tracie Kreunz

18. Willkie
Michelle Boydston
Jessica Dratt
Elizabeth Gibson
Angie Songstad

19. McNutt
Hannah Arbuckle
Jamie Hickey
Andi Kemper
Heather Zagnit

20. Collins
Aline Gubrium
Erika Gubrium
Katrina Quicker

21. Alpha Delta Pi
Natalie Davidenkoff
Jennifer Myers
Leah Querimit
Sydney Ray

22. Alpha Epsilon Phi
Stephanie Darchowsky
Amy Spiegelglass
Jennifer Summers

23. Chi Omega
Cara Avery
Jill Burndeen
Laurie Eagle
Ali Satlo

24. Human Wheels
Stephanie Farmer
Kate Fitzpatrick
Imme Kersten
Constance Spray

25. Alpha Xi Delta
Jennifer Fuelling
Jenny Lewsader
Alison Stricklin
Jennifer Van Huffel
Kimberly Weddle

1995

1. Kappa Alpha Theta
Julie Beck
Greta Hoetzer
Maggie Mathews
Ali McGregor

2. Kappa Kappa Gamma
Staci Bloomberg
Sarah Grimm
Gina Murray
Michelle Reynolds

3. Gamma Phi Beta
Kelly Canull
Cindy Irvin
Kristi McNally
Kim Stewart

4. Alpha Gamma Delta
Julie Biros
Kristin Menger
Elizabeth Roney
Sheri Sprau

5. Landsharks
Molly Housman
Kathryn Kothe
Julie Schmalz

6. Delta Zeta
Holly Andrews
Allison Bradbury

Anne Lee
Molly Terrell

7. Team College Life
Tanya Diehm
Jen Fermin
Jodi Greenwalt
Nicole Tucker

8. Zeta Tau Alpha
Jen Beyst
Michelle LeVeque
Michelle Meier
Kristi Pawski

9. Wright
Jody Foss
Biddy Hubman
Amy Kellerman
Cheryl Koch

10. Pi Beta Phi
Brenda Ford
Shannon Gregory
Gabrielle Popovich
Kendal Silva

11. Alpha Chi Omega
Lisa Braun
Katie Cangemi
Trisha Hipskind
Carrie Sisk

12. Roadrunners
Jessica Dratt
Megan Gavin
Maryann Lekas
Susan Stapleton

13. Delta Gamma
Sarah Moore
Julie Quatmann

Melissa Tagliareni
Tracey Thomas

14. Forest
Shannon Clemens
Janel Frantz
Amy Kallner
Angie Songstad

15. Delta Delta Delta
Jill Allsop
Niki Gray
Tara Kurtz
Chrissy Ryan

16. Kappa Delta
Jill Byus
Lisa Cibelli
Susan Doninger
Heidi Queck

17. Phi Mu
Natalie Banta
Laura Hartman
J. Leigh Johnson
Jill Laffer

18. Alpha Xi Delta
Mandy Dickman
Sarah Krooswyk
Darcy Schulenberg
Alison Stricklin

19. Sigma Delta Tau
Amy Kaufman
Sharna Marcus
Katie Pollock
Mindy Ziffren

20. Alpha Phi
Tonja Hellman

Jenni Smart
Shelly Terry

21. Chi Omega
Darci Harrold
Lisa Heyworth
Lyndsey Hillis
Amy Young

22. Delta Sigma Pi
Sarah Bryant
Erin Campbell
Dawn Clarner
Jen Hollingsworth

1996

1. Kappa Kappa Gamma
Sarah Grimm
Gina Murray
Michelle Reynolds
Amanda Watts

2. Alpha Chi Omega
Lisa Braun
Katie Cangemi
Lesley Hobbs
Carrie Sisk

3. Roadrunners
Megan Gavin
Kari Hendrickson
Maryann Lekas
Susan Stapleton

4. Kappa Alpha Theta
Julie Beck
Maggie Mathews
Alison McGregor
Sarah Steele

The Little 500

5. Landsharks
Joy Jones
Kathryn Kothe
Emily Morris
Becky Peters

6. Alpha Gamma Delta
Katie Heffernan
Kristin Menger
Casey Roth
Sheri Sprau

7. Delta Gamma
Katie Baker
Lisa Its
Hillary Thompson
Tamara Walczak

8. Wright
Biddy Hubman
Amy Kellerman
Andrea Wolff
Deana Zemke

9. Teter
Susan Bein
Abigail Cooley
Lauren Dorosz
Stefanie Smith

10. Delta Zeta
Carrie Brustad
Krista Gibson
Anne Lee

11. Kappa Delta
Amy Clark
Susan Doninger
Suellen Garr
Denett Jablecki

12. Alpha Phi
Julie Drinkwater
Tonja Hellman
Karen Rick
Shelly Terry

13. Team Unique
Jennifer Gress
Paivi Puntila
Denise Stats
Shannon Swanson

14. Zeta Tau Alpha
Jen Beyst
Kris Kilbrun
Shana Smith

15. Alpha Xi Delta
Elizabeth Kar
Amy Powlen
Sharon Siegel
Laura Summers

16. Pi Beta Phi
Shannon Gregory
Erica Lesniak
Angela Messerli
Kim Season

17. Gamma Phi Beta
Kelly Canull
Angela Ott
Karla Walawender

18. Phi Mu
Katie Barszcz
Heidi Gillig
Kristi Mirobelli
Stephanie Sage

19. Alpha Delta Pi
Jill Antisell
Jeanne DelGiorno
Heather Kinnard
Caitlin Smid

20. Sigma Delta Tau
Jill Finkelstein
Amy Kauffman
Katie Pollock
Mindy Ziffren

21. Delta Delta Delta
Sari Andalman
Courtney Emerick
Leigh McLauchlan
Chrissy Ryan

22. Delta Sigma Pi
Dawn Clarner
Kelly Gowland
Susan Hoffa
Holly Scheumann

23. Alpha Phi Omega
Crystal James
Kelly Kerr
Amy Kraft
Kelly Schulthise

1997

1. Roadrunners
Megan Gavin
Jeanie Leinweber
Keri Nevile
Susan Stapleton

2. Kappa Alpha Theta
Julie Beck
Carey Brown

Vanessa Hirtzig
Sarah Steele

3. Phi Mu
Katie Barszcz
Bethany Beck
Janet Kiefer
Alison Roy

4. Alpha Gamma Delta
Katie Heffernan
Jamie Kaczmarek
Jaima Reising
Casey Roth

5. Kappa Kappa Gamma
Mary Elizabeth Andrew
Suzanna Bero
Jennifer Downing
Amanda Watts

6. Delta Gamma
Katie Baker
Kim Ballard
Kristen Hoehne
Paige Peters

7. Alpha Chi Omega
Hannah Arbuckle
Jamie Hipskind
Lesley Hobbs
Courtney Laychak

8. Landsharks
Jennifer Glombicki
Emily Morris
Rebecca Peters

9. Alpha Delta Pi
Jeanne Delgiorno
Heather Gathercole

Caitlin Smid
Jen Szypezak

10. Gamma Phi Beta
Amy Suits
Karla Walawender
Teal Walker
Katherine Zlatic

11. Alpha Xi Delta
Katie Drake
Elizabeth Kar
Nicole Mozden
Amy Powlen

12. Pi Beta Phi
Shannon Aeschliman
Kelly Akin
Elissa Freeman
Allison Russell

13. Kappa Delta
Angela Haskett
Lisa McLean
Heidi Queck
Jordan Smith

14. Chi Omega
Jill Blackford
Lindsey Hawkins
Megan Quigley

15. Wright
Christy Holtkamp
Amy Kellerman
Kari Krause
Andi Wolff

16. Briscoe
Erin Fields
Erin Hill

Denise Stats
Caroline Wolfberg

17. Delta Zeta
Sara Gailble
Kimberlee Haney
Jami Long
Emily Rush

18. Team Z
Mary Bates
Melissa Hake
Angie Songstad
Jill Zbrzezny

19. Collins
Kathleen Cyr
Aimee Fraulo
Kristen Friend
Tara Walhart

20. Alpha Phi
Stephanie Miller
Karen Rick
Darcy Ross
Becky Stuart

21. Delta Delta Delta
Veronica Fife
Tara Kurtz
Lauren MacNaughton
Chrissy Ryan

22. Sigma Delta Tau
Julie Golding
Melanie Muscoplat
Amanda Scheier
Mindy Ziffren

23. Mezcla
Abigail Cooley
Lori Prindle
Siri Sitton

24. Foster
Lara Behrmann
Pamela Cornes
Elizabeth Groves
Indya Watts

25. Teter
Marisol Cisneros
Nicole Egendorfer
Lisa Levin
Peggy Nebriaga

26. Zeta Tau Alpha
Brittany Morris
Kristi Pawski
Elizabeth Slamkowski
Katherine Spear

27. Alpha Kappa Psi
Susan Jackson
Gina Kandris
Angela Pastorino
Kelli Vollmer

28. Tortues
Olivia Bressy
Melanie Hobbs
Jessica Minton
Turiya Simic

29. Alpha Phi Omega
Elana Berkun
Michelle Dyke
Genell Lewis
Kelli Warner

30. Alpha Epsilon Phi
Heather Deitchman
Melissa Goldstein
Monique Klugman
Amy Pierson

1998

1. Kappa Kappa Gamma
Elizabeth Andrew
Suzanna Bero
Jennifer Downing
Lisa Roessler

2. Chi Omega
Lindsey Hawkins
Megan Quigley
Rae Raffin

3. Kappa Alpha Theta
Nicole Duggan
Anne Holterhoff
Margaret Molloy
Sarah Wilson

4. Alpha Chi Omega
Ashley Grossman
Lesley Hobbs
Kelly Maher
Stefanie Spreen

5. Landsharks
Nicole Daluga
Jennifer Glombicki
Marni Jo Mooney
Emily Morris

6. Roadrunners
Laresa Ingram
Kori Neville
Susan Stapleton
Tara Walhart

7. Alpha Gamma Delta
Jennifer Cooper
Jamie Kaczmarek

Jaima Reising
Casey Roth

8. Phi Mu
Katie Barszcz
Bethany Beck
Janet Kiefer
Alison Roy

9. Delta Gamma
Katie Baker
Alison Forti
Christy Holtkamp
Elizabeth Kouba

10. Wright
Mecca Adams
Niki Gauger
Amy Glaser
Kari Krause

11. Pi Beta Phi
Kelly Akin
Mollie McCollum
Elizabeth O'Dell
Kristen Watts

12. Vayu
Carrie Caraco
Tricia Fleming
Sally Hulett
Adrienne Puttet

13. Team Elite
Olivia Bressy
Erin Fields
Jessica Minton
Elizabeth Steinmetz

14. Team College Life
Amy Hufty
Jaime Schutte
Cindy Sims
Jessica Talaga

15. Perigee
Carolyn Brustad
Anne Lee
Heather Maupin
Leonida Tansinsin

16. Delta Zeta
Lisa Braundis
Kim Haney
Jill Harkness

17. Alpha Phi Omega
Melissa Hake
Kelly Kerr
Kelli Warner

18. Alpha Xi Delta
Katie Drake
Tara Feichter
Jessica Jones
Nicole Mozden

19. Delta Delta Delta
Andi Booker
Veronica Fife
Angela Jones
Lauren MacNaughton

20. Alpha Phi
Amy Aulick
Jodi Knauer
Jennifer Lamka
Becky Stuart

21. Sigma Delta Tau
Carly Izenson
Angie Luke
Jill Stein
Mindy Ziffren

22. Zeta Tau Alpha
Kara Anderson
Lisa Hausler
Liz Slamkowski
Katie Spear

23. Alpha Kappa Psi
Susan Jackson
Gina Kandris
Laura Richardson
Kelli Vollmer

24. Oz
Erin Clarkin
Abigail Cooley
Lauren Dorosz
Laura Wood

25. Backdraft
Jennifer Consorti
Tracy Porter
Rebecca Wellons

26. Delta Sigma Pi
Jennifer Briar
Christeen Krueger
Laila Motiwalla
Andrea Rucano

27. Army ROTC
Christine Hansen
Michelle Kistner
Micki Roessner

28. Alpha Delta Pi
Jessica Chait

Heather Gathercole
Ilene Potasnik
Cristina Winslow

29. Teter
Marisol Cisneros
NiCale Rector
Phrosini Samis
Jessie Taylor

30. Foster
Sara Freeman
Amanda Hickman
Kellie Richardson
Indya Watts

31. Briscoe
Megan Hamelmann
Amy Robb
Hima Tadoori
Heather Ward

32. Alpha Chi Sigma
Stacy Bennett
Ericka Dreesen
Rebecca Hilbrich
Jessica Pramuk

1999

1. Kappa Kappa Gamma
Elizabeth Andrew
Suzannah Bero
Katy Hair
Lisa Roessler

2. Kappa Alpha Theta
Nicole Duggan
Anne Holterhoff
Erin Hudson
Sarah Wilson

3. Alpha Delta Pi
Emily Derkasch
Heather Gathercole
Sara Herman
Cristina Winslow

4. Phi Mu
Bethany Beck
Kara Kenney
Janet Kiefer
Allison Rufatto

5. Pi Beta Phi
Amanda Boehmer
Mandy Pettibone
Erin Reiter
Kristen Watts

6. Team Athena
Jessica Burns
Erin Fields
Caitlin Skinner
Christine Weiss

7. Chi Omega
Lindsey Hawkins
Melissa Hayes
Megan Quigley
Rae Raffin

8. Roadrunners
Ellen Hall
Christine Johnson
Erica Schilke
Jill Zbrzezny

9. Alpha Phi
Amy Aulick
Marie Baker
Andrea Corso
Jennifer Urbanski

10. Gamma Phi Beta
Jennifer Abel
Angie Beier
Stephanie Hinshaw
Jennifer Wallrab

11. Oz
Erin Clarkin
Lauren Dorosz
Amy Howard
Jennifer Milosavljevic

12. Cycledelics
Mercedes Collins
Niki Gauger
Amy Joyce Glaser
Lisa Marie Paine

13. Delta Delta Delta
Andi Booker
Shauna Correll
Leslie Fine
Angela Jones

14. Alpha Xi Delta
Tara Feichter
Megan Lambeth
Nicole Mozden
Megan Weber

15. ConFuoco
Megan Abell
Robyn Faike
Leslie Gilmore
Katie Wyatt

16. Delta Zeta
Lisa Braudis
Jill Harkness
Abbey Kaser
Melissa Mongoven

17. Forest
Laura DeSana
Amanda Fleming
Lauren Naset
Sarah Nessler

18. Landsharks
Shannon Bazur
Daphne Houze
Venus Mc Coy
Keely Stevens

19. Vayu
Melanie Hannon
Sally Hulett
Adrienne Putteet

20. Alpha Chi Omega
Katie Binz
Lindsay Grabb
Jenny Kniptash
Amy Mink

21. Delta Gamma
Susan Binder
Sarah Crider
Lindsay Ems
Kristin Fenton

22. McNutt Cycling
Lisa Goranson
Leifschon Pattengale
Kathryn Peck
Erin Shelly

23. Alpha Phi Omega (Women)
Alissa Gerrish
Bobbie Pollard
Jennifer Schmitt
Amy Stiller

24. Alpha Gamma Delta
Stephanie Farnsworth
Lisa Meyer
Katie Pennamped
Amy Walters

25. Team College Life
Torri Barco
Erika Braun
Kellie Parker

26. Briscoe Blaze
Catie Crossland
Sharada Nethaway
Caitlin Sullivan

27. Zeta Tau Alpha
Mary Beatty
Beth Burnett
Carrie Klene

28. Kappa Delta
Kelly Gustafson
Tania Hults
Katie Perschon

29. Delta Sigma Pi (Women)
Jennifer Briar
Andrea Bucano
Megan Hakes
Laila Motiwalla

30. Foster 4ce
Sara Freeman
Kristen Meyer
Rebecca Roberts
Indya Watts

31. Super Teter
Kelli Antes
Gretchen Finn
Kelly Sutliff

32. Teter Cycling
Marisol Cisneros
Phrosini Samis
Jessie Taylor

The Little
500

Photo Credits

The author, Indiana University Press, and the IU Student Foundation wish to extend their thanks to the photographers who contributed to this book and whose work adds so much to our presentation

Arbutus, by Douglas Benedict, p. 119 (left); by Nadia Borowski, p. 119 (right); by Jim Hudelson, p. 114; by Richard Schultz, p. 142; by Mic Smith, pp. 120 (right), 140; by Chris Usher, p. 129 (both); by Jensen Walker, p. 154.

Martha Armstrong, pp. 54, 67, 69 (both), 104. Martha Armstrong by Dave Fryer, pp. 37, 61.

Bloomington Herald-Times, p. 127. By Dave Schreiber, p. 110; by John Terhune, pp. 111, 116 (right), 139 (both).

Bill Brissman, p. 81 (left). Bill Brissman by Jerry Clark, p. 81 (right); Bill Brissman by Robb Gutowsky, p. 80; Bill Brissman by Janet Witek, p. 78.

Jim Cusick, p. 28.

Indiana Alumni Magazine, pp. 86, 87 (center and right); 89 (top, left and right), 93, 95 (all), 96, 97, 101, 120 (left), 154; by Michael Gard, 150 (upper left).

Indianapolis Star and News, pp. 18, 24, 26, 116 (left), 147, 150 (lower right).

IU Archives, pp. 11 (large), 12, 39, 41, 59, 79, 84, 89 (bottom), 90 (both), 91 (right), 92, 100.

IU Photographic Services, pp. 4, 5, 7, 8, 20 (left), 21, 31, 52, 53 (both), 124 (both).

Randy Johnson, p. 229. *Copyright © by Randy Johnson.*

Dave Price, p. 118 (both).

Dave Repp, p. 42, 47, 71, 72, 107, 126, 131, 132, 133 (both). *Copyright © by Dave Repp.*

G. Ralph Scott, p. 10 (lower left, right), 11 (small), 15.

Moose Walterhouse, p. 30.

Howdy Wilcox, pp. 2, 10 (upper left).

All other photos are by the IU Student Foundation.

The Little
500

Index

book and jacket designer
Sharon L. Sklar

printer and binder
Four Colour Imports

compositor
Sharon L. Sklar

typefaces
New Baskerville with Univers Display